D1556063

THE JUDITH DURHAM STORY

COLOURS OF MY LIFE

GRAHAM SIMPSON

For Mahlia
Here's proof that little girls' dreams sometimes do come true

This edition first published in 2003 by
Virgin Books Ltd
Thames Wharf Studios
Rainville Road
London
W6 9HA

First edition published in Australia in 1994 by Random House Australia Ltd

Copyright © Musicoast Pty Ltd, 1994, 2003

The right of Graham Simpson to be identified as the Author of this Work has been asserted by him in accordance with the Copyright, Designs and Patents Act, 1988.

A catalogue record for this book is available from the British Library.

ISBN 1 85227 038 1

Typeset by Phoenix Photosetting, Chatham, Kent
Printed and bound in Great Britain by CPD Wales

Judith Durham website: www.judithdurham.com

CONTENTS

FOREWORD BY LYNN REDGRAVE

It was a rainy day. It often is in London. Shooting on *Georgy Girl* was complete and editing was well under way. I received a phone call from the producer of the film, Otto Plaschkes.

'Lynny,' he said, 'we've had what we think is a great idea. We've commissioned a title song for the film. Jim Dale and Tom Springfield have written it and we're going to record it with The Seekers.'

It sounded perfect to me. Judith Durham, with that clear, warm clarion call of a voice. There could not have been a better choice for the sound that would introduce Georgy to the film's audience. The group recorded the song in London, where they were doing a series of concerts, and the film's director, Silvio Narizzano and I went to see them perform.

Of course they were a group, a wonderful group, but I honestly have to say that it was Judith who held my attention. Perhaps I saw myself in her. I know she has said that she felt that way about me when the film was screened for her. We were born the same year and, although our lives have followed different paths, I have felt a kinship with Judith ever since those strange heady days in the sixties when we were young and all things seemed possible. *Georgy Girl* changed my life and I have always known that a big part of the film's success was thanks to the title song. Most particularly to Judith.

We met again a few years ago, when I was performing my one-woman play, *Shakespeare for my Father*, at the Melbourne International Festival. After the performance, there she was, in my dressing room. My singing alter ego. Her appearance unchanged by the years. With what joy we embraced. Life can be so strangely magical. Two older women, not girls any more but feeling like girls at that moment. Meeting again, reaching out across the years and recognising what they have both meant to each other.

– Lynn Redgrave
February 2003

FOREWORD BY
THE DUCHESS OF YORK

I will always remember my first meeting with Judith Durham.

We met in London in 1994 and I, like so many others, was struck by Judith's warmth and her vibrant personality. Nevertheless, there was an underlying sense of intense sadness. Judith's beloved husband, Ron, who was in Australia, was very close to dying from the devastating illness that is motor neurone disease. Judith desperately wanted to be by her husband's side, but was committed to a punishing schedule of interviews preceding one of The Seekers' UK tours.

Shortly after we had met, I flew to Australia on a charity fundraising trip. I had been so touched by Judith's plight that I wanted to visit the man who meant so much to her. Ron Edgeworth was in hospital in Melbourne – he was unable to speak and virtually unable to move. I remember being shown a video of him playing the piano and it was clear that he had been an extraordinarily talented pianist. The tragic irony of his situation in his fight against this terrible debilitating disease was that it was the use of his hands that he was to lose first. Ron died a week after I had visited him. I am privileged to have had the chance to meet him and will always remember his dignity and courage.

Despite the geographical distance between us, my friendship with Judith has remained strong over the years and it is an honour to write this foreword to *The Judith Durham Story: Colours of My Life*. It is a wonderful book, which tells the story of a courageous woman who has faced both triumph and disaster in her life but throughout has remained steadfast in her beliefs. I am delighted that the book is now being published in the UK so that many more people can read the compelling story of Judith's life.

– Sarah, Duchess of York
February 2003

FOREWORD BY SHELLEY BOVEY, JUDITH DURHAM'S MANAGER

My memories of the Judith Durham of the sixties are far more vivid than of any other female pop star of those great years. She was the girl I wished I could be. I had a weight problem and thick glasses; she, on the other hand, was beautiful and had the best voice I had ever heard. I used to watch her on *Top of the Pops* and think that if I looked and sounded like her, I wouldn't have a worry in the world. Ever! When I saw her live at The Talk of the Town in 1968 I was far too shy to speak to her afterwards. I got the other Seekers' autographs but Judith was a goddess in my eyes and therefore not to be spoken to like ordinary mortals.

I also sang and played the piano and was considering a career in music. I think Judith's awesome brilliance was a factor in my thinking that I'd never make it; instead I became a writer.

So if anyone had told me then that Judith Durham thought she was overweight and had a serious problem with her image, that she suffered with low self-esteem and was often very troubled, I'd have laughed in disbelief.

But it was true, as I learned first-hand when I finally met Judith many years later to interview her for a magazine. I heard her in concert first, and the passage of time, the fact that she was now middle aged, had done nothing to diminish that incredible voice. It took my breath away and touched the depths of my emotions, just as it had when I was young and raw.

Afterwards she told me of the struggle she'd had; how difficult it had been in the sixties when female pop stars were expected to look like Twiggy and she felt she didn't measure up, literally. It was an astonishing revelation to me, though I couldn't help but notice how very slim she had become. At the time I was writing a book about weight loss and I invited her to contribute to it; thus began our professional relationship.

It did not take long for me to learn that Judith is an astounding and extraordinary person who has the gift of affecting people at the deepest level. Her music has been found to possess profound powers of healing, and indeed nothing else had enabled me to overcome a lifelong flying phobia. I had long ago given up thinking I would travel, yet such is the inexplicable magic of Judith's music that I have now heard her sing in the Sydney Opera House.

Judith and I have now worked on many different projects in several different capacities, and this culminated in her asking me to be her manager. And what I am doing now is more than I could have dreamed of in those days when I was too shy to speak to her. I thank the cosmos that I did not pursue my own career in music, as a far more important, inspiring and rewarding mission was in store for me.

Graham Simpson has given us a great gift. His story, so beautifully and truthfully told, has brought Judith the woman to life, taking her far beyond the artist on stage. This is the Judith I know and love so well, and through this book you will feel you know her too.

– Shelley Bovey
February 2003

Tributes to Judith Durham

'Judith Durham, like Karen Carpenter and Eva Cassidy, possesses the purest voice in popular music. When she recorded one of my songs I was so flattered and loved her version. She made the song her own – a very enviable talent.'   *Sir Elton John*

'A lot of people sing well – very few have individuality – there's only *one* Judith Durham!'   *Sir Cliff Richard O.B.E.*

'Judith Durham has one of the purest sweetest voices that, as of today, no one else has been able to emulate.'   *Lulu*

'When Judith was my guest on *Surprise, Surprise*, I saw how much her warm personality and natural approach to her music mean to her fans. That 'surprise' meant a great deal to one man. Judith never forgets who put her where she is today. She is a woman after my own heart.'   *Cilla Black*

'Judith has a unique voice full of power and clarity. I think she is a top-class talent.'   *Helen Shapiro*

'Together we happily celebrate a new direction for our "little sister". The voice that bonds The Seekers sound and their songs into the hearts and lives of our many friends takes off again on its own. What another splendid journey it will be. Your "boys" will always be watching and applauding from the wings wherever you may be.
    Much Love. Athol Guy, Keith Potger, Bruce Woodley   *The Seekers*'

'For me, Judith has always been a great solo artist. That beautiful jewel of a voice cuts right through, and everything around it serves as a setting for its purity of purpose. I am and always have been a Judith Durham fan.'   *Sandie Shaw*

'It should be remembered that Judith Durham was the first internationally famous Australian singer since Dame Nellie Melba, with a possible exception of Joan Sutherland. Judith Durham and The Seekers gave musical expression to an era of charm and innocence we will never see again.'   *Barry Humprhies*

ACKNOWLEDGEMENTS

For such a long time, Judith Durham's life story has been a book waiting to happen. It annoyed me for years that her biography hadn't been written, for it's a book I've always wanted to read.

That it would be I who would be asked to write the Judith Durham story was a surprise to me, and yet obviously destined to be.

Judith and I met in 1972, but our paths crossed only occasionally until 1990, when a tragic car accident rekindled our friendship. By that time, I was earning my living as a music journalist and that, combined with my knowledge of and interest in Judith Durham and her music, possibly made me the natural storyteller.

It was an awesome task for someone who'd never actually written a book! It took a deep breath, an amazing amount of hard work and help from some very special people. Whom to thank first has been my biggest quandary in writing this book.

First and foremost I want to thank two people, without whom this book would be much lighter in detail.

The first is Paul Clayton-Lea, my childhood penfriend from Ireland. Paul was a big Judith Durham fan and had systematically collected British and Irish memorabilia from Judith's years in The Seekers. As a member of The Seekers' UK fan club, he had saved every newsletter. Paul spent some time in Australia as a teenager and, before returning to Ireland, he sent me his entire collection, figuring it would be in good hands! Without it, the coverage of those monumental years in Judith's career would never have been so comprehensive. Now a priest and teacher in Northern Ireland, Paul remains a great admirer of Judith's work and finally managed to meet her in 1994.

The second is Tim Hubbard, who, as a teenager in England in the 1970s, ran the Judith Durham Club. Tim's amazingly detailed monthly newsletters formed the template for a major portion of the book and saved me endless hours of research. Tim is now an award-winning BBC radio presenter and a renowned author himself.

Strange to think that I've never met these two people, and yet their contribution to this biography is enormous.

I thank my agent Margaret Gee, who knew so well what was involved in writing a book, and took care of business. Thanks also to John Kovac,

Judith's former manager, and the many kind and generous people in Judith's life who allowed me to interview them and shared with me their memories.

It's been a pleasure to work with Virgin Books, and my special thanks go to editors Stuart Slater and Mark Wallace and the whole Virgin team.

My own family and friends lent support and encouragement every step of the way. Mum and Dad (Nancy and Phil) and my sisters Jennifer and Anne – thanks for putting up with my endless playing of Judith's music over the years! My love and gratitude always to so many truly wonderful friends – the McKays, the McCleans, the Scotts – and, of course, my lifelong friend Kay Sharples, who introduced me to Judith Durham that first time, backstage at the Comedy Theatre in Melbourne in 1972.

I'd also like to mention Michael Salmon, whose talents I so admire. And my good friend Frank Howson – what a pleasure it was to introduce him to Judith, knowing their association would result in beautiful music.

What a privilege it has been to meet Shelley and Alistair Bovey and hear Shelley's astonishing tale of courage. Amazing faith and extraordinary ability have led Shelley quite naturally into her new management role and Judith's career could not be in better hands.

I don't know how to begin to thank my wife, Jacqui Johnson. She had her life turned upside down, a peaceful existence interrupted by a bloody big book. She put up with a part-time, often distracted husband and never complained when she was asked to listen, read, check facts or arrange interviews. When Jacqui said 'I do' in the early eighties, she wasn't expecting to spend her tenth wedding anniversary with Judith Durham, but she was incredibly gracious about it. Jacqui joked that Judith and I would probably be working when our twentieth rolled around. It's just around the corner, and guess what . . .

Then there's our daughter Mahlia, my special girl, whose response as a youngster to Judith and her music reminded me so emotionally of what this remarkable woman and her gift of song have meant to me over the years. I'm taken back to Mahlia's early years, when, having seen one of Judith's *Thank You Melbourne* concerts in 1991, she spent weeks recreating the stage magic in her room, her hair swept to one side and singing 'Colours of My Life'. It's a special part of our relationship I'll always cherish. Mahlia is now a performer in her own right, and I am enormously reassured to know that Judith was one of her earliest role models. What a start!

I want to thank Ron Edgeworth, without whom this story might never have been so adventurous. When the writing commenced, Ron had already begun to be affected by the progression of motor neurone disease. Over the months, it continued to diminish many of his abilities, but never his enthusiasm for this book. Although at times it taxed him, he always made the effort to contribute, as determined as Judith that the story should be told accurately and honestly.

And, of course, there's Judith Durham herself. After analysing her entire life and condensing it into this book, I find it really hard to find just a few words to sum up the special place she has in my heart. Judith has been a big part of my life since 1965, when I was ten years old and heard 'I'll Never Find Another You' for the first time. I was instantly captivated by the most beautiful voice I'd ever heard, and, more than three decades later, I still get that same thrill hearing her sing.

Getting to know Judith Durham and telling her story has been one of the great pleasures of my life. Had someone told me back in 1965 that she would one day share the intimate details of her life with me, make me lunch or sing to me on my birthday, I'd have laughed at them.

That she and I have ended up such wonderful friends means more to me than I can adequately express.

It's a small gesture by comparison, but this book is my way of saying thank you.

– Graham Simpson, 2003

PROLOGUE

It is around seven in the evening on 30 April 1993 and, as is normal at this time of year in Australia, it's a warm night in Perth. People of all ages are beginning to arrive at the Perth Concert Hall. Old people who haven't been to a live show in years mingle at the souvenir stand with young children seeing their first big concert. In the queue for programmes, teenagers wearing heavy-metal T-shirts rub shoulders with people in their thirties, forties and fifties.

Something special is happening tonight, something that transcends all barriers. It must be special to have resulted in this many expectant faces.

Backstage, backing musicians sit together, tuning up and telling jokes. Caterers clear away dirty dinner plates as an overawed delivery man, armed with bouquets of flowers for the star of the show, enquires where he should leave them. Road crews are doing last-minute production checks, while a tour manager pores over a computer screen. When the audience is seated, manager John Kovac springs into action and hypes everyone up with the same manic fervour that pulled this event together in the first place.

The house lights dim and thousands of pairs of eyes focus on a suspended video screen that takes these faithful fans on a visual stroll down memory lane. The unforgettable images of the sixties flash across the screen and the audience watches in silence. A plucking guitar plays the melodies of the songs these fans have never forgotten, the songs they've come along to hear once more tonight.

Three men have been getting ready to help recreate magic. Once in the corridor, they begin the short walk to side-stage. In the dressing room nearest the stage, assistant Irene Ruffolo makes a final check that the dresses needed tonight are all in place, while the lady whose name is highlighted on the marquee outside the venue checks her fringe one last time. She takes a quick sip of water and one last grape, and now she too is ready. A vision in pale pink, Judith Durham hurries down the corridor and joins her three partners in the wings.

As the visual display comes to an end, the voice of George Fairfax fills the hall with the opening announcement. 'Tonight, as part of their twenty-five-year silver-jubilee reunion, they're back together again:

Athol Guy, Keith Potger, Bruce Woodley and Judith Durham – The Seekers.'

And so it begins. The four walk on stage to a tumultuous welcome. They bask in a flood of gold light as the adoring audience cheers and whistles. Then all is quiet as they start to sing the gospel song, 'When the Stars Begin to Fall'. Tonight, although her voice is as pure and strong as it always has been, Judith Durham is unusually nervous. A solo artist for a quarter of a century, she has seldom suffered performance anxiety, but tonight is different. Tonight, for the first time since 1968, she's a group member again, and she knows how much rests on her shoulders for this performance and through the long months ahead.

As The Seekers move through the songs that made the group a household name in the sixties, the audience is transfixed, reminded of how timeless these classics are. Tonight, they're witnessing something they thought they would never see again.

They're elated that the picture they see in front of them is just the way they thought it should always be. What they don't realise is what a difficult decision it was for Judith Durham to become a Seeker again after so many years.

So firmly was she entrenched in people's minds as the girl in The Seekers and so comfortable was the public with that happy group picture, that carving her own musical identity became one of the greatest challenges of Judith's life. Unless they saw her solo concerts, Seekers fans never really forgave Judith Durham for leaving the group so suddenly, and she would be reminded over and over again in the ensuing years just how much she had disappointed them.

The public image of The Seekers had always been of a happy bunch of young Australians with the world at their feet. But, despite the group's success, Judith Durham was lonely, unhappy and unfulfilled, although she never let her fans know that. To the casual onlooker, she was the lead singer of Australia's most successful singing group, the first group to sell a million records, the first to reach Number 1 in Britain and the first to top the American charts.

The Seekers dominated the charts between 1965 and 1967, replacing the likes of The Rolling Stones and The Kinks in the top spot. The group knocked The Beatles from the top of the British Top 40 at the height of Beatlemania, selling more records in one year than the lads from Liverpool. Constantly in demand, Judith had met royalty, performed in some of the world's most prestigious venues and shared with her three associates the honour of being named Australians of the Year in 1968.

But Judith Durham was a reluctant pop star. Despite the phenomenal success The Seekers enjoyed, her four years with them involved anguish and heartache as well as the thrill of succeeding. Judith saw herself as overweight and unattractive and she was forever at odds with the direction her musical life was taking.

Ultimately, Judith knew she had to leave The Seekers in order to spread her wings as a person and as a performer. Before joining the group, she had already enjoyed success as a singer in her home town of Melbourne, and she yearned for that independence and musical fulfilment once again. She had certainly given more years to The Seekers than she ever envisaged when she set sail with the band for a working holiday in England. But the decision to leave The Seekers was every bit as difficult for Judith as the decision to rejoin in 1993. However, having decided to leave, she was able to look forward to exploring the musical universe that lay outside the confines of The Seekers' sound.

In 1969 Judith married her musical director and pianist, Ron Edgeworth, and together they roamed the world as musical gypsies, performing all types of music. Judith found enormous satisfaction in making music with Ron, and together they travelled on a spiritual path that finally gave Judith the fulfilment she hungered for.

Judith enjoyed more than two decades of personal and professional growth as an international concert artist and emerged as a songwriter in her own right. But, as the years passed, she began to realise that her former partners felt that they had been cheated. Perhaps now, before it was too late, there were bridges to mend. Judith's happiness was also permanently clouded by the knowledge that so many of the public felt she'd let them down by taking away something that had meant so much to them. However, it took a tragic car accident in 1990 before she finally decided that she should try to make amends for their sense of loss. After many months of soul-searching, Judith finally agreed to give those faithful fans what they'd wanted for so many years. It's mostly for them that she's standing on stage at the Perth Concert Hall tonight.

And those fans couldn't be happier. Tonight they're hearing songs they know and love, as well as new songs written for the tour and some The Seekers have never sung before. Songs like 'One World Love', 'Keep a Dream in Your Pocket', 'Devoted to You', 'I Am Australian' and 'You're My Spirit' sit comfortably with perennials like 'I'll Never Find Another You', 'The Carnival Is Over' and 'Georgy Girl'. That sound, that full-on four-part harmony that only Judith, Athol, Keith and Bruce can create, is as synonymous with the sixties as miniskirts and man's first walk on the moon, and it is a tribute to the musicianship of these four people that it can so successfully translate to the nineties.

For two and a half hours, the Perth audience ARE transfixed. Three encores and several standing ovations later, The Seekers are back in their hotel rooms, preparing to do it all over again tomorrow. Before the Australian and New Zealand leg of this reunion tour is over, they will have sold nearly one hundred concerts before moving on to Britain.

It has taken Judith Durham half her life to come full circle. Ultimately, she will have to leave The Seekers again, but the difference is that this time she won't have guilt to suffer. This time she'll move on with all her dues paid in full. Hopefully, Judith will have been forgiven, and for the second time in 25 years she will pick up the threads of the solo career she put on hold to become a member of The Seekers. What remains unanswered is whether those satisfied Seekers fans really do understand why Judith Durham shattered their dreams in 1968. One of the aims of this book is, finally, to explain why.

Judith's journey through life has been dotted with professional achievements and career triumphs. She has explored many different styles of music, flourished as a songwriter and consistently thrilled concert audiences on her own and with Ron. It is for these accomplishments that the public know and love her. What they have never known before is how many dreams Judith Durham set out with as a young girl, and how much sacrifice and suffering she went through to realise those dreams.

Through Judith's post-Seekers career, she and Ron overcame giant obstacles with their great love for each other, their spiritual beliefs and their unshakable faith in each other's abilities. Now, in the 1990s, with so much they could have looked forward to together, they were faced with the greatest challenge of their lives – coming to terms with Ron Edgeworth's fatal illness. But like every challenge they encountered in their marriage, they faced it together with humour, dignity and courage.

Judith Durham's story is as inspiring as it is moving. For more than thirty years, she has shared with us her gift of song and, in so doing, she has touched our hearts. Here, for the first time, she shares with us the intimacy of her remarkable life, and her honesty will touch your soul.

1. STARTING OUT

Tell me white dove,
Where will I find the olive tree?
For just one branch,
I'd search my whole life through,
I've heard them say,
A greener land is waiting there,
Where people wake and find,
Their dreams come true.

– 'THE OLIVE TREE'
TOM SPRINGFIELD AND DIANE LAMPERT

It was in 1938 – the year before World War Two broke out – that William Alexander Cock married his sweetheart, Jessie Hazel Durham. They had met some eight years earlier when Bill was working as an office boy with the Shell company and had caught the eye of the pretty young stenographer, Jessie Hazel, or Hazel, as she preferred to be known.

The teenagers were sweet on each other, but Bill was determined to carve out a career for himself. When the chance came for him to become a sales rep with a Melbourne electrical company, he grabbed it. His new position meant a good deal of travel and, throughout their courtship, he was often on the road.

They became engaged in 1938 and were married in Scots Church, Melbourne, on 22 December that same year. After a brief honeymoon, Bill and Hazel returned to Melbourne and moved into a solid red-brick home at 897 Mount Alexander Road, Essendon.

Because of the threat of war, Bill had been posted to a Royal Australian Air Force (RAAF) base in North Victoria before their marriage, and it was during one of his weekend leave visits late in 1940 that Bill and Hazel's first daughter was conceived. Beverley Hazel Cock was born on 21 May the following year. The year ahead was a tough one for Beverley's mother Hazel. She had earlier contracted pyorrhoea in her gums and the only treatment in the 1940s was to have all her teeth removed. The anaesthetic during the four-hour operation left Hazel with asthma, which would gradually worsen over the years and, ultimately, claim her life.

Bill's next posting was to Canada for training with the RAAF, and this left his wife and daughter, both asthmatics, at home fending for themselves. Beverley's baby eczema was so bad that at nights Hazel would pin her tiny arms to the sheet in her cot to prevent her scratching and making the condition worse.

Later, Bill was transferred to England, where he became a flight lieutenant in Bomber Command, and then a navigator with Pathfinder Squadron Number 83, serving over Germany. Formed in 1942 by Sir Arthur Harris, the Pathfinders were a pool of exceptional airmen from which crews would be drawn to lead other pilots on their missions. The Pathfinders' characteristic feature was their emphasis on aerial bombing, in which the centres of towns would be the targets for nocturnal raids.

Bill would later be decorated with a Distinguished Flying Cross for displaying courage, fortitude and devotion to duty.

In the early years of the war, before joining the Pathfinders, Bill was allowed leave from Canada to visit his family back home in Australia, and during one of these visits, in 1942, Hazel conceived for a second time. Alone again, Hazel delivered another daughter in Llandyssil Private Hospital in Essendon, at two minutes past midnight on 3 July 1943, an astrologically significant moment.

Hazel had decided that, if she had another girl, she would name her Prudence, but after giving birth she changed her mind and named her second daughter Judith Mavis. Hazel's parents, Anthony and Jessie Durham, who were living in the beachside town of Rosebud, returned to Melbourne and moved in with Hazel to help with the children. Judith's grandfather was of Greek descent, having been born Antoney Demetre Pannucca to Dimitri Antoni Paniocto (a.k.a. Pannucca) and Emily Trin Paniocto (née King). While still a child, he assumed the name Anthony Durham after his father died and his mother married Francis Durham. It would be almost three years before little Judy would meet her father, and, in the interim, she bonded closely with her grandfather, Tony.

'Mum told me that at first I felt much more attached to Grandpa when Dad came home from the war,' Judith recalls. 'I quite emphatically wouldn't accept Dad at first. He always figured in my life after that and he was always there for me, but I never really trusted him early on. I remember him teaching me how to swim, and me worrying so much that he'd let me drown. But he was so dependable for his family and so hard working.'

Judith believes part of that initial uneasiness was because Bill felt some disappointment that his second child wasn't a son. 'I think Dad always wanted a son,' she says. 'He was very conscious of his name being carried on. He had two girls and the name Cock couldn't be continued. It did disappoint him, I feel. I took an interest in the things he did around the house, like mowing the lawns and clipping the hedge, even changing a tyre. I remember early on trying to be a tomboy so that Dad and I could relate on another level.'

It wasn't until Judy was five, when Bill's talent for playing the piano helped sow the seeds of her lifelong dedication to music, that a bridge between them was really established. Bill's sister Beatrice had been a singer and Bill, who'd had lessons for only a year, often accompanied her when she sang in public. Later, he taught himself by the Shefte method, but he confined his playing to parties.

'Whenever we had guests to dinner or people around for a party, Dad would play the upright German piano in the lounge and everyone would sing,' says Judith. 'He was great socially, always holding the floor and cracking jokes. On the piano, his party pieces were "The Wedding of the Painted Doll" and "The Doll Dance", both difficult pieces. He could have been a professional entertainer, he had a real love of it.'

Home from the war in 1945, Bill settled back into domesticity, with his nine-to-five job as a salesman with Noyes Brothers. As with so many returned servicemen of the era, the trauma of war and its effect on him were probably never addressed. And, like so many of them, he would never share his feelings about what he'd been through, despite his daughters' requests for stories about the war. Whenever they asked what he did in Germany, Bill would always reply, 'I dropped a bomb on a wolf!' To Bill, the war was behind him and he automatically resumed his dutiful role as head of the family.

Now Bill was home, Judith's grandparents returned to their home in Rosebud. For the next few years, the Cocks would spend each summer with them in their small weatherboard home on the beach. It was a typical old-style Australian house, with its wood stove and outdoor lavatory, or 'dunny'. Off the veranda was a sleepout, where Judy and Beverley would sleep. The girls spent many happy hours playing and building sandcastles on the beach and, at other times, had fun making fairy wings out of old newspapers, having tea parties with their dolls or trying to mix fairy paint from flowers in the garden.

As each summer ended, the Cocks moved home to the city and Judy and Beverley returned to Essendon State School. By now, both girls were suffering chronically from asthma and skin disorders. Already prone to fevers, Judy had caught measles at age four and the illness led to a lung condition, later diagnosed as bronchiectasis which, to lay people, sounds like a smoker's cough. (It is a dilation of short sections of the air tubes in the lungs, and causes excess mucus production, in turn causing coughing.) For the rest of her life, Judy would be plagued by this condition.

Determined to find a treatment for her daughters, Hazel took Beverley and Judy to see an infant dietician, who initially suspected that Judith may have been suffering from lead poisoning.

'We would wait hours to see this dietician, Miss Nesbitt,' Judith recalls. 'Sometimes, we'd be sitting in her waiting room with Mum for up to two hours at a time. I remember her talking to Mum about lead poisoning and asking me whether I sucked my pencils at school. My nails were very hard and Mum was alarmed that I would cry whenever she tried to cut them.'

Once lead poisoning was discounted, Miss Nesbitt treated both girls' asthma by modifying their diets to the point of blandness. They could eat only starch-reduced Procera bread and Beverley was given a powdered glucose sugar to use instead of cane sugar. Throughout their childhood years, wheat germ, fish, mushrooms, parsnips and many other foods were off limits. At Easter, they could have only the tiniest piece of chocolate Easter egg each day. Judith says, 'It was probably worse for Beverley. Her diet was very restricted because of her eczema and she would literally have to go to birthday parties with just an apple to eat.'

Bill and Hazel tried to ensure the girls didn't bring on an asthma attack by overexerting themselves. Luckily, indoor pursuits – such as sewing, crafts and, in particular, playing the piano – became very much a part of the girls' lives. Bill and Hazel recognised Judy's musical ability from an early age. She could sing nursery rhymes in perfect tune from the age of two, when she also composed a little song of her own, and she could pick up complete songs after hearing them just once or twice on the radio. 'When I was five, I just loved a song I'd heard called "Forever and Ever". I can still sing it through to this day. And another song I loved singing was "Twenty-Four Hours of Sunshine", as well as the very first advertising jingle I ever heard, for Kellogg's Corn Flakes.

'In 1948, I can remember getting on the piano with Beverley and we'd play "Chopsticks" and "Johnny Wash Your Father's Shirt",' Judith says. 'The enjoyment I got from it was just overwhelming. I so desperately wanted to be able to do what Dad could do on the piano that I'd sit there for hours.'

With a sick wife and two delicate daughters, Bill Cock had to make many sacrifices, both professionally and personally, and after paying medical and chemist bills, there was little left over for luxuries. To save money, Hazel made things like cakes, scones, pies, jams, mint sauce and mayonnaise, while Bill grew tomatoes and silver beet (a vegetable grown mainly in Australia and New Zealand). With help from her mother, Hazel made most of the girls' clothes – mostly matching dresses with gathered, puffed sleeves. As much as Bill wanted to pay for ballet lessons and other such extras, he simply couldn't afford to. But, with a piano already in the house, he needed only to pay for lessons. When Judy was six and

Beverley eight, they began formal piano lessons up the road in Essendon with Miss Bendall.

'I was a bit disappointed after that first lesson,' Judith says. 'We played a little bit on the piano and then we had to do some theory and I found that terribly tedious. I just wanted to play. I wanted the instantaneous fulfilment of performing, even at that age.'

Beverley and Judith continued their lessons for a few months before Bill came home from work one night late in 1949 with the news that he'd been promoted to branch manager of Noyes Brothers, and the family would be moving to Hobart early in the new year. Initially, Hazel didn't welcome the move. Tasmania was so far away from her family and friends and the climate so cold, but she realised that it was a wonderful opportunity for Bill. In the weeks ahead, Hazel and the girls said farewell to their friends while Bill sold the house and took care of all the arrangements.

And so the Cocks began a new decade in a new town, and for Judith and Beverley, the six years ahead would be filled with happiness. After renting for a short time, Bill applied for a war-service loan and was able to buy a half-completed spec home. The family moved into their neat, white weatherboard home in Brown's River Road (now 145 Kingston Highway), Taroona, just five miles from Hobart. Bill named the family's new home Merryhaven and proudly painted it on the front of the house.

Initially, Beverley and Judy were enrolled in the local Albuera Street State School, but neither adapted well. 'It was an awful experience,' Judith says. 'I remember the concrete playground and how different the kids were from the friends we'd made at school in Essendon. For a start, they all seemed to talk dirty and I was bullied quite a lot. I'd just turned seven, but I was still very small. I remember they used to make fun of our surname, Cock. We'd never encountered that before.'

Before long, they'd been taken out of the state system and moved to the exclusive girls' school, Fahan, in Hobart. Of the school's two headmistresses, it was Miss Morphett who encouraged arts and drama and at last Judy could shine. Along with a strong academic focus, Fahan had a drama group, a choir, a madrigal group and piano tuition.

Throughout her school years in Tasmania, Judy was often ill and missed school, particularly in winter. 'I was very prone to fevers,' she says. 'I could wake in the morning and be fine, but by evening my temperature would be very high. I'd get asthma, earache, hives. I spent a lot of time in bed, playing solitaire or reading or making something.

'I had to be very careful at school. In winter, I sat in the classroom with a blanket behind my chair. I wasn't able to compete in things like the cross-country races, because it would trigger asthma. In those ways, I had to be very cosseted.'

While the family were in Tasmania, Judith was admitted to hospital to have her tonsils and adenoids removed, as was the custom for children in those days. Looking forward to the jelly and ice cream that invariably followed such surgery, Judy cheerfully said goodbye to Hazel. However, an hour later, her mother returned to take her home again. A polio epidemic was rampant at the time and the doctors were concerned young Judy might become its next victim. Perhaps luckily for her singing, Judith never had the operation.

It was in those early days at Fahan that Judy Cock first got the chance to perform in public. When Miss Morphett wrote and produced the annual school play based on the story of Snow White, Judy was quietly confident of being cast in a major role. 'Of course, I desperately wanted to play Snow White,' Judith recalls. 'I knew I could do it well, but I just wasn't glamorous enough for it. Instead, they cast me as the mirror! All I was required to do was to sing a reply to the witch when she looked in the mirror and said her "mirror, mirror on the wall" bit.'

But Judy's big moment, before a packed house in Hobart's Theatre Royal, was a disaster. When her cue came, she was downstairs in her dressing room playing cards. 'Miss Morphett was furious,' she recalls. 'The lyrics of the song I had to sing, just before the interval, were quite important because it moved the plot forward, but I wasn't there to deliver them. As these huge, heavy curtains closed, Miss Morphett made me stand behind them, although nobody could see me, and sing unaccompanied. Everybody was standing up and moving to the foyer for the interval and, gradually, they became quiet as they heard this tiny, frightened voice singing. I was terrified. It was a very traumatic experience.'

The following day, Miss Morphett phoned to apologise for what she'd done. All was forgiven, but Judy never forgot her humiliation. At the same time, she also learned a valuable lesson about acting responsibly in theatre. It would be some time before Judy had the opportunity – and the courage – to try again. But, sure enough, the chance did come. One afternoon, bursting with pride, she ran home from school and told Hazel the good news: she'd been chosen to play the principal rat in the school's production of The Pied Piper.

'I got to actually perform in public this time, and it was very exciting,' Judith says. 'I wore a rat costume and I had to walk to the front of the stage and sing "I dreamt I was a happy rat in that, in that, in that delightful dream". The play ran for three nights and of course, true to form, I got asthma and had to miss the first night. The understudy went on in my place, but I performed for the other two nights.'

While taking advantage of these opportunities in drama, Judy honed her keyboard skills with the school's piano teacher, Miss Cox, and joined the choir and madrigal group under Walter Stiansy, the conductor of the Hobart Symphony Orchestra, who also taught at Fahan. Both were impressed with Judy's musical abilities and often she was singled out.

'I was in class one day and someone came in and told the teacher that Mr Stiansy wanted me to come and sing for the senior school in the next building,' Judith says. 'I went over and stood in front of them all and sang the koala song from the *Songs for the Young Australians* suite. Another time, he had me up in front of the class and asked if I had perfect pitch. I didn't understand what he meant, so he asked if I could sing an A without hearing the note on the piano first. It turned out I couldn't, but, because he was impressed with me, he tried to give me experience and let other people hear what I could do. The same with Miss Cox. I was always asked to play piano when a pianist was needed for something at school. I was asked to play for marching practice and hymns during morning assembly.'

For the next few years, Judy absorbed herself in music, playing the piano for hours on end and singing for family and friends. From the time she was nine, music was striking a strong emotional chord.

'I can vividly remember my first experience singing and playing a song that I'd never heard before,' she says. 'It was Christmas 1952 and Beverley and I received our first sheet music. Beverley got "Any Time" and I got "When You're Smiling". I sat down and read as I played. It was the first time I played something my teacher hadn't taught me. It was a fascinating experience for me, reading and singing all the words and accompanying myself. A whole new world opened up to me. It was the complete experience of a performance for me. As soon as I'd played mine, I had to play Beverley's, too. I became quite avid. I'd become so quick at sight reading that I just consumed whatever music I could get my hands on. Eventually, I had stacks on top of the piano and, each school holidays, I'd work my way through them. One stack was classics, one was musical comedy, one was pop songs of Mum and Dad's era and the last was my school music. It took hours every day, but I kept at it. It was like a hunger in me.'

It was when Judith heard the instrumental 'Waltz of the Flowers' from

Tchaikovsky's suite *The Nutcracker* that she first became aware of how much music could move her. 'I first heard it on the radio and just had to get the music,' she recalls. 'It affected me very strongly; it was an incredible feeling. I just wanted to be part of it. I didn't know what it was at first, so I remembered the melody and sang it to the girl who worked in the sheet-music shop. Luckily, she knew the name of it.'

By the time she was ten, Judy was able to play more advanced material such as 'Bumble Boogie', 'Kitten on the Keys' and 'Nola'. She had even mastered a little of the Fats Waller material that Bill was so adept at, even though her tiny left hand couldn't stretch a full octave and she had to perch on the edge of the piano stool so her feet could reach the pedals.

'I picked up a lot from Dad,' Judith says. 'He had some old wartime stuff, mostly chord charts, and some of those songs were really great. Things like "My Hat's on the Side of My Head". It was such an exciting thing for me, chomping out the chords and singing "I've got a wonderful feeling ..." My lessons were very disciplined, very classical, so coming home to this big adventure was terrific. I was discovering all this interesting stuff from the twenties and thirties and I just couldn't get enough.'

Beverley didn't share Judy's dedication to the piano. She continued her lessons and did well in her exams, but didn't discover the emotional release that Judy was finding so satisfying. Beverley played piano very well and could remember music a lot more easily than Judy could. However, while Judy would sit at the piano for hours and hours, Beverley would play for a while and then want to get up and do something else.

'I think she saw me blossoming with music and she just figured I was going to be the musical one,' Judith says. 'That's the way it is with siblings. On the other hand, Beverley was very attractive and later on, by the time I reached my teenage years, I had this huge complex about my appearance.'

Those years in Tasmania were happy times for the Cock family (and Judith's feelings of isolation were assuaged every now and again when the family flew home to Melbourne). Bill was enjoying his new job and his increased responsibilities, and he was even elected to the Kingston Council. Hazel, although always ill, seemed to settle reasonably well.

Judith and Beverley had lots of friends in the neighbourhood, among them the Partingtons, the Actons, the Ludlams and the Floyds. 'We played with Robin Partington and his two brothers a lot and next to us were the Actons – two girls and a boy,' says Judith. 'All up, there were about ten or twelve of us and we'd play ball with them or cycle to the local township to buy ice cream. We'd all try riding with no hands or doing tricks on the bikes. I got to a stage where I could stand with one foot on the bike seat and one leg out behind me as I went down a sloping gravel road! Then we'd all go to the beach. Robin and his mates would snorkel around the rocks. We'd be freezing, teeth chattering and lying on the river's sandy shores watching them in their rubber suits. Other times, we'd walk up to the caves through the bush behind our house. There were some terrific times. Hobart was a marvellous place for us to enjoy our childhood. I still think it's a great place to live.'

Val Partington, mother of Robin, John and Reginald, is now in her eighties and she remembers Judy Cock as a short, plump girl who was always lively and anxious to play music.

'The Cocks were a very united family,' Val Partington says. 'Bill was a real scream, a natural comedian and very much the life of the party, but Hazel was a sick woman. The kids all had a lovely time together. They'd pack a picnic lunch some days and all of them would go off to the beach and stay there all day. About four o'clock in the afternoon, when the wind began to spring up, they'd come home ravenous.

'Judy's musical ability was there from a very early age. She was a happy little girl, even though her health wasn't very good. I remember her when she was about seven sitting on a couch with her feet barely touching the floor, being asked what she was going to be when she grew up. "I'm going to sing," she said. She always knew what she wanted to do.'

In 1954, Queen Elizabeth II became the first reigning monarch to set foot on Australian soil when she and the Duke of Edinburgh toured between February and April. Bill's position as a Kingston councillor afforded him certain prestige in the community and, when the Queen and the Duke visited Hobart in late February, Bill and Hazel were invited to the royal ball. For Judy and Beverley, this was like Cinderella – but it was happening in *their* family. 'Mum had a really beautiful dress,' says Judith. 'We used to love seeing her dressed up. We were so excited, we went to see the royal couple at nine different locations. When they sailed down the Derwent past our house, we stood and took photos. It was an incredibly important event in our lives at that time.'

By the time Judy was twelve and Beverley fourteen, this happy chapter in their lives was drawing to an end. Noyes Brothers was moving its head office from Hobart to Launceston, and, as manager, Bill was expected to relocate. However, knowing that Hazel's health was deteriorating in the cold climate and how much she missed her family and friends, he passed on the promotion and accepted the position of sales manager back home in their Melbourne office.

'I remember Mum telling me we were going back to Melbourne because of Dad's job,' says Judith. 'She knew I'd be leaving my friends and understood how difficult that might be, but she sold me on the belief that there would be some good opportunities for my music on the mainland.'

By way of compensation for the sadness of moving away from Fahan and their friends, Judy and Beverley had two things to look forward to when they returned to Melbourne in 1956: the introduction of television and the Olympic Games. Bill's involvement in the electrical industry meant that he was able to bring equipment home, and, from the outset, there was always a television set in the house. The first was a 21-inch black-and-white AWA set with 'rabbit ears' as its aerial, and on that set the family were able to watch the 1956 Melbourne Olympics as they were broadcast live. Judy devoured as much TV entertainment as she could, and recalls endless fascination with singers and pianists.

'I particularly remember watching Liberace on TV and wishing I could play the piano like he could,' she says. 'It was a thrill many years later to meet him and watch him performing live. I watched *The Mickey Mouse Club* and always felt I could do what the contestants were doing. I identified very strongly with any kind of performing on television.'

But the intrusion of television didn't distract Judy from her own musical pursuits. She continued her piano lessons and regularly added new sheet music to her collection. Although Bill brought home the family's first record player around that time, Judy never really found as much pleasure listening to records as she did in her hours at the piano.

Briefly renting a house in Denmark Street, Kew, Hazel and Bill enrolled the sisters in nearby Ruyton, an exclusive girls' grammar school. While its curriculum wasn't as artistically progressive as Fahan's, it nonetheless afforded Judy plenty of opportunities to express herself creatively. She became a member of the choir and leader of the madrigal group, and took part in the drama group's productions. Beverley, being that little bit older, had begun to lose interest in the piano and, being far more socially outgoing than her younger sister, she had discovered parties!

Not long after the family had returned from Hobart, the girls were invited to a teenage party, a first for Judy. 'I was thirteen at the time,' she recalls, 'and I remember taking all my sheet music along with me. I was so used to being asked to play for people at parties that the music automatically went with me.

'When I got there, I soon discovered they weren't the least bit interested in hearing me play the piano. They were playing postman's knock and I got into a situation with this boy, and I had to go outside with him and let him kiss me. I heard him telling his mate it was like kissing his sister! I was so embarrassed. It was an awful experience for me. For the first time in my life, I felt like I didn't fit in. Before that, I'd always had my music and everything in my life was ordered and happy.

'It happened again with my first dancing class. The boys were lined up down one side of the room and the girls down the other. The girls had to wait for a boy to ask them to dance. Every other girl was asked before me. There was only me and this one guy with bifocals and pimples, and he very reluctantly sidled up and asked me to dance. I felt like I was the ugliest girl on earth. Even he didn't want to dance with me – and he was ugly! I remember making a conscious decision then to try to work on my personality to make up for what I believed I lacked in looks.'

The beginning of Judy's teenage years changed for ever her innocent perception of life and love. Ever since she was three years old and madly in love with the boy who lived next door, she had romance in her heart. And she desperately loved the romance in music. Judy wanted Prince Charming to love her, just as he did in the songs.

'When I was a little older, I would be singing songs about making love, without any idea of the sexual connotation,' Judith says. 'Making love, to me, was romance, like the prince kissing the princess. Then, when I was ten and Beverley twelve, Mum took us to the local library, where she found us a book on the facts of life and talked us through the basics. This was my first realisation that Dad had had something to do with my birth. Up to that point, I had no idea. I knew Dad was Dad, but I thought Mum just had babies by herself. I had an argument with Dad one day and I blurted out to him that, if Mum hadn't married him, he wouldn't be my father. Of course, they then realised I knew nothing about the facts of life and that triggered the sex education.

'It came as a big shock to me that romance and love weren't something that fell from the stars in heaven! I found the reality quite sordid at the time. That wasn't how I'd ever pictured it in my mind. Until then, romance hadn't been dependent on my being attractive enough to arouse interest from a boy. Somehow I thought he would just love me.

The other realisation was that I had absolutely no idea how to make myself look attractive to the opposite sex.

'The day I turned fourteen I wore lipstick for the first time and started wearing those wonderful frilly, stand-out petticoats. But, from that point on, life became more difficult for me. I was suddenly in an area of competition where I had never been before because my music had always singled me out. People had seemed to like me for who I was and I didn't ever feel the need to compete. That all changed and I began to feel horribly inadequate, something I had never experienced in any other area of my life.'

To camouflage these feelings, Judy threw herself into her schoolwork and extracurricular activities. She began playing tennis every Saturday afternoon and became quite good at it, and she took to sewing and knitting with a vengeance. That same year, she got her first kiss. Things were looking up!

'Before the kiss, I got my first wolf whistle,' Judith says. 'I was in shorts and these boys whistled at me out of a passing car. I couldn't get over it! I went straight home and told Mum.'

Judy was slim – hula hoops were all the rage at the time and she would try for hours to master all its tricks – but she wasn't glamorous, and she desperately wanted to be. Much as she would have liked to have long hair, as Beverley once had, her hair was still short, with a side parting and a clip. She still adhered to the advice of a hairdresser back in Essendon, who had told Hazel that Judy's hair was too thin to grow long. But that whistle made her feel like a million dollars. Then came her first kiss.

'He was a boy in my dancing class and I got him to like me,' she says. 'He asked me to the ball with him and he kissed me. It was very exciting. But, after that, I had trouble making the people I was attracted to reciprocate my feelings. I guess I was quite shy, still am in that area. But I found it very difficult. I was watching my friends being asked out on dates but it wasn't happening for me. I'd go to dances with girlfriends and come home alone. It often used to make me feel depressed.'

The only safety valve Judy had was music, a place she could escape to when her social life was lagging. By now, her piano playing was very advanced and, while still at Ruyton, she was accepted as a student under Ronald Farren-Price, who taught classical piano at the Melbourne University Conservatorium.

'I was so proud when I found out he was prepared to take me on as a student,' Judith says. 'That whole experience of going to the Conservatorium and having lessons on a grand piano was absolutely thrilling. The piano I'd been playing on at home all those years had a very heavy action – although I didn't know that at the time. When I got on the grand piano, I was amazed because my standard was actually higher than I realised as it is so much easier to play a Steinway. And of course Ronald Farren-Price himself was so lovely. I had a complete crush on him. He was a wonderful teacher because of his passion and understanding of music and his ability to communicate to me the intricacies of music that I hadn't appreciated before. He opened my ears to Bach, to that contrapuntal form of writing, and the richness of Rachmaninov. I felt I was a real pianist when I got to that point.'

For her sixteenth birthday, Judy was given mascara, but she asked Hazel if it would be all right to exchange it for sheet music of the Rachmaninov Concerto No. 2. She couldn't wait to play it. As time went on, Judy became more and more convinced that her future lay in music, although exactly where, she wasn't sure. She didn't feel she had the looks or the image required to become a popular singer, so instead she set her heart on a future in either musical comedy or opera. Hazel had promised Judy that at eighteen she could begin having her voice trained for opera, and that was enough to keep her going.

When the subject of careers was raised in the Cock household, Bill pointed out to both his daughters that they would need to earn a living by the time they left school. Beverley had not made up her mind where her future lay, so she decided to stay on and finish matriculation in the hope of winning a scholarship to university. But Judy was certain her career would be in music, and she was prepared to dedicate herself to it. On Hazel's advice, Judy finished her leaving certificate and left school a year early. It was on Hazel's suggestion that Judy used that year to complete a secretarial course at the Royal Melbourne Institute of Technology, so she had something to fall back on should her musical aspirations not pan out. Then, the following year she could find a job and pursue her dream. To make it easier, her parents agreed to continue paying for Judy's lessons with Ronald Farren-Price.

While Judy was soon making great progress in what would eventually become her professional life, her private life was somewhat different – certainly as far as romance was concerned. Judy just couldn't seem to find her Prince Charming. This, combined with the fact that it had been a couple of hectic years with more and more homework and ever-increasing piano and singing, led her to seek solace in food. To cope with the workload, she had begun to nibble while she studied – a sandwich here, a quick snack there. When she started putting on weight, she became depressed and ate to console herself. The workload was taking its toll on her health, too, and she had to be careful because, two years earlier, a bout of fever had developed into pleurisy and pneumonia and she had spent weeks at home in bed, recovering.

For Judy, this was the beginning of a vicious cycle of dieting and weight gain that would not be broken for some years to come. She dreamed of glamorous stardom and dearly wanted to emulate Judy Garland, Brigitte Bardot and Elizabeth Taylor, her heroines of the silver screen. But gradually her waistline thickened and the matronly bust line she thought she saw in the mirror made her miserable. This was the beginning of a dilemma. If her shape meant she couldn't be a beauty, should she set her sights on being a musical-comedy star like June Bronhill, or an opera star like Maria Callas? Or should she just have another packet of biscuits and keep on worrying about it?

By now, the fifties were drawing to a close and Judy was about to enter the sixties with her personal life in turmoil. But her dogged determination to compensate for what she saw as her inadequacies meant her professional life was surely going to flourish.

Judy Cock may not have had love-struck boys glancing longingly in her direction, but, by hook or by crook, she *was* going to be noticed.

2. THE VERY LONGEST JOURNEY

The very longest journey
Must begin with just one step,
But you have to have a little dream to start.

–'HOLD ON TO YOUR DREAM'
JUDITH DURHAM

Australia in the sixties was a decade of startling contrasts and an era of change. It was a time of liberation, when youth culture would finally make its mark. The wave of rock 'n' roll music that had taken hold in America in 1952 finally hit Australia in 1955, following Bill Haley's performance in the film *The Blackboard Jungle*. It reached its peak at the end of 1959 and then suddenly abated. The Australian charts reflected the music that middle America was listening to: the lilting, safe sounds of Perry Como, Johnny Mathis, Pat Boone and the Platters. America's rock rebel Elvis Presley was gaining a foothold, vying for the top spot in Australia with local rockers such as Johnny O'Keefe and Col Joye and the Joy Boys. The new decade was greeted by Chubby Checker's 'The Twist', which triggered a revolutionary dance craze. Then there was surf music, invented in California, which became all the rage. But not for everyone, and certainly not for Judy.

One television show Judy had particularly enjoyed watching over the years was *Swallow's Juniors*, a talent show, and she closely identified with Janice Taylor, who often sang arias on the show. As she watched the participants go through their paces, Judy realised she could do that, too, and, early in the year, she successfully auditioned for the programme and was invited to appear. For her television debut, Judy sang 'Velia' and for the semifinal she sang 'Princess of the Dawn'.

'I still had no real musical direction, other than the belief that I was going to be operatically trained,' Judith says. 'I remember having to make a conscious decision about what to sing. I knew I should probably sing something using my soprano voice but, at the same time, Beverley and I had started to sing Everly Brothers songs as a duet. We were learning songs by Buddy Holly, the Platters – lovely, melodious songs – and the romance of Johnny Mathis records thrilled me. It was a bit of a conflict, but I eventually decided to play it safe, and settled on the soprano.'

The semifinal was won by two ten-year-old electric-guitar players and Judy was crushed. 'That was my first real lesson in the foibles of show business,' she says. 'In my earlier years, I'd believed that the harder you tried, the more you would succeed, but now I was learning that trying hard didn't necessarily bring you anything. I felt my talent was potentially as good as theirs, if not better, but their "gimmick" enabled them to win. It's the things that capture the public's imagination that win, at least with that kind of show.'

Losing was a big blow to young Judy's confidence. She couldn't believe she hadn't won, because she had sung so well. It knocked a lot of the drive out of her and she didn't think she would ever have the confidence to go through something like that again. But, five months later, she was back in front of the cameras in an afternoon programme on Channel Nine called *Toddy Time*, compered by Hal Todd. This time, though, she decided she wouldn't go it alone, but would perform with Beverley.

Having made themselves matching dresses, the sisters appeared before the cameras with Judy seated at the piano and Beverley standing beside her. By now they were both getting into material by the Kingston Trio, and, after their perennial 'Sentimental Journey', they segued into 'Lonesome Traveller'. This time the experience was much more satisfying for Judy.

At the start of 1960, with her seventeenth birthday still a few months off, Judy Cock enrolled in a secretarial course at the Royal Melbourne Technical College (RMTC), her dream of becoming an opera star now uppermost in her mind. At the same time she was continuing her piano study at Melbourne University with Ronald Farren-Price. Through another student she met there, Judy landed her first professional musical engagement, playing piano for a ballet school in the city's Pink Alley.

'I did that for quite a while,' she recalls. 'I'd go along once a week and play for all the ballet students. I used to wish I was one of the dancers, but of course I was a bit too fat. In Hobart, one of my friends used to teach me ballet. I was very good at doing the splits and could do one or two fouettés. I loved it, but Dad couldn't afford ballet as well as piano. I also wanted to learn gymnastics. If I have any regrets in life, it is that I didn't master those two loves, ballet and gymnastics.'

Still yearning to sing publicly, Judy took part in the annual revue staged by the RMTC dramatic society, playing piano and singing 'Zing Went the Strings of My Heart' and 'Birth of the Blues'. For fun, she and Beverley sang the duets 'Bei Mir Bist Du Schön' and 'Sentimental Journey' billed as the Nightingale Sisters with the added legend, 'Oh Those Golden Tonsils!'

Judith says, 'I wanted to play in a jazz band and I had the opportunity while I was still at the tech. One of the guys there who was forming a band invited me to join and asked if I wanted to play modern jazz or trad. I'd never heard of the terms at that stage, and I was so embarrassed. I did go to his house and play piano, while he and two other musicians played drums and bass, but it just didn't gel quite well enough for a professional career!'

In 1961, with a year of secretarial training behind her, Judy went looking for – and found – her first job, as secretary to the pathologist at the Eye and Ear Hospital in Melbourne, where, for a forty-hour week, she was paid nine pounds (Australia didn't go metric till 1966). It was a little on the low side for a fully trained secretary, but she had her own office next to the pathologist in the research laboratory and she enjoyed the work. During her final school year, Judy had won the senior science prize for biology, one of her favourite subjects. When she first started looking for employment, Hazel suggested she utilise this talent and become a laboratory technician, but the training took time and she would earn barely enough to support herself for the first few years. So, instead, Judy settled for a secretarial job, working closely with two senior technicians and two laboratory assistants. But still she yearned to sing.

By now, Judy's lung condition had worsened and, although she didn't smoke, her chronic 'smoker's cough' had become a major concern. She underwent a diagnostic bronchogram and recalls it as an extremely unpleasant procedure. 'The doctors thought there was a possibility I might have TB,' Judith says. 'They gave me a drug that made me feel extremely nauseous and then I had my lungs pumped full of this stuff that would help show the problem area in the X-ray. I was supposed to remain conscious throughout all this, but it was very difficult. I was rolled around quite a lot then walked to a screen and was X-rayed, over and over again. Afterwards, all they could tell me was that I had bronchiectasis! I could either stay on antibiotics, or have part of my lung cut away, but, as that wouldn't guarantee that the problem wouldn't recur, I decided to live with it. After the [bronchogram] operation, I was very, very sick. All this stuff they'd pumped into me had to come out again and the only way of doing it was coughing it up. These days, doctors actually commiserate with me if I tell them I had a bronchogram and assure me the procedure isn't done any more.

'The doctors also recommended physiotherapy, but, unfortunately, it was going to have to be Mum who would administer the daily pummelling, and she was gasping for air herself.'

Hazel's health had indeed deteriorated and by 1961 she had incessant lung problems. She was using cortisone on a daily basis and required an oxygen tank in the house, which was where she now spent almost all of her time.

Despite her health problems, and with Beverley's encouragement, Judy was now starting to take an interest in the burgeoning jazz scene in Melbourne. 'We'd already started going to church dances,' Judith says. 'I'd go with a group of girls. These were very wholesome places to go, very old-fashioned dances where you'd do the foxtrot or a waltz. Halfway through the evening there would be a supper dance, where you'd hopefully get asked to dance by someone nice, and then you'd have supper with them in the dance hall, and then the dance would continue. If you were lucky, someone would ask you for the last dance and that boy would escort you home.

'Then Beverley introduced me to jazz dances and all of a sudden it wasn't the "Pride of Erin" any more. These were jazz venues, like Dante's Inferno, Jazz Centre 44, Hernando's and Campus, where the music was hot Dixieland, blues and gospel, and the audience was full-on, stomping and cakewalking. There'd be two thousand people stomping and the floor would move. I just loved it. The music was striking a real chord.'

It saddens Judith that the jazz dances of the early 1960s remain unchronicled in music history. Before The Beatles arrived in the early sixties and changed youth culture permanently, jazz was all the rage in Melbourne and yet there is no real pictorial record of the period.

Jazz's revival in the city can be traced back to 1949, when the Australian jazzman Graeme Bell and his band topped the hit parades with numbers such as 'Black and White Rag' and 'Smokey Mokes'. Until 1949, big bands and ballroom dancing were all the rage and there was plenty of work for musicians, provided they could play barn dances and waltzes. Then square-dancing replaced ballroom dancing and, with less work available, musicians made their own employment by inventing the jam session. Jazz musicians organised their own parties and would play more to keep in practice than to make money. It would be the Melbourne Jazz Club, formed in 1957 as a nonprofit organisation, that would finally provide these dedicated players with regular work.

At the same time, casual dances were popular in Melbourne and, taking their lead from the Melbourne Jazz Club, they became known as clubs. Musicians were organising these events on an ad hoc basis and, when they caught on with the jazz crowd, promoters were quick to jump in.

'Jazz was so incredibly popular,' Judith says. 'There was a real cult movement in those days. Town halls were literally packed to the rafters every weekend with teenagers. It was crude entertainment in a way, but it had a real character of its own. It had its own fashion – corduroys, sloppy joes and desert boots. You'd knit yourself a jumper, using very big needles and a special stitch to end up with a fisherman's rib. The very tight corduroys were a bit like the leggings that are in fashion now. You wore them as tight as you could stand, with the big jumper over them. Then you'd top it all off with a duffel coat!

'The jazz shows were very uplifting and we'd stomp and cakewalk all over the joint. When they were over, everybody went off to a coffee lounge. You maybe had a beatnik boyfriend, and went off for coffee and a toasted cheese sandwich after the dance. It was the in thing to do.'

During the Easter holidays of 1961, Bill took Hazel and the girls to the seaside resort of Lorne, and it was there that Judy won a talent contest for ragtime piano and, later, met a boy named Michael O'Connor. Michael was jazz crazy and introduced Judy to this new and very exciting music. He also introduced her to his friend Ken Farmer, a drummer, and, before he knew it, he'd made a match.

Judy really flipped over Ken. He was fanatical about jazz and, in a bid to encourage Judy to try her hand at singing jazz, he lent her his collection of Bessie Smith records. Hearing them that first time turned Judy Cock's life around.

'I was so knocked out by this music,' she says. 'It was also my first realisation that girls could sing jazz. We'd all been going to dances and seeing people like Paul Marks singing with the New Orleans Jazz Band, so I knew men were singing jazz, but until I heard Bessie I didn't realise women could do it. I was very influenced by the blues singers Bessie Smith and Ma Rainey, and also by the gospel singers Mahalia Jackson, Sister Rosetta Tharpe and Sister Lottie Peavey, whom I'd also started listening to. Ken gave me the lyrics to some of the songs and I'd learn them at night while I was making dresses, listening to the records and trying to imitate them.'

Judy also learned of a hot jazz singer on the Melbourne circuit named Judy Jacques, who sang with the Yarra Yarra Jazz Band. She watched Judy Jacques work and made up her mind: she was going to have a stab at this jazz-singing thing if it killed her. The start of her operatic training was just three months away by now and, before then, she needed to satisfy her curiosity. She'd found something that truly moved her and she desperately wanted to find out whether she could use it to move others.

Her mind made up, Judy learned three blues songs – 'St Louis Blues',

'Reckless Blues' and 'See See Rider' – and went out one Saturday night with Beverley to the 431 Club at 431 St Kilda Road in Melbourne. The band was not a jazz band as such, but instead played more mainstream jazz material. This wasn't how she pictured her debut, but, as the night wore on, Judy finally plucked up the courage to ask the band leader if she could sing her three songs with them. 'He looked me up and down,' says Judith, 'and then he turned me down. I suppose I looked an unlikely singer and he didn't think I'd be any good. I went somewhere else after that and got knocked back again.'

Much to Judy's dismay, Ken Farmer had decided to sail overseas with the New Orleans Jazz Band. En route to his going-away party, Judy and Beverley popped into the Memphis Club in Malvern. This time Judy actually got somewhere. The University Jazz Band, made up of a bunch of guys from the university, were playing that night and Judy decided that their trombonist, Vin Thomas, looked the most approachable. She asked if she could sing with the band and Thomas casually asked her to come back the following week. She didn't get to sing that night, but at least this wasn't a knock-back! When she arrived at Ken Farmer's party, the University Jazz Band had arrived there too and Judy ran into Vin again. He seemed impressed that she knew these people in the jazz world and he repeated his invitation to come along the following week.

It seemed a long week at the Eye and Ear Hospital before that Saturday night arrived, but finally Judy was up on stage, singing the three blues songs she'd learned. 'I was wearing a tight black skirt, made out of a pair of Dad's old trousers, my old Ruyton school jumper with the sleeves cut off and a fringe braid around a low neck I'd cut in the front and back,' Judith remembers. 'I stood there with my eyes closed and my hands at my side. I had trouble with some of the words because these were Bessie Smith songs and I found her pronunciation difficult to understand – she was using that idiosyncratic language of the twenties that black American blues singers used – but somehow I got through it. The feeling was absolutely fantastic. I felt an instantaneous fulfilment and the applause afterwards was just incredible. People seemed to love it and the band was very complimentary.'

Kemble Miller, the Memphis Club's promoter, certainly loved it. After just one song, he walked up to the bandstand and gave Judy four pounds, telling her he'd give her another five if she returned the following week. Five pounds was as much as the professional musicians got for the night and it was more than half Judy's weekly wage from the Eye and Ear Hospital.

Judy couldn't wait to get home and tell Hazel that not only had she sung with a band, just as she had been dreaming she would, but she had been paid for it, too. Hazel was pleased, but concerned that Judy shouldn't strain her voice. After all, opera training with the very eminent Henri Portnoj was only a matter of weeks away.

John Tucker, one of the University Jazz Band members, was aware of Judy's limited jazz repertoire and offered to help her build a more substantial one. Many nights in the ensuing weeks, Judy would join him after work and together they would work out chords for Bessie Smith, Ma Rainey and Mahalia Jackson songs. Before long, Judy had her own chord book, which travelled from gig to gig. That same chord book would prove instrumental in changing her musical direction more than a decade later.

'Judy was a natural,' remembers Kemble Miller. 'Judy Jacques was the big drawcard of the day, but Judith was a more powerful singer. We actually upgraded the sound system to do justice to her voice. She was able to evoke the style of the blues singers of the day and she had great depth as a vocalist. She ended up getting five pounds a week from Memphis, but I always felt we could never pay her what she was worth.'

As much as Hazel encouraged Judy's fun, she remained very concerned that Judy would strain her voice trying to sing over the jazz bands. *The Sound of Music*, starring June Bronhill, was playing in town and Hazel took Judy backstage to meet the star and ask her advice. June told Hazel that jazz singing could ruin Judy's voice for opera and warned her to be very careful. From that point on, Judy determined to exercise the entire range of her soprano voice and later began weekly lessons with a local singing teacher, Freda Northcote.

For the five weeks leading up to Christmas 1962, Judy sang at Memphis with the University Jazz Band. Then Kemble Miller decided to replace them with Frank Traynor's Jazz Preachers, the hottest jazz act in town. Traynor played trombone and his Jazz Preachers included some of Melbourne's finest: Ade Monsbrough on clarinet, Roger Bell on trumpet, Graham Coyle on piano, Neil MacBeth on drums, Les Davis on banjo and Ron Williamson on sousaphone and string bass.

By now Judy Cock was aware of the sexual connotations of her surname. She was used to innocent schoolyard jokes about 'cock-a-doodle-doo', but now she was working with jazz musicians who were making different sorts of jokes. Before the advertising posters were printed for Memphis, Judy changed her name.

'I was pretty innocent about all that stuff,' she says. 'When I realised what the musicians were joking about, I decided I'd better do something about it. That, and the fact that *The Sound of Music* was still on at the Princess Theatre and whenever I passed, I would try to visualise my name up in lights on the marquee. Judy Cock just didn't seem to fit the picture. I didn't need to give it much thought. I'd always liked Mum's maiden name, Durham, and just went for that. I was aware, though, that it might have hurt Dad's feelings, because I knew how proud he was of his name. He even used to spell it out when he answered the phone. He'd say, 'Cock, C-o-c-k.' I think initially it might have upset him, but he told me later that, when he was nineteen, he'd considered changing it himself.

'I remember once I'd made the decision, I dropped off some dry-cleaning and gave my new name – Judy Durham. I used it again, of course, when I picked the clothes up, just to see how it felt. It felt weird, as if I was being dishonest and using a bogus name, but, after I'd used it a few more times, it started to feel like a good decision.'

In securing the services of Traynor's band, Miller let it be known that Judy Durham came with the job. 'Frank's band had the biggest name at the time,' Miller recalls, 'and he wouldn't have a bar of a vocalist. He just wasn't interested. But he was impressed when he heard Judy. We had an elevated stage and we ended up building a small substage so that she could be out amongst the crowd, who by now were coming along just to hear her. She ended up with a very big following. I remember how hard she worked on stage. She was really just a young kid, but she seemed to take everything in her stride. Suddenly she was in the company of hard-drinking musicians, but she never seemed daunted by it.'

Judith enjoyed the company of these musicians. They were older and more experienced than she was, but they were always very nice to her. She remembers well Traynor's initial reluctance to use a vocalist. 'In a way, I was sort of thrust on Frank,' she says. 'He'd done one of our nights with the University Jazz Band, playing piano, so he knew who I was and what I sounded like, but he didn't particularly want a singer.

'I was quite in awe of working with Frank's band because I knew what strong views he had on the way jazz should be played and set very high standards for the musicians who worked with him. He had a very aggressive nature, but he was very nice to me. I know he wasn't too sure how it would go, but after that first performance, when the audience responded so well, he relaxed. I came to realise that he respected my musicianship and, after a while, he invited me to sing regularly with his band at the Melbourne Jazz Club. That, to me, was the sign that I'd really made it.'

Graham Coyle, the pianist with the Jazz Preachers, had heard of Judy Durham before he ever played for her. 'I'd heard very high praise for this new young vocalist and I was very interested to hear her,' Coyle recalls. 'I'd been disappointed before by singers who came with great recommendations and I was expecting to be let down again, but Judy Durham really had the goods. She had a very dynamic approach and a vibrancy I hadn't seen in any other Australian singers at the time. She was an absolute natural as a jazz singer and what I remember most of all is that smile she always had when she sang. She always got a great reaction from the audience – they really took to her.'

By now, Judy Durham's name was getting around. As well as singing with Frank Traynor's band at Memphis on a Friday night, she was invited to sing with Sny Chambers' Bayside Jazz Band on a Thursday night at Downbeat, above Bob Clemens' record store in Russell Street. Soon, she was singing regularly with the big-name bands of the day. She sang with the John Hawes Jazz Band at the Purple Eye on Sunday afternoons and again with Sny Chambers at Black & Blue, a regular spot at the Balwyn RSL club. It was at Black & Blue that Judy first heard Jim Smart's Ragtime Four playing 'Maple Leaf Rag'. She was eager to borrow the music and play the real ragtime of Scott Joplin. It was so intricate and challenging compared with the Winifred Atwell rags she'd played as a child.

However, despite its popularity, jazz wasn't recognised by the mainstream media. Radio stations picked up on it to a point, especially 3XY in Melbourne, but television wouldn't touch it. *Bandstand*, the hip teenage TV music show of the time, would never present a jazz band, only the pop stars of the day. Judy Jacques was seen on TV, but only with her Gospel Four and not the jazz band. Jazz was never exposed in the mass media the way popular music was.

The new excitement she felt meant something had to give and it was during this year that Judy made the decision to wind down her piano studies. Already she'd achieved her A Mus. A, having been awarded the Associate Diploma in Music from the Melbourne University Conservatorium in 1961, a qualification beyond matriculation, which wasn't quite a Bachelor of Music, but was an excellent teaching qualification. She'd then moved from there into the first year of her two-year study for her licentiate.

'By the time I'd discovered jazz, piano was taking a real back seat,' Judith says. 'I found I didn't have the time to do the proper practice. I made a choice at that point to plateau at that level of piano playing. I felt I'd gone as far as I needed to go. I didn't want to put in endless hours unless I was going to be a concert pianist and I just felt I didn't have the dedication any longer to achieve that technical precision. Doing licentiate would have required many hours more each day to practise, where my method of practice was usually just to play everything through once and just enjoy myself. The teachers never knew that. I'd just roll up for the lesson and play and they'd tell me my practice had been very good, whereas I'd really only sight-read it and played it through once or twice since the previous lesson.

'I could see that, because I had a full-time job and was singing in my spare time, there just wouldn't be enough hours left to fit in practice for licentiate, which eventually requires between four and six hours a day. I realised I wasn't going to be that sort of performer. I was more into the instantaneous fulfilment of just playing songs and pieces that I loved, rough as they were. In that way I was fairly impatient. I enjoyed making music for myself and sitting at the piano for hours, but actually to take a piece and go over it and over it and perfect it, I'd never been that kind of music student.'

Ronald Farren-Price remembers Judy as a sweet girl, full of life. 'She had a very good ability,' he says. 'If she had wanted to dedicate herself, she could have excelled as a concert pianist.'

Judy also decided that she didn't have the discipline to study opera, having now found something that gave her such spontaneous satisfaction. 'As a child, I had listened to Anna Russell, the failed opera singer who'd become a comedian,' Judith explains. 'She turned her failure into entertainment. I remember it striking a chord. I've never been a stickler for technical perfection. My aim is very high, but never to perfection. I'm happy just to be able to share music with people and get it out in an adequate way. For that reason, I would have been totally unsuited to opera or a concert pianist's career. It's just lucky for me that the jazz era came along and I just got swept up in it, away from opera. Otherwise I would have been stuck in something I would have probably found very frustrating, having to specialise in just one style. Besides, it would have destroyed the natural timbre of my voice and many aspects of my singing that people seem to enjoy.'

For a time, Judy was romantically involved with Frank Traynor, and, when things got more serious, Frank invited Judy to live with him, something frowned upon in conservative Melbourne in the early sixties. It was an invitation she didn't accept.

'Frank was a bit bohemian and at the time he was setting up a folk and jazz club on the corner of Little Lonsdale and Exhibition Streets in

Melbourne,' Judith says. 'He lived upstairs and his plan was to use the downstairs section as a jazz joint. He had an old piano in there and some barrels for people to sit on. He actually taught me to play "Pine Top's Boogie" on that piano. Frank finally did get the club off the ground and for a while it became the in place to be seen after dances and a well-known place in Melbourne for musicians to go and jam. You could get coffee and crumpets – all innocent stuff.'

With her musical life apparently sorted out, Judy realised it was time for a job change. She'd been working as a secretary at the Eye and Ear Hospital for two years now, and while the job remained reasonably interesting, she was still earning only nine pounds a week.

'Mum and Dad were actually encouraging me to move on,' Judith recalls. 'Mum felt I'd been there long enough and was starting to become part of the furniture. I approached an employment agency and asked them what they might be able to offer me. That same afternoon they sent me for an interview for a position as secretary to the market research manager at a place called J Walter Thompson. They didn't tell me it was an advertising agency. If they had, I wouldn't have gone because it would have seemed too sophisticated for me. I went along for the interview and when I got out of the lift and saw their big J WALTER THOMPSON ADVERTISING sign, I thought it wasn't for me. But seeing I was there, I thought I'd do the interview anyway.

'When it was over, I walked away feeling I was far too unworldly and unglamorous to land that sort of job. The next day, the market research manager who'd interviewed me rang and told me I'd got the job. I started there on sixteen pounds a week, almost double what I'd been earning at the Eye and Ear Hospital.'

On her first day at J Walter Thompson, Judy found herself chatting to some of the other secretaries and, when she mentioned she was a singer, they told her one of the account executives was Athol Guy, who sang with a folk trio called The Seekers. The name was familiar to Judy. Her sister Beverley had been working as a receptionist at Channel Nine for more than a year and once, when Judy was talking to her on the phone at work, Athol Guy had walked in. Athol was looking for a female singer and knew of two singers who might be suitable – Judy Durham and Judy Jacques – although he hadn't seen either of them. Beverley mentioned to Athol that her sister was Judy Durham and handed him the phone.

'Athol seemed to know of me and I told him I was singing at Memphis and Downbeat,' says Judith. 'He said he'd come along and see me some time. Of course he never got around to it. When one of the girls told me he was working for the same company as me, I just bowled along to his office and introduced myself to him. We had a bit of a chat and he invited me to come along and have a sing with the group for fun that night at the Treble Clef, which was a coffee house in Toorak Road. He told me that Bruce, one of the guys in the group, would pick me up and drive me there.'

Little did Judith know that she would develop an immediate crush on Bruce Woodley, the tall blue-eyed guitarist, which would last for quite some time. Alas, it was unrequited! By day, Woodley worked for the rival advertising agency, Clemengers, and Judy knew of him as a one-time member of Morris Plonk's Moonshine Five, who'd shared bills with her on Downbeat concerts. When she arrived at the Treble Clef, she was surprised to find that the third member of the group was Keith Potger, an assistant producer with ABC Radio, whom she'd already seen on television.

'In 1956, I'd been to my one and only football match,' Judith says. 'It was St Kilda versus Hawthorn and I was there with Beverley and Robin Partington, who was in Melbourne on leave from the navy at the time. I'd seen Keith Potger on television with his group, the Escorts, and one of Beverley's girlfriends was going out with another of the boys in the group. Beverley pointed Keith out in the crowd behind us at the match. I thought he was really dishy and just watched him all the way through the game. He was so good-looking, I couldn't take my eyes off him.'

What she didn't know was that The Seekers had, until recently, been a quartet and the fourth member, Ken Ray, had left to get married. Ken's voice was higher than those of the other three and that was why Athol, Bruce and Keith were considering a female singer to replace him.

'I was surprised when I heard they'd replaced me with Judy Durham,' Ken says. 'I had always thought their plan was to replace me with another male singer. I didn't mix in jazz circles and wasn't really aware of Judy as a singer, but she certainly gave them that little extra that enabled them to make it internationally. I have no regrets about leaving The Seekers. We'd never have made it as an all-male group.'

That first night with The Seekers at the Treble Clef was Judy's first taste of sophisticated Melbourne nightlife. Never before had she set foot in a Toorak Road restaurant and she found the experience awesome. But, as always, although she might have been shy of her surroundings, her absolute focus was the music. Aside from a couple of songs that crossed the boundary from folk to jazz, Judy was unfamiliar with the folk material The Seekers were singing.

'I just sort of sat in and winged it,' she recalls. 'The boys did a few songs on their own, like "Born About Ten Thousand Years Ago", which I didn't know, but I found I could pick the songs up and join in on harmony by about the third chorus. We also did "This Train", "Kumbaya", "Wreck of the Old 97" and "Sinner Man". I'd been listening to Joan Baez a bit by that stage, so I already knew "Little Moses" and "All My Trials", and we also did "Down by the Riverside" and "Banks of the Ohio".'

The night ended well. Judy was pleased to find not only that most of the audience had enjoyed themselves but that the boys appeared happy with the way things had turned out, too. There was a twelve-pound fee that was split four ways, so Judy also managed to walk away with an extra three pounds. It was a lot less than she would have earned on her own, but it was a lot of fun.

'There was never actually a formal offer made to me to join the group,' Judith says. 'The boys just asked me if I'd like to come along the next week. Bruce continued picking me up on Monday nights and I'd sit in with them. Part of the appeal to me was this social side of Melbourne that I'd never seen before. I'd look at the menu and see things I'd never even heard of before. It was an education for me, a look at that sophisticated element of society which I never felt part of but was fascinated by nonetheless. But if Athol had said to me in the first place, "We're looking for a girl to join the group – would you like to come along and audition?" I don't think I would have gone. My head was still very much into jazz and classical music. Effectively, I was auditioning for the group without even knowing it.

'I remember about a week after that, I was talking to Beverley and I told her I didn't think The Seekers needed a girl singer. I thought they sounded very good on their own and they were all very good-looking. Musically, they had enough going for them without a fourth member and it struck me that they should have asked someone pretty and slim, to give them that glamour aspect, to look trendy. I found it strange that they thought I might be able to fill that role, but Beverley suggested it might just be that they thought I was a good singer.'

Later, the boys told Judy that, before her chance meeting with Athol, they had been considering offering the job to Judy Jacques. 'I don't think Judy ever knew that,' Judith says. 'I doubt whether she would have done it, just as I probably wouldn't have if I'd known they were looking for something permanent. We were both into what we were doing and The Seekers' approach was considered very commercial to the purists, like a sell-out.'

Judy Jacques did know she was being considered for the job, but wouldn't have been interested had an offer been made. 'I was a very serious blues and gospel singer,' Jacques says. 'I was dedicated to that type of music. I thought The Seekers' style was a bit lightweight and, besides, I didn't want to digress from what I was doing.'

In December 1962, the three male Seekers boarded a Sitmar cruise liner bound for Fiji, to work as shipboard entertainers for the round trip. The boys decided not to take their new lead singer with them: first, she had not long started work at J Walter Thompson and a fortnight's holiday wouldn't have been possible; and, second, she hadn't yet worked up a repertoire with them. During the two weeks they were away, Judy travelled nightly to Phillip Island for a two-week guest appearance at a jazz dance in Cowes.

Back in town, Judy continued to appear at the Melbourne Jazz Club. She was also in demand elsewhere and was often guest vocalist with the top bands of the day, including John Hawes' Jazz Band and Sny Chambers' Bayside Jazz Band. Aside from the Melbourne Jazz Club and Memphis, she'd guest with them at the Check Jazz Club in Essendon, the Red Arrow Jazz Club in Canterbury, Black & Blue and the Purple Eye.

In March, Judy was to accept a booking that would cap her achievements to date and, ultimately, mean more to her than all her triumphs throughout the sixties. Bob Clemens, who promoted the Downbeat shows, invited Judy to appear at Downbeat's Moomba Concert at the Sidney Myer Music Bowl in Melbourne. Judy accepted, on the condition that she could sing 'The Lord's Prayer'.

'I'd seen Mahalia Jackson sing "The Lord's Prayer" at the Newport Jazz Festival in the 1958 film *Jazz on a Summer's Day* and just wanted the chance to sing it. I thought singing it at the Bowl would be a marvellous experience. On the night of the concert, I was singing with Sny Chambers' Bayside Jazz Band and, when the set finished, I remained on the stage with the band's pianist, Doug Sermon. Doug started playing and I was singing "Our Father, which art in Heaven" and I could hear all this muttering down the front. I thought to myself, My God, what have I done? Then Doug dropped his chord book and I almost died, but I kept singing and, all of a sudden, something started happening. Everybody stopped talking and it was terribly quiet. I finished the song with the audience completely hushed. I got the most incredible emotional rush singing that song, the actual physical and emotional experience of bringing it to reality like I'd pictured it in my mind. I was transformed in a way. I was able to hit these high notes that normally would have been a great strain on me, but they just came out.

'When I finished singing, there was pandemonium. I could see people rising to their feet all the way up the slope in front of the Bowl, appearing to come forward in a concertina effect. I had been told there were nine thousand people there and they were just going crazy. One man just leaped on stage, so full of emotion, and he hugged me. I felt dazed when I walked off the stage, hearing people chanting. I couldn't make it out at first, but then I realised they were saying, "We want Judy!" and I thought they meant Judy Jacques, who was also on the bill.

'People backstage assured me they were calling out for me, so I went back on to this tremendous cheer and did a few more songs with Sny's band. I was on a huge high for the rest of the night. Artistically, it is still the most moving experience I've ever had.'

Bill Haesler, who'd co-founded the Melbourne Jazz Club with Traynor's first wife, Pat, and who was president while Judy was singing with Traynor's band, was there that night.

'I was one of the people in tears backstage after her performance,' Haesler admits 'It was very moving and her singing brought the house down. I'd always thought she was a great singer – she'd taken to it like a duck to water. Earlier on, we'd all tried to help her out by loaning her records so she could learn new material. She always went well with the crowds, and at the Memphis Club and the Purple Eye, where the crowds were younger, they'd cheer her.'

Three days after her Moomba performance, Judy was a featured guest at the Downbeat folk and jazz concert at the packed Melbourne Town Hall and would appear on the bill several times that one night. She sang with John Hawes' Jazz Band, then with Sny Chambers' Bayside Jazz Band and did a set playing piano with her own ragtime quartet. She sang with Athol, Keith and Bruce and the billing was 'Miss Judy Durham and The Seekers'. The same night, Judy joined Alan Lee, the vibraphone and percussion player, to sing with his quartet. Lee was performing Duke Ellington's *Black, Brown and Beige Suite* in its entirety and asked Judy to sing the Mahalia Jackson song 'Come Sunday' as part of the suite.

That was the song Judy chose to sing on the top-rating television programme *In Melbourne Tonight*. A member of the audience at Downbeat had anonymously recommended her to the show's producer Frank Sheldon. A spot on *IMT* was a real feather in her cap: host Graham Kennedy was the hottest thing on television and his nightly Channel Nine show was essential viewing. As it turned out, however, it was not one of the highlights of Judy's career. Confident as she felt with Laurie Wilson playing organ for her, Wilson was a long way from her in the studio and Judy had not worked this way before. She was the last performer of the night and by then Kennedy was probably bored. For his introduction, Kennedy said, 'We will now present to you Judy Durham and Laurie Wilson and they will render for you – that means tear apart – "Come Sunday"!'

As if that weren't enough, Judy had only to see a playback of the show for all her insecurities to start surfacing again. Her hair was all wrong; she'd worn blue when she should have worn black; she looked big. She wasn't Cinderella and TV wasn't a ball!

Still dividing her time between her jazz work and The Seekers, Judy had started rehearsing with her folk-singing friends in a bid to work up a full repertoire. By now, the four were listening to The Weavers and The Limeliters and adding Negro spirituals such as 'When the Stars Begin to Fall' to their act.

By mid-1963, Judy Durham was doing quite well financially. She had a full-time job as a secretary at J Walter Thompson, where she earned sixteen pounds a week. She was picking up three pounds with The Seekers on Monday nights, four pounds for Downbeat and five pounds each from Memphis, the Melbourne Jazz Club, Black & Blue and, on Sunday afternoons, the Purple Eye. Her fee for a one-off appearance had leaped to ten pounds. Later, the workload would become even heavier.

'I ended up juggling the two careers,' says Judith. 'At one point, Keith would pick me up after my first set at the Melbourne Jazz Club, drive me to Rob's Carousel Restaurant, where I'd do a set with The Seekers, and then he would drive me back to the Jazz Club for my second set. It was a very busy time. I was still holding down a full-time job, making all my own stage and day clothes, and learning new material.'

Keith Potger's job as a radio producer with the ABC meant he had access to a recording studio and facilities, even though he wasn't allowed to appear on television with The Seekers because ABC employees weren't permitted to hold second jobs.

During lunch hours and weekends, the group got together in an ABC studio and recorded some of their folk songs, including 'This Train', 'Children Go Where I Send You', 'Kumbaya', 'South Australia' and 'This Land Is Your Land'. Judy also sang solo on 'All My Trials' and 'Little Moses'. The tape was essentially made so they could hear how they sounded, and they also hoped it might come in handy in securing them further bookings. Years later, Keith Potger would strike a deal with the

Philips label and those demo tapes would be released as *The Seekers' Golden Collection*, much to the surprise of the rest of the group.

Through Keith, Judy was invited to be the featured singer with the international pianist and arranger Arthur Young, who was orchestrating a series called *A Man and His Music* for the ABC. Nine years earlier, Judy had heard Young's classical piano recordings broadcast on radio and could hardly believe this celebrated concert artist was in her parents' living room, playing her dad's piano! Young had visited Judy at home in Georgian Court to go through material for one of the programmes in the series, which was to feature the music of WC Handy. Judy already knew 'Basin Street Blues' and 'I Wish I Could Shimmy Like My Sister Kate' and she learned 'Chantez-Les-Bas' and 'Beale Street Blues' especially for the show. The programme gave Judy her first taste of working with a sixteen-piece orchestra. She was nervous, but loved the experience.

Frank Traynor had invited Judy to sing a track on an album he was recording with the Jazz Preachers for the local label, W&G Records. W&G was a two-family company – the Whites and the Gillespies – who'd been pressing radio serials on sixteen-inch transcriptions before starting their own record label in 1955. Judy was interested, but the record company wasn't familiar with her work and wanted to hear her before agreeing to record her. Traynor sent her along to see Ron Tudor, A&R man and publicity director at W&G, and she took with her the only recordings she had of her singing – not jazz, but in a Joan Baez style – on those Seekers tapes. She asked him to play 'All My Trials' and 'Little Moses' but, of course, Tudor played the entire tape.

On 19 April 1963, Tudor wrote the following letter to Judy:

Many thanks for the opportunity of hearing the tapes of your work that you submitted. Our selection panel listened closely to the tapes and have instructed me to advise you as follows:

(1) The solo numbers by you are very well performed but we doubt the commercial sales appeal of this type of material, due mainly to slow tempo.

(2) The up tempo numbers with the group early on the tape are excellent and if you could get together with the group on a batch of material of this nature we could quite easily be interested in producing a record of this nature.

Ron Tudor remembers The Seekers first being brought to his attention by the late John McMahon, the then programme director of Radio 3UZ.

McMahon, in turn, had learned about them from the bandleader Tommy Davidson, who ran the Treble Clef. Having heard the tape, Tudor knew this girl had something special. 'Judith has the most beautifully penetrating voice,' he says. 'There's something about her delivery that commands you to listen. She had that ability then and she's never lost it. It's an indescribable voice, with a tonal quality that is quite remarkable. It's very rare to come across a talent like Judith's.'

At a later meeting, Tudor told Judy he was happy for her to record a track with Traynor's band and also offered her a seven-inch extended-play record of her own in addition to an entire Seekers album. She was pleased but a little disappointed that there was greater interest in the group. Naturally, she wished she could have made an album on her own.

In being offered recording contracts, it didn't occur to her to seek legal advice. 'I took Athol back into W&G for a meeting to discuss the contract, and I remember walking down the street later and asking him what we would be called,' Judith says. 'I just assumed that, because they were The Seekers and I was Judy Durham, we'd be called Judy Durham and The Seekers. But Athol didn't like that idea; he wanted us to be known simply as The Seekers. I remember feeling a bit strange about that because my name was already so well known in Melbourne, but I didn't have the confidence to speak up. Dad was a bit concerned about the contract because, the way it was worded, W&G had our worldwide rights and in return we were being paid some incredibly low royalty rate, like two cents per copy sold. Dad asked Ron Tudor to change the territory for my EP to Australia and New Zealand only, but The Seekers album wasn't done the same way.'

On 17 August 1963, Judy entered W&G's recording studios in West Melbourne and recorded 'Jelly Bean Blues', 'Papa De Da Da', 'Muddy Water' and 'Just a Closer Walk with Thee'. 'Jelly Bean Blues', with its three-part melody, featured Roger Bell's blues trumpet accompaniment. Traynor, in cover notes for the EP, remarked on Judy's performance: 'The maturity and power of her voice are remarkable and compare with classic blues singers of twice her age.'

A week later, she returned and put down 'Moan You Mourners' and 'Trombone Frankie'. Judith had found both songs on Bessie Smith records and they had become popular favourites when she performed live. 'Moan You Mourners', a pseudo-spiritual, had been recorded by Smith in June 1930. In that same session, Smith had also recorded the rhythmic spiritual 'On Revival Day', which Judith would record two decades later. 'Trombone Frankie' was the track that Traynor had wanted

Judy to sing for his album *Jazz From the Pulpit*. It was, in fact, a variation on the song 'Trombone Cholly', first recorded by Bessie Smith in New York City in March 1927. Cholly was really her idiosyncratic pronunciation of Charlie, her trombone player Charlie Green, and a lasting tribute to his skill as a blues accompanist.

'Frank Traynor was [born under] Leo and was the leader of the band, and he wanted the song to be about him,' says Judith. 'That was my first experience of creating lyrics because I had to change part of the song. Bessie sings, "He moans just like a cow" and I changed it to "He leads the Preachers now".'

Judy had a cold during both sessions and was unhappy with the way 'Muddy Water' sounded. She asked for it to be withheld, but it would eventually find its way on to a Frank Traynor EP, *Apex Blues*. 'Trombone Frankie' appeared on Traynor's *Jazz From the Pulpit* album, and Judy's own EP, simply called *Judy Durham with Frank Traynor's Jazz Preachers*, featured, 'Moan You Mourners', 'Papa De Da Da', 'Jelly Bean Blues' and 'Just a Closer Walk With Thee'. In the cover photograph, shot during a performance at the Melbourne Jazz Club, Judy was wearing the cut-down school jumper she'd first worn at Memphis.

'I recall Judith being quite shy early on, almost wary,' says Ron Tudor. 'She may have had some misgivings about recording, but she really seemed to enjoy those sessions with the Jazz Preachers.'

Graham Coyle, who played piano on all Judy's sessions, recalls the means the engineers used in 1963 to achieve echo. 'You'd hang a microphone from a hook in the ceiling of the toilet,' he says, 'which was down the passage past the studio. When we needed echo, we'd just open the door and the microphone in the loo would provide it!

'Because this was jazz, we never got by on just one take. We'd normally do three or four, sometimes up to fifteen takes. Judith seemed to enjoy herself recording. She wasn't prone to error, so the retakes were usually because someone in the band had missed a note.' Of course, these were the days before overdubs, when discs were recorded and mixed live.

The EP was released, and Judy was excited and proud of her newfound status as a recording artist. Her fans loved the record and today it is a rare collector's item. Judy returned almost straightaway to W&G to record The Seekers album. The material they'd selected was a combination of songs they were already singing in their sets and more polished versions of songs they'd put down in the ABC studios.

'When the Stars Begin to Fall' and 'This Train' were favourites from the

Treble Clef, and they added to them the gospels 'Dese Bones G'wine Rise Again' and 'The Light from the Lighthouse', 'Run Come See', which was about the sinking of the *Pretoria* off the Bahamas in 1929, and 'Kumbaya', the time-honoured African spiritual. Keith contributed his arrangement of 'Chilly Winds' and they added a touch of bluegrass with 'Katy Cline'. Judy's solo on the West Indian version of the spiritual 'All My Trials' faithfully reproduced the version by Joan Baez, whose records had greatly influenced her folk singing. The group also included 'The Hammer Song', which was penned by Pete Seeger and Lee Hays and had become a popular recording choice for folkies. Hays was the author of another track, 'Lonesome Traveller' (which the Nightingale Sisters had sung on *Toddy Time*). The only Australian folk song to make it was 'Wild Rover'.

In these same sessions, The Seekers also recorded the so-called Queensland version of 'Waltzing Matilda', but it was not included on the album. Instead, it was released as a single after the group's ABC version of it was played on Malcolm Searle's radio programme on 3AK. Searle invited listeners to phone the studio if they thought it was worth recording. More than a thousand people phoned and W&G saw a golden opportunity. They issued it as a single and backed it with 'Just a Closer Walk With Thee', and it was billed as being by The Seekers featuring Judy Durham. It reached the bottom end of the Australian Top 100 and won a 3AK Edison Award.

Athol, Keith and Bruce travelled up the New South Wales coast to Whale Beach to play their single to the Kingston Trio's Dave Guard, who had settled in Australia. Guard saw Judy's name on the record and, assuming she was freelancing, sent her a telegram asking her to get in touch to discuss forming a group with him. Judy was thrilled and made a mental note to pursue the idea when time permitted.

With the album complete, the group returned to W&G's studios and recorded a couple of 3AK jingles that Keith Potger had written, and also sang backings for other acts. Collectors can find these early background sessions on W&G tracks by Johnny Chester and Johnny Mack.

'It never occurred to us that there was something special about a vocalist who could sing jazz and folk so well,' says Ron Tudor. 'It was something rare, but we just thought she could sing anything. We didn't realise at the time what a unique talent this really was.'

Introducing The Seekers was settled on as the album's title but, by the time it was ready for release, the group realised that, because Keith was still employed by the ABC, he couldn't be pictured on the cover lest his 'second job' be revealed. For the photo session, original Seeker Ken Ray returned and took Keith's place. It was only later, when the four Seekers gave up their jobs and turned professional, that the album was rereleased with Keith in his rightful place.

Introducing The Seekers was favourably received when it was released in November 1963, as was their first *In Melbourne Tonight* appearance, singing 'This Train' to promote it. The Melbourne *Age* wrote, 'In their first release for W&G, these attractive artists have, in our judgment, attained a standard right up in world class ... one cannot pass on without a special word of praise for Judy Durham's especially sweet singing.'

The *Herald* also singled Judith out: 'One of the highlights is the girl singer Judy Durham. She has a warm voice which suits the folk field.' The *Listener-In TV* positively glowed: 'What makes the singers is their lack of pretension. They are not trying to sound like anybody else and they are not trying to take their own brand of folk songs to some high and mighty art form.'

The group's work prospects were beginning to look up. Through Federal Hotels, Athol's client at J Walter Thompson, the group managed to secure a five-week booking at the Federal Hotel in Melbourne, marking their first experience in cabaret. The five-week season in Melbourne went so well that Federal Hotels offered The Seekers a further two-week engagement at their very exclusive Brisbane hotel, Lennons, where they would earn £100 a week between them. Athol had also managed to persuade another client, the Italian cruise-ship line Sitmar, to book The Seekers on three cruises as shipboard entertainers. The first would be a repeat of the earlier Fiji turnaround the boys had done; the second would be to Tonga; the third would be to Tokyo for the 1964 Olympic Games. In lieu of payment, they were to sail to London with a ten-week turnaround before returning in time for the Tonga and Tokyo cruises.

It was at this point that the four Seekers realised that the immediate future looked busy and promising and they agreed to throw in their day jobs. From the start of 1964 onwards, The Seekers were a professional singing group.

'I remember what a big thing it was for us to be flying to Queensland for this engagement and getting all-expenses-paid accommodation,' says Judith. 'Brisbane was like a lovely tropical country town in those days and terribly hot. The old Lennons was a very classy hotel and we were able to have amazing meals for nothing. Back at the Treble Clef, the boys sometimes traded their three-pound share of the fee for a meal, so this was a big step up!'

Dennis Lowrey was playing piano with Burt Weller's house band at

Lennons when The Seekers first arrived in town. He remembers there were three acts nightly in the hotel's Rainbow Room and, on this occasion, The Seekers were bottom of the bill.

'I'd never heard of them when they first showed up,' Lowrey says. 'We had rehearsals on a Monday afternoon, and I remember meeting all three acts that day. Judy struck me as very shy, whereas the three boys were quite outgoing. But, once I got to know her, she relaxed a little. It was a different story on stage. The Seekers were the opening act and Judy was very good. She had a pure bell-like voice, and she always hit the note, something you didn't always get. They were very well received. Lennons was very much the in place in Brisbane then and it attracted a society crowd who responded very well to The Seekers and were more receptive than they usually were to newcomers.'

On the two weekends they had in Queensland, the four drove down to Surfers Paradise for a spot of sightseeing and Judy's first attempt at water skiing. The stint in Brisbane was fun but gave Judy her first taste of being lonely. She was away from her family and friends and, being a girl on her own, felt she was out on a limb. All the group's meals were provided free at Lennons and Judy took full advantage of the perk. Through the week she would have pancakes and maple syrup for breakfast and filet mignon or T-bone steak for dinner. By the time the weekends rolled around, she'd be feeling guilty and would starve herself for two days. She was conscious of her weight problem, but so often found it hard to resist temptation.

At this time Judy began to think about her name again. She was aware that her mother had always wanted her to be Judith, but she was also aware that Hazel used the more formal name when she was cross with her. 'I'd started watching *The Saint* on TV,' she says. 'There was a character in one episode called Judith and it seemed to suit her. She was a very cool-looking character and being called Judith seemed very cool to me. I changed my name to Judith from that point on.'

Returning to Melbourne, The Seekers appeared on *IMT*, this time singing 'Just a Closer Walk with Thee' and 'Cotton Fields'. They resumed performing at local venues and Judy performed a few last jazz jobs on her own. Early in March, she had a one-week booking at the Pennville Club in Coburg and then returned the following week to sing with The Seekers.

The group fulfilled the first part of their Sitmar agreement by singing their way to Noumea, Vila and Fiji, where they added the traditional Fijian song 'Isa Lei' to their repertoire. The cruise director on that trip was Roger Henning, now a successful Sydney businessman. He remembers that The Seekers were a spectacular success at sea. 'They provided real quality entertainment. They were very normal, natural people to deal with and the passengers on that cruise loved them. Because they were working at night, the members of the group would sleep in the afternoons. I remember one time I organised a treasure hunt called "Find a Seeker", where the passengers had to go searching for one of the members. They all got dragged out of bed and they took it very well, although Bruce Woodley wasn't very impressed, I seem to recall!'

The cruise complete, the band returned home and before long, with the end of March looming, The Seekers began to pack again, this time for their sea journey to England. Dave Guard of The Kingston Trio rang Judith from interstate and spent forty minutes on a trunk call, trying to persuade her to join him, but she had to tell him she was off to England and wouldn't be able to do anything until she returned.

'I knew that the trip was only for ten weeks and that was what convinced me to go,' Judith says. 'I'd be able to come back and pick up where I'd left off with my career and maybe do something with Dave. Until now, I'd been a bit embarrassed about singing with The Seekers, at least in front of my jazz friends. I enjoyed it, but it wasn't the image I necessarily wanted people to have of me. I saw myself as very hip and a bit offbeat and that didn't sit with the image of The Seekers. When I told my jazz friends I was going overseas, I was relieved that they saw it as The Seekers enabling me to get a free trip to England and were all for it. They saw it as a real lurk. One of the jazzers actually came and saw me off at the ship and offered me a job singing at the jazz club he intended setting up while we were away. In my mind, I was going to be singing there in less than three months. Staying longer in England never occurred to me. I packed only summer clothes because I envisaged being away just those few weeks.

'Originally Sitmar had offered us a trip to Italy, but when it was changed to England I was even more pleased, especially as I could meet up with Beverley, who was already over there. I had planned to save up and go to London the following year, after having my 21st at home with Mum and Dad. Beverley was 21 when she went there and I planned to do the same thing.'

For Judith, a ten-week singing holiday lay ahead, but, as she would find in about six weeks' time, things don't always go the way they're planned. She was not to make it home for that family 21st-birthday celebration. Instead, she would become one of the most popular and successful singing stars in the world.

3. SAILING TO STARDOM

And we see the culmination
Of their efforts and their dreams,
There's no limit to the things that can be done.

– 'HOLD ON TO YOUR DREAM'
JUDITH DURHAM

The Seekers said farewell to their families at Station Pier in Melbourne and boarded the SS *Fairsky* on 28 March 1964, bound for England. When Athol had made the deal with Sitmar, they had asked if the group could play for shipboard dancing. For fear of losing the booking, Athol had unhesitatingly said they could play dance music. This was news to the others!

For Judith, this was unexplored musical territory. Initially she felt uncomfortable, but her innate ability to rise to any challenge conquered those feelings and soon she was having a ball. In many ways she was reminded of when she used to play for all those singalongs when Hazel and Bill had friends over.

'When we found out we were supposed to do more than just sing folk songs, we had to learn how to do the other stuff,' she says. 'We had a few rehearsals before leaving Melbourne, with me on piano, Keith and Athol playing electric instruments and Bruce on drums. Once we were on board, we started playing for the dances at night. We did a Beatles medley and a few instrumental things like "Walk Don't Run". The passengers loved it. Keith had been a real rocker and he loved the opportunity to sing rock songs. We were also called on to play for barn dances, so out came a lot of my old sheet music.

'We learned to become all-rounders in a very short space of time. The way it went, we'd play the dance music down one end of the ship and then at the other end, in the lounge, we'd be singing our folk songs in a sit-down situation.'

Except for the fact she sang at night, Judith was just another passenger. With the boys or with friends she'd made on board she spent her days having morning coffees in the bar, sunbathing on the top deck, writing letters home and playing the piano. It was the perfect start to what she hoped would be the perfect holiday.

There were several stops on the way to England, the first of which was Singapore. In Colombo, where Keith was born, the group met his relatives and shared a curry breakfast with them. Then the ship sailed through the Suez Canal. Disembarking at Aden, while the ship continued on up the canal, the group made their way with other *Fairsky* passengers to Cairo and then picked up the ship at Port Said. In Cairo, Judith was able to ride a camel and fulfilled a dream of exploring the Great Pyramid. Only later did she realise what a wonderful experience this had been, but, in 1964, she knew nothing about the reputed power centres of the earth.

On 21 May 1964, five weeks later, the SS *Fairsky* berthed at Southampton. The Seekers had finally arrived in England, on Beverley's birthday.

'We took the train from Southampton to London and I was hit by the unbelievable sense of history,' Judith says. 'I'd read about some of those famous buildings and I'd seen pictures of them, but now I was seeing them for real and I remember being struck by how old everything was. We didn't have buildings that old in Australia, of course. The lovely lush greenery we saw from the train was just stunning, and all the beautiful little houses with thatched roofs. Everything appeared to be on a smaller scale than Australia, but it was all so picturesque.

'My classic tourist *faux pas* happened on that train trip to London. As we were pulling into Waterloo, I saw a huge clock and asked the boys what it was. They thought it was hysterical that I hadn't recognised Big Ben and they still laugh about it to this day. "What's that big clock?"!'

Once in London, Judith was reunited with her sister for the first time in more than twelve months. She was overjoyed to see Beverley again and thrilled to be in England, such a long way from home. She'd had fun on the voyage and maybe the group would get a bit of work in London. But it didn't look as if it was going to be easy. The Beatles and The Rolling Stones were monopolising the album charts in a city that was beat crazy, while they were an Australian foursome harmonising on folk songs. Still, there might be the odd booking or two before they were due to head home.

Before setting off on the voyage, at the suggestion of the Australian entertainer Horrie Dargie, Athol had contacted Graham Kennedy, who helped him obtain a kinescope of The Seekers singing 'Just a Closer Walk With Thee' and 'Cotton Fields' on *IMT*. Athol parcelled it up with their *Introducing The Seekers* album and the group's biographical details and sent them ahead to London's famous Grade Organisation, hoping to pick up a little work in their ten-week turnaround period. With it was a letter of introduction from Dargie, whose Horrie Dargie Quintet had earlier worked for the Grades. Dargie had been employed by Melbourne's

Channel 0, which was about to begin transmission, and, coincidentally, they sent him to London at the same time as The Seekers to scout talent for the television spectacular that would mark the station's debut.

It had been prearranged that the group's instruments would remain on board the *Fairsky* because they were to entertain Sitmar executives the night after their arrival. However, unbeknown to them, the Grade Organisation had managed to get them a spot that same night on *The Tonight Show*, BBC TV's evening current affairs programme. This created quite a quandary.

'The boys actually had to borrow instruments to appear on *The Tonight Show*,' says Judith. 'We went on and sang "With My Swag All on My Shoulder", the angle being that we were Aussie singers who'd just arrived in England by boat.'

The Grade Organisation had assigned one of its agents to handle The Seekers personally. Eddie Jarrett, who handled the agency for Cliff Richard and The Shadows and Frank Ifield, and acted as London and European representative of Australia's Tivoli circuit, saw potential in the four young entertainers from Down Under and was determined to get them work. First, however, they needed somewhere to live. Beverley was sharing a bedsitter in Earl's Court with her schoolfriend Anne and, by coincidence, the room next to theirs was vacant. Judith had arrived in London with four hundred pounds and so was able to afford the two pounds and three shillings a week rent.

'I moved straight in,' says Judith. 'It was just one room on the fifth floor, with a skylight and no window. We shared the kitchen annexe out in the hallway and the bathroom was one floor down. I was very happy and the freedom I felt being away from home for the first time really affected me. The first thing I did was buy a sewing machine so I could start making myself some clothes.'

The boys weren't quite as fortunate. They were virtually broke, and, during those early days in London, they all shared a one-room bedsit.

The Seekers' BBC TV appearance had given Eddie Jarrett enough clout to have the group included on a variety bill at the Queen's Theatre in Blackpool and on 2 June – less than a fortnight after they had set foot on British soil – they were supporting Freddie and The Dreamers for a six-night run, playing twice nightly. Also on the bill were The Don Riddell Four, Don Arrol, Howard De Courcy, The Avons, The Mighty Avengers and a pop trio called The Trebletones. Judith heard The Trebletones play over the speaker in her dressing room, but took little notice of them. She was too shy to come out of her dressing room most of the time, preferring to hide in her shell. It would be a few years before she took a second look at the group's lanky piano player, Ron Edgeworth!

'Performing in a venue like the Queen's Theatre was just extraordinary for me,' Judith says. 'To be in the theatrical environment that I'd been so mesmerised by as a child was fantastic and we were really quite unprepared for something so big so quickly. I was travelling to the venue with a tiny suitcase the size of a hatbox, with my dresses, shoes and tambourine all crammed in. When we did the rehearsal for the show, the lighting guy asked me what makeup I'd be wearing. I told him I'd probably wear my street makeup, which is what I'd done back home in Australia when we were singing at the Treble Clef. He looked at me a little oddly and explained that I really should be wearing stage makeup because the lighting would just take away all my colour. The other mistake I made was to wear a different dress every night. The lighting man was going crazy, especially as one dress was green and, as I was to learn quickly, green doesn't light well and should be avoided at all costs.'

The show was a prestigious one, but there was very little glamour attached to it. 'We'd checked into bedsitters in Blackpool in this old house that we soon learned had no bathroom. There was a bath in the back yard, but they'd never got around to installing it. When we told the landlady we wanted a bath, we got a real surprise. She told us we'd have to catch the Number 59 bus down to the public baths! So that's what we did. We each paid for a bath and the charge included the use of soap and a towel. There was another place we stayed in around that time, which did have a bath, but the landlady would remove the hot tap at night in case anyone tried to have a hot bath late at night without paying for it!'

During that week in Blackpool, Judith had seen an advertisement for a Sunday evening charity show at the Blackpool Opera House organised by the Jewish Committee for Aiding Deserving Societies. Produced and directed by the Grade Organisation, it was to star some of Britain's big-name acts, including Tito Gobbi, Tommy Trinder, Ronnie Carroll, Acker Bilk and his Paramount Jazz Band, Susan Lane, Millicent Martin and – particularly of interest to Judith – Dusty Springfield.

Horrie Dargie was in Blackpool on business at the time and he and Judith went to the Opera House to buy the group's tickets to the show. Judith was recognised at the box office by a Grade Organisation representative. Assuming Dargie was their manager, he told him Susan Lane had come down with laryngitis and had to cancel, leaving a vacancy on the bill. Would The Seekers be interested in stepping in, seeing that they were already in Blackpool? Would they ever!

'He asked me how much money The Seekers would want for stepping in,' Dargie recalls. 'I told him they'd take whatever Susan Lane was going to be paid, which turned out to be 60 pounds. When we left the theatre, we went straight to Blackpool station, where the boys were checking in their luggage for the trip back to London. I told them to start unpacking straightaway because there was a show to do that night.'

The Seekers appeared between The Executives and Acker Bilk and, according to a Blackpool press review, 'got one of the best ovations of the night'. Horrie Dargie was impressed by their performance. 'They went very well, considering how big some of the other names were,' he says. 'They were a contrast – three clean-cut boys and a sweet, beautiful girl. The audience loved them.'

Their performance attracted a column piece in *Melody Maker*, one of the leading music publications, which also mentioned that 'Myra' and 'With My Swag All on My Shoulder', recorded the previous year for W&G in Australia, had been released in Britain on the Oriole label. It was reviewed in *The World's Fair*, whose reviewer wrote, 'The sound they make is good enough to top any chart – a C&W sort of Springfields. It is so polished, it glitters.'

In the coming months, The Seekers would often be compared to The Springfields, a folk trio formed in the early sixties and made up of brother and sister Tom and Dusty Springfield, and Tim Field. In 1961 and 1962, The Springfields had minor hits on the Philips label with 'Broadway' and 'Bambino'; then in 1962, Field left and was replaced by Mike Hurst. The following year, the trio hit the charts in a big way with three Top 40 entries: 'Island of Dreams', 'Say I Won't Be There' and 'Come on Home'. That year, The Springfields split up. Tom Springfield, who'd written most of the trio's material, concentrated on his songwriting and production, as did Hurst, while Dusty launched a solo career that soon made her one of the top female performers in Britain. By the time The Seekers supported her at Blackpool, Dusty had already reached the Top 5 in Britain and Top 20 in Australia and America, with 'I Only Want to Be with You'.

'I had looked forward to seeing Dusty Springfield at the Opera House – that was one of the reasons I was buying tickets,' Judith says. 'Then, when we were included on the bill with her, I made sure I was able to watch her and see how she did things. I still expected that before too long I'd be a solo performer again and I was watching to see how she worked and the sort of material she was doing. I was quite in awe. I remember talking to her secretary, who told me the sky-blue skirt Dusty was wearing had been specially made for the show and cost forty pounds. It seemed so incredibly extravagant to me. I was still making my own clothes on the sewing machine in my bedsitter!'

Newspaper articles claim that Dusty Springfield saw The Seekers perform in the Opera House show and mentioned them to her brother Tom as a possible vehicle for the sort of material he was writing. At the same time, Keith – who was looking to buy a twelve-string guitar – made contact with Tom Springfield, and Eddie Jarrett clicked to another possibility.

Once back in London, Judith was shown around the city by her sister, who delighted in taking her to jazz clubs to see some of the big-name jazz stars Judith had only ever heard on record. One evening, while exploring the London streets with Beverley, Judith stumbled across a coffee lounge in Soho called Act One, Scene One. They went inside and noticed Long John Baldry having his astrology chart plotted by an old man with a long grey beard. Both sisters by now had an intense interest in astrology and couldn't resist the opportunity to have their futures told.

'His name was Ernest Page,' Judith recollects. 'We paid him five shillings [25 pence] each and he got out his books and meticulously started doing our charts. He knew my star sign was Cancer, the home body, and the first thing he said to me was that he couldn't understand what I was doing on the other side of the world, so far from home. He then went on to pinpoint my personal qualities – prophetic insight, maternal instinct, tenacity of purpose, difficulty with travel, mood changes, creativity – all of which were correct. But what really intrigued me was his insistence that I would have success, major success, in February 1965. That was only seven months away. He also told me I would have a "love marriage", a truly exceptional marriage. I never saw Ernest again, but I always kept the chart.'

In seven months' time, Judith would learn how prophetic Ernest Page's first prediction had been, but it would be several years before the second prediction came true.

Before long, Judith was sitting in with Ken Colyer's band and thoroughly enjoying the experience. The London jazz scene was different from that of Melbourne, but Judith still felt quite at home in it. In London in those days, jazz was often presented as a sit-down affair where people went to listen, not to dance. Most venues were clubs, unlike in Melbourne, where they were mostly halls. It had been some months since Judith had sung jazz and that familiar rush returned. 'It was such an accolade, being allowed to sing with Ken Colyer,' Judith says. 'He was so complimentary after I'd sung, I was on Cloud Nine. And I'd met Sammy Rimington through Beverley, who was a big fan of the band. Sammy was just seventeen, at the beginning of his career, and he was regularly playing with Ken. He was such an amazing player.' Judith had no idea then, but a decade or so later Sammy Rimington's name would be famous in the jazz world and he would be her clarinet and sax player.

Acker Bilk and his Paramount Jazz Band were also immensely popular in Britain at the time. Bilk had already had ten Top 40 hits in Britain, including 'Buena Sera', 'That's My Home' and the Number 1 smash, 'Stranger on the Shore'. Having worked on the same bill with Bilk in Blackpool, Judith was confident enough to ask if she could sing with his band too.

'I sang three songs one night with Acker Bilk in a London club,' Judith says. 'I finished with "We Shall Not Be Moved", which I'd always sung in my jazz shows, and it brought the house down. Acker and his manager came up and talked to me after the show. They told me the band had been booked for a radio broadcast in Scandinavia and he invited me to go along as their singer, but I felt obliged to tell them about The Seekers and how we were being handled by the Grade Organisation. And that was the end of that.'

This final realisation that her jazz singing days were over, at least for the time being, tugged at Judith's heart. 'I felt that my loyalties lay with the guys while we were in England. I felt that I really couldn't carry on a second career in jazz, much as I missed it. I thought, image-wise, it would be very confusing for the public. So I reluctantly had to let it go.'

Judith didn't have long to dwell on her lost jazz opportunities. The Seekers were starting to make waves and, within a fortnight of their appearance in Blackpool, they were offered a television spot supporting Buddy Ebsen – most commonly known for his role as Uncle Jed in TV's *The Beverly Hillbillies* – on a *Sunday Night at the London Palladium* bill. That show was staged, and televised, on 21 June. 'It was a major booking for us,' says Judith. 'We actually had to audition for that one. That same day, while we were backstage at the Palladium, I met Eddie Jarrett for the first time. Up till then, he'd done all the group's business with Athol. When I met him, I felt like I'd known him for a long time. I automatically called him Eddie and not Mr Jarrett, which I would usually have done in those days with someone who was older than me. The audition was successful and we got the booking. We went very well with the audience and it stuck in my mind how many people seemed to have seen the telecast. The very next day, I went along to see Mickie Ashman's band with Beverley and sat in again. All the guys in the band and the audience had seen the TV show.'

Over the next couple of months, The Seekers travelled the English countryside, appearing in small northern clubs before two or three hundred people. 'We often did more than one show a night,' recalls Judith. 'We'd do a short set – about fifteen minutes – at one club and we'd get a hundred pounds between us. Then we'd jump in the van we'd bought and drive several miles to another club for another set. It was a slog, but it was an adventure at the same time.'

Eddie Jarrett was hearing nothing but good reports about the group's performances and contrived a way to keep them on British soil. He called Judith into the office one day with Athol, Keith and Bruce and told them he could book them solidly if they would agree to stay longer in Britain. To prove it, he would sign them on the spot for a sixteen-week summer season in Bournemouth, almost twelve months away. Judith was confused. She could see this was a major group commitment and would mean temporarily giving up her dream of becoming a star in her own right. On the other hand, she was beginning to enjoy the adventure and wondered where it might lead her. She enjoyed life in London and spending time with Beverley, and, although she missed her parents, she didn't want to disappoint her three singing partners, who were keen to stay while there was work. Instead of boarding the *Fairsky* and returning to Australia on 30 July, The Seekers tore up their tickets and history was written.

Judith turned 21 on 3 July 1964. The group was out of town the day before, so Judith began celebrating at two minutes after midnight Australian time, the time she'd been born. She enjoyed one party with Beverley and Bruce Woodley's relatives in Hampshire, and the next day in London she partied with Bev and her friends and the three Seekers. That night, she phoned Hazel and Bill back home in Australia and had to summon the courage to break the news that things were looking good for The Seekers and she had decided to stay on in Britain indefinitely. In persuading The Seekers to stay in Britain, Eddie Jarrett had dangled some tempting carrots. The sixteen-week season the following year at the Winter Gardens in Bournemouth could be secured and there was a Christmas pantomime in the wind. These were good, solid bookings and Judith was convinced that sticking to her original plan and returning to Australia would be letting everybody down when there was so much work ready to be lined up.

'I felt awful making that call,' Judith says. 'I felt bad for Mum and Dad because they weren't with me on my birthday and I felt worse telling them I wasn't coming home. A couple of weeks later I reluctantly phoned Dave Guard in Australia, to tell him I wasn't coming home and therefore wouldn't be able to so some group work with him, as we'd planned before I left.'

The Seekers landed another major booking supporting Max Bygraves at the Winter Gardens Theatre in Bournemouth and, two weeks later, they were added to the bill of a variety show headlined by the honky-tonk pianist Winifred Atwell at the Hippodrome in Brighton. Also on that bill were the magician David Nixon and the singer Mark Wynter, but it was The Seekers who were singled out in reviews. The reviewer for the *Evening Argus* wrote, 'The show was nearly stolen by an Australian quartet, The Seekers, with a programme of folksy material put over in a thoroughly professional manner.'

With the Bournemouth season finished, The Seekers commenced a week with Mark Wynter at the Hippodrome in Birmingham, supporting The Applejacks, whose two records – 'Tell Me When' and 'Like Dreamers Do' – had been Top 20 successes earlier in the year. Again, they were noticed by the critics. A review in the Birmingham *Evening Mail* said, 'From Australia come a folk-flavoured group known as The Seekers. Watch their progress in this country. They are on a winning ticket.'

They certainly were. The group had been noticed by Ronnie Carroll, who had shared the bill with them back at the Blackpool Opera House, and they were signed as regular guests on his new weekly ATV series, *Call in on Carroll*. The Seekers were to sing two songs each week on the programme, which also included the singer Janie Marden and the Jack Parnell Orchestra as regulars. This new series featured many of Britain's biggest names as guest stars, including Dusty Springfield and Dickie Valentine.

'It was just terrific doing that show,' says Judith. 'It was great for me because they made costumes especially for me. They knew I was weight-conscious and what I was comfortable in, and so they'd make these nice waisted dresses that looked great on TV. They also spent about an hour each week on my makeup, glamorising me a bit. I'd never been terribly interested in things like makeup, so to have someone else do it for me thrilled me to bits. They had ways of shading my cheeks with makeup and I learned a lot. For the first time, I started feeling more confident about being on TV.'

Each Friday morning, The Seekers would meet in Studio D at ATV's Elstree complex for rehearsals and wait around for the show to be prerecorded. The Seekers performed two numbers each week, usually folk songs and the occasional gospel from their stage act. The group was a hit with the viewing public and hailed by the critics. Eddie Jarrett was able to secure more and more club bookings for them, in addition to their residency on *Call in on Carroll* and a hectic schedule of radio broadcasts. By now, Athol had taken tapes of The Seekers around to the major British record companies, but nobody had shown any particular interest in signing them. One Sunday afternoon, while the group was at a party, Keith bumped into an old friend who was now employed by the World Record Club and before long an offer was made. The Seekers got a bad deal, having been offered a royalty of only around 2 per cent, but it was a start. With Keith Grant appointed as their sound engineer and Cyril Ornadel as executive producer, the group went into Olympic Studios with just a one-day booking.

Judith didn't question the financial side of the contract. She was impressed to be making a record for the World Record Club. Hazel and Bill had been members in Australia and had bought some orchestral records and a Maria Callas album, which had inspired Judith to aim for a career in opera. Much later, in 1994, a former executive of the World Record Club in Australia met Athol Guy. As they shook hands, he thanked Athol profusely, explaining that he had been able to retire on the proceeds of those Seekers records. Everybody, it seemed, got rich from Seekers records. Everybody but The Seekers!

The songs the group settled on for this first English-recorded album were 'The Wreck of the Old 97', their version of 'Waltzing Matilda', 'Cotton Fields', 'Lemon Tree', 'Gotta Travel On', 'With My Swag All on My Shoulder', 'Isa Lei', 'Whiskey in the Jar', 'Five Hundred Miles', 'Gypsy Rover', and 'South Australia'. Judith was also featured on 'Plaisir D'Amour' and 'Danny Boy'.

'We did that first album literally in one day,' Judith recalls. 'We went in at ten in the morning and all stood around the mikes and did the material we'd been performing for months, back since the Treble Clef days. We'd rehearsed the material well and all felt so exuberant during the sessions that we finished by seven o'clock that evening and all went out for a curry! Because I'd been watching my weight, I'd actually been on a four-day fast, just drinking black coffee. My fast ended with the curry that night. It's a wonder I survived the onslaught.

'We listened back to the tapes a few days later and we realised there were a few rough bits in there, so we decided we'd go back into the studios and redo a few of them. But we didn't come up with anything that was better than what we'd done originally. The album had been created in a really good atmosphere and the mood sounded so good. We did something like forty-three different takes of "Wreck of the Old 97" before we decided to just leave it as it was!'

The album was released simply as *The Seekers*, with a black and white photo of the group taken on Westminster Bridge as its cover. The photo was taken early one freezing London morning and Judith draped a homemade woollen coat around her shoulders, over her homemade sleeveless summer dress. She pleaded with the photographer not to get the coat in the shot but, needless to say, he did. On the album cover, much to her horror, she appears to be wearing an old-fashioned shawl.

The album was well received by the public, who were enjoying this new Australian group on TV every week, and, more importantly, it was well received by the World Record Club. Grant, Ornadel and the WRC's Sir Norman Lonsdale were particularly taken with Judith's singing and very quickly a second World Record Club album was suggested. Judith was to perform six solo tracks on the album, with an orchestra conducted by Bobby Richards. Again, Judith wondered about the billing. If half the album featured her solo and the boys weren't being featured on all the tracks, it somehow didn't seem right to call it *The Seekers*. She insisted that the boys make their audible presence felt, at least with 'oohs' and 'aahs', to make it truly a Seekers record.

Judith would find out years later, after Hazel and Bill had a casual chat with a record company executive in Australia, that the World Record Club had actually requested that the album be released as 'Judith Durham and The Seekers'. The boys had never let Judith know that this opportunity had been presented and that they had turned it down.

For the session, the group looked beyond their usual repertoire for material. The quartet was, at this point, in accord on the material they performed. They would, on occasion, argue the toss on chord structures, but picking the songs in the first place was never a problem. They chose the American gospels 'This Little Light of Mine' and 'We're Moving On', the beautiful Scottish folk song 'The Water Is Wide' and the spiritual 'Well Well Well', and they recorded the Negro blues 'Chilly Winds' and 'Kumbaya' again. The group also covered Bob Dylan's war protest song 'Blowin' in the Wind', which had been a hit the previous year for Peter, Paul and Mary, and a children's lullaby called 'Morningtown Ride' written by Malvina Reynolds, which Keith had found on an album by the American folk band The Limeliters. For her solo numbers, Judith picked another Malvina Reynolds song, 'What

Have They Done to the Rain?', a very early protest song about the damage atomic testing was causing to the environment, and her own arrangement of 'Lady Mary', an English ballad that was adopted by America's early settlers. The producers requested that Judith sing the New Hebrides love song 'Eriskay Love Lilt'.

Once again the group entered Olympic Studios and the experience remains a delightful memory in Judith's mind as 'one of the most emotional musical experiences I've ever had in a recording studio. It was the first time I'd ever sung on my own with strings and it was very moving for me. The string section was small, it wasn't much at all, but Bobby Richards had written the most beautiful arrangements and I was so enjoying that feeling of singing on my own again. I was almost in tears during that session, particularly recording "Lady Mary" and "What Have They Done to the Rain?" I still get emotional when I hear them today. I've always been very proud of those recordings.

'My only regret was not being able to sing the lead on "The Water Is Wide". It was a song Bruce knew and loved and he wanted to sing it, but I remember being in the studio and feeling sad that I wasn't able to sing the melody. I always thought it would be a perfect song for me.'

The decision was made to release the album as *Hide and Seekers* and, like its predecessor, it was a critical success. Judith continued living in her Earl's Court bedsit, while Beverley and her schoolfriend Anne moved out of theirs and into a flat in West Kensington with two girls who had travelled on the ship with them from Australia. Out of the blue a call came from Bill at home in Australia. Hazel, as well as suffering her chronic asthma and emphysema, had become terribly depressed. With both her daughters living thousands of miles away, there was nothing much left in Hazel's life. Her doctors feared that her depression and loneliness would shorten her life even more than her illnesses would. That phone call placed enormous pressure on the two sisters and there was a choice to be made: Bill said that one of them would have to go home to Australia.

'It was a dreadful predicament to be in,' Judith says. 'Beverley could see that The Seekers had a lot of bookings ahead. Out of the amazing goodness of her heart, she elected to return home to Mum. It was such a huge wrench for her really. She absolutely loved London, even though she was living on a shoestring. But she figured she'd been there for almost eighteen months and I'd only been there about six months, so she made the decision to return. It would have been so difficult when she got back. Her life would have changed so dramatically. Here she was at 23, suddenly back home in Balwyn with Mum and Dad. No more of the London pub scene she loved so much. There was not much jazz in Melbourne, because The Beatles had exploded by then. I was so grateful to her for making it easy for me, but I felt guilty about it and I missed her terribly. Suddenly, I was on my own again.'

Beverley's friend Anne was also going home and the two decided to make a real adventure of their return trip. They cashed in their return ship's tickets and spent the money on air tickets to Australia, via Canada and the United States.

'I cried solidly all the way to Toronto,' Beverley says. 'They gave us free champagne and I just cried the whole time, because I was leaving London, because I had to say goodbye to Judy and Mum was sick, and I didn't know what was waiting for me at home. From Toronto, we went to New York, then Florida, New Orleans, San Francisco and Samoa before arriving back in Melbourne. I hadn't been home in Melbourne long before I started to feel suffocated. I'd had nearly two years of freedom and here I was, back in a three-bedroom house in Melbourne with a mother who treated me like I'd never been away from home. It was a very difficult time.'

In London Judith moved out of her bedsit and into the West Kensington flat that Beverley had vacated. Beverley's friends Val and Pat were still living there, which meant Judith now had the company of girls her own age. Sharing the flat above them were bass player Ronnie Mathewson and guitarist Jimmy Douglas, two members of Alex Welsh's well-known jazz band. Judith struck up a friendship with them and, on occasion, sat in with Welsh's band. One night, she was invited to a party at Ronnie and Jimmy's and it was on the stairway that she met a part-time actor named John Ashby and the two struck up a friendship. Portsmouth-born Ashby had been a steward in the merchant navy and had done a stint in the RAF before settling in London working in a variety of jobs and picking up occasional acting roles as an extra. After that party upstairs, Ashby became Judith's first British boyfriend. Before long, she introduced him to Athol, Keith and Bruce. The four men got along well and, shortly afterwards, he became The Seekers' road manager and, later, tour manager.

'A couple of years later, at a party, John had his palm read by a Chinese fortune-teller,' Judith recalls. 'John was told he'd become an important entrepreneur one day, and he just scoffed. Interestingly, he's now a well-known entrepreneur in Britain and his management company has looked after Cilla Black and Petula Clark.'

By now, Eddie Jarrett had struck up an association with Tom Springfield. Having seen from the sales of the World Record Club albums that there was a ready market for Seekers records, and wishing to give them a clear identity on the airwaves, Jarrett was anxious for them to find some new, original material. Who better to provide it than the man who'd written hits for The Springfields? Jarrett had given Springfield copies of the previous Seekers albums and asked him to go off and write something.

In October, The Seekers appeared with Cliff Richard and The Shadows, Kathy Kirby, and The Dave Clark Five in the *Sun's* All-Star Pop Concert at Wembley Pool. But, the night before this biggest booking to date, Judith's health problems took a turn for the worse. Her bronchial cough was always present, but nothing this serious had happened before. While Judith was making last-minute alterations to her outfit on the sewing machine, she dropped a pin and, as she bent to pick it up, she coughed and expelled blood.

'I just freaked out, totally,' Judith says. 'I was just so scared. I thought I was going to bleed to death. I knocked on my neighbours' door and told them what had happened. They called a doctor, who came and checked me out and prescribed some antibiotics. The bleeding was very, very bad and I probably shouldn't have worked, but I didn't want to let anyone down on such an important show, so I turned up, full of pills, and sang.'

Fragile as she was, Judith managed to get through the performance without any major problems, but didn't feel well enough to stay after the show. 'The guys were very excited to be on this particular bill. I told them I was on antibiotics and wanted to go straight home, but they tried to kid me along. They said, "You'll be OK, Jude, you're all right." But I wasn't. It shocked me that they didn't understand what I'd been through. Performing on that show was very risky for me under the circumstances, but they didn't seem to realise I'd done it so that we wouldn't have to cancel. The guys didn't want to leave, so I ended up getting a cab home.'

Not long after, Judith received a call from Jarrett's office. Tom Springfield had indeed written a song for the group and the boys had all heard it. All that remained was Judith's approval.

The song was 'I'll Never Find Another You'.

'I'd been to the dentist that day,' Judith recalls, 'and hadn't gone into Eddie's office, so he put Tom on the phone and he sang the song "I'll Never Find Another You" for me. My initial reaction was that the song sounded a bit square. Until now, we'd really been singing mostly folk songs and this was a slightly old-fashioned pop song. I remember being surprised, because it had never occurred to me that The Seekers might become a pop group. This was an area I was totally unfamiliar with and it didn't seem to me that it was the sort of song I could get much feeling out of. It was very pleasant, but I didn't necessarily think it was right for the group.'

The decision was taken out of Judith's hands. Despite their not having a record contract, Jarrett and Springfield paid two hundred pounds and booked The Seekers into EMI's Abbey Road Studios on 4 November, to record 'I'll Never Find Another You'. For the B-side, Eddie suggested that the group record one of their own arrangements of a song in the public domain and the boys looked to Judith to suggest something. She came up with one of her favourites from her own jazz repertoire, the gospel 'Open Up Them Pearly Gates'. Jarrett had told the group he'd booked a photographer for the session and, that night, Judith set her alarm for six the next morning so she could wash her hair for the photos, then promptly slept right through it.

'The next thing I knew, it was about ten o'clock and the phone was ringing,' says Judith. 'It was Eddie frantically asking me why I wasn't at the studio. The boys had been there since early on, and the backing tracks for the song had already been put down. He told me he'd pay for a cab so I could get there in a hurry. That's what I did. I went straight in and recorded the vocal with the guys.'

'I'll Never Find Another You' and 'Open Up Them Pearly Gates' were recorded on a four-track machine, with Tom Springfield producing and directing them from the booth. These were still early days in recording and, as usual, to achieve the right vocal balance, the four Seekers stood around a microphone. Athol would move two steps back, Judith would move one step forward and so on.

Confident they had a hit on their hands, Jarrett and Springfield had become partners in their own production company, FXB Productions, named after Springfield's favourite silent movie star, Francis X Bushman. Shy Judith asked Jarrett at the outset if she could put some of her own money in, but Eddie refused point-blank. Jarrett did the rounds of record companies with the now-completed tapes, but didn't find many expressions of interest. The Animals reached Number 1 with 'House of the Rising Sun' not long after The Seekers arrived in London and the charts were dominated by The Beatles, The Rolling Stones, The Supremes and The Moody Blues.

Despite an uphill battle trying to convince the industry's movers and shakers that this quaint quartet from the colonies stood a ghost of a chance, Jarrett eventually managed to persuade EMI Records to distribute the single. The company released the record on their Columbia label on 4 December 1964, but still there was no contract in place. It seemed odd to Judith that the record would be released without signatures on a contract, but this turned out to be only the lull before the storm.

The Seekers, by this time, were rehearsing for their first British pantomime. They'd been signed to star in a winter season of *Cinderella*, which opened at the ABC Theatre in Stockton-on-Tees on Christmas Eve. Judith was looking forward to spending Christmas in the north of England and, possibly, enjoying a white Christmas, but she'd been disappointed when she learned she wouldn't be playing the principal role in the pantomime, even though she accepted that she wasn't pretty or slim enough. Even the initial request for her to understudy the Fairy Godmother was rescinded. The part of Cinderella was to be played by Susan Lane, whom The Seekers had replaced in June on the Blackpool Opera House bill. Judith was cast as the lady's maid, Jeannie, while Keith was Dandini and Athol and Bruce played the broker's men, Mr Near and Mr Farr.

'I really didn't have a role in *Cinderella*. It was very frustrating for me. I had a bit part as the lady's maid, but I desperately wanted to be playing Cinderella. After being the principal rat in *The Pied Piper*, where else would I aim?' laughs Judith.

'The way pantomime worked was the speciality act had small roles in the show and then did their own fifteen-minute act at the end. We were the speciality act and our name was used to draw crowds, but mostly we just sat around backstage waiting to do our bit. I did enjoy the show, though. Susan Lane was very beautiful as Cinderella and the two older guys who played the ugly stepsisters, Syd and Max Harrison, were just brilliant. We opened on Christmas Eve, and at midnight, it started to snow! It was great. I was staying in a room in a pub and the guys were staying in a house, but we all got together the next day and had Christmas dinner with their landlady.'

It was only a matter of days after *Cinderella* had opened that Eddie Jarrett really began putting pressure on Judith to sign a contract for the record. 'I'll Never Find Another You' was receiving a helping hand from an expatriate Australian called Alan Crawford, who played it on the pirate station Radio Caroline. It debuted at Number 48 on the British Top 50 on 9 January 1965, the same day that The Beatles reached Number 1 with 'I Feel Fine'. The heat was now on in earnest. Stalling for time, Jarrett told EMI that The Seekers were signed to FXB Productions, which was not the case: FXB had recorded the tracks, but no contract had ever been drawn up.

'Eddie just confronted us with a contract, as a *fait accompli*, saying it had to be signed immediately,' Judith says. 'It was a terribly legal document and I had trouble understanding it, but I was aware that there was no provision in there for us to receive a decent royalty from Eddie if we were really successful recording artists. The guys didn't really question the contract and they all signed and I remember talking to Athol about it. I asked him what would happen in the event that we sold a million records and he just laughed. He mocked me a bit and said, "Well I suppose they'll give you a bonus."

'The boys all signed and started trying to persuade me to sign. I guess they were getting impatient, but I just didn't want to sign something that didn't seem fair to me. I rang Eddie and he just pressured me more. I rang Mum and Dad in Australia and told them I didn't know what to do. Dad was concerned that the contract was for four years and he suggested I get in touch with my cousin Tom, who was a lawyer in London. But I was in Stockton, in the middle of a show, at Christmas – I didn't have time to consult lawyers. I ended up in tears, with the guys at me constantly to sign and, eventually, Eddie told me if I didn't sign, he'd just tear up the contracts and resign as our manager. I was backed into a corner. Because the record was going up the charts, I had no choice but to sign.'

One of the things that concerned Judith was that The Seekers were required to sign the contract jointly and severally. To her, that meant that, if she wanted to pursue a solo career in under four years, she would still be tied to Eddie at a poor royalty rate. In the back of her mind, she really believed she would return to her solo career before too long. The Seekers had become more than a ten-week holiday for her, but she didn't expect to be with them for that much longer. Judith had always believed she would be a big star one day and it was possible her voice could be on million-selling records within the four-year contract period. She thought maybe she could sing as well as Dusty Springfield, Cilla Black and Sandie Shaw, and they were all topping the charts. It could easily happen to her too.

'For all I knew,' she says, 'I might have left The Seekers and be married with kids after that time and I'd have had no chance to continue my solo career on a decent royalty rate. If I was solo within that four years, I wouldn't have the freedom to choose the record company I might want as a solo artist. The negotiation went on for three days. I did manage to have part of the contract altered to say The Seekers would receive not less than three-sevenths of whatever FXB received. But, in the end, I had no choice but to sign it. I would have been letting everyone else down and that also weighed heavily on my mind.

'The boys now realise how unfair the deal was and, financially, we all suffered, but of course we didn't have hindsight then. Not long after I signed the contract, I did get in touch with my cousin in London and he told me I'd been right: that by signing that deal I was effectively signing up my possible future solo career before it had even begun. That freaked me out even more.'

There was no turning back now for Judith Durham. She was part of an increasingly popular group with a recording contract and a single on its way up the charts. This was shaping up to be a fairytale success story and hundreds of aspiring pop stars would gladly have swapped places with her. But Judith had never set out with stardom as part of a group in her sights and, while the year ahead was filled with professional promise, it seemed to Judith that her life was now very much out of her control.

4. POP GO THE CHARTS

Maybe I'll stay here, maybe I'll go,
I don't know what to do.

—'CAN'T MAKE UP MY MIND'
JUDITH DURHAM AND DAVID REILLY

On 25 January 1965 Judith Durham was back in London, having completed a very successful season of *Cinderella* in Stockton-on-Tees. 'I'll Never Find Another You' was starting to take great strides in the charts. Each week, the group would travel to Manchester to appear on the BBC's *Top of the Pops* to perform the song, sharing the set with many of the big names of the time.

The Seekers were often confused with The Searchers, the four-member male group. Once, Judith recalls the producers recoiling in horror when they realised they had allocated one dressing room for all four Seekers. This, they felt, would never do – a young girl alone with three male pop idols! They solved the problem by putting her in a dressing room still being used by Tom Jones!

By the start of February, 'I'll Never Find Another You' was nudging the Top 10 and on 19 February The Seekers did the unthinkable: they reached the Number 1 spot on the British charts, knocking The Kinks and 'Tired of Waiting for You' back to second spot. Below them both were 'You've Lost That Loving Feeling' by The Righteous Brothers, 'Game of Love' by Wayne Fontana and The Mindbenders, 'Keep Searchin'' by Del Shannon, 'Don't Let Me Be Misunderstood' by The Animals, 'The Special Years' by Val Doonican, 'Funny How Love Can Be' by Ivy League, 'It Hurts So Much' by Jim Reeves and 'It's Not Unusual' by Tom Jones.

In making it to Number 1 on the *Melody Maker* charts, Judith became the fourth female singer in their history to reach the top. Before her were Cilla Black, who did it twice with 'Anyone Who Had a Heart' and 'You're My World'; Honey Lantree of The Honeycombs, who did it with 'Have I The Right'; Sandie Shaw, who did it in 1964 with 'Always Something There to Remind Me'; and, that same year, The Supremes, who did it with 'Baby Love'.

Seizing the top spot in beat-crazy London was no mean feat. That year, three artists – The Beatles, The Stones and Dylan – would share the Number 1 spot on the album charts all year, along with the soundtrack of *The Sound of Music*. The three rock acts reflected the spirit of the sixties while *The Sound of Music* was a Hollywood wonder of the decade, which came and conquered and just wouldn't go away.

The release of 'I'll Never Find Another You' had created a problem in Australia, where W&G Records still had the domestic rights to The Seekers' recordings. It was released on Columbia through EMI in Britain and Europe, but it was issued in Australia on W&G's familiar light-blue label. In Australia, it reached Number 1 on 10 March, replacing '20 Miles' by Ray Brown and The Whispers. 'I'll Never Find Another You' had stayed at the top in Britain for three weeks, before being knocked off by Tom Jones with 'It's Not Unusual'. In Australia, it also held Number 1 for three weeks, being dislodged on 31 March by The Beatles' 'Rock 'n' Roll Music'. EMI Australia handled the local pressing of W&G products and realised they were losing money by not having Australia covered under The Seekers' contract. It took time, but eventually EMI purchased the Australasia rights from W&G. Until that happened, Seekers singles continued being issued on W&G in Australia. Those hits weren't able to appear on Australian album releases by EMI, but made it onto a W&G compilation, *The Seekers Sing Their Big Hits*, which also included material from their debut album, *Introducing The Seekers*. W&G sold the British rights to that album to Decca, who renamed it *The Seekers* and issued it to cash in on the UK success of the EMI single. It entered the British album charts the same week as the group's first Columbia album, but stayed only a week.

'A while after The Seekers arrived in England, Athol Guy rang me and told me they had the chance of signing with EMI,' says Ron Tudor. 'W&G negotiated with EMI and we retained their Australian rights for the period our original contract had left to run. Ron Gillespie of W&G did the deal with Decca. A couple of the guys in The Seekers were angry with us for releasing that album in England, but, because we had worldwide rights to it, it was our prerogative.'

Eddie Jarrett also had to stave off possible competition from the World Record Club. He had heard that the WRC was planning to release 'Morningtown Ride', from the *Hide and Seekers* album, as a single. Two thousand copies were ready to go out at the same time as EMI released 'I'll Never Find Another You'. Jarrett managed to convince the World Record Club that as The Seekers' contract stipulated only their two albums, they really had no right to release singles. It could possibly have been contested in court, but the WRC fell for it and the song remained an album track. Two years later, when Jarrett realised the song's potential, he had The Seekers rerecord it so that FXB and EMI owned the rights.

On a personal level, Judith was overwhelmed by the success of 'I'll

Never Find Another You'. She hadn't been particularly satisfied with her vocal performance and its success intrigued her. When John Ashby arrived at her flat to tell her it had jumped from Number 3 to Number 1, she burst into tears. Far from being carried away with her own success, Judith figured that a Number 1 record would earn her enough money to make life back home in Balwyn a little more comfortable for Hazel and Bill. She was also excited by the realisation that Ernest Page, the grey-bearded astrologer from Soho, had been right. It was mid-February and this was certainly major success. Perhaps, then, his other prediction of a truly extraordinary marriage might come true. Reaching Number 1 meant a sudden and unexpected invasion of Judith's privacy. Requests for interviews poured in from all over Britain as well as Australia and Europe and it was Judith Durham they all seemed to want to talk to. Judith was instantly thrown into the spotlight, appearing on the front pages of newspapers and being recognised wherever she went. Suddenly, she had become public property and she was not at all comfortable with her newfound celebrity.

In addition, the stress of constant performing was taking its toll and Judith still felt guilty about Beverley's return home and missed her terribly. Judy wasn't able to get to know anyone well, apart from her flatmates and the three men she worked with. John Ashby was a close friend, but being away so often meant she had no close female friends to confide in.

In recent months, Judith had become even more caught up in her habit of eating comfort food to assuage her insecurities, and within six months of stepping off the ship, her weight had risen from ten to ten and a half stone. Judith was now a pop star and with that came greater expectations of her. She was suddenly in a league of female performers like Dusty Springfield, Cilla Black and Sandie Shaw, all of whom had trendy images, wore glamorous clothes and, most depressing of all, had trim figures. Here was Judith Durham, the reluctant overweight pop star who ran up sensible dresses on her sewing machine, thrust into a world where appearances were paramount. In her previous career as a jazz singer, it didn't seem to matter how she looked, as long as she could move people with her music. The big names of blues, gospel and opera that Judith so admired were all known for their impressive figures. Because of this, Judith had felt part of the genre's in crowd, but she was instantly at odds with the world of pop. Soon, the arrival of Twiggy on the fashion scene would have an instant impact on pop culture and girl pop stars would be expected to be thin and pretty.

'By then, I saw myself as square, I suppose,' Judith admits. 'I thought the music we sang was square and I just couldn't see how I'd be able to master the art of being fashionable. Seemingly overnight, I couldn't go anywhere without being recognised. People would stare and I'd get very embarrassed. I constantly worried about how I looked and felt bad that I was fat. So I'd go home and feel miserable and then eat some more. At the same time, I was picking up articles and, while they said nice things about my singing, I was being referred to as dumpy or homely. I remember being cut to the quick by one headline I read that said, WHEN WILL JUDY DURHAM GET WITH IT? Another newspaper said, "She looks more like Queen's Pudding than King's Road". I used to ask the boys constantly how I looked, wanting reassurance, and they'd say I looked fine. To them I was just a worrier, but I had a picture of myself indelibly etched in my mind and it took a long time to change that. I really sympathise with young girls today who have those insecurities. When you dwell on what you see as physical faults, you really go through a lot of suffering.'

Being naïve, Judith didn't understand that these criticisms weren't affecting the popularity of the group in any way. The fact that she wasn't a glamorous, untouchable sex symbol only served to make her more endearing to fans. It would take twenty years before she would realise how many men around the world had been in love with her. But Judith was going to be too busy to dwell for too long on what she saw as her inadequacies. The Seekers were still appearing on *Call in on Carroll* and making constant appearances on the TV pop shows of the day, most often the BBC's *Top of the Pops*, and doing a seemingly endless string of live radio performances. Coming up was the group's most prestigious booking to date: The Seekers had been signed for a cabaret season at the plush Savoy Hotel in London.

The Seekers opened their three-week season at the Savoy on 22 February with a short act that featured 'This Little Light of Mine', 'Light from the Lighthouse', 'Well Well Well', 'Just a Closer Walk with Thee' and, of course, the hit the audiences wanted to hear, 'I'll Never Find Another You'. Only days later, The Seekers were booked to appear on an all-star bill for the *Daily Express* Record Star Show at Wembley's Empire Pool, staged to raise money for the Stars' Organisation for Spastics. Appearing with the group would be Tom Jones, PJ Proby, Sandie Shaw, Dusty Springfield, Long John Baldry, Kenny Ball and his Jazzmen, Elkie Brooks, Billy J Kramer and The Dakotas, Lulu, The Merseybeats, The Pretty Things, Them, and The Zombies. The Seekers were scheduled to follow

The Pretty Things, who'd had two Top 10 hits in the previous year with 'Don't Bring Me Down' and 'Honey I Need'.

'Following The Pretty Things seemed a bit bizarre to me,' Judith says. 'We seemed such a contrast. We were very aware that we could get booed, but we didn't go badly. We did a very short spot, maybe two or three songs.'

Although 'I'll Never Find Another You' was still high in the charts, Jarrett and Springfield were aware there was nothing in the can to follow it. Back in his Chelsea flat, Springfield had come up with another song he thought would suit The Seekers perfectly. He called it 'Downhearted Blues'. Tom sang it to the group and, while Judith liked the music, she thought it sounded more happy than downhearted. She liked the tune, but wasn't taken with the chorus, which went 'I'm so downhearted, oh, so downhearted, wasting my lifetime away over you. I feel so downhearted, oh, so downhearted, wasting my lifetime away.'

'He'd used the words "a world of our own" at the end of the verse and I suggested to him that we could turn it into a happy song by using "we'll build a world of our own" as the first line of the chorus,' Judith recalls. 'He went away and came back with the song as we know it today. I really liked the song and thought it suited my voice. I'd had time to become accustomed to this Seekers sound with "I'll Never Find Another You" and this was very much the same sort of song. It fascinated me that Tom had added percussion to "I'll Never Find Another You" after we'd left the studio. We'd never had anything to do with percussion, outside of my playing the tambourine and Keith's uncle's conga drum on "Myra".

'What Tom did is part of what gives the song such a distinctive sound. He did the same thing on "A World of Our Own". He was very influenced by sounds he heard at the Rio Mardi Gras, which he went to every year, and he was always bringing back interesting percussion instruments.'

Tom presented Judith with an autoharp to play on the track. Judith found it was similar to a zither. It had chords printed on it and, by holding down a particular button, she could automatically pluck the right combination of strings to form the chord. Judith learned to play it in the studio when The Seekers returned to Abbey Road to lay down 'A World of Our Own' and its B-side, the old gospel song 'Sinner Man'.

Judith was happier with the outcome of this new single than she had been with 'I'll Never Find Another You', although she was aware how similar people thought it was in sound to the first single. By now, The Seekers were earning reasonable money from concerts, although she never really knew exactly how much. But their high earnings attracted an even higher tax rate, and, after tax, The Seekers were banking two shillings [ten pence] in the pound. To offset their tax level, Jarrett persuaded them to form a company, known as Seekers Musical Enterprises, from which the four members drew a weekly salary of £35.

The Seekers were about to take part in another major showcase. Having been voted Best New Group in a poll conducted by the music publication *New Musical Express*, the group was added to the bill of the annual *NME* Poll Winners' Concert, staged at the Wembley Arena on 11 April and televised a week later. This time they were in even more distinguished company. Appearing with them were The Beatles (who recorded 'Help!' two days later), The Animals, The Bachelors, Cilla Black, Georgie Fame, Wayne Fontana and The Mindbenders, Ivy League, Tom Jones, The Kinks, The Moody Blues, Rockin' Berries, The Rolling Stones, The Searchers, Sounds Incorporated, Dusty Springfield and Twinkle.

'We went pretty well, I seem to recall. [The actor] Clint Walker presented us with the *NME* Best Newcomers award on stage. I had to walk up to him and shake his hand, this towering person who was legendary to me because he'd been the star of the television series *Cheyenne*. I remember saying to him, "How do you do?" So Melburnian! And he mumbled back, "Mahty fahn, ma'am, mahty fahn." Backstage, I was overwhelmed by the screams and the sheer power of the crowd. It was so incredibly loud. We were almost a novelty act on that bill, I suppose. We didn't get booed or anything, but we didn't get the screams either. Backstage, we were very close to The Beatles and I do remember they were wearing those mustardy suits with high Mandarin collars. Of course, I was far too shy to speak to them, or to anyone else, but they were very close to us. We were all kind of mingling in one area.'

'A World of Our Own' was well received by the critics. *New Musical Express* called it 'a contagious toe-tapper ... commercial folk of the highest order', while *Melody Maker* referred to their 'unmistakable sound' and added 'they do sound like the dear old Springfields and Judith has a very, very nice voice'. The group performed the song on TV's *Top of the Pops* and *Saturday Club* and headlined *Sunday Night at the Blackpool Opera House*, playing two shows with Russ Conway.

Later that week, they opened a one-week cabaret season at the renowned Mr Smith's in Manchester before accepting a booking at Greasbrough Social Club, a working men's club in Yorkshire. On this bill, they were supported by Mandy Rice-Davies who, with Christine Keeler, had helped blow the lid off the British establishment in 1963 with her involvement in what became known as the Profumo Affair. Their involvement with the then war minister, John Profumo, saw them enmeshed in a scandal that combined those two most potent of taboos: sex and national security.

'I had to share a dressing room with Mandy and I had no idea of what to say to her,' says Judith. 'She was very pleasant, but I was uncomfortable around her. She came from a totally different world to me. The shows themselves were a real experience. We were performing a lunchtime show, which was staged just after the customers had played bingo. It was so naff! They'd be calling the bingo numbers – "all the legs eleven" – and then that would all finish and, before they introduced us, they'd make their announcements. One performance sticks in my mind. We were waiting to be introduced and we heard an announcement that went something like this: "It 'as coom to ahr attention that soom of ahr members 'ave bin relieving themselves against t'west wall of t'cloob. This 'as got to stop. Now a little shush please for t'Seekers."

'The shows themselves went quite well,' Judith continues. 'The northern audiences used to think it was unusual that we'd sing gospels like "Just a Closer Walk with Thee", but they were usually very quiet while we sang them. It was in these sorts of working men's clubs that we really paid our dues.'

At the end of April, The Seekers left for Ireland for an eight-day ballroom concert tour that kicked off at City Hall in Belfast. In just over a week, they played eight cities.

'What I remember of that tour was the wilderness of the Irish landscape, and how boisterous the audiences were,' Judith says. 'It was a different type of atmosphere to anything we'd encountered before. It was a fairly arduous tour, with a lot of ground to cover. The dressing-room situation was abominable. There were never adequate facilities in these venues and I had to get dressed and made up under very stressful conditions. I do remember that in Ireland we had our first real screaming audiences. We were very popular there and got screams like The Beatles did back in England. Keith was popular with the girls in Ireland and they'd scream even louder for him.'

The hysteria on this tour spilled over into their personal appearances and police were called in to control the crowd that turned up to greet The Seekers when they opened the Singer Sewing Machine Company's new record bar in Belfast.

The group returned from Ireland on 3 May with just over three weeks remaining before their return home for an Australian tour. 'A World of Our Own' had entered the British charts on 1 May and, five days later, the group appeared on *Top of the Pops* to sing 'A World of Our Own' and to receive their second gold disc for 'I'll Never Find Another You'. The song had reached Number 1 in Britain and Australia and Number 4 in America, and had sold more than 1.75 million copies.

Earlier in the year, 'I'll Never Find Another You' had been released in America through EMI on the Capitol label. Repeating and consolidating The Seekers' instant success, the song helped push the disc past a million sales. Not only had Judith and the boys become the first Australian group to reach Number 1 in Britain, they'd also become the first Australians to crack the US Top 40.

Capitol in America was anxious to have an album to release in order to capitalise on the success of this fresh new group of Aussies. With nothing up their sleeves, The Seekers had given them *Introducing The Seekers*, but it was rejected by the Americans, who wanted an album filled with more songs like 'I'll Never Find Another You'. So, on top of the hurried follow-up to the single, The Seekers were faced with having to record an entire album with very little time for planning. Tom Springfield had given them tapes of other people's songs to listen to during their Irish tour and it was from these that the final selection was made.

With Springfield in the producer's chair, the group went back into the studio and laid down twelve tracks. Having already recorded 'Blowin' in the Wind', they chose two more Bob Dylan songs, 'Don't Think Twice It's Alright' and 'The Times Are A-Changin', and rere-corded Woody Guthrie's 'This Land Is Your Land'. They drew on American folk history again for 'You Can Tell the World' and Judith's jazz background for 'Just a Closer Walk with Thee', marking the third time Judith had sung it on record. They covered Jo Stafford's 1950s hit 'Allentown Jail' and the relatively new Canadian ballad 'Four Strong Winds', and a beautiful ballad they'd heard on a Clancy Brothers album, 'The Leaving of Liverpool'. With only a little songwriting expe-rience behind him, Bruce Woodley contributed two tracks to the new album, 'Don't Tell Me My Mind' and 'Two Summers'. Judith was well acquainted with 'Two Summers' by the time it came to be recorded. After getting stuck writing it, Bruce had knocked on Judith's door and asked her advice. She helped him construct the song's middle eight. Stuck for an extra track, Tom Springfield asked the group to write something, but no one had anything to offer. For fun, they included the old ragtime folk instrumental 'Whistlin' Rufus', which gave Judith the chance to play the piano again.

The twelfth track for British release was, of course, 'A World of Our Own', which was the title of the album in Britain. (But, because the rights to 'A World of Our Own' were owned by W&G in Australia, a replacement track was needed, and six months later, when the album was released Down Under, it included 'We Shall Not Be Moved'. In Australia, the album was called simply *The Seekers*.) The cover featured a shot of the group running down the Eros steps in Piccadilly Circus, with Judith wearing the leopard-print, rabbit-lined coat she'd splashed fifty pounds on at Fenwicks of Bond Street when the group had decided to stay in the UK for their first British winter.

Before departing for Australia in May, The Seekers managed to squeeze in a night off and went to see Bob Dylan play at the Royal Albert Hall. The four Beatles also attended the concert. This was, effectively, the first contemporary concert Judith had ever been to. She remembers being surprised how informally Dylan was dressed for a Royal Albert Hall show and how devoted his audience was.

Judith was certainly aware of Dylan. The Seekers had covered several of his songs that had been popularised in America by Peter, Paul and Mary, but the growing protest movement in America had passed her by. Because of her cloistered upbringing, Judith saw the world as a peaceful place. Her father had fought in a war that was now over and, the way she saw it, harmony prevailed.

'I really had no understanding of the revolution that was happening in America,' Judith says. 'I read about protests in America, but I didn't really understand what they were protesting about. I had no knowledge of oppression, not for many years to come. I had a totally warped view of all that. The importance of Bob Dylan's lyrics never struck me at all. But then I didn't evaluate song lyrics much in those days. To me, the emotional content, melody and chord structure in the music was the most important thing and I didn't take much notice of lyrics at all. Lyrics were a means of getting the notes out! I always listened to the music first and, if I liked the music, then the secondary thing was whether the lyrics were nice to sing. I judged Dylan more then as a singer, which was a mistake. I appreciate him enormously now, as a songwriter and interpreter of music.'

On 15 May, just a few days before The Seekers were to leave for Australia, 'A World of Our Own' reached Number 1 on the *Disc Weekly* charts and in so doing ended The Beatles' four-week run with 'Ticket To

Ride'. Also in the Top 10 that week were 'King of the Road' by Roger Miller, 'Where Are You Now?' by Jackie Trent, 'True Love Ways' by Peter and Gordon, 'Bring It on Home to Me' by The Animals, 'Pop Go the Workers' by The Barron Knights, 'Wonderful World' by Herman's Hermits, 'Oh No, Not My Baby' by Manfred Mann and 'Subterranean Homesick Blues' by Bob Dylan.

The Seekers had little time to promote the song before they boarded the aircraft that would take them home to Australia for the first time in twelve months. Eddie Jarrett, ever aware that the group needed some time to catch up with family and friends, accepted the only possible offer that would get them back to Britain in time for their sixteen-week Bournemouth season. The offer was from the Australian promoter Kenn Brodziak, whose Aztec Services had toured The Beatles so successfully the previous year. Brodziak's company specialised in double and triple bills, mixing acts according to their chart ranking at the time. That year they toured Manfred Mann, The Kinks and The Honeycombs on one bill; Cilla Black, Sounds Incorporated, Mark Wynter and Freddie and The Dreamers on another. Brodziak had built up a close relationship with Jarrett, having negotiated with him to tour Cliff Richard and The Shadows in 1961.

Calling the tour 'The Big Show', Brodziak brought The Seekers home on an unlikely double-headed bill with The Dave Clark Five, who had recently reached the Top 5 in Britain with their hit 'Bits and Pieces'. Also on the bill were support acts Tommy Quickly, a Brian Epstein protégé who'd had a minor UK hit in 1964 with 'Wild Side of Life', and a local duo, Bobby and Laurie. In three weeks, The Seekers would play seven concerts and tape a half-hour television show for Melbourne's HSV Channel Seven.

The Seekers and The Dave Clark Five flew into Perth at two in the morning on 25 May and the next night their tour kicked off at Perth's Capitol Theatre. Judith's inexperience as an international traveller was painfully obvious to her on that 36-hour flight from London to Perth, with stops in Rome, Delhi, Bombay, Madras and Singapore.

'I'd never been on a long flight before. I left London wearing my nicely pressed linen dress and matching coat and by the time we reached Delhi, our third stop, I was frantically trying to stop it from getting too creased. It never occurred to me that we'd be landing and taking off again for thirty-six hours, going through about five different climates. I didn't even think to pack my toothbrush or deodorant as part of my hand luggage, so you can imagine the state I arrived in. Even though we landed at two in the morning, there were a lot of teenagers at the airport. Thankfully, we didn't have to do a press conference.'

The combination of The Seekers and The Dave Clark Five had seemed like a curious one to Judith, who couldn't understand why The Seekers couldn't headline their own tour. 'I felt that, instead of returning home on the strength of our own hits, we were tagging along on someone else's tour,' she says. 'We didn't make a lot of money from that tour and it wasn't a very compatible bill. We got along OK with the guys in The Dave Clark Five, although I didn't have a lot to do with them. I remember being very embarrassed when a photographer had me sitting on Dave Clark's knee for a photo. We had massive crowds waiting to greet us at all the capital city airports, but it never dawned on me that we were "stars". I just saw it as Australians being supportive of their own. I really didn't comprehend the level of success we were having at that point.'

From Perth, the bands flew to windy and rainy Melbourne for a show at Festival Hall that night. It was at Essendon Airport, just down the road from where Judith was born, that news cameras caught her reunion with Bill, Hazel and Beverley after twelve long months. But, despite Eddie Jarrett's well-intentioned plans, there was little time for relaxation.

'The demand on our time was just extraordinary,' says Judith. 'Any spare moment we had seemed to be taken up with television, press or radio interviews. It was literally a whirlwind and I remember Mum and Dad being very concerned about my health. After one of the Melbourne shows, Mum mentioned to me that she didn't think I was singing as well as I used to. She knew my singing backwards from those endless hours at the piano, and, to her, my voice sounded different, not as relaxed. But we'd come in from London, only days after having recorded an album and that was very strenuous for me.'

The Melbourne concerts went well enough. At one of them, the leading Melbourne DJ Stan Rofe presented The Seekers with miniature replicas of their gold-disc award for 'I'll Never Find Another You'. It might have seemed odd that Rofe, who hosted a very up-to-the-minute rock-music programme on 3KZ, would be honouring a group like The Seekers, but there was a connection. Rofe recalls that The Seekers came to see him at 3KZ after they'd recorded 'Waltzing Matilda', looking for a little airplay. But he was Stan the Man, the Rocky Jockey, and he made it clear that he couldn't help them if they didn't play rock 'n' roll, a stance Judith thought was particularly unfair.

'I told them I didn't like folk groups,' Rofe says. 'Judith said to me that day that I'd live to be sorry I hadn't helped them, and that night, in front of seven thousand people, she reminded me of it very publicly before digging me in the ribs. Their show went very well that night. They were superb and, even though I wasn't a fan of that sort of music, I had to admire what they did.'

Press reviews were favourable, with the *Age* writing, 'A capacity audience at Festival Hall gave the four Melburnians a welcome back that the group will long cherish ... It was a ticker-tape reception, with streamers, stamping feet and sustained hand-clapping.'

Stadiums manager Richard Lean Jr told the Melbourne *Sun* that the audience for The Seekers and Dave Clark Five had created the most noise since the previous year's Beatles concert at Festival Hall.

On their second day in Melbourne, from the Fitzroy Teletheatre, the group recorded a thirty-minute special for HSV7, which was screened early in June as part of the station's *Big Show* series. The following year, the footage would be incorporated into a TV special called *The Seekers at Home*.

Judith was also delighted to find during this homecoming that her sister Beverley had announced her engagement and would marry the following year. Now working as secretary to a professor in the Department of Semitic Studies at the University of Melbourne, Beverley had fallen in love with Barry Sheehan, a high school teacher who was studying for Bachelor of Education degree.

'I liked Barry instantly,' Judith says. 'I felt very close to him, like I'd known him all my life. We were staying at the Southern Cross Hotel in Melbourne, where The Beatles had stayed the year before. It felt very posh to me to be in Melbourne, a few miles from Balwyn, in the best hotel in town. When Beverley had worked at Channel Nine, she had invited me to go with her to the telecast of the opening of the hotel. Two years later, here I was, a guest, ordering room service and feeling so self-conscious of the cost of room service for a snack for Mum and Dad after all their scrimping and saving. I think they were thrilled for me, though.'

The Seekers moved on to Adelaide, where they played Centennial Hall, then flew on to Brisbane for one concert at Festival Hall. After that it was on to Sydney for two final concerts at the Stadium. The four Seekers had their parents flown to Sydney in a bid to secure at least some time with them before leaving Australia again, but between rehearsals, press conferences, interviews and the concerts, free time was minimal. Intercity rivalry between Melbourne and Sydney was nothing new and The Seekers fell victim to it in a big way. A review in the *Sydney Morning*

Herald after their first show delivered an axe blow in comparing them with The Dave Clark Five: 'The Seekers proved pallid and unexciting by comparison. On songs like "Don't Think Twice It's Alright", "Kumbaya" and "This Little Light of Mine", their approach was unimaginative, their harmonies unchallenging. Only Judith Durham gives the group any distinction.'

Judith clearly remembers someone in the audience this night, calling out during a quiet moment, 'Go back to Melbourne!'

After the final concert in Sydney, the group had just one day to spend with their families in Melbourne before flying out of the country again. Like Athol Guy, Judith had contracted laryngitis and was confined to bed while a visa problem was sorted out. So much for quality time with the folks!

The Seekers flew out of Australia on 6 June and, en route to England, arrived in America, where they had been booked to appear on the top-rating *Ed Sullivan Show*. 'I'll Never Find Another You' had already cracked the US Top 5 and now 'A World of Our Own' was edging its way into the Top 20.

'America was an amazing experience for all of us,' Judith recalls. 'We stopped in Hawaii in transit and then it was straight on to New York. I immediately thought of the photos Dad had taken of New York when he'd been there during the war. I was seeing America through my parents' eyes in a way. I was so sad that Mum wasn't able to travel and I would look at these different places we visited and try to imagine how Mum would have enjoyed them. I always kept a spare aerogram in my bag and would be writing letters to Mum and Dad whenever I travelled, in trains, planes and the back of cabs.

'This was 1965 and, of course, neither Australia nor England had anything in the way of skyscrapers, so that's one thing that jumped out at me when we got to New York. We didn't have a lot of time to sightsee because we had three days of rehearsals, and that was another shock. America was so union-conscious. If I wanted my microphone stand moved, even two inches, I couldn't do it myself. They had someone employed to do that and he had to do it, or there'd be trouble. I also had my first experience of being made up for television by a man. That had never happened before!'

The actual show was broadcast live from Hollywood Palace in New York and, true to form, Ed Sullivan was being difficult: he was surly and unfriendly. His introduction to The Seekers and 'I'll Never Find Another

You' was brief and, when they'd finished singing, Sullivan spoke with them and asked that they give his regards to an obscure Australian sportsman.

'Tom Jones was also on that show with us,' recalls Judith. 'I remember there was a big furore over his gyrations and they wouldn't shoot him from the waist down. We spent a bit of time with Tom in New York and we went to a party he had in his hotel suite after the show. I really hoped Tom might fancy me, but I was too shy to say very much to him. Everyone at the party was doing go-go dancing, like the swim, and, although I always had a go, I never quite mastered anything beyond the twist and the cakewalk.'

The Seekers returned to Britain in the second week of June – only days after The Beatles were awarded the MBE – and had only a few days to settle in before opening the long-awaited sixteen-week season supporting the comedian Arthur Haynes and the cabaret singer Yana at the Bournemouth Pavilion. This was the booking that Eddie Jarrett had secured the previous year as a means of enticing the group to stay in England indefinitely. Of course, the season had been booked at their 1964 price and, for four months, The Seekers would be performing twice nightly for £250 pounds – between them!

'I was incredibly whacked by the time we got back to England,' Judith remembers. 'I didn't have a home to go to because I'd vacated my flat before we went to Australia. In the meantime, my friend John Ashby had found a big house for us all in Bournemouth and had moved my things into it. Keith found a place of his own.

'I just wasn't happy doing that Bournemouth season. For a start, the money was terrible because we'd been committed to it a year earlier; and, secondly, we really should have been headlining by then. Instead, we were playing support to Arthur Haynes and Yana. But the worst thing was that this show included a production number for which we had to wear special costumes and sing a parody of a Tommy Steele number. The song meant absolutely nothing to me and we weren't being The Seekers. The boys didn't have instruments and we were just going through the motions, wearing these silly costumes. I thought it was wrong for the image of the group and, musically, it was very unsatisfying for me. I didn't want to know about it, but we were obligated to see it through.'

The Seekers opened at the Bournemouth Pavilion on 24 June. Their opening night was a resounding success, despite the fact that their sound system packed up during their performance. Playing twice nightly, The Seekers did a brief set that opened with 'You Can Tell the World', which was followed by 'Blowin' in the Wind', 'A World of Our Own', 'The Times

They Are A-Changin", 'I'll Never Find Another You' and 'Cotton Fields'. For one month at the start of the season, the group were also to appear on Sunday nights at the Princess Theatre in Torquay, headlining a variety bill.

Judith celebrated her 22nd birthday during the season and Russ Conway, who was appearing at a rival theatre, came along to her party. John and the three boys gave Judith a bicycle. She spent many happy but lonely hours riding around Bournemouth, while Athol, Keith and Bruce sported their newly acquired Jaguar XK150s!

Early in the season, Judith began to suffer from nasal polyps, which made it difficult for her to sing. She was exhausted from the Australian and American visits, very unhappy with the Bournemouth show and still feeling self-conscious about her weight and appearance. Her nights were spent sitting up late sewing stage dresses, missing her parents and still in conflict about being a member of a group. Judith became very depressed during this time. She woke up in tears one morning, not long after her 22nd birthday, and realised then that things were starting to get out of hand. She couldn't stop crying, to the point where a doctor was called.

'I felt so bad, so incredibly miserable,' Judith recalls. 'The doctor diagnosed nervous exhaustion and put me on a tranquilliser called Librium, but what he didn't tell me was that I shouldn't drink alcohol while taking them. On Bruce's birthday, I had two drinks and just collapsed. I had to be put to bed. It was then I realised that I had a big problem. Life was just too much to cope with and this helpless, continuous crying started again the next morning.'

Judith's doctor was called again and this time he prescribed five weeks off, with a stint in a nursing home. He said Judith should spend two weeks in the nursing home and three weeks convalescing, with no demands placed on her. 'It meant pulling out of the Bournemouth show, but I had to do it,' Judith says. 'I was also concerned that, while I was in hospital, they'd feed me up and, after consciously trying to lose weight, make me put it all back on. Luckily, I had a very sympathetic nurse. I actually enjoyed being there, being in a situation where I didn't have to do anything in particular. I just wanted to lie there.

'While I was there, the doctors decided to remove the nasal polyps, which was another positive thing. I felt sorry for Mum and Dad, though. They'd been very concerned, because the hospital stay had been widely publicised and there were some very exaggerated newspaper stories about why I was in hospital.'

Eddie Jarrett was even more concerned. Judith's illness meant not only a disruption to the Bournemouth season and the cancellation of the Torquay dates, but a scheduled taped appearance for US TV's *Red Skelton Show* also had to be called off. What if the nasal polyp operation affected Judith's voice? What if her bout of nervous exhaustion led her to leave The Seekers?

The Australian pop group Take Five had stood in on the Bournemouth bill for the first few days after Judith's hospitalisation, but The Seekers were contracted and it was The Seekers the show's promoters wanted.

Aware of Judith's fragile state, Eddie gingerly raised with her the subject of finding a temporary replacement. That way, the Bournemouth season could continue. While she vaguely felt that having a replacement for her, or for any member of the group, was wrong, Judith agreed to the proposition and auditions for her replacement were held. Of the forty applicants, a 23-year-old Scottish singer, Ellen Wade, was chosen. In a strange twist of fate, Wade had to cancel her first week with the group because of laryngitis, and Take Five were back on the bill.

'I never really felt comfortable with what happened,' Judith says. 'Once I was out of the nursing home, the doctor recommended that I go on a holiday somewhere, so I asked John Ashby to take me to a quiet seaside resort. We ended up in Majorca of all places, teeming with UK holidaymakers! All I wanted was to be anonymous somewhere, so it was a bit of a shock; but, once I adjusted to it, I enjoyed myself. When we got back, I asked John to take me along to the Bournemouth Pavilion one night and we stood up the back and watched the boys and Ellen performing as The Seekers. The show was very good and I went away thinking, Well, they don't really need me after all. I guess it didn't do much for my self-esteem.'

Judith rejoined The Seekers early in September for one final Sunday night Princess Theatre engagement. The next night, she took over from Ellen Wade at Bournemouth Pavilion and completed the season. 'Eddie was there at the Torquay show to find out how I was feeling,' says Judith. 'He seemed to have some doubts about whether I wanted to continue with the group, which I thought was very strange. I felt my allegiance at that stage was very much with the boys and the last thing I wanted to do was desert anybody. If I'd had my wits about me, perhaps I should have taken the opportunity to start my solo career. I was always thinking of everyone else's feelings and I didn't think I would have the support of those closest to me if I was to make a move.'

Towards the end of the Bournemouth season, The Seekers squeezed in an appearance at the annual Pop Show held by the Marquis of Bath at his stately home, Longleat, sharing the bill with Georgie Fame and Adam Faith. This was another of those occasions when Judith was completely in awe of other performers. As far as the charts were concerned, she was as big a name as Adam Faith, but she was able to muster the courage to have only one brief exchange with him.

Now Judith was back after her illness, Jarrett had to remind her that it had been some time since The Seekers had topped the charts with 'A World of Our Own' and now was the time to re-enter the studios. Tom Springfield had made a special trip to Bournemouth during the Pavilion season to present to the group a couple of songs as possible new singles. One was called 'Hummingbird', the other a ballad called 'The Carnival Is Over'. The latter was inspired by the latest of Springfield's many trips to Rio during carnival time. He had adapted the melody from an old Russian folk song, 'Stenjka Razin', but half the tune was his own composition and the lyrics entirely his own work.

'Tom sang both songs to us and the boys seemed to favour "Hummingbird",' Judith says. 'I felt the most overwhelming emotion when I heard "The Carnival Is Over". It was inconceivable for me to think we wouldn't record it. It was such an obvious song for us and it would have broken my heart if I couldn't have sung it.'

Back into the Abbey Road studios went The Seekers, with Bobby Richards, who had orchestrated their World Record Club album, on board as the arranger. 'It was the first time I'd ever tried to really put pressure on the group, as far as material was concerned,' says Judith. 'I felt in a way as though I was stepping out of line, but I was convinced in my own mind that "The Carnival Is Over" was the right song for us and I pushed and pushed for it. I adored the arrangement done by Bobby Richards and I had a lot of pleasure singing to it. After the break I'd had, I returned in pretty good voice and we knocked the session over very quickly. It was a tremendous feeling, working with a string section and meeting up with Bobby Richards again. His work on the *Hide and Seekers* album was inspiring.'

Judith felt so daunted on occasions, during sessions, when her ideas differed from those of the boys. At those times, she felt she wanted to leave the group. For someone with strong feelings about music and the way it should be presented, it was difficult for her to have to compromise her artistry for the sake of her three male partners. She felt, as she still does today, as though she was frustrated and suffocated at those times, in contrast to the happy-go-lucky camaraderie she enjoyed with the rest of the group for the majority of their years together.

Richard Lush, who now lives in Sydney, was assistant engineer to Peter Vince at Abbey Road from 1965 to 1973, working on sessions with The Beatles, Cliff Richard, Manfred Mann, Freddie and The Dreamers and Cilla Black. Lush worked on several Seekers sessions at Abbey Road, and he attributes the group's success to the combination of their musical ability and Tom Springfield's songs.

'The songs The Seekers recorded were good songs and they still are today,' Lush says. 'Judith Durham is a great singer, one of the few in the world who consistently sings as well in the studio as she does on stage. The Seekers were very professional and always came into the studio very well prepared. The sessions were usually fun, although I remember the odd bit of tension. Judith sometimes had her own ideas of how a song should be done, which wasn't always the same as the boys'. There were often three-way negotiations between Judith, the boys and Tom. There was never a slagging match, but certainly a few differences of opinion. Tom was a real perfectionist. Mixing a Seekers song always took a long time because Tom would mix it up to thirty different ways and take the tapes away to listen to them. He was finicky to the point of distraction sometimes.'

With the new single now recorded, The Seekers went on to top the bill at the Cardiff Commonwealth Arts Festival Variety Show, supported by Eden Kane and The Downbeats. They then took part in a special 'Pop from the Commonwealth' series at London's Royal Festival Hall. Brian Epstein had arranged a 'Pop from Britain' concert starring Gerry and the Pacemakers, Georgie Fame and The Blue Flames, The Moody Blues and Cliff Bennett and The Rebel Rousers. The following week The Seekers represented Australia, with support from all corners of the Commonwealth. An odd line-up indeed for a pop concert!

The reviews for this show were raves. The Cardiff-based Welsh daily, the *Western Mail*, wrote, 'They're a vibrant lot, full of self-confidence but never brassy, crisp without losing touch or warmth towards the audience'; while the Australian Associated Press (AAP) reported, 'The Seekers stole the limelight ... [the] audience of about 2,000 clapped, cheered and shouted for minutes before the Australians had sung a note.'

But the show doesn't stand out in Judith's mind. 'It was a fairly unsatisfactory experience,' she says. 'But at least it meant we got to play the Royal Festival Hall, even if it was a variety bill. We always seemed to play the venues the Grade Organisation booked, like the

Palladium or the Talk of the Town, so effectively [that] we were never allowed to become a London concert act, despite the success we were having with records. We did concerts around the country and overseas, in concert halls, but not in London. Sadly, we were more of a cabaret act there.'

In the few days Judith had off after the 'Pop from the Commonwealth' shows, she moved into a semidetached house in Richmond, which John Ashby had rented for them both. Judith could never bring herself to tell her parents how close she and John had become. Their relationship was almost like a marriage, although, it being the sixties, setting up home together was not the done thing and Judith was always worried about who might come knocking on their door. By the time the twelve-month lease was up, she preferred to find her independence again. They had spoken of marriage, but Judith felt uncertain – for the time being, anyway – of whether she had found her perfect match.

Soon after moving into the house, she was caught up in The Seekers' appearance on ATV's *The New London Palladium Show* with Shirley Bassey. 'Once again I was in awe,' Judith says. 'Being on a bill with Shirley Bassey was incredible for me. It was a bit like being on a bill with Dusty. These women were real stars to me. They had all the clothes and their appearance was fantastic and their acts were so well put together. Shirley Bassey on that show presented herself so well and sang so magnificently. I bought her album. I didn't buy many albums, but I definitely bought that one. It never occurred to me that I was equally as famous as these artists and that the missing element for me was experience and expertise as a soloist.'

Just a few days later, EMI issued 'The Carnival Is Over' as a single, backed with the gospel 'We Shall Not Be Moved', which had been recorded in the same session in one take. It was released in a month that saw new singles by The Rolling Stones, Tom Jones, Sonny and Cher, Gerry and The Pacemakers, Peter and Gordon, The Moody Blues, Billy J Kramer, Georgie Fame, Lulu and Wilson Pickett. For The Seekers, this was a crucial release. They had reached Number 1 with their first and second singles, but this third one would effectively make or break them. There was a degree of scepticism within the music industry about The Seekers: many believed that their success so far had been a fluke and they were seen in some quarters as a bit of a novelty act. This third single, if successful, would silence the critics, but recording a lush ballad was definitely a risk. Even riskier was the fact that The Seekers wouldn't be around long to promote it.

With the Bournemouth Pavilion season finally complete, The Seekers opened a one-week variety stint at Liverpool's Empire Theatre the night after their Palladium Show, followed by two week-long stints in other Empire theatres in Manchester and Bristol. These shows were all extremely well received and critically acclaimed, and reviews for 'The Carnival Is Over' were very favourable. The single entered the British Top 40 on 6 November 1965 and The Seekers were able to make several BBC radio appearances and perform the song on *Top of the Pops* before flying to Holland for one day to record a television appearance. The following day, they travelled on to Ballymena for the start of their second Irish tour, which moved through twelve cities.

'The Carnival Is Over', meanwhile, was gliding up the charts, knocking out of its way hits by The Yardbirds, Cliff Richard, Hedgehoppers Anonymous and Elvis Presley. On 27 November it jumped six spots and dislodged The Rolling Stones' 'Get Off of My Cloud' from the Number 1 spot. The Stones fell to Number 2 and below them were 'Yesterday Man' by Chris Andrews, 'My Generation' by The Who, '1-2-3' by Len Barry, 'It's My Life' by The Animals, 'Tears' by Ken Dodd, 'Positively 4th Street' by Bob Dylan, 'Here It Comes Again' by The Fortunes and 'Yesterday' by Matt Munro.

There was something special about 'The Carnival Is Over', something about Judith's singing that made people cry. Her instinct about the song had proved right and finally she felt the kind of pride she'd experienced earlier as a solo artist when, through her performance, she was able to move people. She received letters from fans all over the world, remarking on how emotionally touched they had been by the record. As a bonus, the record's success enhanced Judith's popularity in a major way.

'The Carnival Is Over' remained at Number 1 in Britain for three weeks before being replaced by The Beatles' 'Day Tripper'/'We Can Work It Out'. Because of The Seekers, The Beatles failed to debut at Number 1 for the first time in two years and their manager Brian Epstein was furious. He told *Melody Maker*, 'The chart must be made up of figures from fish shops.' Within a week of 'The Carnival is Over' reaching Number 1, The Seekers were voted Best New Group of 1965 by *New Musical Express*. Back home in Australia, the song also topped the charts, dislodging 'Que Sera Sera', by Normie Rowe and The Playboys.

'"The Carnival Is Over" made me realise for the first time just how big our record sales were,' Judith says. 'Eddie Jarrett was getting the daily figures as they came in and, at one stage, we were selling ninety-three thousand copies a day in England. That was monumental. At the time the song reached Number 1, we were in Paris, appearing at the Olympia on a very famous radio show. I just loved Paris, although we didn't get the chance to see much of it during that trip. I don't think the audience could care whether we were there or not. None of our records were particularly big hits in France and I don't think we really appealed to the French people.

'Aside from that Paris show and a week of cabaret in Majorca, we never really played on the Continent at all – outside of television shows in Holland and Germany – which used to baffle me. It seemed we were always just booked in London on variety bills and only did a few concerts outside London. We kept on having this incredible chart success, but the UK audiences never saw us as an international concert act – although, when we were away, we did big concerts in America, South Africa, Australia and New Zealand.'

That chart success paid off in 1965. The Seekers, in the *New Musical Express* half-year points table, came in at Number 1 (with 552), ahead of Sandie Shaw (481), The Beatles (367), Cliff Richard (359), The Rolling Stones (342), The Animals (330), The Kinks (317) and Them (312). An amazing feat, considering they were in competition with The Beatles' 'Day Tripper' and 'Help!' and The Stones' 'The Last Time', 'Satisfaction' and 'Get off of My Cloud'. The Seekers finished the year second to The Stones (836), but ahead of The Beatles (760), The Animals (656) and Sandie Shaw (649). The group rounded out the year with their own half-hour BBC2 television special, *An Evening with The Seekers*, and as special guests on the BBC's *Tonight in Person*, as well as their own Seekers Show at Birmingham Hippodrome. This time they were headliners, with support from The Applejacks and the comedian Frank Berry. Also on the bill again were The Trebletones, whose piano man was Ron Edgeworth, but still his path had not crossed Judith's. Despite her achievements, she was still too shy to make conversation with other artists, preferring the sanctuary of her dressing room.

One thing that was definitely changing was Judith's weight. The intense media focus on her prompted a concerted effort to curb her eating and, early in the year, she'd managed to lose five pounds. Before long, she felt confident enough to buy off the rack and throw away her girdle. Sheer willpower saw her replacing breads, biscuits and ice cream with steak or whole Dover sole, and slowly her weight dropped so that by the end of 1965 she had lost over fourteen pounds.

The Seekers ended 1965 at the height of their popularity. In just eighteen months, they'd become one of the biggest pop groups in

Britain, and Australia's greatest success story. They had the world at their feet and the year ahead was filled with promise. But for Judith the next twelve months would see her back in hospital and fighting an escalating emotional battle to keep hold of her identity.

5. STORMING THE WORLD

Why do all the boys just pass you by?
Could it be you just don't try,
Or is it the clothes you wear?
You're always window shopping
But never stopping to buy
So shed those dowdy feathers and fly.

– 'GEORGY GIRL'
TOM SPRINGFIELD AND JIM DALE

Because of the success of their 1965 Australian tour, The Seekers were planning to head back home again in 1966, under the banner of Kenn Brodziak's Aztec Services – and this time they would headline.

Judith was looking forward to this tour very much. It had been almost a year since the Cock family had been reunited and she was missing her Mum and Dad and Beverley. Beverley's wedding was coming up on 6 February and, knowing she was a bundle of nerves about it, Judith wanted to be there for her. The tour, she hoped, would give her that chance. But first there was a new single to be recorded, and another marriage.

Through Alan Paramour of Lorna Music, Bruce Woodley had met Paul Simon in London. Simon was a fledgling singer-songwriter who, with his musical partner Art Garfunkel, made up the American duo Simon and Garfunkel. The two had a recording contract with Columbia Records and were on the verge of chart success.

Paul Simon and Bruce Woodley wrote the song 'Red Rubber Ball' and offered it to the American group The Cyrkle. This group was managed briefly by Brian Epstein and were hired as supports for The Beatles' first US tour. Despite the fact that Epstein had publicly dismissed The Seekers' success as a fluke, he was well aware of the commercial appeal of this new style of harmony singing and dabbled in it on the side. Along with The Cyrkle, Epstein had previously put together a Seekers-type instrumental group called The Silkie, comprising two male guitarists, a male string bass player and a female lead singer, who'd formed a folk group while they were all still students at Hull University. In August 1965, The Silkie recorded Lennon and McCartney's 'You've Got to Hide Your Love Away', with John Lennon producing, Paul McCartney playing guitar and George Harrison providing the Judith Durham-style tambourine playing. The song reached Number 28 in the British charts and Number 10 in America before the group sank without a trace. Even with Epstein's power and connections in the music industry, The Silkie didn't have the public appeal of Judith, Athol, Keith and Bruce.

Epstein had greater success with The Cyrkle. Their recording of 'Red Rubber Ball' didn't chart in Britain or Australia, but it went all the way to

Number 1 in the American charts. Flushed with their initial success, Simon and Woodley penned two further tracks, 'I Wish You Could Be Here' and 'Cloudy', which would appear on a later Seekers album. Aware of The Seekers' phenomenal success in the British charts and their need for a new single, Paul Simon had contacted the group late in 1965 and had let them know he had a couple of songs they might be interested in. They were 'I Wish You Could Be Here' and 'Someday One Day'.

'Paul was visiting London at the time and he contacted Tom Springfield,' says Judith. 'We all went around to Tom's flat to meet him and listen to him sing these songs he had for us. I just loved "The Sound of Silence", which he also played, but, just our luck, we couldn't have it. Paul said he had just found out that, while he was in Britain with Art, the record company in America had added bass, drums and strings to their version of the song and had released it as a single. Paul was furious because he wanted the song to be left acoustic, but ultimately it became their first chart hit and reached Number One in America. Although we liked "I Wish You Could Be Here", we decided it wasn't a potential single, so that really only left us "Someday One Day", which I didn't particularly like. The lyrics didn't mean much to me, but we were short of material and we needed a new single, so we just went into the studio and cut the song, with Tom producing.

'I don't recall any emotional experience recording the song. It was more a mechanical process, just singing it parrot fashion. I recall it was quite a hard song to sing, still is. One thing I did like about it was that chord change right at the end. Harmonically speaking, it's very clever. These days, because the audiences love it, I've shared their joy whenever we've sung it. Paul is a very clever writer and I appreciate his lyrics so much more now.'

The Seekers recorded 'Someday One Day' early in 1966, and followed the session with a two-show, one-night stand at the De Montfort Hall in Leicestershire, supported by The Rockin' Berries and Mrs Mills. Mrs Mills was an overweight, jolly woman who played the piano with great gusto. Judith knew she could probably play Mrs Mills right off the stage, but she was also aware that her piano playing was getting sadly neglected. It seemed to be used only when the group needed a novelty; no one took it seriously.

The De Montfort Hall show was packed and again The Seekers were ecstatically received. The *Leicester Mercury* wrote:

> The hall was packed to capacity for both performances and the appreciative audience demanded encores at the end of the show.

Although individually fine entertainers, the group must surely owe its success to the incomparable Judith Durham, who really didn't need a microphone to reach the ears of those sitting at the back.

Only a matter of days later, on 22 January, Keith Potger married Pamela Powley, a British swimming star who was ranked fourth in the world for the 100-yard breaststroke event, having swum for Great Britain in the 1957–8 season. The wedding, held at St Michael's of All Angels, a tiny eleventh-century country church in Sopley, took Judith by surprise.

'I was aware that Keith was going out with Pam, but the wedding seemed to come around very quickly,' she says. 'Pam was very much Keith's companion and I didn't really have an enormous amount to do with her. I do remember thinking how the structure of the group had changed, much like it must have done for The Beatles when John Lennon married Cynthia [Powell]. Like, suddenly, there's five of us. Pam always looked beautiful. She was very slim and very well dressed, all the things I wasn't. Being as complex-ridden as I was, I saw Pam setting a standard that I wanted to emulate but couldn't. She was two years older than me and a lovely person, but we didn't really do anything together outside the group.

'I did emulate her on one thing, though, and I'm grateful to her to this day. She used the Mary Quant style of eye makeup – shadow in the socket – and I adopted that technique. I still use a lot of black matt shadow on my puffy eyelids, to give the impression of a socket. From 1966 on, I felt I could at last compete in the big-eyes department. Dusty Springfield always had that Clara Bow image and it worked brilliantly for her. She got away with even more black than I could. But thank you, Pam Powley – you changed my life without knowing it!'

The wedding was attended by the three unmarried Seekers, with Athol Guy as best man. Police were out in force as hundreds of Seekers fans packed the grounds and the church doors had to be locked, as fans surged forward and threatened to take all the pew space. 'Keith and Pam looked just beautiful,' Judith recalls. 'We were walking to the church with fans barricaded either side of us and I was aware of this huge response to us.'

Just eight days later, The Seekers – and the new Mrs Potger – set off to Australia for their second national tour, supported this time by the British star Mark Wynter ('Venus in Blue Jeans', 'Go Away, Little Girl'), the New Zealand band The Librettos and local stars Bill and Boyd, and Marcie Jones and The Cookies. Judith admits a bit of a crush on the incredibly smooth Mark Wynter. 'All the girls loved him,' she says. 'He always got a tremendous reaction from the females in the audience when he performed. We worked with him quite a lot.'

In preparing for this tour, Judith had lost a little weight and, when she changed her hairstyle, she inadvertently became a trendsetter by creating a new fashion that would be slavishly copied by teenage girls in both Britain and Australia.

'I'd been worrying about my hair for quite a while,' Judith recalls. 'When we first got to England, it wasn't terribly long so it just hung either side. But, by the time it had grown longer, we'd had the three Number One hits and we'd moved away from pure folk music, so it looked a bit too folksy down both sides, especially with the formal, full-length stage dresses I was wearing by now. It was a bit of a dilemma for me, because my only other option, if I wanted to look more sophisticated, was to wear it up.

'I was considering doing that before the Australian tour, but I had a bit of dermatitis on the back of my scalp and it would have been noticeable if I'd put my hair up. The only way I could see around it was to sweep it around to one side, something I'd tried briefly when I was sixteen after seeing a Brigitte Bardot movie and thinking it looked glamorous. I needed something really simple that I could do myself, because I never enjoyed going to a hairdresser. It always seemed a waste of a day to me and it was expensive. Besides, I never knew exactly how I'd look when I came out. The experience I'd had doing *IMT* on my own had been a disaster when I had a beehive and, years before that, Mum took me to a hairdresser who gave me an "onion cut", which I hated. So I started cutting my own fringe way back in the early sixties and still do it today. But I didn't realise at the time what a trademark the whole one-sided hairstyle would become.'

Judith and the boys touched down in Sydney on 1 February, only days before Beverley's wedding and the start of The Rolling Stones' Australian tour. At their first press conference, Judith had to deny rumours that the group were on the verge of breaking up, following Keith and Pam's marriage. The following night, the group opened their tour at Perth's Capitol Theatre, where, according to the *West Australian*, they 'presented the zenith in pop folk music'. Two days later, they played Adelaide's Centennial Hall, and then, on 5 February, they arrived to a screaming crowd at Melbourne's Essendon Airport. More and more now, The Seekers were getting the type of reaction from fans that the other, hipper bands were getting. The Seekers' fan club membership was swelling and, to their hometown fans, they were conquering heroes.

Although they were not performing until the 8th, these next few days were very busy. On Sunday, 6 February, the group attended a blessing of Keith and Pam's wedding, held after evensong at St Martin's Church in Hawksburn, and, the next day, Judith was one of three bridesmaids at her sister Beverley's wedding to Barry Sheehan at St Peter's Church in Melbourne's Eastern Hill.

'Coming back to Melbourne and seeing Beverley again was a very emotional experience for me,' says Judith. 'Knowing that I'd be back home on tour at the time of the wedding, she'd sent me the material and the pattern for my bridesmaid dress, so I was prepared. It was great how I matched up with the other two bridesmaids – our cousin Sheila and Beverley's close friend Anne, with whom she'd travelled to England.

'But poor Beverley was just a bundle of nerves. She'd made her own lovely dress and looked really beautiful, and she had handled all the arrangements herself. But it really was so much to take on and, even though I wanted to help her enjoy her wedding, I felt a bit helpless, having arrived so late.'

On top of all this pressure was the fact that the press had caught wind of Judith's inclusion in the bridal party and newspaper photographers turned up. 'But I thoroughly enjoyed the day,' Judith says. 'It was the realisation that Beverley was actually getting married.' Beverley made sure her younger sister caught the bouquet.

Bill and Hazel had yet to meet John Ashby, Judith's boyfriend of eighteen months. Hazel had asked Judith about him and had shown concern that he was a good enough suitor, but Judith gave no indication that she was thinking about marriage.

'I did wonder if maybe one day I would marry John,' Judith says. 'I was disappointed when Eddie apologised to me about John not coming to Australia as our tour manager, because Mum and Dad and Beverley wouldn't be able to meet him. Besides, I was obviously going to miss him while I was away. We had been secretly living together in the Richmond house and, while the morality of that bothered me, I still believed that we were committed to each other. It gave me a degree of companionship, domesticity and protection. I had a great affection for John and we were very close.'

The morning after Beverley and Barry's wedding, The Seekers

attended a civic reception in their honour and met Lord Mayor Beaurepaire at a Melbourne Town Hall reception before flying to Sydney later in the day for a press reception at the Chevron Hotel, thrown for them by EMI Records. The company's managing director presented them with gold discs to mark the sale of 50,000 copies of 'The Carnival Is Over' in Australia. Then it was back on the plane to Melbourne for their first concert at Festival Hall.

Festival Hall in the sixties was a huge barn of a place and into it were crammed 8,000 cheering people, stretched out mostly on either side of the stage, which was along a wall. Known mostly for staging title fights, Festival Hall was not the best place to see The Seekers, but in 1966 Melbourne didn't have a decent concert venue. It didn't seem to matter. In a review headed ROWDY HOMECOMING, The *Age* wrote, 'It was clear that The Seekers ... were being given a heroes' welcome home.' The Melbourne *Herald* wrote:

> How much more polished and at ease the group seemed to be since they last sang from that stage ... Easily and sweetly they swung into the gospelling 'When the Stars Begin to Fall'. But what a night it was, when the stars began to rise.

Judith performed a second Festival Hall concert with The Seekers in Melbourne on the 10th, before flying to Tasmania with Bill and Hazel. There, Judith's proud parents held a big reunion for old friends and neighbours at Wrest Point Hotel. In the little spare time she had, Judith drove with Hazel and Bill to see Merryhaven, their old home, and Hazel was amazed to see that the curtains she had made by hand all those years before were still hanging in the windows.

The group played the Albert Hall in Launceston on the 11th and Hobart's City Hall on the 12th. They returned to Victoria for one concert in county Ballarat and three days later they were in Canberra for a Civic Theatre concert that saw the *Canberra Times* comment, 'The Seekers captured the Canberra audience in a way which previously had been reserved for artists with the glitter of foreign nationality.'

On 17 February, The Seekers were back in Sydney, where they were once again at the mercy of a mocking press. The *Daily Telegraph* reviewer sniped, 'The big square sound arrived at the Stadium last night ... their smooth, characterless rendition of folk orientated pop tunes hasn't improved with age.' Two concerts – in Newcastle and Brisbane – remained, before The Seekers were to leave Australia for New Zealand.

It was in Newcastle that what has become their infamous press breakfast took place. The group had arrived in Newcastle, yawning and bleary-eyed, and headed straight off to breakfast. Suddenly, the press burst in and started filming them and Bruce, in his usual inimitable way, let them know quite strongly that they were intruding. The press abruptly packed up and walked out. Only later were they informed that they were supposed to be guests of honour at this 'press breakfast'.

The Seekers' first tour of New Zealand was a major success, with rave reviews for all shows. On 25 February, while The Seekers were still in New Zealand, EMI Records in Australia released 'Someday One Day' as a single, some four weeks ahead of its British release. The song reached Number 15 on the Australian charts, the first Seekers record since 'I'll Never Find Another You' to miss the Top 5. Even their World Record Club recording of 'Morningtown Ride', released by W&G as a single in Australia, had peaked at Number 5 the previous year.

The Seekers arrived back in Australia in the second week of March to be filmed for a television special – *The Seekers at Home* – being made by Channel Seven. The group shot footage near Melbourne for the special, singing 'Morningtown Ride' on Victoria's historic steam train *Puffing Billy* in the Dandenong Ranges, and 'Someday One Day' on the beach at Black Rock. Further footage was shot in a studio, with Mark Wynter as their guest.

The following day, The Seekers took part in *Music for the People* at the Myer Music Bowl, performing before a record 110,000 people, the largest crowd in the twenty-year history of the annual concerts. Little did Judith know that, the following year, The Seekers would break their own crowd record. Sharing the stage with the Australian Symphony Orchestra, conducted by Hector Crawford, The Seekers performed just four songs – 'Someday One Day', 'The Carnival Is Over', 'The Water Is Wide' and 'We Shall Not Be Moved' – and were given a standing ovation. The reaction brought back happy memories for Judith of her jazz show and her own standing ovation at the Bowl just three years earlier.

With this, their best-attended show, behind them, the group had only a couple of days to rest before flying to London on 18 March, the day 'Someday One Day' was released in Britain. The reviews for this first non-Springfield song were mixed. *Melody Maker* wrote, 'Not as catchy as their others. People won't go around singing this in the street, it's too rushed'; while *Disc Weekly* insisted it would 'be a big hit. Written by Paul Simon, it goes along at a fair old lick, with The Seekers singing with their usual enthusiastic skill.' Even *New Musical Express* predicted it would be a hit.

'It's peppy, bright, fast-moving and a compulsive toe-tapper,' its review read. 'Clearly a hit.'

Clearly, it wasn't. Judith's initial concerns about the song proved fatalistic, with 'Someday One Day' peaking at Number 11 in the British charts, breaking their run of Number 1 hits. 'It didn't surprise me at the time because I didn't like the song much and I didn't think it would be a major hit for us. I just didn't feel any emotion when I sang it.'

Softening the blow, The Seekers learned that a compilation album called *The Seekers Sing Their Big Hits*, which had been put together by W&G, had gone gold in Australia, making them the first Australian group to reach gold on album sales.

Two days after arriving back in England, The Seekers were sharing a bill with Roy Orbison on ATV's *New Palladium Show*. By this time, Orbison had had twenty UK hits, including 'Only the Lonely', 'It's Over' and 'Pretty Woman', all of which had reached Number 1. 'I can still see Roy Orbison now, dressed in black with his sunglasses on during the rehearsal,' says Judith. 'I wasn't a really big fan of his, but I was impressed by this incredibly emotional, tearful voice. He had an overwhelming sadness about him which really struck me while I sat in the seats out front, watching him rehearse.'

The following day, The Seekers were to add yet another award to their mantel of trophies. While in Australia the previous month, the group was advised that they and The Rolling Stones were winners of major Carl-Alan Awards, presented annually by Mecca for outstanding services to ballroom dancing. The Seekers were named Most Outstanding New Group of 1965, while The Stones picked up the Most Outstanding Group award. The presentations were made at a gala ball at the Empire Ballroom in London's Leicester Square by the ballet star Dame Margot Fonteyn.

'That presentation meant a great deal to me,' says Judith. 'I was just thrilled to be meeting Dame Margot and she was very complimentary to me. She was one person I considered legendary and I was knocked out that she knew who I was and appreciated what I was doing. She was such a big star in the arts and I held her in great esteem. Meeting her meant more to me than meeting The Beatles would have, if you see what I mean. I actually went over to her table after the presentation and sat down and had a chat. That's something I'd never have done previously, but I felt much more of an affinity with her than I did with anyone in the pop world. She commented on my dress and said how lovely it was.

'I was thrilled because I had designed it and picked the fabric out myself, even though all my dressmaking by now had been delegated to a wonderful girl named Val, with whom I'd struck up a rapport at the ATV studios in Elstree during all the Ronnie Carroll and Mark Wynter shows. Val was single-handedly more responsible for my boost in self-confidence than anyone else. She would painstakingly nip in a quarter of an inch here and a half-inch there as I gradually lost weight.'

The Seekers made a surprise appearance in April at London's top showroom, the Talk of the Town in Leicester Square, deputising for the American singer Vikki Carr, who'd come down with laryngitis. Their performance was a critical smash and, as a result, The Seekers landed their own five-week season at the Talk in August. Again, Judith couldn't see that she was probably even more famous by now than Vikki Carr was. She marvelled at Vikki Carr's wardrobe, left hanging in the star's dressing room in her absence, and compared them with her own folksy ones, so suited to The Seekers show. Judith was a long way from seeing herself as a 'real' star.

Next came a flying visit to Paris and Hamburg for TV shows, and it was in Hamburg that Judith suffered another serious bout of depression. The home-loving girl once again felt out of place in these strange surroundings and she couldn't wait to leave.

Back in London, the group taped television guest spots and began production on four fifteen-minute ATV mini-specials called *A Date with The Seekers*. ATV, who obviously saw The Seekers as wholesome entertainment for the mums and dads, knocked up a little farmhouse setting with a veranda and a rocking chair. The group would sing three or four songs in each show. However, despite their success, it wasn't prime-time viewing. It was something for the folks to watch late at night with their nightcap, if they were still awake. Judith enjoyed doing the shows, but, more and more, she longed to be doing something on her own, to be stretching her talents beyond group singing and, maybe, making a name for herself.

At the same time, however, Judith's self-image was so bad that she even considered plastic surgery after The Seekers had topped the charts. Even as a teenager she was preoccupied with her small eyes. She would sit in darkened cinemas with her cheeks sucked in and her eyes wide open, hoping that if she sat that way for long enough, it might result in hollow cheeks and train her muscles to widen her eyes!

Judith had lost around a stone in weight and was now nine stone ten pounds, but she still felt matronly and found it difficult to get hold of clothes that flattered her large bust. It was such a problem for Judith that she consulted a Harley Street plastic surgeon, who arranged for a bust-reduction operation to take place within a few days. During the same appointment, she discussed the idea of some cosmetic surgery, to slim down her face, which the surgeon advised against.

'I'd confided in Eddie Jarrett,' Judith says. 'He strongly advised against both operations. On one hand, he pointed out that there were literally thousands of pretty models whose faces weren't memorable. It was people like Barbra Streisand, with unusual faces, who stuck in people's memories. He tried to make me understand that one of the greatest assets anyone can have in show business is a unique appearance. On the other hand, he had made his own enquiries through a doctor friend whose wife had undergone a bust reduction and had become paralysed. He was very concerned this rare complication might happen to me. Besides, the doctor was convinced that, if I continued to lose weight, my bust line would naturally reduce as well. I took Eddie's words very much to heart, but still wasn't sure whether to go ahead with it or not.'

The decision was made for Judith when a Fleet Street reporter rang her home the next day and asked if it was true she was booked in for a bust-reduction operation. Mortified at the possibility of her private anguish being emblazoned across newspaper front pages, she denied everything and promptly cancelled her operation. She'd just have to keep losing weight.

May 1966 was another exciting month for Judith Durham. The Seekers had been named *New Musical Express'* Best New Group of 1965, and were included in the *NME* 1965–6 Poll Winners All-Stars Concert presented by Maurice Kinn at the Empire Pool in Wembley. On the bill were The Beatles, in their last ever concert performance, and The Rolling Stones, making their first concert appearance in two years. Also performing were The Yardbirds, The Who, The Spencer Davis Group, Roy Orbison, Dusty Springfield, The Walker Brothers, Crispian St Peters, Herman's Hermits, The Overlanders, The Fortunes, The Shadows, The Alan Price Set, Sounds Incorporated, Cliff Richard and the group Dave Dee, Dozy, Beaky, Mick and Tich.

By this time, Cliff Richard had been an established star for eight years, since 'Move It' reached the Top 5 in 1958. The Seekers' runaway success came as no surprise to him. 'They had a style that was very refreshing,' he says. 'Judith had such a distinctive voice and they had a knack of always finding the most commercial songs for their style of music. They were a group you could recognise immediately when their songs were played on the radio.'

A five-night stint at the Stockton Fiesta followed before The Seekers were guests of the Variety Club of Great Britain's Golden Disc Luncheon at the Dorchester Hotel on Park Lane. Appearing with them was a veritable *Who's Who* of variety performers – Harry Secombe, Vera Lynn, Jackie Trent, Liza Minnelli, Tom Jones, Ronnie Carroll, Val Doonican and Georgie Fame.

'Funny to think just ten days earlier we'd performed with The Beatles and The Stones,' says Judith. 'Being on a bill with them didn't mean that much to me, but meeting Vera Lynn at the Dorchester was a great thrill. I couldn't believe I was actually meeting this woman whose music I'd listened to and tried to emulate when I was a child, and that she would know who I was. We met Liza Minnelli, too, that day. She was a new star at that point and she seemed quite reserved, compared with how I now know her to be.'

Once again, it was time for The Seekers to make a new album, but this time they weren't going to be as rushed as they were making 'A World of Our Own'. Bruce Woodley had written a couple of tracks for this new LP and Judith had fallen in love with Paul McCartney's song 'Yesterday'. The album was also to include cover versions of a couple of recent hits that originated on the West Coast of America.

However, because The Seekers had undertaken a five-week weekend tour of Britain, the recording sessions had to be squeezed in on their days off. The tour was a great success and, whether they were playing in 800-seaters or 3,000-seaters, they constantly pulled capacity houses.

While The Seekers were roaming the British countryside, Beverley and her husband Barry had arrived in London, having cut short their European honeymoon because Beverley had been ill. She had been suffering from nervous exhaustion leading up to the wedding and the subsequent travelling had taken its toll. When a doctor was called, he diagnosed chickenpox. Beverley and Barry moved into Judith's Richmond house in her absence. When Judith arrived home after the tour she was delighted to see them, but, the moment she learned Beverley had chickenpox, she went straight into worry mode. It was, after all, a contagious disease!

The decision had been made to return to Tom Springfield for material for the group's next single and, during this tour, The Seekers recorded a lush new Springfield ballad, 'Walk with Me'. A second recording session had been set for 'Georgy Girl', the title song of the forthcoming Otto Plaschkes film starring James Mason and Lynn Redgrave. But, during rehearsals late in May, Judith was taken ill and rushed to Victoria

Hospital in Kingston with acute appendicitis, where an emergency appendectomy was performed. Sharing headlines with Peter Quaife of The Kinks, who'd been seriously injured in a car accident the same week, Judith's hospitalisation was seen as major news and articles appeared around the world, with varying degrees of accuracy.

As a result of the operation, Seekers concerts in Stockton, Carlisle, Gloucester, Exeter and Plymouth were cancelled, along with a scheduled appearance on Dickie Valentine's TV show. 'I didn't know whether I really needed to have my appendix out,' says Judith. 'I had this terrible pain and thought it may even have been indigestion, because I'd eaten bananas, which was unusual for me. But they examined me and told me it was my appendix and that it had to come out. Apparently, it was badly infected. Knowing what I now know about nature cure, I might not have had it out. But here I was, suddenly whipped off to the Kingston Clinic. Bev and Barry came to see me, which was terrific, and I remember I got loads and loads of letters from people, along with some of Beverley's wonderful shortbread.'

Among the telegrams that sat on Judith's bedside table was one from Dusty Springfield, which read, 'Lot and lots of sympathy. Hope you feel better very quickly. This is a very unfunny telegram because laughing hurts don't it love?' It was signed 'Tom's Sister'. 'I was very surprised to get that telegram,' Judith says. 'It was lovely of Dusty. It still seemed odd to me that these other people in the entertainment industry, these stars, would know what I was doing and would care how I felt.'

About three weeks later, Judith rejoined The Seekers for their week-long season back at Greasbrough Social Club, where the patrons were known to relieve themselves against the walls! They went on to a triumphant return season at the Bournemouth Winter Gardens, where their supports included a young Australian duo named Pat and Olivia. Olivia Newton-John was a Melbourne girl whose first prize for winning a radio talent competition in Melbourne was a trip to England. Judith would learn many years later that Olivia had been a school student of her brother-in-law, Barry. Pat Carroll was another Melbourne singer seeking to make it alone in Britain. Both singers knew Athol Guy and had met Eddie Jarrett, who suggested the two girls team up. Through the Grade Organisation, Eddie was able to have them added to the bottom of the Bournemouth bill.

'I remember them performing in bell bottoms, doing choreography while they were singing,' Judith says. 'We saw Pat and Olivia socially in London a few times, but they had more to do with the boys in the group.

Olivia was going out with Bruce Welch of The Shadows at the time, and they'd all get together. I was a bit in awe of Olivia. She was so pretty, still is. So was Pat. They were both so slim and fashionable!'

A week-long cabaret engagement followed in Palma, Majorca, at the Tagomago Club, and the booking sticks in Judith's mind for a couple of reasons. 'That was the time Keith and Pam lost all their luggage,' she says. 'The airline had mislaid it and Pam had to go through the whole week without her own clothes. She came down to meals with a sheet beautifully tied, with the flair she had, like a toga. She just had to make do and she did it very well.'

'I'd also started to get tired of forever doing cabaret and clubs and the Tagomago Club in Palma wasn't my idea of the type of place we should have been playing. We'd had five Top 40 hits, three of them Number Ones, and we'd had hits in America and Australia, too. We should have been doing international concerts by that time. We should have been a concert act, but Eddie just kept booking us in the safe theatre venues and clubs like this one. We forever seemed to find ourselves up north. Greasbrough Social Club, really! Mr Smith's in Manchester.

'We were on variety bills, never given a whole show to ourselves. It was ridiculous. When we did our second summer season at the Pavilion in Bournemouth in 1966, on a variety bill for six weeks, we went to see Peter, Paul and Mary at the Bournemouth Winter Gardens. They were carrying the show on their own. They were the stars of the show and that's how I felt it should have been for us.

'I went down the road in Majorca and saw Shirley Bassey perform. She was playing at the biggest and best club, the in venue. I felt we could have carried a full show on our own, in concert, but Eddie said, and I distinctly remember this, we shouldn't do more than fifty minutes anywhere, that it would be too much. But, with the talent we had between the four of us, each of us could have done a bit of something on our own as well, and that would have been very fulfilling for me.

'Eddie was a great manager, but his background was as an agent for the Grade Organisation, and the tradition of English theatre was very important – cabaret, the clubs and variety. You did your pantomime at Christmas, because it was a good, solid booking to see you through winter, and then, when the weather got better, you followed the crowds to the beach areas and did a three-month booking. That was your employment and everything else was a bonus. It's something everyone did, but it usually changes when you have a hit record. You take one step up from it, but we never did.'

The Beatles, whose record sales in Britain had been matched by The Seekers the previous year, had moved into arena concerts, playing venues like the Shea Stadium in New York. They'd stepped into the big time, leaving The Seekers singing away on the variety circuit. They weren't alone: the circuit was also a way of life for groups such as The Bachelors, The Honeycombs and The Applejacks. The difference was that The Seekers were now major recording stars.

Immediately after the Majorca season finished, The Seekers were featured guests on *Blackpool Night Out*, another of those variety shows that were quietly irking Judith. After week-long seasons in Stockton and Blackpool, The Seekers followed Johnny Mathis into a five-week engagement at the Talk of the Town on 22 August. Deputising for Vikki Carr had paid a dividend!

'I didn't get to see him at the Talk of the Town, but I did meet Johnny Mathis when we worked together on a TV show,' says Judith. 'That was another big thrill for me. His records in the fifties meant an awful lot to me, those beautiful, emotional songs I loved, like "Wonderful Wonderful" and "Chances Are". I liked him as an artist, but was again very in awe. But I thought it was terrific that I'd been able to meet him.

'I was very much aware we were following him in at the Talk. It really was *the* showroom and it was just about the biggest booking a nightclub act could get at the time, on a par with getting the Palladium. The Talk of the Town presented shows very, very well. Everything was very grandly put together and there was the house band – the Burt Rhodes Orchestra – who were terrific and worked with some of the biggest names in show business. It was very much a "star" venue. The room had a lovely feeling about it and the big black stage was magic, the way it was built with the audience surrounding it. That booking also marked another transition for us. We'd had orchestrations done to augment the orchestra, so we were playing with a full band, rather than the acoustic show we did everywhere else. It was a disciplined experience, actually performing with a band and a conductor. The band was brassy and there were strings, and these elements were not familiar to me in a Seekers act. We had a much fuller sound. But I enjoyed the pure showbiz of it. It felt very glamorous. I don't know that I'd like to be stuck in it, but it was fun and a change from those variety bills. But it still didn't alter the fact that we should have, by now, been playing concerts.'

A *New Musical Express* writer seemed to echo Judith's instincts when he wrote:

The Seekers are the best act of their kind I have ever seen. The Talk of the Town is undoubtedly London's best cabaret room. But somehow the marriage didn't happen. Don't get me wrong, The Seekers were great! But they gave a concert in a nightclub.

During the group's season at the Talk of the Town, they'd previewed their new single 'Walk with Me', using the orchestral backing. The song was released while they were at the Talk. 'I absolutely loved the song,' Judith recalls, 'but I didn't see it as a Seekers song. I remember hearing it when Tom only had the music and he asked us to try to help with the words. I came up with some lyrics for him, which, of course, were totally unacceptable. But it was my first real try at real composition and I think of it now as the crawling I did before I learned to walk. I saw "Walk with Me" as more of a solo vehicle for someone than a group song. I felt that Tom had written it possibly with my voice in mind, but it didn't work as a group song. It didn't suit strumming guitars. I thought perhaps it might have fared better if someone like Shirley Bassey had done it. I realise now I should have recorded it solo, as none of the three boys like it at all and I love it. When we recorded "Walk with Me", I recall thinking it would not have the same level of success as say, "The Carnival Is Over", but still liking it very much.'

The critics seemed to love it, although again the *New Musical Express* echoed Judith's concerns. Their review read, 'Seekers come up with a different, vaguely disturbing new sound. I say disturbing because it's so hard to place exactly what the difference is.' *Disc Weekly* wrote, 'A poignant rock ballad, written by Tom Springfield, beautifully harmonised by The Seekers with several Judith Durham solo passages. Isn't it amazing how her voice stands out, just as did Dusty's in The Springfields?' *Record Mirror* also gave it the thumbs-up: 'A slower than usual but thoroughly charming performance. Must be a hit, possibly Top 5. Excellent singing from Judith Durham.' The *Manchester Evening News* predicted it would be The Seekers' fourth Number 1, while even the *News of the World* was showing approval. 'Haunting ... fine solo singing by Judith.' But still Judith wasn't convinced.

'Walk with Me' peaked at Number 10 in the British charts, faring better than 'Someday One Day', but failing to get The Seekers back to Number 1. 'There seemed to be some concern within the record company about whether "Walk with Me" was a good enough record to follow "The Carnival Is Over",' Judith says. 'I know it was remixed before it was released, so there must have been some discussion about it. I can remember watching *Juke Box Jury* and being thrilled to see Engelbert Humperdinck, who said it wouldn't matter what that girl sang, Judith is just a wonderful singer. That did wonders for my self-esteem at the time. It was like I felt when Dusty sent me the telegram in hospital – it was recognition by my peers.

'It was very difficult for Tom by this stage, I imagine. We couldn't, as a group, sing love songs and it didn't sit well with our image to sing anything sexually suggestive, so he was stuck with neutral ground. We needed songs almost with spiritual overtones and of course arrangements that basically suited guitars. As a song, I loved "Walk with Me". I loved that middle eight. We were rehearsing it at my place in Richmond at the same time as we were rehearsing "Georgy Girl" and Beverley was there. She thought "Georgy Girl" was the obvious hit, whereas I didn't relate to it as much on a musical level.'

Springfield's lack of scope as far as Seekers songs was concerned meant he was unable to give them anything for their new album. Aside from covering 'Island of Dreams', Tom's early hit for The Springfields, and featuring 'Georgy Girl', which he'd written with lyrics by the actor Jim Dale, the album featured modern material and covers. Bruce Woodley contributed a new song, 'Come the Day', and co-wrote two others with Paul Simon. One was a cover of 'Red Rubber Ball' and the other was 'I Wish You Could Be Here'. Judith recorded 'Yesterday' as a solo, along with her cover of the French singer Françoise Hardy's UK hit from earlier in the year, which she loved, 'All Over the World' ('Dans le Monde en Entier'). The boys covered PJ Proby's 'Louisiana Man', which Lonnie Donegan had played for them at a dinner party at his home. Turning again to America, the group selected Pete Seeger's 'Turn, Turn, Turn' – a 1965 American chart-topper for The Byrds – and The Mamas and the Papas' 'California Dreamin'', a Top 5 US hit from earlier in the year.

Completing the twelve was the gospel-tinged 'Well, Well, Well', which had previously been recorded by Peter, Paul and Mary and by The Seekers for the World Record Club.

'I saw Françoise Hardy singing "All Over the World" on TV and thought how much I'd like to sing it,' Judith recalls. 'It had a beautiful piano accompaniment and I really liked it. I wanted to play piano on it. I was also struck by what a beautiful song "Yesterday" was. I saw Paul McCartney sing it on his own on *Blackpool Night Out* on TV. He stepped forward from The Beatles and just sang it on his own, playing guitar. It was just the most beautiful song.

'I bought The Beatles' *Rubber Soul* album and Beverley and Barry gave me *Sergeant Pepper*. I didn't have a great record collection in those days. I'd bought Dusty's album and I had a Tom Jones album that I really loved, but not a huge collection. I bought "It's Not Unusual" as a single, and "You've Lost That Loving Feeling" by The Righteous Brothers. Can you believe I was actually buying records? I even bought some of The Seekers' records. It never occurred to me that, as one of the artists on the EMI label, I could just ask them for a copy, or several copies. I didn't want to bother anybody, so I sometimes went into the shops and bought The Seekers' albums to send home to Mum and Dad. I don't think I even had a complete set of our records. I missed getting some of the singles at the time.

'I remember feeling anticipation when The Beatles were releasing a new record and discussing the different tracks with people, but I was never a sort of "normal" Beatles fan. To me they were a really musical group, very talented. I liked their production, which was mainly due to George Martin. His arrangements had so much classical influence, like whole concertos, and of course I related to that. There were intricacies in their recordings that fascinated me. I always admired their inventiveness, the way they progressed with the times.

'There was something very clever about someone who could construct a song like "Yesterday" with such simplicity and yet it could be so beautiful. I loved recording it, just as I loved recording "All over the World".'

The rest of the material on that album Judith didn't particularly care about, one way or another. The group was making a transition and yet she wasn't a motivating force in that transition. When Judith recorded 'California Dreamin'', she had no idea what she was singing about. It was so American, a foreign language to Judith, who sang it more or less phonetically. It was interesting to sing, but she was still at a stage where she didn't really care what she was singing, just as long as the record got made. The Seekers were in the studio and had to put down tracks. 'California Dreamin'' sounded OK for harmonies, so they recorded it. They just had to get that album out before too much time slipped away.

In September with the album finally in the can, Judith received some disappointing news. Ernest Page, the astrologer who'd predicted her success in 1964, had died. 'That made me very sad,' Judith says. 'I'd done an interview with *New Musical Express* earlier in 1966 and mentioned Ernest Page and the journalist decided he'd like to do a feature on him. So they found him in Hyde Park, where he lived, gave him the birthdays of twelve personalities, including Paul McCartney and Elvis, without letting him know who they were, and got him to map their charts and analyse their personalities. He was remarkably accurate of course and it ended up a major feature in *NME's Summer Annual*. Ernest was knocked out by it, very rosy-cheeked at his new notoriety. They took his picture and everything. Not long after that, the journalist rang me and told me they'd found him on one of the benches in Hyde Park. He'd died in his sleep, in the sun.'

Judith had little time to dwell on Ernest's passing, for The Seekers had landed the most controversial booking of their career. Coming up at the end of the month was a five-week tour of South Africa for African Consolidated Theatres, and dates in Rhodesia and Kenya for Twentieth Century-Fox. In accepting the tour, The Seekers would become the first British-based pop group to visit Rhodesia since the rebel breakaway government of Ian Smith took power the previous November.

Among the group's supports was the British harmonica virtuoso Tommy Reilly. Judith didn't know the first time she met him just how significant he would become in her life in years to come. Also on the bill were the comedians Hope and Keen, the sons of Syd and Max Harrison, who'd appeared with The Seekers as the Ugly Sisters during *Cinderella's* Stockton season. Judith was happy to learn that John Ashby, with whom she was still having a relationship, would fly out with The Seekers as tour manager, and they departed for Johannesburg late in September and opened on 26 September.

'South Africa's similarity to Australia struck me as we flew into the country,' says Judith. 'The brick houses with the tiled roofs, the gum trees. I had difficulty singing in Johannesburg because of the altitude. It was so high, there was very little oxygen. I ended up with a big saliva problem, constantly having to swallow. Getting used to that rarefied atmosphere wasn't easy for me, because of my lung trouble, and I got headaches initially.'

From Johannesburg, the group moved on to Cape Town, Durban, Pretoria, Port Elizabeth, East London and Bulawayo, playing to sell-out crowds at all venues. 'The audiences were very, very enthusiastic,' says Judith. 'We got incredible press wherever we went. They seemed to love us.'

They certainly did. In Pretoria, their reviewer wrote, 'The Seekers know how to make the show-business billy boil and they stand high on the list of Australia's most important exports.' A *Daily Dispatch* review of their performance in East London claimed, 'The Seekers would be just another group if it was not for the folksy voice and vibrant personality of Judith Durham'; while Durban's *Daily News* championed their show at the Playhouse with 'Judith is the star that twinkles brightest ... The Seekers are a perfect team, a harmonious gang of diggers who struck gold and who are working together to mine it.'

Judith heard during the tour that there had been a request for The Seekers to sing for a black audience. Judith would have loved to do it, but this was still considered a no-no in 1966 in South Africa.

The group moved on to Rhodesia, played their shows and flew straight on to Nairobi. That was when disaster struck. With four shows at the Kenya Cinema completely sold out, The Seekers disembarked to be greeted by the news that their work permit had been rescinded by the Kenya Immigration Department and their shows had been cancelled. The Seekers were given no official reason for the ban, other than the assurance that the decision had been reached jointly by the Kenyan government and the Australian High Commission. The ban made newspaper headlines around the world, thrusting The Seekers into controversy for the first time in their career.

'We found out that, politically, we were a terrible threat to the Kenyan government,' says Judith, 'because [Jomo] Kenyatta, the prime minister of Kenya, was one of the twelve black African nations' leaders. We had performed in South Africa and Rhodesia, which were segregated, and to have us play in Kenya would make Kenyatta look as though he was endorsing apartheid. He couldn't afford to compromise his integrity by aligning himself with the southern countries, so we had to be barred. Of course, I didn't really understand the apartheid problem then. I was totally separated from the colour problem and just wanted to think of myself as a nonpolitical entertainer.

'We were entertained a fair bit in South Africa by wealthy whites and I recall black people serving the food. The ladies of the house all seemed to have such big thighs, because they didn't do any work, I supposed. They always seemed to sit.

'Eddie wanted to keep the ban very hush-hush because he felt it might be a bit too controversial for our image. It was the first time anything really dramatic had happened to us as a group, presswise. There was a lot of publicity about it in Africa and Australia, but Eddie managed to squash most of it in England. As usual, I did what I was told. I was content to be controlled and, when Eddie told me not to say anything publicly, I said nothing. It never occurred to me that as a group, we could have helped raise public awareness of apartheid.'

Not only could the group not perform, but the government wanted The Seekers out of the country as soon as possible. That day, John Ashby's brother Tony, who lived in Nairobi, still gave a welcoming party for The Seekers, and, because their four-day all-expenses-paid sojourn at the wildlife reserve Tree Tops had to be cancelled, he quickly arranged for the group to visit a local wildlife reserve. From the safety of the car she was travelling in, Judith delighted in watching the zebras, giraffes, elephants and lions all in their natural surroundings. But, when the driver had to get out to see to the car, everyone panicked as a lion took a lingering and very interested look in the direction of the vehicle. The driver jumped back in a lot faster than he had got out!

The group spent one night in Kenya and departed for London, having called off their six-day holiday in Mombasa, which would have marked the end of the tour. The day they left, the *East African Standard* ran a story headed SEEKERS LEAVE 'VERY UPSET', in which Ashby was quoted as tactfully saying, 'Originally we intended only to perform in South Africa, but there was an option in the contract and we accepted an invitation to play in Kenya. We were asked to come here.'

There was little time for regrets when the plane touched down at Heathrow Airport: only days earlier, Judith had been elated to hear that The Seekers had been asked to perform before the Queen Mother at the forthcoming Royal Command Performance variety bill at the London Palladium; they'd landed another of those 'good, solid winter pantomime bookings' for Christmas, as the stars of *Humpty Dumpty*; their new album was about to be released; and a Christmas single needed to be recorded.

Judith's favourite yet most vocally challenging of Bruce Woodley's songs was 'Come the Day'. When Bruce first sang it to the group, it was written as a slow song but Judith suggested it would sound better up-tempo. That was how the group recorded it and it became the title track of their next album, which drew favourable reviews from the music press. *New Musical Express* wrote, 'What a polished folk group this is ... Judith Durham, one of our better girl pop vocalists, is heard to advantage', while *Melody Maker* claimed, 'This shows just why The Seekers are so far ahead of their rivals. No other group has a lead singer to compare with Judith Durham.'

With this album, The Seekers were taking their first serious steps away from the confines of folk music. This album comprised contemporary songs in the folk idiom. They had also gone back into the studios to rerecord 'Morningtown Ride' as a single, so that the new rights to it would be held by FXB instead of the World Record Club. The group recorded their stage favourite 'When the Stars Begin to Fall' as the song's flip and it was issued as The Seekers' Christmas single on 18 November, four days after their Royal Command Performance.

Meanwhile, Judith had virtually no time to think about what to wear for that show. 'It was such a prestigious event and I wanted to look just right,' she says. 'As long as I'd been in London, I'd admired a shop in Baker Street called Mary Fair and had dreamed of the day I might be slim enough to do the clothes justice. Each dress was a one-off and for the Talk of the Town I'd bought a lovely pink chiffon dress with white chiffon bodice and pink trim, but this time I needed something more sophisticated. I was in luck. Two days before the concert, I found a silver lamé dress there that fitted me perfectly.'

The group made their royal debut in illustrious company. Sharing the bill with them were Judith's heroes, Juliet Greco and Henry Mancini, as well as Sammy Davis Jr, Matt Munro, Des O'Connor, Jerry Lewis, Gilbert Becaud, Kenneth McKellar, Gene Pitney, The Bachelors, Wayne Newton and Frankie Howerd.

'It was a very exciting time,' Judith recalls. 'We spent all day rehearsing at the Palladium, which is just a beautiful theatre. I remember watching Jerry Lewis rehearsing from the side of the stage. It was an incredibly long rehearsal and he was being very fussy. Everyone was getting very edgy, because time was slipping away. I received a telegram while I was in my dressing room, from Mum and Dad back home. It read, "Tonight we feel we really are the parents of a star", and it made me cry. We did three songs and then bowed the way we were all shown, once to the royal box. You weren't supposed to look at the box until you bowed. Then there was the finale and the line-up backstage to meet the royal party.

'I'd bought myself a pair of silver leather gloves from Harrods to wear with my dress, but I wasn't sure about the protocol of wearing them. I remember asking Henry Mancini, who was next to me in line, and he thought it would be OK. The Queen Mother was very nice. She told me we had an act that appealed to all ages and that we were one of her favourites. We also met the Duke and Duchess of Kent and the young Duke of Gloucester.'

For their set, The Seekers performed 'This Little Light of Mine', 'Morningtown Ride' and 'Come the Day'. *New Musical Express*, in reviewing the television special made of the concert, singled the group out. 'The Seekers got a warm welcome and show they deserved it ... In a mainly male cast, Judith Durham was an oasis of feminine appeal.'

Meanwhile, 'Morningtown Ride' was shaping up to be the vehicle that might propel The Seekers back into the Top 5. Its reviews were all favourable. *New Musical Express* said it was 'attractively harmonised in The Seekers distinctive style' and noted 'the in-crowd will dismiss it as corny, but it's easy on the ear'. *Disc and Music Echo* asserted, 'Judith's pure voice is ideally suited to this number'; while *Melody Maker* wrote 'The unmistakable Seekers approach makes it a sure-fire hit.'

And sure-fire it certainly was. In the last week of December, 'Morningtown Ride' jumped to Number 1 in the British charts. Below it were 'Sunshine Superman' by Donovan, 'Green, Green Grass of Home' by Tom Jones, who'd been at Number 1 the previous week, 'What Would I Be' by Val Doonican and 'Save Me' by Dave Dee, Dozy, Beaky, Mick and Tich.

One of the many groups who followed in The Seekers' footsteps and left Australia in search of fame and fortune were The Easybeats, who were in the Top 10 that week with 'Friday on My Mind'.

'Morningtown Ride' earned The Seekers a silver disc from *Disc and Music Echo* and went on to sell more than a million copies. Malvina Reynolds, the 66-year-old American housewife with a PhD who'd penned the song, had much to thank The Seekers for: they'd also recorded her 'What Have They Done to the Rain?' on their *Hide and Seekers* album.

Just as The Seekers were in pantomime when 'I'll Never Find Another You' was storming the charts, so were they when 'Morningtown Ride' reached the top. They'd opened the ten-week season of Tom Arnold and Bernard Delfont's production of *Humpty Dumpty* at the Bristol Hippodrome on Christmas Eve. This time, The Seekers all had roles as well as their own speciality act at the end of the show. When Eddie Jarrett had asked the group to do another pantomime season, Judith was reluctant, feeling they'd already had one experience and were now major stars. When Jarrett persisted, she told him she'd only be interested if she could play the principal female role. Jarrett arranged it, but Judith was self-conscious that she had to audition. But she got her wish and was cast as Mistress Mary Quite Contrary, while Athol, Keith and Bruce were the barrow boys Jack, Peter and Bluey. Judith's leading man was the handsome British actor Tony Adams, as Tommy Tucker, and the comedian Ted Rogers played Simple Simon. The Welshman Wyn Calvin was Humpty Dumpty.

The Seekers broke all box-office records with *Humpty Dumpty* and got some of their best notices. *New Musical Express* wrote:

It seems everyone at Bristol Hippodrome is a fan of The Seekers, those four young Australians whose names in lights shine out over the title *Humpty Dumpty* on the theatre's canopy. But whether everyone was perfectly satisfied with the way they had been fitted into the show is another matter ... It is when the script calls on them to sing to their own accompaniment in the last fifteen minutes of this three-hour show that they really come into their own! ... It seems The Seekers must claim most of the credit for the fact that the pantomime advance bookings at Bristol are not merely big, but vast!

The Seekers took time out from *Humpty Dumpty* to appear as panellists on TV's *Juke Box Jury* and also appeared in a concert to aid the Aberfan disaster. While The Seekers had been in South Africa, half a million tons of black coal waste from a mine in South Wales had slithered down a mountainside in October 1966, killing 144 people, many of them children, in the town of Aberfan and, with a proud Welshman as their manager, The Seekers were naturals for the charity bill.

In the end-of-year bestselling charts, The Seekers came first, beating The Beatles and The Rolling Stones for singles sales. Not bad, considering The Beatles had 'Paperback Writer', 'Yellow Submarine' and 'Eleanor Rigby' in 1966. In *NME*'s end-of-year popularity polls, Judith was knocked out, to be placed sixth in the British Female Singer category above Marianne Faithfull, Shirley Bassey and Helen Shapiro, and thirteenth in the world female ratings. In the British Vocal Group category, The Seekers were fifth, ahead of The Spencer Davis Group, The Small Faces, The Who, The Kinks and The Troggs.

The Seekers ended 1966 with *Come the Day* at Number 3 on the album charts and 'Morningtown Ride' at Number 1 on the singles chart. Two and a half years after being thrust into the spotlight, Judith was finally feeling better about herself. But while her nagging doubts about her appearance and her image were abating, they were replaced with concern that The Seekers – with a success story to rival just about any of their contemporaries – were still considered a novelty act on the variety circuit. She still felt trapped by the group. Her voice was topping charts and figuring strongly in the popularity polls, but she had no real identity.

She was still, to a large degree, 'that girl in The Seekers'. A face without a name.

In *NME*'s end-of-year issue, Judith spoke of her new year's resolution. She wrote, 'My resolution is to try to become even better adjusted to the life I lead in show-business. I am also going to try to make sure I am continually appreciative of all the good things that have happened to me.'

6. THE HIGH PRICE OF FAME

Don't be so scared of changing
And rearranging yourself:
It's time for jumping down from the shelf.

– 'GEORGY GIRL'
TOM SPRINGFIELD AND JIM DALE

Judith Durham thoroughly enjoyed the season of *Humpty Dumpty* in Bristol. Far from being like her first pantomime stint in *Cinderella* when she was pressured into signing a contract she had doubts about, this time she was relaxed and happy. As well as a Number 1 single and a Top 5 album, she'd made a new friend.

'It really was a magic ten weeks,' Judith says. 'I was still a Seeker, but the pantomime also gave me the opportunity to do something on my own. And I had a wonderful friendship with my leading man, Tony Adams. He was terrific. I can't thank him enough for the friendship he showed me. On stage, he was great to work with. We had our little dance routines, we had to fall in love, all that fairytale stuff. I just loved it. Humpty Dumpty was in love with me, too, and I danced and sang with him. It was like a fairytale for me for those ten weeks. A dream come true in a way. I got carted off by the giant green ogre in the scene of terror, carted off over his shoulder, screaming. It was such a lot of fun.

'Tony was very theatrical, a wonderful dancer and musician. We would share music after the show and on the weekends. We'd get together on the piano and sing theatrical songs. Tony was teaching some of the cast jazz dancing and I joined the classes. We went for walks all over Bristol; it was a real change for me to be with somebody who I had so much in common with. I wasn't able to share that kind of love of the theatre and that kind of music with Athol, Keith and Bruce. It was the other side of me that they never really saw. On our long walks, it used to amaze Tony how often I was recognised. He had a pair of glasses with plain glass in them, as a disguise, and after a few days, he gave them to me, saying he thought I might need them more than he did!'

Judith was still going out with John Ashby, but he didn't have that musical background either. He never did understand that hunger in Judith to express theatrical music and to share the love of music with somebody else, knowing that that other person was experiencing the same emotions. It was while Judith was in Bristol, staying in a Clifton Spa Hotel apartment, that she was visited by Tommy Reilly, the harmonica player who'd supported The Seekers on their South African tour. Tommy wondered whether Judith would mind meeting his son David, who was trying to get recognition as a songwriter.

'Tommy was another wonderful artist,' Judith says. 'It was great seeing him again. He really is the world's greatest virtuoso of the classical harmonica, yet he did a marvellous act in variety theatre. I felt we had a real affinity and I loved spending time with him in South Africa. I wasn't sure how I'd be able to help David, because I didn't see myself as a songwriter, even though I'd influenced the way "A World of Our Own" and "Come the Day" turned out and I'd helped Bruce with "Two Summers" and later with the middle eight of "Chase a Rainbow". But I decided to give it a go and I really enjoyed working with David. He always said what valuable contributions I made. We wrote nineteen songs together and went into a studio and made demos of them. I even did duets with David on a couple of them and I asked Bobby Richards to do the arrangements. We signed a publishing deal with a company called Sunbury Music. One of those songs, called "So Much More", was recorded in Swedish and "Colours of My Life" became a bit of a classic for The Seekers. That song was even used in a Belgian detergent commercial!

'I always felt these songs that I wrote with David were his inspiration. He would come up with the concept of the song and the style of lyric and I would add to them, rather than go in with something of mine in the first place. Collaborating with him and having my name as co-writer on those songs certainly helped David's career, but, at the time, he helped me enormously. He effectively started me off as a songwriter.'

Among the songs born of the Reilly–Durham partnership were 'The Non-Performing Lion Quickstep', 'Again and Again', 'Memories', 'Can't Make Up My Mind' and 'Colours of My Life', all of which Judith would later record. Reilly went on to make an album of his own songs and, more recently, to write film music and film scripts.

It was also during this Bristol pantomime season that Judith was surprised to hear the news that Capitol Records had released the group's *Come the Day* album in America retitled *Georgy Girl*, and had lifted the song as a single.

'I always thought of "Georgy Girl" as an album track,' Judith says. 'I never considered it might be a single. It all started when Otto Plaschkes had approached Eddie about our singing a song over the credits of his new film *Georgy Girl*. He said he was a very big fan of the group, and he wanted us to do the theme. He'd finished the film and wanted to enter it in a German film festival, so he needed the song in a bit of a hurry to play over the credits.'

Before making the decision to record the song for the movie, The Seekers went to see a private screening of *Georgy Girl* in Soho, and at that stage there was another song over the credits, by a male singer. The film touched a nerve with Judith, who was stunned how closely she identified with the title character played by Lynn Redgrave.

'It was the story of my life, really,' Judith says. 'I couldn't believe it. I related so strongly to Lynn Redgrave's role, and wished I could have played it. In the opening scene she's been to a hairdresser and is so unhappy with the way they've tried to make her look that she runs into a subway bathroom and washes it out under a tap. That scene was just me to a T! I'd been to a hairdresser especially for my appearances that first time on *In Melbourne Tonight* back in 1963 and they did this awful beehive and I clearly remember wanting to put my head under a tap and wash it all out, but there just wasn't time.'

Eddie Jarrett was happy to have The Seekers singing the title song to *Georgy Girl* on condition that Tom Springfield could write something more suitable for them. Plaschkes agreed and Springfield wrote the song and then teamed with the actor Jim Dale, who wrote the lyrics. There were two sets of lyrics written and recorded for the film. One opened the film and the other closed it, over the credits. When the film was released with the song, it was evident it was a hit waiting to happen, so The Seekers recorded a special version as a single for America and it was included on *Come the Day*.

'I quite liked the song, but it did nothing for me emotionally,' Judith says. 'It was actually quite difficult to sing, because of the huge range. I had to have Keith singing the lower notes with me. I never really understood why people liked it so much. It was the same with "I'll Never Find Another You". Nice songs, but it amazed me that they became so incredibly popular and endured for so long. One thing "Georgy Girl" did have going for it was great production. It was a very well-made record. And Tom was very creative with that whistling opening. He had a professional whistler come into the studio and do that.'

Georgy Girl, although a British film, was extremely successful in America and its popularity stretched to its theme song. The decision to release it as a single was a wise one. The American trade papers loved it, with the music industry bible, *Cashbox*, calling it 'the surprise hit of the year'. Indeed it was: by the second week of February, The Seekers had notched up another first when 'Georgy Girl' reached the Number 1 spot on the American charts, displacing The Monkees' 'I'm a Believer'.

Within a matter of weeks, The Seekers' *Georgy Girl* album had cracked the US Top 10 and the tune was nominated in the Best Song category for the upcoming Academy Awards. In addition, the American music magazine *Record World* invited 4,000 DJs to vote for a series of awards and the Top British Record award was shared by The Seekers for 'Georgy Girl' and The New Vaudeville Band's hit 'Winchester Cathedral'.

EMI in Britain was watching the American charts closely and saw a dollar to be made. With 'Morningtown Ride' still in the Top 40, they issued 'Georgy Girl' as a single on 17 February, the same day Shirley Bassey's 'The Impossible Dream' and Herman's Hermits' 'There's a Kind of Hush' were released. Again, reaction to The Seekers was positive. 'Folk music at its sparkling best,' wrote *New Musical Express*. 'A gay, toe-tapping rhythm, and The Seekers at their most scintillating.' *Record Mirror* contended, 'Somehow parts of it don't sound so Seekerish, yet when Judith is dominant it's alright again', while the *Melody Maker* reviewer begrudgingly wrote, 'I don't like them, but they always get a hit. I like Judith Durham, actually. She has a good voice, but I don't like the whole sound. This will be a hit, I'm afraid.'

News came through from Eddie that The Seekers had been invited by the Academy of Motion Picture Arts and Sciences to sing 'Georgy Girl' on the television broadcast of the Academy Awards. However, the group's contract with the pantomime bound them and they were not released from it. It was a bitter blow for Judith, who was stuck in Bristol with the boys while Mitzi Gaynor took her part and presented the song for an international television audience of millions of people.

'Georgy Girl' went to Number 2 in Britain and Australia and Tom Springfield flew alone to America for the Academy Awards presentation. The Oscar for the Best Song went that year to 'Born Free', making it the first time Britain had won the award in the 39-year history of the Oscars. Again there was no time for The Seekers to bask in the glory of their latest chart success. At the end of the *Humpty Dumpty* season they were aboard a plane headed for Australia, where a $100,000 one-hour colour television spectacular with HSV7 awaited them.

The Seekers landed in Sydney on 7 April and this time their airport arrival was a major event. 'I guess in the minds of Australians, and particularly the Sydney people, we'd truly made it because we'd had an American hit,' Judith says. 'I remember we commented on the amount of fans, television cameras and photographers at the airport. In particular, we noticed how much more respectful the Sydney press was. We were no longer just Melburnians to them: we were an international singing group. We were also very much aware that we were back in Australia. It seemed odd to get off a plane and see men in Bermuda shorts with long socks and people with sunburn!'

Whisked away to the privacy of a VIP room, where a press conference was held, Judith was once again left to field questions about those ever-increasing rumours that The Seekers were about to split up. She told reporters, 'There's no truth in these rumours and we hope to stay together at the top for several more years.'

No expense was being spared by HSV7 for the special, which they had titled *The Seekers Down Under*. Basically a travelogue of Australia, it was being shot in colour for possible sale to British and American networks. The Seekers would film fourteen songs around the country, at locations in Canberra, Melbourne, Sydney, Surfers Paradise and the Barossa Valley. Produced by the *In Melbourne Tonight* producer Norm Spencer and directed by Mike Brayshaw, the special required 1,716 pieces of film equipment weighing 1,200 pounds.

Filming commenced in Canberra, where The Seekers travelled by car around the international consulates to a backdrop of 'A World of Our Own' and then performed 'The Times They Are A-Changin'' in Canberra Civic Square. They were filmed on the steps of Parliament House meeting Australian prime minister Harold Holt, who was quoted in daily papers as saying he had longer hair than the three male Seekers!

In Sydney, the group performed 'The Water Is Wide' at the Spit, aboard a 35-foot yacht, and then sang 'Someday One Day' on the site of the as yet unfinished Sydney Opera House. While in Sydney, The Seekers attended a record-company reception, at which they were presented with gold disc awards for their *Come the Day* album, which had sold more than 50,000 copies in Australia. Having moved on to South Australia's Barossa Valley, the group performed 'Turn, Turn, Turn' and 'Red Rubber Ball' during grape harvesting at Lyndoch winery. In Surfers Paradise, on Queensland's Gold Coast, the group were filmed singing 'We Shall Not Be Moved' while heading a cavalcade of vintage cars from Surfers to Coolangatta, driving a 1909 Renault. Police were required to control the crowds who'd gathered along the way to watch. Later, at the Beachcomber Tiki Village motel, they were filmed at a mock-up *luau* (a Hawaiian food feast), performing 'Isa Lei' and 'Myra'.

Still in the hinterland, Judith was filmed at the top of the four-hundred-foot Purlington Falls, in the midst of the subtropical forests of Springbrook, singing 'The Olive Tree', the new song written by Tom Springfield with lyrics by Diane Lampert.

In discussions about which song Judith would feature as a solo in the special, the boys had remembered 'The Olive Tree', which Tom had written around the time of 'Walk with Me'. When Tom was asked for his permission for Judith to sing it, he agreed on the condition that it be released as a single, which became the reason Judith would release her first solo single later in the year. But she had no idea when she recorded the song how much it would change her life and that it would one day be instrumental in her meeting her future life partner.

'I enjoyed the experience of filming, still do,' Judith says. 'What I recall most of all was being out in the sun for so long each day. It was very hot, and we'd come from an English winter, don't forget. Suddenly we were being confronted with blowflies, and when you're driving around in an open-top car and things like that it's hard to keep your hair in place. I was lucky I had a good makeup artist working with me, but I wasn't terribly prepared for the special, as far as wardrobe was concerned. I remember being taken to Paula Stafford's shop on the Gold Coast and picking up a muumuu, quite the fashion then, and several of the dresses that I wore for the filming, but I had to borrow Mum's blouse for the Barossa Valley sequence. Mum and Dad were with me in Queensland. They were actually in the last of the vintage cars in the cavalcade scene, and again at Tiki Village they were on the balcony overhead while we were filming the two songs. John Ashby was with us; in fact, he's the one driving the tractor in the Barossa Valley when we walk through the vineyard singing "Turn, Turn, Turn".'

The Seekers Down Under was Channel Seven's biggest undertaking to date, not only financially, but logistically as well. The producer Norm Spencer admits the show was made available for sponsorship and presold to General Electric before the station would commit to such an expensive project. 'We'd never done anything like it before, so we were virtually learning as we went along,' Spencer says. 'The cameraman and the director went to the locations the day before the rest of us arrived and set up the shots. We had a rough script, but everything was more or less made up as we went along.'

Gordon Bennett was chief cameraman on *The Seekers Down Under*. Today, he laughs when he recalls the magnitude of the event. 'To pull together a unit of people to travel around Australia with a singing group was not an easy task,' Bennett says. 'Unlike today, forward planning was not television's strong suit. We had a lot to get done in a very short time. It was incredibly hot while we were filming at Parliament House in Canberra and freezing cold when we were filming the summery sequence at Tiki Village on the Gold Coast. It was a complete reversal of the usual weather patterns in those places.'

It was only when The Seekers began location rehearsals for 'Isa Lei' and 'Myra' at Tiki Village, that the crew realised the group couldn't move properly. 'They could certainly sing, but none of them really had any idea of how to move,' Bennett says. 'In the end, Norm Spencer flew Joe Latona, who was the hot choreographer of the day, from Melbourne to teach them some basic moves.'

In the midst of filming *The Seekers Down Under*, the group were required to fly back to Melbourne for a gold-record presentation from EMI and, once again, they were invited to appear at *Music for the People* at the Myer Music Bowl, during Melbourne's annual Moomba festival. The film crew decided to shoot it as the special's Melbourne sequence.

'When we flew back in to Melbourne, there was a motorcade from the airport,' Judith recalls. 'The press had reported the route we'd be taking and, all the way from Essendon Airport, people came out of their homes and lined the streets, waving at us. I had a feeling it was going to be a special visit.'

Appearing with The Seekers for this concert were the Royal Australian Navy Band, who played Tchaikovsky's *1812* overture during the first half of the programme, and the Australian Symphony Orchestra conducted by Hector Crawford. Supporting The Seekers was Crawford's wife Glenda Raymond, who sang selections from *The King and I*. Judith was thrilled to meet her, having admired her soprano voice on television for so many years.

The Seekers were not scheduled to perform until 3.15 in the afternoon and yet crowds started gathering at the Bowl as early as six in the morning. By ten, the Bowl was swamped with tens of thousands of people jostling for a space in the sun. By the time The Seekers walked out on stage, the Bowl had virtually disappeared under a sea of 200,000 people, the largest crowd in the venue's history. In fact, The Seekers pulled the largest concert crowd in Australia's history and to this day they still hold the record for the largest concert crowd in the southern hemisphere.

'It was a big occasion anyway, performing with a symphony orchestra and the navy band, and I felt nervous walking out on to the stage. There were musicians everywhere behind us, so it wasn't like our normal show, where we had the stage to ourselves. And the scene in front of us was awesome, this vast sea of faces, people cheering. I would love to have been out there myself, to have some sense of what it was like to be in a crowd that big. I've spoken to many people over the years who were there and they tell me what an amazing experience it was. It was also touching that these were families coming out on a Sunday to see us sing in the gardens.'

Having waited for hours to see The Seekers, the crowd was treated to just fifteen minutes of them, in which time they performed 'Come the Day', 'Morningtown Ride', 'Red Rubber Ball' and 'The Carnival Is Over'. For an encore, they sang 'Georgy Girl' and received a standing ovation, but, despite twenty minutes of fans screaming 'We want more', the group did not return. Aware it was a free concert and that they were the special guests, the group had worked out only a fifteen-minute spot and had no more musical arrangements for the orchestra. They weren't to know that people would start queuing from six o'clock in the morning and would wait up to ten hours in the heat to see them.

'When we finished "Georgy Girl" and went downstairs, we could hear this incessant yelling and clapping,' Judith says, 'but there was nothing we could do about it. We stayed backstage for quite a while and then tried to leave in a car, but getting out of there was difficult. We were mobbed and for the first time it dawned on us all just how popular we were. Somehow we didn't see ourselves on that level, but being mobbed like that was like something out of a Beatles newsreel clip, not a Seekers one. Even though it's not perhaps the most ideal concert situation to be in – singing outdoors can be very difficult, particularly when your mouth gets dry – it's been a memory I've always treasured. It was such a show of support from our own people.'

Two days after the Bowl concert, The Seekers attended a cocktail party held in their honour by EMI Records. Their proud parents stood by as the four entertainers were presented with gold-disc awards for 'Georgy Girl', which by now had sold more than 2 million copies internationally (it would eventually sell 3.5 million copies). Footage from the EMI reception and the Myer Music Bowl – which had been televised by Channel Seven on the day – completed the sequences needed for *The Seekers Down Under*, although the chief cameraman, Gordon Bennett, recalls some trickery being brought into play. 'We had a disaster on the day of the concert,' he admits. 'One of our cameramen ended up with nothing on film and we were short when it came to editing the concert footage for the special, so we used cutaways from the 1966 Bowl show for that sequence!'

The special was screened in black and white shortly after The Seekers had returned home, attracting an audience of more than 2 million and drawing a rating figure of 67, which beat the previous record of 58 set four years earlier by Channel Nine's *BP Super Show*, starring Elaine McKenna. To this day, The Seekers hold that record as well.

No other Australian television special has ever attracted such a high rating. Before its public debut, the special was shown at Parliament House in a private screening for all members of Parliament, organised by the Minister for Tourism, Don Chipp. The following month, the Australian Prime Minister, Harold Holt, took a copy of the special with him to America and showed it to President Lyndon Johnson in a private screening at Camp David. The President reportedly loved The Seekers and responded by showing Holt a colour movie of the LBJ ranch in Texas!

Because of public demand, the special was repeated in Australia late in 1967. However, Channel Seven first had to edit out the sequence where the group chatted to Holt on the steps of Parliament House. (On 17 December 1967, Holt disappeared, presumed drowned, at Shelley Beach in Portsea, Victoria.)

Judith was later to learn that US networks had offered Channel Seven US$80,000 for the American rights to screen the special, but this was knocked back. The special did eventually make it on to American and British TV screens, but there was never any mention of payment for the group outside of the two screenings in Australia. More and more, Judith was realising that The Seekers were making vast amounts of money for other people, but very little for themselves.

'That's just how it seemed to be at the time,' Judith says. 'Someone made a lot of money out of the special, but it wasn't us. It all felt wrong to me, and I had Dad forever questioning the financial side. He could see that all this work we were doing didn't translate to a healthy bank balance. By this time, of course, we were major drawcards. We'd had all the Number One records, knocking The Beatles and The Stones off. We were pulling big crowds; we'd topped the American charts; and "Georgy Girl" had been nominated for an Academy Award. We came back and did this TV spectacular, pulled two hundred thousand people to the Bowl and yet, when we got back to England, Eddie had us booked on another variety bill at the Bournemouth Winter Gardens. We'd go back into England and settle back into being a novelty act again.

'I also discussed with Eddie the fact that, after all the hits, we should have been the stars on television shows. We were forever appearing on TV, but we always seemed to be the opening act. We were never given the closing spot of the night, the star spot we had every right to. Eddie used to tell me he had an awful fight on his hands to get anything more than the opening spot because of the sort of music we did. The producers saw us as a "bright opener", but our standing on the charts contradicted that. The producers wouldn't want us to close the show, but we were always used as the drawcards in the advertising of the show. We were usually the biggest names on these shows by far, and they used that to their advantage; but, come show time, there we were, the opening act.

'It also struck me as odd that the only concert we did in Australia in 1967, at the height of our popularity, was the Myer Music Bowl – and that was a free show. I remember thinking that we could pull two hundred thousand people but we weren't getting anything for it. Whenever Eddie booked a tour for us in England, America, South Africa or Australia, it was always for a flat fee. I'd talk to him about it, suggesting that perhaps we should have been on a percentage, a door deal. That way, if we pulled a huge crowd, we made more money and if the attendances were down, too bad. To me, it seemed fairer that way, but Eddie always erred on the side of caution.'

Because of that caution, Eddie never took The Seekers to a higher level. By 1967, with several Number 1 hits behind them, The Seekers should have been headlining their own concert tours, not only in England but throughout Europe and America, but it was a step they were not to take in the sixties. They should also have been able to tour Australia more often, but Jarrett was intent on keeping them as much as possible in the United Kingdom.

Before leaving Melbourne, The Seekers were special guests at the *TV Week* Logie Awards, staged that year on the SS *Fairstar*, a Sitmar liner docked at Station Pier. The *Fairstar* was the sister ship of the *Fairsky*, which had taken the group to England in 1964. The group won a special Logie that night for their promotion of Australian talent overseas.

'I remember the Logie awards and thinking how out of touch I was with what was happening in the Australian television industry,' Judith says. 'We'd effectively been away from Australia for three years and all the people winning the major awards that night were new to me. I had my photograph taken for one of the newspapers with Vic Morrow, who'd been specially brought from America by *TV Week*, but I had no idea who he was. I'd never seen an episode of *Combat*. Later, I was sitting with

Graham Kennedy and I recall his asking me how I thought the papers would react if we announced that night that we were getting married!'

Graham Kennedy also remembers the moment. 'It was a line I was using a lot in those days, with varied success!' he says.

Two days after the presentation of the Logies, The Seekers flew back to London and, two days after arriving, opened a four-week season at the London Palladium. This was their fifth appearance at the Palladium and for the first time, The Seekers were the headlining act. Among their supporting acts were the comedians Mike and Bernie Winters and the Nitwits, the clarinettist Des Lane and the comedian Frank Berry. The Seekers should by now have been playing major concerts, as The Animals were, but for now they had to be content with their other supporting artists, a dove act and Tanya the Adorable Elephant!

For Judith, there was an overpowering feeling of loneliness during that season. The three boys had been given the star dressing room and Judith's room was a long way from where they were. She seemed to spend all her time sitting in her dressing room on her own. People seldom dropped by for a chat. John Ashby joined her sometimes, but he spent much of his time with the boys. Judith would simply turn up, sit around until show time, perform and then go home alone. Here she was, a major star, and her only real company was Tanya the Adorable Elephant!

During the season, backstage negotiations took place for The Seekers to make their movie debut in a proposed film starring Bing Crosby, to be shot in Switzerland. *New Musical Express* named it as *The Great St Bernard* and reported that, if the deal was clinched, it would feature two specially written Tom Springfield songs for the group to sing.

'We were quite keen to do it,' Judith says. 'We'd got to the stage where we were about to meet Bing Crosby, although nothing had been signed. But there was a problem with our itinerary and we couldn't have done it until much later, but unfortunately, by then, there wouldn't be enough snow in Switzerland for what the producers needed, so we had to drop out. The film was never made.'

The Seekers wound up their Palladium season by topping the bill on ATV's *Palladium Show*, this time supported by their old friend Lonnie Donegan, who was making his comeback. Within days of closing at the Palladium, the group was on a plane bound for Canada, where they represented Australia at Expo '67, the World Fair in Montreal. They arrived at Montreal International Airport on 18 May and met up with Ed

Sullivan and his wife, who had just flown in from New York. On the tarmac, they took full advantage of the photo opportunities, with Sullivan pictured serenading them with a guitar.

The Seekers were booked to headline the 'Pop Goes Australia' concert series at the Expo Theatre on the banks of the St Lawrence River. Their supporting cast was all Australian and included the comedian Rolf Harris, the pop singer Normie Rowe, the boomerang thrower Frank Donnellan, the jazz instrumentalists Don Burrows, George Golla and John Sangster, and Bobby Limb as MC. The Seekers made their second appearance on US TV's *The Ed Sullivan Show*, singing 'Georgy Girl' in a live cross from the Expo Theatre.

'The actual Expo was fantastic,' Judith says. 'We went to all the pavilions and I can distinctly remember feeling very proud to be an Australian. It really hit me for the first time what it meant to be Australian, that realisation that we really had made a big contribution to Australia's cultural image overseas. We did our week at the theatre and it was very well received. Frank Donnellan, the boomerang thrower, was terrific. Boomerangs are so dangerous but he managed to throw it out right around the indoor auditorium, over the heads of the audience several times and catch it. It was something uniquely Australian and I didn't question at the time why a white man should be illustrating how a boomerang works. There were no Aborigines in the show at all. Odd to think now that people then were presented with a white Australia.'

The Seekers were taking part in the first live television transmission to Australia, where homegrown fans had to sit up until three in the morning to see them. That night, they were invited to a performance by the Australian Ballet Company, who performed Robert Helpmann's ballet sequence based on Aussie Rules football. Later there was a reception and Judith met Marie Collyer, the opera singer she'd admired for so long and was flattered to find that Collyer admired her voice just as much.

When Judith walked in, Robert Helpmann turned around and started singing 'Georgy Girl' to her! Rolf Harris gave her one of his drawings and Australia's Prime Minister Holt made a point of engaging Judith in a chat.

Judith enjoyed spending time with Bobby Limb and Rolf Harris and, sensing she was among friends, allowed her newly arrived tape of 'The Olive Tree' to be played over the PA in the theatre, to gauge people's reactions. Everyone, she thought, seemed complimentary, but Limb remembers the incident differently.

'We were sitting in the empty Expo Theatre one afternoon,' he says, 'when Judith's solo song, "The Olive Tree", came over the sound system.

I immediately felt a real tension with the three boys. It was a very uncomfortable feeling.'

Judith had had mixed feelings about recording 'The Olive Tree'. 'On one hand, I thought it was a beautiful song and it was exciting to think that I might be able to do something on my own again, especially featuring piano. Bobby Richards, my favourite, wrote a sweeping orchestral arrangement for those beautiful strings. But at the same time, I was worried about it. I wasn't convinced that the guys were all that happy about it because it looked as though I was stepping away from the group. But, ultimately, EMI agreed and for me it was such a great experience going into the studio and doing something by myself. I went in and did it and wasn't overly happy with the outcome. I don't know why, really.

'I got the feeling that, although the guys and the record company approved of my doing a solo record, they more or less viewed it as a means of keeping me happy, letting me have a little fun. No one seemed to take the record all that seriously; there was never a big push behind it. It just sort of limped out and got airplay and then just petered out, although I still get so many requests for it today.'

The Seekers returned to Britain, where a five-week season at the Bournemouth Winter Gardens awaited them. They also flew back to controversy, after news of Judith's impending solo single leaked out. 'The Olive Tree' was released on 9 June 1967, and inevitably it reactivated those rumours that The Seekers were on the verge of breaking up. Newspapers around the world carried reports that Judith was preparing for a solo career, which was strenuously denied by both her and Eddie Jarrett. Judith hadn't realised she would end up in a press skirmish when she agreed to record the song as a solo single. She hadn't realised, also, that she would be seen to fail if it wasn't a hit. Guileless as it seems, she was simply happy to release it in the hope the public would enjoy it.

In a moment of weakness, Jarrett told a reporter that the rumour was 'basically correct' and, in a statement to Britain's Sunday Mirror, Judith said, 'It's inevitable that eventually I shall make a split with The Seekers. But it would only happen if the three boys convinced me that they could make a replacement without it hurting their career.'

The music press was delighted with Judith's solo effort. BEAUTIFUL JUDITH DURHAM DEBUT, read the headline in New Musical Express, which went on to write, 'A gorgeous folksy tune ... the gal's voice is as clear as a bell ... it's bound to click.' Record Mirror was equally impressed, claiming, 'It's a beautiful song . . . Judith is tremendously popular and this will obviously be a hit.' Not long after its release, Judith performed the song on BBC TV's *Top of the Pops* – a show that also featured Eric Clapton, Procol Harum, The Hollies, Petula Clark and Traffic. *Disc and Music Echo* called her 'the star of the show'. On 2 June, a prerecorded appearance on *The Des O'Connor Show* was broadcast, in which Judith performed 'The Olive Tree' and then joined O'Connor for a duet on 'Somethin' Stupid', which had topped the charts two months earlier for Frank and Nancy Sinatra.

'I thoroughly enjoyed that experience, too,' Judith says. 'I was actually doing something on my own, for myself, and I loved the freedom. Working with Des was fun. He took me out for dinner in Bournemouth and, when he took me back home, I remember John Ashby was hovering around and seemed concerned that I'd gone out to dinner with somebody else. I was still going out with John at the time, but I didn't see us as going steady. It had crossed my mind previously that perhaps John and I would get married but, as time went by, that thought faded. It just wasn't a relationship that looked like it would lead to anything permanent. During the Bournemouth season, we shared a house with Athol and Bruce, but, because there wasn't a commitment, I didn't see anything wrong with my going out with other people. John didn't seem to like it too much, though.'

'I think John thought Des O'Connor was keen on me and maybe that's right. I admired him musically and liked the twinkle in his eye. He was a good performer, and our voices blended very well. Dinner was very enjoyable, but nothing more came of it.'

By the time The Seekers came to open in Bournemouth, 'The Olive Tree' had debuted on the British Top 40. It peaked at Number 31 and then disappeared. Part of the reason was that, early in July, EMI recalled the single, issuing a statement from Tom Springfield explaining that he wasn't happy with the final mix and wanted it reissued with a slightly faster tempo, even though several thousand copies had already been sold. By the time it was rereleased, the momentum had been lost. Judith was disappointed, but in a way it was almost a relief because she had found the media speculation about her ongoing role in The Seekers uncomfortable and she felt Eddie's and the boys' interest in the song's success was negligible.

On top of this, she was back at Bournemouth Winter Gardens, slogging away on another variety bill for a set fee. There was also the question of the next Seekers single to consider, and another album that year, plus an American tour and a return trip to Australia for the group's first full concert schedule since 1966. At least this time, though they were once again headlining a variety bill, The Seekers were presenting a more musically challenging show. The decision was made to change their standard stage act, which Britons had been seeing – with the odd song shuffle – for the past year.

Supported this time by Tommy Reilly and the Australian comedian Ted Rogers, who'd worked with them in *Humpty Dumpty*, The Seekers decided to utilise fully the house band – the Johnny Hawkins Orchestra, conducted by Gordon Rose. They integrated full orchestral backing for several numbers, including 'The Olive Tree', and introduced a new approach to their stage presentation. Athol and Keith revisited their early rock 'n' roll years by playing 'Runaround Sue'; Bruce took the solo spotlight for 'I Wish You Could Be Here'; and Judith not only got her own solo spot with 'The Olive Tree', but also played 'Maple Leaf Rag' on piano and performed 'We Shall Not Be Moved' as a solo in true trad-jazz style. It always brought the house down and gave her a kick.

Beverley and Barry had moved out of Judith's Richmond house some time before The Seekers played Bournemouth. Beverley was expecting her first baby in June and their new flat was unsuitable for children. While the group was out of town, Judith arranged for Beverley and Barry to stay in Athol Guy's flat while she paid for Athol to stay in a hotel. While Beverley and Barry were staying at Athol's, their first son, Anthony, was born. It was a big thrill for Judith and she was at Beverley's bedside the next day, after returning to town.

'I felt very emotional about Beverley's baby, much the same as I felt when Beverley and Barry got married,' Judith says. 'Tony was just gorgeous, so perfect and beautiful. It was incredible, holding him for the first time. But, for myself, I was never what you'd call clucky. I suppose I just assumed that I'd get married one day and have children, but I'd not had a lot to do with small babies and was never that comfortable with them. John Ashby was very good with Tony as a baby and I remember thinking that he'd make a good father, but having a child wasn't on my list of priorities.'

During the Bournemouth season, The Seekers had returned to the recording studio in London, having selected as their new single, a Kenny Young song called 'When Will the Good Apples Fall?' The song had been recorded and released earlier in the year by the British singer Ronnie Hilton, but had done nothing. Young, who had already penned The Drifters' 1964 hit 'Under the Boardwalk', had hit on the perfect harmony-group formula.

It was always difficult to find material for the group that accommodated their harmony style and suited their image. 'When Will the Good Apples Fall?' was yet another step away from the safety and suitability of Tom Springfield's tailor-made songs.

New Musical Express, as usual, glowed. Its reviewer made 'When Will the Good Apples Fall' the Record of the Week, saying:

> Beautiful. Another great hit for this group . . . Judith Durham takes the lead with that crystal-like voice of hers and the boys join her in the erupting choruses. What more can I say? The Seekers are back, and won't the chart know it soon!

Disc and Music Echo was more circumspect: 'A beautiful song, well produced,' its review ran, 'but it is just an ordinary, straightforward sound. It didn't do anything for me, although one can only marvel at Judith Durham's voice.'

But it was *Melody Maker*, which had previously waxed lyrical about The Seekers' recording output, that seemed to sum up Judith's feelings more precisely: 'More stirring stuff . . . which will doubtless be another success . . . but I wish The Seekers would become a little more adventurous. As an established group, they could afford to take a few risks. Another safe hit.'

The times, they certainly were a-changin' in London and, by 1967, The Seekers desperately needed to reassess their image in order to remain competitive. It was one thing to take on the beat groups in 1964 and contend with the likes of The Beatles, The Stones, Billy J Kramer and The Dakotas, The Dave Clark Five and Manfred Mann, but it was another thing entirely by late 1967 when their chart-topping rivals were The Monkees, The Foundations, The Bee Gees, Scott McKenzie and The Love Affair. Pop music was teetering on psychedelia and, if The Seekers didn't get a move on, they were going to slide from wholesome to old hat in an awful hurry.

By reaching only Number 11 in Britain, 'When Will the Good Apples Fall' was sending a message to The Seekers. It was time to update – or else. But the question remained: where would the new material come from? Tom Springfield's well appeared to have run dry and The Seekers were painfully aware that their image needed to be hipped up. Although it was never intended, the industry perception of The Seekers was that they approached only Tom Springfield whenever the need to record arose, which tacitly inhibited other songwriters from pitching new material at them. Judith was later to hear that The Bee Gees had written a song in late 1966 that they thought was perfect for The Seekers. Maurice Gibb related to Judith how they'd wanted to pass it on to The Seekers to consider for recording, but had heard there was a kind of Tom Springfield monopoly on the group and assumed he would just keep coming up with more hits. The song The Seekers missed out on was 'Massachusetts', which went on to become a Number 1 hit for The Bee Gees the month before 'When Will the Good Apples Fall' peaked at Number 11. The Bee Gees had earlier headed straight for Eddie Jarrett for management when they arrived from Australia. Jarrett turned them down, a move he probably lived to regret.

Another time, an American fan named Christopher Miethe contacted Judith and told her he'd written a song that he was desperate for her to record. Miethe had inherited $10,000 and was prepared to spend it all on seeing his dream come true. When Judith pointed out that she wasn't in a position to record without the group, Miethe agreed that his song 'Brothers and Sisters Everywhere' could be recorded by The Seekers. Studio time was booked and the group began recording, but the deal fell through then Miethe refused to sign over his publishing rights to FXB.

The quandary over new material became more pronounced as the pressure mounted on The Seekers to make a new album. It had been more than a year since *Come the Day* had been recorded and in that time there had been just one major hit single. In August, just prior to The Seekers' American campus tour, it was announced that the group would soon be starting work on a new album featuring mostly material by Bruce Woodley and Judith Durham, and, at this stage, Tom Springfield was still attached as producer.

'Tom presented us with a very sensible list of twelve perfect Seekers-type songs,' Judith says. 'One of those songs was "Adios Amor", which Jose Feliciano went on to record, and there was another song called "Carnival" from the film *Black Orpheus*, which was very haunting. But, ultimately, we decided the songs were too square, too typically Seekers, and we definitely wanted to change our image by this point. We weren't quite sure what the change would entail, but we knew something had to happen.'

Imagine the degree of frustration Judith was feeling by this stage, with people believing The Seekers was all she ever did and all she ever aspired to. She was perceived as unsophisticated and unsexy, and she desperately wanted people to start thinking there was more to her than The Seekers allowed her to reveal. She wanted to be more hip, more up-to-date, but she was still very much 'that lovely girl in The Seekers'.

'It's a bit like Julie Andrews wanting to do a film with swearing in it after finding herself typecast as Mary Poppins,' Judith explains. 'Or Olivia Newton-John finally shaking that girl-next-door image by doing "Physical". I was sick of being seen as this sweet girl in that nice group who had a lovely voice. I was capable of more than that. I felt, as an artist, I had so much more to offer. I never knew so many men were already in love with me and I truly believed I was unattractive to the opposite sex, from a romantic point of view.

'But I felt sad that our relationship with Tom ended. We explained that we wanted to do songs other than those he'd suggested and he just had to tell us in the end that there was nothing more he could do for us. Oddly enough, there wasn't a definite split with him, or anything. We just sort of drifted apart. We didn't have any sort of party for him, or let him know in any way how much we appreciated what he'd done for us to that point. It was just that, suddenly, Tom wasn't in our lives any more.'

The Seekers didn't seem to understand fully how Springfield had created their hits through his innate ability to conceive music that suited their sound. The bonus was that he was also able to bring that sound to fruition in the studio. Springfield had injected much of his personality into the group's hits and was therefore an integral part of their commercial success, a fact they heartily acknowledge in hindsight. The Seekers probably hurt Springfield's feelings, but they were oblivious of it at the time. They were completely focused on their need for an image change and, while The Beatles had managed it very successfully, it was a lot more difficult for a 'wholesome' group like The Seekers.

Springfield was philosophical when asked to comment on the end of his association with The Seekers. In a London press interview at the time, he said, 'We've had a good run. Now I feel the time is set for us to go our separate ways. I don't want boredom to set in and I feel I could run dry of fresh and original ideas for the group, so it's best that we end the association. The split is completely amicable all round and I'm sure the break will do us all the world of good from a creative point of view.'

After closing in Bournemouth, The Seekers spent most of August rehearsing and recording material for their forthcoming album, squeezing in appearances on TV's *Juke Box Jury* and the BBC's *Billy Cotton*

Band Show. Eddie Jarrett severed his ties with Tom Springfield by buying Tom's share of FXB Productions. Keith Grant, who had sound-engineered The Seekers' first World Record Club album in Britain years before, returned for the new album, and Bobby Richards once again handled the orchestral arrangements. The sessions were already booked at Olympic Studios with Grant engineering, so in the end the four Seekers produced the album in collaboration with him.

It was Grant who suggested to Judith that she might consider recording the Jacques Brel-Rod McKuen song 'If You Go Away'. Another track settled on for the album was 'Cloudy', the song Bruce Woodley had written earlier with Paul Simon. They also settled on Woodley's 'Chase a Rainbow (Follow Your Dream)', 'Rattler', 'Love Is Kind, Love Is Wine', 'Angeline Is Always Friday' and 'The Sad Cloud', and Keith Potger's 'All I Can Remember'. Tom Springfield was co-writer with Gary Osborne and Bob Sage on 'On the Other Side', which also made it on to the album, as did the group's cover of Paul Simon's '59th Street Bridge Song' ('Feelin' Groovy'), which had been recorded by Simon and Garfunkel as an album track.

To Judith's great delight, the two other tracks to make it were 'Can't Make Up My Mind' and 'Colours of My Life', which she had written with David Reilly.

'David and I sang them to the guys and they seemed to like them,' Judith says. 'I had no resistance from the boys to introducing my own songs, which was great. Funnily enough, I never thought "Can't Make Up My Mind" was a particularly good song, but we were short of material so it ended up making it. The material Bruce wrote for that album was very good. We took longer recording this album than previous ones. We seemed to get through about two tracks a day, but we still had no album title.'

Meanwhile, a London photographer, Rob Whitaker, who had made his name by taking the more avant-garde shots of The Beatles that were being published in 1967, returned to shoot more Seekers photos in a bid to beef up their image. Whitaker had been introduced to the group by Keith Potger and had already worked with them, shooting the cover of *Come the Day* in Richmond Park, near Judith's house.

'Rob Whitaker had some very innovative ideas for us and I saw the sessions with him as a means of moving away from that firmly entrenched vision of how The Seekers looked,' Judith says. 'He did some abstract things with us, with him lying on the ground while we all jumped in the air and other shots that got away from the four of us just sitting nicely and smiling. He took some shots of me running, while he ran in front of me pointing the camera behind him. He did some photos of me even earlier than that, while we were in Bristol doing *Humpty Dumpty*. I always liked the shots he took: they had more depth to them than our standard publicity shots. He came on tour with us after that Bristol season and ended up coming along on our last Australian tour.'

Whitaker showed Judith his choice of cover shots for the album and, taken with the greenery that surrounded the group's head in the photo, she suggested the album should be called *Seen in Green*. Judith was still going out with John Ashby at this time, but she found herself attracted to this bohemian photographer, whose company she so enjoyed.

Around the same time as *Seen in Green* was recorded, Judith re-entered the studios to make her second solo single. While little promotion had been done for 'The Olive Tree', it had nonetheless cracked the Top 40 and the decision was made to give her another try. Eddie had negotiated a separate royalty deal for Judith as a solo performer.

For this second solo outing, Judith decided on two songs she'd written with David Reilly. The A-side was an upbeat pop song called 'Again and Again', while the flip was an almost Seekerish song called 'Memories', for which she used the vocal backing of The Mike Sammes Singers.

'"Again and Again" was an out-and-out pop song and possibly not the right choice in hindsight,' Judith says. 'It moved along at a frantic pace and I found myself competing with the orchestra, who swamped me a bit. In order to deliver a real pop song, I changed the inflection in my voice and that ended up making it sound contrived. I enjoyed recording "Memories", although it felt odd singing with another group. Mind you, The Mike Sammes Singers were very tuneful and the track ended up sounding very good. When I think about it now, "Memories" should perhaps have been the A-side and "Again and Again" should have been demoed for some other singer to record.

'I was very much aware that people were viewing my solo records as my instigating a solo career, which wasn't the case at all. I saw the solo singles as a means of doing something outside the group, but I wasn't necessarily looking for hit singles. I mean, it would have been nice if they'd been more successful, but I just wanted the enjoyment and fulfilment of doing something on my own. Unfortunately, that was not the public perception and, when the records didn't work, it was seen as my failure. So I'd failed as a solo performer before I'd even left the group.'

But there was little time for regrets: The Seekers were off to America.

The group arrived in New York and opened their tour on 30 September. Their concert at Santa Monica Civic Center received a favourable review:

> The quartet was consistently excellent, obviously enjoying their music and each other . . . Judith Durham's voice was, of course, the major attraction and rightly so. Miss Durham also added a bit of glamour wearing a short white jewel-edged dress, changing halfway through to a long peach-coloured crêpe gown. Her lead singing on 'Turn Turn Turn' brought extended applause, as did The Seekers' two US hits.

Further dates, including concerts in North Dakota, Florida, North Carolina and New York followed until 27 October.

It was a low-key but successful tour and Judith particularly enjoyed Santa Monica. There, she finally met Dave Guard of The Kingston Trio, with whom she'd talked of forming a group back in 1964. Guard picked Judith up at her hotel and together they drove around Santa Monica sightseeing. She didn't know it then, but Dave Guard – and America – would be back in her life six years later.

'The crowds were very good, but we weren't the centre of attention presswise,' Judith remembers. 'We were told we'd left our run a bit too long after "Georgy Girl", yet it had only been six months since it had been on the American charts. We had a comedian opening for us most of the time, but on one show, in Connecticut, I think it was, he was replaced by Stan Getz as our support. Another time, we had Neil Diamond as our opening act. His career was on a bit of a downturn at the time, and I recall thinking how depressed he seemed to be.'

On one American show, the group ended up without a support act and had to do the entire thing themselves. A two-hour show for The Seekers was a big challenge, because they had always obeyed Jarrett's wishes and done a maximum of fifty minutes. The show went well and seemed to confirm Judith's opinion that the group was more than capable of carrying a whole concert on their own. There was an irony in the fact that they were new to American audiences, and yet they were concert stars. In Britain, they were major stars and yet they were seen as a variety act. And in America their concerts were being greeted with standing ovations, something that seldom happened in Britain or Australia.

While in America, The Seekers also appeared on TV's *The Mike Douglas Show* performing 'Georgy Girl'. 'We did a sound check for that show and then a rehearsal,' says Judith, 'and while we were rehearsing someone came up to me and told me Mike Douglas wanted to say hello and ask me a favour. I went over to him and he said, "I hear you're a blues singer" – and I was just floored. He'd found out somehow that I used to sing blues and jazz and it turned out he loved the music. He asked me to sing him a blues, there in the studio! So I stood with the pianist and sang "Reckless Blues" for him, just around the piano. It wasn't broadcast, of course, but it was a really big buzz for me. He was very complimentary, as Americans always have been whenever I've sung the blues.'

The group returned to Britain on 5 November and went straight into a taping for *Top of the Pops*, sharing the evening's bill with Traffic, The Small Faces, Cliff Richard, Engelbert Humperdinck and The Supremes. On 1 November, EMI had released *Seen in Green*, complete with the new image created by Robert Whitaker. Not only did this new Seekers offering feature a full orchestral backing, a gatefold sleeve and very contemporary material, but Judith's long dresses and the boys' suits had disappeared. Instead, the shots featured Judith Durham wearing jeans, with her hair tied back. For the first time, The Seekers looked cool.

The press was very accepting of this new look, but, from this time on, they increasingly seemed to single out Judith as the focal point of the group. Again, nothing was said among the group members, but Judith could sense their discontent. *New Musical Express* wrote, 'First-class album from the so professional Seekers, with Judith Durham's voice outstanding. She is superb ... so good that you wonder how she would get on as a solo singer. Very well, we'd say.'

One person who was not impressed with the record was Paul Simon. In an interview with *Record Mirror*, Simon was asked about The Seekers' covering of '59th Street Bridge Song' and The Bachelors' recording of 'Sound of Silence', and instantly distanced himself. 'The Seekers and The Bachelors ... What kind of image are we getting with our songs being recorded by groups like that?' he asked. Far from being slighted, Judith understands his reservations. 'The Seekers were very square and Paul was very hip and artistic, so I can quite understand how he felt,' she says. 'He saw his songs as works of art, I'm sure – real poetry set to music. Then along come The Seekers, who do a lollipop version of one of his works of art. He makes money from it, but he still sees his creation being ruined. If I put myself in his shoes, I understand completely. Having artists like us and The Bachelors use his material was just something he wouldn't have expected to happen. I can imagine Tom Springfield might have felt the same way when he learned Nick Cave had recorded a cover version of "The Carnival Is Over".'

As well received as *Seen in Green* was – it reached Number 15 in the British charts – nothing from it was released as a single. Ironically, 'Colours of My Life' and 'Love Is Kind, Love Is Wine' would later become perennial favourites with fans and would be issued as singles after the group had broken up.

The Seekers returned to Olympic Studios and recorded two more tracks as a Christmas single. The A-side was another fairytale-type song called 'Emerald City', written by Kim Fowley and John Martin and based on the 'Ode to Joy' from the final movement of Beethoven's Symphony No. 9. The flip was a song they'd heard on an album by an American female singer, called 'Music of the World a-Turnin'', for which Judith's old mates from Alex Welsh's jazz band were brought in to provide backing. Sadly, the masters of this recording are lost. Only years later was it revealed to the group that the 'John Martin' credited as co-writer of 'Emerald City' was, in fact, none other than Keith Potger. Keith took a nom de plume because he didn't want the group to feel obliged to record one of his songs.

With *Seen in Green* released to the public on 1 November, it seemed a strange marketing ploy by Jarrett and EMI to release Judith's solo single 'Again and Again' just two days later. To release 'Emerald City' just three weeks after that was sheer madness.

'For some reason, they just swamped my record,' Judith says. 'It could even have been a deliberate move, I just don't know. If not, then it seemed to be an ill-thought-out plan, releasing three lots of product within three weeks. If Seekers fans were waiting for something new from us, they'd be likely to run out and buy our new album and single, but they probably wouldn't think to buy something featuring just me. I was virtually forced into competition with myself.'

Judith wasn't able to promote the single properly, either. Her one and only plug was singing the song live on *The David Frost Show*. The Seekers weren't in London when 'Emerald City' was released, having travelled to Glasgow for a season at the Alhambra Theatre. The record attracted excellent reviews, but again Judith was being singled out. The reviewer for the *Liverpool Echo* was impressed:

Judith Durham is in complete control of the vocal activity. Indeed, we don't hear much from the rest of the group. Miss Durham delivers the lyrics in a pure voice which sounds as though it was recorded way up high in a clear night sky.

Despite the critical acclaim of both 'Again and Again' and 'Emerald City', neither was a hit. 'Again and Again' missed out on charting altogether, while 'Emerald City' spent only one week in the charts, peaking at Number 50. It was the first Seekers single not to reach the Top 40 – and it was also to become the last Seekers single to chart. Before flying to Scotland, The Seekers appeared on one more Palladium TV show on an all-star bill that included The Rolling Stones and Tom Jones. The day after the show was broadcast, newspapers carried scathing attacks on The Rolling Stones, who'd caused a fuss during the filming of the show by refusing to mount the roundabout with the other artists for the familiar finale. Mick Jagger, incensed at the controversy the group's stand had caused, told *New Musical Express*, 'The same thing happens every week on this show and we don't want to conform to what has gone before.'

'For some reason, I knew The Stones weren't going to do it,' Judith says. 'It was probably a bit of an unprofessional thing to do, given that if you did the show you were expected to do the finale, but I can understand why The Stones wouldn't do it. It just wasn't appropriate for their image. I mean, there was this carousel on the stage with letters spelling out "Sunday Night at the London Palladium" and each person on the show got allocated a letter. You'd stand behind the letter and the carousel would revolve as we waved to the audience while the credits rolled. It just wasn't something you could imagine The Rolling Stones doing. That was the sort of thing The Seekers did!'

The group ended 1967 rated fifth in the *New Musical Express* end-of-year Top 10. They were outsold this year by The Beatles, The Beach Boys, The Monkees and The Bee Gees, but they managed to come out on top of The Troggs, The Stones and The Dave Clark Five. In the Top Albums of 1967 chart, *Come the Day* came in eighth, a place higher than The Rolling Stones' *Between the Buttons* album. The group's last television outing for 1967 was a pretaped appearance on the Christmas edition of *Juke Box Jury*. When it screened, the pop impresario Jonathan King wrote of the group, '. . . the four innocent Seekers, like gentle Australian sheep, bleating at the foggy world around.' This, from the man who'd recorded 'Everyone's Gone to the Moon', the Number 1 hit on the 1965 corn parade. Judith, Athol and Bruce flew out of London on 20 December, headed for Australia, where a national tour and yet another big-budget TV spectacular awaited them. As Keith Potger's new son, Matthew, born on 6 December, was required to be two weeks old before he could travel out of the country, Keith and Pam would spend Christmas in London before joining the rest of the group Down Under. Despite the fact that their greatest accolade as a group was still to come, the cracks in The Seekers armour were now beginning to show. Judith was becoming more and more disenchanted with life inside the group and their grip on the charts was beginning to slip. For Judith Durham, 1968 would be a pivotal point in her professional – and personal – life.

7. THE SPLIT

Open up this cage towards the sun,
For just this skyline pigeon,
Dreaming of the open, praying for the day,
When she can spread her wings
and fly away again,
Fly away, skyline pigeon fly,
Towards the dreams you left so very far behind.

– 'SKYLINE PIGEON'
ELTON JOHN AND BERNIE TAUPIN

By leaving England five days before Christmas, Judith Durham was able to enjoy her first Christmas dinner at home since 1962. Two days later, with her three singing colleagues at her side, she was fronting yet another press conference and denying that The Seekers were on the verge of splitting up. The group, she said, planned to stay together indefinitely. Not long afterwards, she was pinned down about her love life by *Woman's Day* magazine, which published a story in which Judith admitted she'd found 'that special someone' in Britain. All she was prepared to share, however, was that her someone special was tall, English and in show business.

She got a shock a few weeks later, however, when Rob Whitaker, who was accompanying The Seekers on their Australian tour, casually mentioned that John Ashby had always been going out with other women back in London. 'I had no idea at all,' Judith recalls. 'My world just fell apart. That was really the beginning of the end of our relationship. We weren't committed in any way, but it came as a shock. It made me very sad to think the guys in the group hadn't told me before this, because they spent a lot of time with John and would have known. It embarrassed me that other people had known, but no one had had the decency to tell me.'

Other things were beginning to rankle with Judith. She was aware by now of tension within the group, partly due to the fact that seldom was a review published that didn't single Judith Durham out as the focal point of The Seekers. While she had no control over what was written, the three male Seekers were starting to get peeved with the way the media continually diminished the importance of their roles.

Athol Guy had recently given an interview to *Everybody's* magazine, in which he remarked that sometimes The Seekers' publicity got a little too much:

We detest sensationalism and people know we do, so perhaps this is why they pick out the group's talking point – Judith's voice. In my opinion, they push this too much. It puts pressure on her and she never wanted it that way. We wouldn't be The Seekers if it weren't for all of us and nobody has been able to put their finger on what makes the difference. So they say 'Oh well, it's because Judith has a lovely voice.' But that isn't really the reason.

'I think the three boys all felt that way,' says Judith. 'It wasn't ego or jealousy: it was their belief that we were all equal players and I agree with that. But I never understood why they would get upset that the focus was on me. That's how it was with groups in the sixties. It would be like Charlie Watts getting upset because all The Stones' publicity revolved around Mick Jagger. There'd be something wrong if every article on The Stones featured Charlie Watts, wouldn't there? The boys are all strong personalities and I accept that it was probably hard for them to take a back seat to somebody else, but their attitude towards me and what was projected as my pivotal role in the group definitely had an effect on me. The irony is, they initially cultivated that image. I was the only girl in the group, I was the youngest and this was the sixties. They were happy to be seen as my protectors and I was the little sister with the sweet voice. As a result, the press homed in on me and gradually resentment started to bubble to the surface.'

In so many ways, Judith's individuality was being suppressed in The Seekers. When they did interviews together, she was never encouraged to express an opinion. She was expected to sit and look demure. On stage, she got to speak only occasionally. Athol was the group spokesman and he did the patter while Judith sang and smiled. Even when the act changed in 1967 and Judith was given her own piano spot, playing her dearly loved 'Maple Leaf Rag', it was a token effort. But by the time it was included in the act it was reduced to a comedy routine with the boys sending it up. On one hand, they'd provided Judith with a new creative outlet but, on the other, she saw her art being demeaned. Worst of all, some of the audiences didn't think Judith was actually playing the piano, so she wasn't being appreciated as an artist in that regard.

While Judith had overcome most of her misgivings about her appearance, she was growing increasingly disenchanted with her life as part of a group. More and more members of the public were encouraging Judith to go solo. Often, she was told she *was* The Seekers, that she didn't need the boys. Why didn't she go out on her own? Each time, Judith would assure them that all four voices were of equal importance to the group sound, but deep down she yearned to have success on her own.

Now there was not only a cloud over her professional happiness, but her personal life had also taken a battering. Judith was able to remain friends with John Ashby, who was still the group's tour manager, but her realisation that she had not been the only love of his life changed any romantic involvement. Judith turned her attentions to Rob Whitaker, whose work she admired and whose company she greatly enjoyed. There was something very cool and modern about this much-respected cameraman, and his lifestyle, typical of the late sixties, intrigued Judith.

London in 1968 was a long way from Judith Durham's experience of Melbourne in the early part of the decade. She left home in 1964, a nice girl from a good family who'd had a good upbringing and had a good sense of propriety. The Queen of Good. And here she was, four years later, a London-based pop star working in an industry that took full advantage of the sexual revolution and the booming drug culture that was sweeping the Western world. Had she dipped her toe into these waters, it would have been like Alice in Wonderland on acid. She never did experiment, but she was certainly curious.

'I was aware of drugs all around me by this time,' Judith says. 'The Beatles were in their psychedelic period and had recorded "Lucy in the Sky with Diamonds" and "Strawberry Fields Forever". Their lyrics were forever being analysed and there was a lot of publicity about LSD. Now, LSD interested me. I'd heard stories about people having trips and I even bought a book on LSD. I discussed it with Rob Whitaker, who I knew had the occasional smoke [of cannabis]. He said if he had LSD one day, perhaps we might experience it together. Part of the reason the group was looking for a hipper image was because of the influence of the whole flower-power thing that was happening around us. There were kaftans and flowers and people experimenting with drugs and sex, and the more it grew, the squarer The Seekers would have looked if they'd stayed the same as they'd always been. We had to move on.

'The sexual revolution fascinated me too, but I was still a long way from being promiscuous. The same with the drugs. If Rob had put any pressure on me I may well have been tempted to try, but he didn't. I have a tendency towards excess, so it could have been disastrous. For so long I'd turned to food for solace but, now that I had my weight under control, I had to fill that comfort void. With a history of overdoing food, I could easily have overdone something else. I didn't drink very often, but when I did I always drank too much. I think it would have been very easy for me to just go to excess with drugs, too.'

The Seekers opened their 1968 Australian tour on 8 January, the first night of a six-night run at Melbourne's Palais Theatre. Supporting them were the local television star Mike Preston and their old friend Bobby Limb. Their slicker, fast-moving stage show went down a storm with audiences and critics. The *Age* ran a review headed GOLDEN WELCOME GREETS SEEKERS, which read:

> To say that last night's audience was biased, prejudiced and totally one-eyed is pointless. They were Melburnians and the young group's rise to success is one of Melbourne's proudest possessions ... The dominant voice of tiny Seeker Judith Durham guided the group into the new rhythms, like potential chart-topper 'Colours of My Life' ... the programme ended with The Seekers bathed, perhaps symbolically, in the flood of gold spotlight that had coloured their entire performance.

'It was a good season,' Judith recalls. 'The thing I thought was odd was going back into a venue like the Palais after having had two hundred thousand at the Bowl the year before. I mean, the Palais seated three thousand people, so we were going through this slog every night for a small audience. It was just Eddie playing it safe again, like he did when he put us back into the Greasbrough Social Club after "Georgy Girl" had gone to Number 1.'

During her time in Melbourne, Hazel and Bill had a serious discussion with Judith. They were concerned that she was being exploited and asked her if she had thought about leaving the group. The way they saw it, Judith was handling most of the media requests and, by working much longer hours than Athol, Keith and Bruce, she was missing out on a social life. Why wasn't she getting more money? She talked things through with her parents for hours and, after leaving Melbourne, realised she was facing one of the most difficult decisions of her life. That decision was mulled over as the workload continued.

The group had three weeks after their Melbourne season ended before they resumed the tour in Sydney. In that time they were expected to break the back of a gruelling film schedule for their next TV spectacular, *The World of The Seekers*.

This time, the special was being made by GTV Channel Nine in conjunction with Ajax Films, a production company the station had just purchased. It was being shot on 35-mm colour film with a view to cinema release. The one-hour special, under the direction of Rod Kinnear, would trace the group's meteoric rise to fame and feature the band performing seventeen of their songs. Unlike *The Seekers Down Under*, which had entailed the rigours of moving around Australia, this new special was being shot mostly in Sydney and Melbourne.

Rod Kinnear recalls that Channel Nine was looking for a vehicle to launch Ajax Films and decided a one-hour spectacular built around the country's most successful music exports would be a sure hit. The Seekers didn't know when the deal was signed that Nine owned Ajax Films.

'Sir Frank Packer was in charge in those days,' Kinnear says, 'and he was always worried about how his station's money was being spent. *The World of The Seekers* cost a lot to make and he was concerned that the money was being well spent. He came by the Ajax studios in Bondi one night while we were mixing, and watched the dream sequence when the group are in wheelchairs. There were a few tense moments while he watched because we weren't sure whether he'd see the humour, but it turned out he loved it. He thought the scene was hilarious.'

Packer may have slapped his thighs, but Judith felt like a hypocrite filming that scene. In it, The Seekers were aged with makeup to look in their seventies, and to set the scene Judith was required to say the line, 'Maybe the group will never break up, maybe we'll be together in fifty years, and then what?' Then what, indeed! In her heart, she had already made her decision but she hadn't had an opportunity to talk to the boys. For now, she remained silent and filmed the scene.

Judith remembers that taping was a solid grind, but she enjoyed the experience. 'The Ajax film crew was terrific,' she says. 'I had a fantastic makeup girl, Gaye Evans, who just did a wonderful job on me. At the end of the filming, the crew presented us all with briefcases with our names on them, to show their appreciation for our co-operation. That's amazing when I think about it now. We thought they were great, too.

'I sang "The Lord's Prayer" in that special, but it took a lot of persuading before I agreed to do it. They wanted to recreate my night at the Bowl in 1963, but it had been such a special moment for me – I didn't think they'd be able to get across just what it had meant. They talked me into it in the end.'

Kinnear recalls nursing Judith through the scene and her great reluctance to recreate that memory. 'Judith is an exceptionally talented singer,' Kinnear says, 'but she was the type who needed to be reassured she was doing a good job. That's not a bad thing. It shows she's thinking about what she's doing. She and the boys were excellent to work with, very professional, but I do remember some tension between them. Judith's attention to detail and the concerns she voiced from time to time seemed to annoy them.'

Midway through the filming schedule for the special, the nation's front pages carried an important story. On 17 January 1968, Sir Norman Martin, chairman of the Australia Day Council, announced that The Seekers had been named Australians of the Year for 1967. The award had been implemented eight years before to recognise any Australian who had brought the most honour to their country in the previous year. For the first time, it was awarded to a group of people instead of an individual. In a statement to the media, Martin said The Seekers were probably the most popular singing group in the world at that time.

'Athol called the rest of us to a meeting and told us he'd known about the award for a couple of days,' Judith says. 'He'd been sworn to secrecy. When the announcement was made, I was terribly proud and thrilled, but it really seemed wrong to me that Athol should have had the privilege of knowing ahead of the rest of us. That broke my heart. It shot down in flames that theory about us all being equals. He should have told the rest of us immediately. It's something I'll never forget, one of those things that really went against the grain. There was an assumption by some of the people around us that I didn't need to be told certain things, and it really upset me.

'We were actually filming a recording-studio sequence at Channel Nine, recreating the session for "I'll Never Find Another You", when the announcement was made and we did a press conference from there. It was plastered all over the papers and I can look at the pictures now and see us all smiling, but I know how shocked I was when Athol called us over and told us he had some good news for us, just before the announcement was made.'

Nine days later, on 26 January, The Seekers were presented with their Australian of the Year 1967 bronze medallions at a special Australia Day luncheon at the Melbourne Town Hall. The presentation was made by the newly invested Prime Minister, John Gorton, who had stepped into the role permanently following the shock drowning of Harold Holt. Gorton and a former Prime Minister, Sir Robert Menzies, both paid tribute to the group, who performed 'A World of Our Own' and 'Georgy Girl' before the presentation of the plaques. Prime Minister Gorton told luncheon guests he was one of millions of Australians who got great pleasure from The Seekers' singing.

'I felt very good at that ceremony,' Judith recalls. 'My parents were able to attend and Mum and Dad felt very proud that I actually met Sir Robert Menzies. I was terribly right-wing in those days, something I'd inherited from Mum and Dad, and Sir Robert Menzies was their favourite politician. I never questioned politics, having been brought up to vote the way my parents did. Athol responded after the speeches and then John Gorton turned to me and asked me to say a few words. I was quite unaccustomed to speaking in public, but I went to the microphone and blurted out something about how we had often sung a song about South Australia, but how nice it would be if someone could write a special song about Australia as a nation, never dreaming I'd write one myself one day.'

With a great deal of filming now behind them, The Seekers picked up their tour in Sydney on 1 February, with a two-night engagement at Sydney Town Hall. Even the usually Seekers-unfriendly Sydney press was won over on this tour. The *Daily Mirror* said, 'The Seekers held the audience spellbound ... after each of the eighteen numbers, the audience broke into wild applause.' The *Sydney Morning Herald*, long accustomed to deriding the Melbourne band, gushed, 'Obviously the soaring voice of Judith Durham is the thrill of The Seekers.'

The group moved on to Canberra for two nights at Canberra Theatre and were invited to lunch with Prime Minister Gorton and Mrs Gorton at the Lodge [their official residence], along with future leader of the opposition, Andrew Peacock, and his wife Susan. The Gortons also attended one of the shows. Later that same day, the group went to afternoon tea at Government House with the acting Governor-General, Sir Rohan Delacombe, and his wife, and were entertained for the afternoon along with their fellow guest, the society photographer Cecil Beaton.

The *Canberra Times* kept the good reviews coming, noting that 'Judy Durham was the star of the evening'. Next came a two-night stint at Brisbane City Hall, followed by regional Victoria dates in Ballarat and Geelong. The Geelong show, the final concert in The Seekers' Australian itinerary, was the one that distressed Judith more than any performance that had gone before. This badly presented show became the straw that finally broke the camel's back.

The performance really summed up everything for Judith in a nutshell. The curtain went up before the group was supposed to be seen and Judith was horrified. It emphasised to her how poorly the group were being presented. Supposedly professionals at the peak of their career, they couldn't even get the stage presentation right. Suddenly, Judith could see how different she was from the boys in her attitudes and approach. She would home in on the details of presentation, but it meant almost nothing to them.

'I was consumed with frustration that things couldn't be done the way they were supposed to. I know my perfectionism annoyed the boys, who just didn't worry about those things. But it reinforced the feeling that I was forever being forced to compromise because I was a member of a group. You're just not a free agent, because, to get by, you needed to agree on everything. I never felt comfortable confronting the boys on something that was not agreeable to them. Yet we had a marvellous relationship when we were all in accord on an issue. They always made me laugh and we had a lot of special, funny moments together. But things changed if I tried to force an issue that they didn't agree with. It was always uncomfortable.'

Judith was still wondering what the future held for her. She was almost 25, had no social or private life to speak of, and was very aware that four years of her life had gone into the group. She had, after all, intended having only a ten-week working holiday with them in 1964. All this discontent had been bubbling away for quite some time, but it was now starting to surface.

The Seekers finished their Australian tour and moved on to New Zealand for a two-week, fourteen-concert tour, to open at the Bowl of Brooklands in New Plymouth on 15 February. There, they set a new attendance record when 15,500 people turned up, breaking the Bowl's previous biggest crowd of 11,000. It was on 14 February – Valentine's Day – while rehearsing for the Bowl of Brooklands opening that Judith Durham finally snapped.

A minor incident during that rehearsal triggered a major emotional reaction and Judith finally summoned the courage to tell her three partners that she would quit. She could no longer put up with the impenetrable wall that confronted her whenever the three boys united against her. It upset her that they would be her dearly loved big brothers only until she attempted to rock the boat.

'It just sort of came out,' she says. 'I was very upset and I just blurted out that I was leaving The Seekers and giving them the required six months' notice that we'd all agreed to several years before. Then I sat in my dressing room, got out an aerogram and wrote a letter to Eddie Jarrett. I told him I was quitting the group in six months. Once that was done, I felt a tremendous sense of relief. I felt it would be easy getting through the next six months, having my artistic freedom to look forward to.'

Interestingly, nobody tried to talk Judith out of her decision. In fact, she remembers no discussion on the subject after she'd announced she was leaving. Judith assumed they thought it would just blow over and that, having let off steam, she'd settle back into her Seekers role.

'I might have thought differently if my name was up in lights,' Judith admits, 'but I had this awful sense all the time of being a quarter of a whole. I wasn't being myself. People didn't really know me. Many of our fans didn't really know my name, but they recognised my voice. It occurred to me long after I'd resigned that the boys believed The Seekers was the thing we should all have aspired to in life, that nothing should have attempted to take its place. But, for the whole four years I was a member of the group, I had thought it was temporary. When I thought of a future on my own, it was a matter of when, not if.

'It was a huge decision for me, and it took a lot of courage. It took all that time for me finally to accept that we were just four very different people. Our personalities, our goals in life, everything we aspired to was at odds with everyone else in the group. That necessity to compromise all the time, on everything, takes its toll after a long period of time and I really do understand how it drives bands to throw in the towel. I've racked my brains in the years since then, trying to work out whether there would have been an easier or fairer way for me to leave the group, but I can't think of one.

'The only conversation I ever had about leaving was with Athol, and it was back in England, several weeks afterwards. He suggested that I should perhaps stay in the group a bit longer, make a solo album while still a group member and wean people on to the idea that I was going solo. But that was unthinkable to me. When I do things, I like to do them one hundred per cent. I couldn't do both, as my two attempts at making solo singles had already proved.'

Judith's decision was made and The Seekers carried on with their New Zealand tour, not leaking a word of her impending departure to anyone. The concerts were a resounding success, but the deal struck for the New Zealand leg of that tour just hammered home to Judith her dissatisfaction with the way The Seekers were being handled. Jarrett had booked them at around a thousand dollars a show between them. Before leaving London, Judith approached Jarrett about it, expressing surprise that the group should be working for a flat fee, considering they were almost certainly going to sell out. Surely they should be on a percentage?

Jarrett assured her it was safer his way. When The Seekers arrived in Auckland, they were shown press photos of people who had been queuing around the block for tickets from six o'clock in the morning. There was no question that the tour was going to pack them in and, if it had been any other group of similar status, they would have been on 80 or 90 per cent of the box office. Instead, The Seekers were singing their hearts out for $250 dollars a night each, while the promoters presumably made a fortune.

The group returned to Australia, where they played a few last dates and headlined a charity concert at the Melbourne Palais with Bobby Limb, the American entertainer Tim Evans, their friends Pat and Olivia, and the Brian Henderson Showband. The concert was to raise money for the Association for the Blind. On this final Australian date, The Seekers were presented with a gold disc by the Victoria Premier, Sir Henry Bolte, for sales of more than 50,000 copies of the album *The Seekers*.

Judith made headlines when her father handed six letters and a telegram that Judith had received in recent weeks to detectives. The writer of the letters gave a Wellington address and the matter was placed in the hands of the Wellington police, who deemed them obscene.

'Nothing like that had ever happened to me before,' Judith says. 'I just thought it was weird. It turned out the man had been released from a psychiatric hospital and he meant no harm. They weren't exactly obscene letters, but I do remember he mentioned knickers. The only other unusual mail I got over the years was from a man in Wakefield Prison. He was quite a fan and he wrote to me. I wrote back, because I thought it might be nice for him to get a letter in jail. I wrote one other time and then got a letter from him, saying he was being released. A while later, I got another letter from him, telling me he'd got into a fight, had attacked someone with a broken bottle and was back in jail! I didn't write any more after that!

'And there was one person who sent me thirty-six red roses every Valentine's Day for three or four years in a row. I even got them in Australia one year. I think he signed his cards John, and, while I never met him, I knew he was the one in the front row with dark hair.'

The group completed the remaining scenes of *The World of The Seekers* and returned to London, where they were soon to open a weekend, one-night-stand tour of Britain, but first they had to keep their record company happy by recording a new single with a new producer. Earlier, Eddie Jarrett had found a new producer for the next record. It would be left in the hands of Mickie Most, a young hotshot producer whose chart credits included hits for The Yardbirds, Donovan, Lulu and Herman's Hermits.

Judith had her reservations. 'Eddie took us all out to lunch to meet Mickie Most and, during the course of the meal, the question of how much Mickie would be paid was raised. Eddie mentioned they'd agreed to Mickie getting four per cent and I nearly choked. For heaven's sake, the whole group's royalty rate had been put up half a per cent from three to three and a half – between us – and here we were, giving the producer four per cent, more than all of us put together. If I'd had a little more business acumen, I might have realised that, if I had an objection, I should raise it with Eddie in private, but I didn't. I just blurted out then and there that I thought it was unfair.'

Jarrett explained that Most was a top producer and received 4 per cent when he worked with people like Lulu, but Judith didn't care. It simply wasn't fair and she made it clear she wouldn't put up with a producer earning more money than the group he was producing. After some haggling, it was agreed Most would work for 3 per cent. Judith still thought it was exorbitant, because Most had no prior success with The Seekers, but 3 per cent was agreed on. 'As a result of that lunch, I don't think I ended up being very popular with Mickie Most,' Judith smiles. 'But he gave me a lift home one day in his yellow Rolls-Royce, and he was very businesslike in the way he approached things.'

Most went off in search of a suitable song for The Seekers to record and, late in March, they entered the studios to record a song he'd chosen called 'Days of My Life' by the songwriter Tony Romeo. For the flip side, they once again plundered Judith's gospel repertoire and came up with 'Study War No More', another name for the old gospel 'Down by the Riverside'.

'Mickie Most was very different to Tom Springfield, in a studio sense,' Judith recalls. 'It was a new studio for us, he set things up very differently to the way Tom did it and, even though we were very accustomed to working with Bobby Richards, Mickie brought in another arranger. There wasn't that homey, family feeling we had with Tom. Mickie was very much the producer: he had a clear idea of the way he wanted that record produced and we just went in and did what we were told.'

Before the record's release, Judith finally asked for – and got – star billing. 'Days of My Life' would be released as 'The Seekers featuring Judith Durham'. The single was issued on 26 April and the first to notice the new billing was the *Watford and West Herts Post*, whose writer remarked, 'What I don't like about it is they've put on the front all posh-like and sort of stuck up, "featuring Judith Durham". I mean to say, as if we didn't know she was the best of the bunch.'

Little did Judith know how much her search for her own identity would be perceived this way by people for years to come.

Mickie Most found himself in the middle of a minor controversy over Judith's separate billing and distanced himself from it. He told the *Glasgow Evening Citizen*, 'It's not my decision. The boys suggested it, but I think it's a good idea. Featuring Diana [Ross] has been good for The Supremes. I'm certain this will be good for The Seekers.' In the all-important music-industry publications, 'Days of My Life' got the thumbs-up. Predicting it would be a 'massive seller', *Record Mirror* noted the difference in production and saw it as 'a number which will go straight into their long list of evergreens'. *Melody Maker* wrote, 'I fail to see how their folksy choice of material can miss … this is certainly going to go right to the top.'

Unfortunately for The Seekers, it didn't. In fact, it didn't crack the bottom of the charts. Even The Seekers' performances of the song on *Top of the Pops*, *Billy Cotton's Musical Hall*, and *The Rolf Harris Show* couldn't lift its sales. The group didn't expect a flop, particularly after Jarrett had sold Mickie Most to them as a production whiz, but a flop it was. It was a pretty song, but there was no interest in it.

A scheduled Seekers tour of America and Canada was postponed by Jarrett, who cited Athol's genuine bad throat as the reason, and a proposed BBC TV series was also canned, reportedly because of contractual differences. The real reason, of course, was that, in three months, The Seekers would cease to be. A series of concerts beginning in late July through Scandinavia had also been booked, but these too were cancelled. Also abandoned was an all-out effort to break The Seekers in the United States. The group had paid $18,000 to a major American publicity company, which was 50 per cent of the total budget for an eighteen-week campaign to promote them in the States. That money was never refunded.

Back home in Australia, *The World of The Seekers* premiered on the Nine Network and was another ratings winner, peaking at 63. The Seekers held the all-time ratings record of 67 for *The Seekers Down Under* and now they held the second-highest rating as well, for *The World of The Seekers*. The special was shown as a colour film in cinemas for a while, sometimes with up to six screenings a day. Many avid fans later admitted to Judith that they had sat through all six screenings.

On 17 May, The Seekers kicked off their final British tour, with the popular pianist Russ Conway as their only support. They appeared twice nightly in one-nighters each Friday, Saturday and Sunday night through the remainder of May and most of June. Over four weekends, they would play Brighton, Portsmouth, London, Birmingham, Worcester, Leicester, Exeter, Torquay, Bournemouth, Hanley, Manchester and Liverpool.

New Musical Express reviewed the tour's opening night at the Brighton Dome and reported, 'The house-full notices went up ... Visually, The Seekers – with the charming Judith Durham, a fascinating, eye-riveting centrepiece – are as fresh as their Australian climate.'

However, despite the good notices, the remainder of the tour wasn't as well attended. The Seekers didn't do very good business at all on that last tour. The 3,000-seater Hammersmith Odeon in London was practically empty, much to Eddie Jarrett's dismay and embarrassment.

'Perhaps we'd been so overexposed on television in recent months that people were taking a break from seeing us,' Judith reasons. 'We desperately needed a hit record too, but didn't have one. Before the tour started, I'd had a discussion with Eddie in which he suggested perhaps we should make it our farewell tour, announce we were splitting and say goodbye on this tour. No doubt, had we done it that way, the tour would have been a sell-out. I told him I would prefer it if the fact that the group was breaking up was kept secret. I felt if the fans knew, they'd be terribly sad and it would have cast a big shadow over all the concerts and also that there would be all this pressure on me to stay. At that time, I had no idea there was going to be a big announcement that this was to be our final show. I had hoped we'd just kind of disappear or melt away, and not announce our intentions to the world.'

During the tour, which she knew would be her last as a Seeker, Judith began coming out of her shell a little more with the people around her. She was still including her solo performance of 'The Olive Tree' in group concerts and its backing required piano. When the tour was being put together, Eddie Jarrett suggested as the opening act The Trebletones, who'd worked with The Seekers before, but Judith didn't like the idea much.

'When Eddie told me The Trebletones would be appearing on the bill, I just said, "Oh, not again! Isn't there anybody else?"' Judith says, laughing. 'Eddie couldn't come up with anybody else, so I was stuck with them. I found out that Ron Edgeworth, their pianist, had actually just left the group to establish a solo career and the leader, Johnny Wiltshire, called him up and implored him to come back for this one final booking with The Seekers. He rang five times and Ron kept turning him down. The sixth time, he accepted.'

The Trebletones were to back Judith on 'The Olive Tree' and, when she walked on stage to rehearse with Ron Edgeworth for the first time, he smiled and remarked, 'What a dolly lady!' Now nobody had ever paid Judith that sort of compliment before. Nobody really said anything to her about her appearance – she was just the sweet Seekers girl. He didn't know it at the time, but Judith got a real kick out of being noticed.

'Little did I know when I recorded "The Olive Tree" that it was going to play such a pivotal role in my life,' Judith says. 'I just loved Ron's talent, his playing was brilliant and very versatile and he was a great sight-reader. The Trebletones had their own spot at the start of the show and Ron had a showcase with them, playing the *Warsaw Concerto* or [the theme from] *Exodus*. I heard him practising in the theatre after hours and realised how dedicated he was. While the three boys sang "Louisiana Man" or "Rattler", I started looking forward to the little chats Ron and I would have while we waited in the wings to go on for my solo spot. He was such a nice person and I felt I could really communicate with him. It was so rare for me to actually strike up conversation with anybody, but I felt so comfortable in Ron's company.'

Judith found this tall piano man very attractive. She wasn't initially thinking of romance, but she admits that, when she first heard his name, she did a mental check on how Judith Edgeworth sounded, and decided it didn't have much of a ring to it! Not knowing that Ron had a fine reputation for embellishing music and adding marvellous fills, she floored him by asking him to play the piano accompaniment exactly the way it sounded on the record!

By the time the British tour ended at the Liverpool Empire on 9 June, Judith had plucked up the courage to ask Ron Edgeworth for his business card. She was careful not to let slip that she was leaving The Seekers, but, knowing he was now freelance himself, she suggested per- haps she might need someone to rehearse with one day back in London. Ron told her he'd try to catch The Seekers' show at the Talk of the Town one night.

Judith had hoped Ron could play piano for her during the engagement, but, as with their previous booking at the Talk, she was obliged to use the Burt Rhodes Orchestra for the four-week cabaret stint. For now, it was farewell to Ron.

John Ashby talked to Judith one day about her leaving the group, and questioned how she would feel if the three guys carried on with a new female singer. It was now that Judith realised she wanted to have her cake and eat it, too. She was curious to know what her singing partners would do, but, as so often happened in the past, she didn't broach the subject with them.

Although the proposed TV series for The Seekers had been scrapped, Jarrett nevertheless went back to the BBC and offered them a one-hour Seekers special, which the corporation jumped at. Already Jarrett had arranged for The Seekers' Talk of the Town show to be recorded as a live album. Mickie Most was named producer of this final album and, still on 3 per cent of royalties, had a gift handed to him on a plate. The group's final week at the Talk of the Town was the week of Judith's 25th birthday. They were to record on three nights of that week and, when the Talk season finished on the Saturday night, they were to do the same show at the BBC studios on the Sunday night for the TV special. And that, as far as The Seekers were concerned, would be that.

Nothing had been leaked by this stage, but during that final week the split was inadvertently revealed and suddenly all hell broke loose. The group had said nothing, but the *TV Guide* had come out that week, boldly listing the special in its programme highlights as *Farewell The Seekers* and the papers just picked it up from there. Judith felt her wish to keep the break-up a secret had been betrayed.

'It turned into a terribly hectic week, very emotional,' Judith says. 'To be doing shows every night and worrying about recording the live album and TV special would have been quite enough, but now we had press everywhere. Yet at the Wednesday night show, which was my birthday, the boys had the audience sing "Happy Birthday" to me and then they brought on this absolutely huge basket of flowers, as tall as me and weighing a ton. It had to be carried off by a stagehand because I couldn't lift it. It was an exhilarating night.'

Backstage, however, Judith would come back down to earth with a thud. Awaiting the group with a television camera and microphone was the Australian television personality Tony Charlton, who was in London filming interviews for broadcasting back home. 'I was thrilled to be talking to him at first,' Judith recalls, 'but then, all of a sudden, the questions started coming thick and fast. Why are you breaking up? How can you do this? Australia is in mourning – won't you reconsider? I just went into shock, realising the absolute enormity of what I was doing. I felt absolutely alone and it now seemed nobody was going to wish me well in my solo career, whatever it may be. The questions were asked of all of us, but the boys stood back and said nothing, so I had to bumble my way through it as best I could. I just felt like the big bad wolf, trying to explain why we were splitting up.'

The Seekers ended up issuing a press statement, simply saying that things were getting too complicated and that the four members believed they should be growing as individuals and not as a group. They told the media that Judith had no solo career plans yet and intended returning home to Australia. Athol was having a holiday and would later work in Australian television; Bruce was off to New York to establish contacts for his songwriting; and Keith was staying in London with his wife and son.

The Seekers ended their Talk of the Town season on 8 July and, on 9 July, filmed *Farewell The Seekers* for BBC TV. The show went well enough and the reviews were glowing. But, with news of the split now well circulated, Judith couldn't shake the feeling that millions of viewers around the world were condemning her.

Athol's final words as a group member came just before they sang 'The Carnival Is Over' for the last time. 'Tonight,' he said, 'the carnival really is over' – and those words knotted Judith's stomach. Backstage, after the group had taken their final bows, Judith burst into tears. People around her just assumed she was crying because she was upset that she'd never sing with The Seekers again, but in reality she was reacting to the strain of that final week.

While they never sang again together after the BBC special – until their silver-jubilee reunion in 1993 – the following day all four now ex-Seekers agreed to be interviewed on a current-affairs programme on British TV and then all that was left was the final reckoning in the accountant's office on 10 July. In a little over an hour, the four musicians were presented with statements of account that neatly summed up what they had reaped from the four years they had spent as one of the world's top singing groups.

'I was always in awe of accountants,' Judith says. 'We'd see an accountant at the end of every financial year, to go through the books for Seekers Musical Enterprises. We were each drawing a salary of about sixty dollars a week and the rest of our money was just ploughed back into the group. At the end of each year, when we got our statements, there just never seemed to be much money there. The dividends were very small. I used to just send my money back to Australia to be banked. Some of it I gave to Mum and Dad to try to make things more comfortable for them. I had no independent advice, of course, so all these pages of figures meant nothing to me, but it always struck me as odd that we didn't seem to have made very much. Money had never been my motivation in my career, but I had Dad in my ear so often, questioning why I was working so incredibly hard for so little in return.'

Judith walked away from The Seekers with about $80,000 to show for her four years in the UK. She was still contracted to EMI Records until November, but, for the first time in four years, she was almost a free agent. The first thing she did was take a ten-day holiday in Europe, her first real break in years. It dawned on Judith when she was planning that holiday that she really didn't have any girlfriends. Beverley and Barry and one-year-old Tony were still living with her and, while Judith would have relished the opportunity to tour Europe with her sister, Beverley was now well and truly tied to motherhood.

'I'd spent four years with three male singing partners, a male manager and a male tour manager,' Judith explains. 'There was just never any time in those Seekers years to establish outside friendships. I ended up going on holiday with John Ashby. We were still close friends and still did things together, but I no longer put my loving trust in him. I enjoyed that time, going down through France, looking at the countryside. There was no pressure on me at all.'

While Judith was away, offers started coming in for her and she returned to an excited Eddie Jarrett, who told her Channel Nine in Australia wanted her to do a TV special, a New Zealand tour had been proposed and there was talk of a Christmas album sponsored by Goodyear Tyres. The offers took Judith by surprise. She had given no real thought to her immediate singing career and was certainly in no hurry to start recording pop songs. She had planned to fly home to Australia alone, get to know her mother and father again and maybe spend a few weeks relaxing and playing the piano, and only then have a good hard think about her future. She told reporters she may even consider going back to being a secretary, a job she had always enjoyed. What Judith hadn't expected was the music world to care about her now that she was no longer with that group they all thought so much of.

The Channel Nine special appealed to Judith greatly. She had never done anything like that in her own right before, and they were talking about a major production – a big-name director, an orchestra and an invited, black-tie studio audience. They were also prepared to fly her home to Australia – another plus. Judith realised she would need a manager. Not knowing what else to do about it, she asked John Ashby to come to Australia to handle the business, and he agreed. Beverley was concerned that Judith couldn't seem to break the umbilical cord that tied her to Ashby.

Judith regretted not seeing Ron Edgeworth during the Talk of the Town season and, summoning all her courage, she phoned him to arrange some rehearsals. Her heart sank when a girl's voice answered. She figured Ron must have been in a relationship and, indeed, it turned out it was his long-time girlfriend. Ron thought about the rehearsals and decided he would happily rehearse with the 'dolly lady' who'd caught his eye a few months before.

'The first time Ron came over to rehearse, I thought I'd better have a snack for him,' Judith remembers. 'I baked a cake and, when he arrived, I offered him some with tea. He asked me if it had wholemeal flour and eggs in it and, when I said it had eggs in it, he wasn't interested. He was the first vegetarian I'd ever met. Coincidentally, I'd recently seen a film called *Marjorie Morningstar* and in it the maiden aunt wouldn't eat anything at the wedding breakfast because she was a vegetarian. Now I'd tried every diet I'd ever heard about in the hope of finding the answer to my slimming problems. After I saw the film, I thought vegetarianism might be worth a try. I bought a book on the subject from the first health-food store I'd ever been into in my life, but hadn't got around to doing anything about the diet.'

Judith was interested to learn about Ron's diet. For most of his youth, he'd been a meat-eater and a typical big-drinking musician. It was relatively recently that he'd become a vegetarian and a nondrinker and he made it his business to be knowledgeable on all aspects of a healthy diet.

That same day, Judith helped Ron complete a composition he'd been working on. 'I asked him if he'd ever written any songs and he played me the melody of "Music Everywhere", but when he got to the last line he just stopped. He'd never finished it. It was such a beautiful song. We finished it right then and there. We got on really well from that first rehearsal and we seemed to have a great musical rapport. We discussed the fact that we both had a blues and traditional jazz background too, although I didn't think I'd ever be singing jazz again at that stage.'

Jarrett had already told Judith that she would need a musical director in Australia, and he suggested Ron. After several weeks of rehearsal, Judith asked Ron if he would be interested in coming to Australia in that capacity, for a minimum of two months. 'He didn't answer straight-away,' Judith says, smiling. 'He seemed to ponder it and, when he said he'd always wanted to go to Australia, I threw in the possibility of a New Zealand tour and he seemed to be warming. The next day, he came back with a list of the "fors and againsts" of going to Australia. The list of "againsts" was by far the longer. We went for a walk in the churchyard opposite the flat and talked about it. And I must admit, it went through my mind that I'd probably never end up marrying anyone like this, because he was a well-established freelance musician in London, and, in addition, Russ Conway had invited him to be the opening act for his summer season and Dusty Springfield had shown great interest in his work. Besides, he was a whole foot taller than me! But, in the end, he said he would come to Australia and be my musical director.'

Ron needed time to organise his overseas trip, so Judith and John Ashby returned to Australia ahead of him, arriving on 4 August. Ashby leased an apartment large enough for Ron to share when he arrived. While the two men didn't socialise much, they got along together and respected each other's professional abilities. Judith went home to Hazel and Bill's house in Balwyn and found her parents anxious for her to invest the money she'd made from The Seekers in real estate. To give Hazel a hobby, Judith had her mother scout around for land, and she eventually bought five acres in Lara, near Melbourne. Later, Judith took the real-estate agents to court, for using her image and the lyrics of 'A World of Our Own' in press advertisements for the remaining Lara blocks.

When Ron arrived in Australia, Judith took a taxi to Essendon Airport to meet him. She was surprised how pleased she was to see this lanky Englishman striding towards her. Under his arm was his beloved practice board, which would remain his dearest possession for years to come. She wasn't sure at first whether to shake hands or kiss him, but decided perhaps she should express more affection than a handshake would reflect. Taking a deep breath, she stood on tiptoes and planted a kiss on Ron's cheek.

In the taxi on the way to town, the two chatted easily. Judith asked the driver to take the most scenic route, but Ron wasn't terribly interested. He was bushed after the long flight and hadn't seen anything out of the window so far that compared with London. After settling into the flat with Ashby, Ron began work on arrangements for Judith's forthcoming New Zealand tour. She soon learned how unconventional Ron's life was. He bought a bike and would cycle daily to Balwyn for rehearsals. After riding for so long in the Melbourne heat, the first thing he would do after arriving was have a shower.

The Channel Nine special, to be directed by Rod Kinnear – who'd been responsible for *The World of The Seekers* – was to have a 48-piece orchestra and eight-voice choir under the direction of Brian Rangott. The repertoire Judith worked out included two songs from her Seekers years, 'Music of the World a-Turnin'' and 'Georgy Girl', as well as 'After You've Gone', 'Cry Me a River', 'Danny Boy', 'Back in Your Own Backyard' and a song written for her by Tom Springfield called 'Nobody but You'. On piano, she played 'Nola' and a Chopin prelude leading into 'My Faith'.

'I had an idea in my mind that I wanted to be a sort of Lena Horne-type performer,' Judith says. 'But I hadn't considered how little experience I'd had, especially communicating with an audience on my own. I'd never really talked to an audience before and here I was going to be standing on a high dais in a miniskirt with a hand microphone, chatting between songs. I was surrounded by a black-tie audience who were self-conscious themselves with all the lights on them. The way the stage was positioned, one half of the audience sat all night staring at the other half. In hindsight, the orchestra and choir would suit me as an artist now, but then it was completely over the top.'

Typical of Channel Nine in those days, the orchestra was just too loud for the artist and the mix was atrocious. The reviews weren't too bad, but ultimately the special was no help to Judith in getting people along to see her subsequent Australian concert tour. Rod Kinnear agrees that the formality and positioning of the audience were a mistake and admires Judith's courage. 'It was a very gutsy thing, taking on that solo special,' Kinnear says. 'It took a lot of courage to step out of the mould people knew her in, so soon after leaving The Seekers.'

Judith's first stage appearance as a post-Seekers solo performer came on 13 October, when she was guest star at the Lord Mayor's Command Performance in Brisbane. With Ron as her musical director, Judith headed a bill that also included the singers Mike Preston and Rosalind Keene, and the husband-and-wife team Bobby Limb and Dawn Lake. An audience of 5,000 people turned out at Brisbane's Festival Hall for the concert. The critics were kind. The *Courier-Mail* wrote, 'Obvious audience darling was Judith Durham ... they were right behind her'; while the *Daily Telegraph* reported, 'If any of The Seekers is to make world fame as a solo artist, Judith Durham will be the one to do it.'

For old time's sake, Judith had stayed the night at Lennons Hotel in Brisbane, and the next day she, Ron and John flew to Sydney and then on to Hollywood. Ashby had negotiated a deal with the Goodyear Tyre company, whereby Judith would become one of a series of international artists to record a Christmas album. EMI had given Judith a release from her contract to make the album, which was called *For Christmas with Love*.

Judith and Ron had bought some Christmas albums by other artists and listened to material. One of those albums, featuring the arrangements of Dick Reynolds, particularly impressed her and she sent ahead to him in America manuscripts for the songs she wanted to record. When she arrived, the whole album had been orchestrated and she was thrilled when she found Ron would be able to play piano on the album. Ron was very impressed by some of the world-renowned names among the American musicians – Herb Ellis played guitar, Pearl Bailey's husband, Louis Bellson, was on drums, while Pete Jolly played organ. The whole album was mixed down to two tracks, as was Capitol Records' way in those days. Had it been multitracked, it could have been remixed for its 1994 international Christmas rerelease. The album was done quickly with Judith singing vocals live in the studio while the orchestra played.

Since arriving back in Australia Judith had made the decision to become a vegetarian and gave up meat, fish and eggs; she also became a teetotaller overnight. She was nowhere near as strict as Ron at this stage, but she had a real interest in improving her health. In Los Angeles, Ron took Judith to some vegetarian restaurants, where they would have wonderful dinners and, later, walk for hours.

In September, Judith, who still continued to drink caffeine at this early stage of her new diet, went to Sydney with Ron to make a television ad for tea. It was during their stay that they first both admitted there was a romantic attraction between them. 'I was very, very happy in Ron's company,' Judith says. 'He was very entertaining. We had easy conversations on all sorts of subjects. He made me laugh and, as a bonus, we had music to bond us even more. Our first kiss was very romantic. We were looking at the moon through the window of a Sydney hotel. Two months had passed since we started working together and neither of us had wanted to change our working relationship for fear of losing something wonderful. But our romance was even more wonderful.

'By the time we'd finished the album, Ron had effectively influenced my whole life,' Judith says. 'I was never really in a situation where I worried about having left The Seekers. In a very short time, Ron and I were literally in a world of our own and I'd left England long behind.'

In the UK, *Seekers Live at the Talk of the Town* had been released and had reached Number 2 in the national album charts. A few weeks later, EMI's hastily put together *Best of The Seekers* gave the group its first Number 1 album. After knocking *The Beatles* from Number 1, *Best of The Seekers* later reclaimed the spot from Cream's *Goodbye* and *Diana Ross and*

The Supremes Join The Temptations. The album would stay in the UK charts for a staggering 125 weeks, but the status of The Seekers in the charts was the furthest thing from Judith's mind. *For Christmas with Love* was finally finished, and featured some of Judith's favourite Christmas songs. Once pressed, the first 25 sets were sent by Goodyear to Australian troops in Vietnam, while the album was launched in Sydney and went on to sell 80,000 copies. Today, it is a very expensive collector's item on vinyl. With the recording of her first solo album behind her, Judith took time out to visit Las Vegas with Ron, in order to check out how cabaret artists in the late 1960s were putting shows together. Among the artists they saw in America were Sarah Vaughan, Ella Fitzgerald, Jerry Lewis and George Shearing.

'We were looking for ways to put an act together and seeing these other artists was very helpful,' Judith says. 'We returned to Australia and Ron was finishing all the arrangements for the forthcoming tour of New Zealand that John Ashby had booked. It was Ron, out of the blue one day, who said to me, "I guess you'll be singing Seekers songs in the show." It just hadn't occurred to me that I would. I'd already made a decision not to sing them on television because I thought it would be wrong, but Ron pointed out that, with the break-up of The Seekers so fresh in people's minds, they'd expect to come along to my solo show and hear at least some of them.'

Judith got around her apprehensions about singing Seekers material by containing the group's hits in a medley and fleshed out the rest of her repertoire with popular tunes of the day, including 'Those Were the Days', 'By the Time I Get to Phoenix', 'Gentle on My Mind', 'Alfie', 'Climb Ev'ry Mountain', 'Help Yourself' and 'Tzena Tzena'. Before leaving Australia, Judith officially opened Radio 3AK's 24-hour transmission and then flew to Auckland with Ron and John Ashby.

At her first press conference, Judith admitted to the Auckland *Sunday News* that life with The Seekers had not been a bed of roses. 'You can't work together without arguments and tension and we had our share of differences,' she said. 'It was pretty tiring at times.' Nor, it seemed for a brief moment, would performing solo be a bed of roses. The first news from Ron to greet Judith on her arrival in New Zealand was that none of the musicians, who'd been booked by the promoter, could read music. Ron was left to find some way of getting the musicians to the stage where they could play for Judith; but in the end he imported a bass player and a drummer from Australia.

Despite these early setbacks, the tour looked as if it would be a successful one. Judith had full houses ahead everywhere, not a bad effort considering she was playing mostly 1,200-seaters. Judith opened her first ever solo tour at the Auckland Town Hall. Her first review, in the *Auckland Star*, wasn't what she expected after an ecstatic response from her audience. 'Her voice did not seem true in non-Seekers material, which was zestless and rather unpolished, her simple manner almost ill at ease,' the reviewer wrote. But after that first night the critics positively glowed. The *New Zealand Herald* wrote, 'She proved once and for all that hers was the voice that carried The Seekers ... there was no room for nostalgia alongside her own soaring talent.'

The glowing reviews continued. In New Plymouth, the *Daily News* critic gushed:

> If Judith Durham ever shakes loose her Seekers past, she will be assured of a niche in the international world of stardom. The audience loved her and realised, possibly for the first time, who was the driving force behind the foursome.

The *Napier Herald's* reviewer was knocked out: 'How long is it since you've heard an audience cheer?'; while the city's opposition paper wrote:

> It wouldn't have mattered had she played Three Blind Mice on a tin whistle – Judith Durham had a near-capacity audience at Napier's Municipal Theatre eating out of her hands last night ... There was only one word for her performance – superb.

The notices seemed to get better and better. In a review headed 'HOUSE ROCKED WITH APPLAUSE FOR JUDY DURHAM', the *Wellington Evening Post* said, 'It was hard to believe any artist could come so close to perfection.'

In Christchurch, Judith was elated to see her name in lights for the first time, and stopped to drink in the sight from opposite the theatre. In interviews, she was often asked about The Seekers and whether she regretted leaving them, but people were usually very receptive to her as a solo artist. She was overjoyed to be working on her own, singing the material she wanted to sing. On one of the bus trips during the tour, she wrote a lyric for Ron's composition 'Music Everywhere' and he was knocked out when she handed it to him. It was the beginning of their complete future collaboration. The only time Judith missed Athol, Keith and Bruce was when she was taking her bows. For so long, she had looked along to see when they were going to bow, so she could co-ordinate with them, and all of a sudden all the applause was for her. Judith sent the rave reviews to Eddie Jarrett, who was still handling her bookings in London, and they were all he needed to get her a three-week nightclub booking as a solo artist at the Savoy Hotel, where The Seekers had gone down a storm just after 'I'll Never Find Another You' had reached Number 1 in the charts.

Before returning to London, Judith would take further steps towards a new, healthy lifestyle by spending two weeks with Ron on a health farm. Despite a disastrous Australian tour, the year ahead would be filled with joy for Judith Durham. Not only would she set out on a spiritual path that would give new meaning to her life, but she would also sign a solo contract with one of America's leading recording companies.

And, before the year was over, she would become Mrs Ron Edgeworth.

8. LET ME FIND LOVE

If I had love,
Pure love in my heart,
Sweet love in my heart,
I would find peace,
Sweet peace in my soul,
I would be free, this is my goal,
Let me find pure love,
Oh let me find pure love in my heart.

– 'LET ME FIND LOVE'
JUDITH DURHAM

In 1968, as Judith Durham was finally resolving to take control of her life and change its direction, Ron Edgeworth was tackling the same personal agenda. He had enjoyed a varied career so far, working in Europe and North America and in Britain with many of the famous big bands of the day, including Ronnie Aldrich, Cyril Stapleton and Johnny Howard. Later, he'd been asked to join the band of the blues guitarist Alexis Korner, who had so influenced The Rolling Stones, and had recorded an album as part of his All Stars band. Through these years, Ron had lived the hard-drinking, fast-living life of a young, single musician, but in the end he found it vacuous. Taking stock, he had radically altered his diet and lifestyle and his quest for meaning in his life had led him to the teachings of an Indian master.

Brought together by music, Judith and Ron were amazed by how much they had in common. He was a confident, humorous and relaxed man and she was an unsure, unrelaxed and unfulfilled woman, but they were impressed by each other's talent and became more and more intrigued by each other's personal search for truth. Ron responded to Judith's vulnerability, while Judith was attracted to Ron's strength and musical affinity. And, to top it off, they both had a passion for Citroëns! Before Ron had arrived in Australia, Judith had begun to experiment with a vegetarian diet. Since then, she had intensified her resolve. She had also raised the issue of reincarnation with her new best friend and was drawn to the depth and simplicity of his beliefs.

'I found myself wanting to discuss spirituality with Ron,' Judith says. 'It was something from my past that had never been completely resolved. We were in musical accord, and I wanted to see if he was interested in spiritual things too. We were out walking in Sydney one day and in a bookshop window I saw a book I'd always loved called *The Prophet* by Kahlil Gibran. I asked Ron whether he'd ever read the book, because I'd found it very interesting, and he said he could show me something a whole lot better than that. Funnily enough, the book I'd bought in London about LSD was also in the window and I asked what he thought of LSD, and he said it was a load of nonsense.

'We got into a discussion about spiritual issues and in the following conversation just about every question I'd spent hours and hours discussing in the corner at parties in my late teens he answered. I wanted to know about life after death and confirm my beliefs about the possibility of reincarnation. Is this all there is? Ron was able to answer every one of those questions for me, because of the path he was following with his Master. Funnily enough, he'd vowed to his mother before leaving for Australia to start working with me that he wouldn't try to talk me into becoming a vegetarian or talk about the path he was on. She didn't want me to think he was weird or anything.'

Ron told Judith that, since he had arrived in Australia, he had been going to meetings and she began going along with him. She was overwhelmed by the way this newfound knowledge filled the void in her life. Judith's upbringing had left her mind open to alternative beliefs about reincarnation. Her grandfather was heavily involved in theosophy and, during Hazel's early years, meetings of the Theosophical Society were held in Judith's grandparents' lounge room.

'Neither Dad nor Mum had really followed any orthodox religion,' Judith says. 'They were married in a church and sent Beverley and me along to Sunday school to give us a basic moral foundation in our lives, but they didn't guide us towards any particular denomination. I had a strong religious belief throughout my childhood. I believed in God and Jesus and I aspired to something very high. I always wanted to be a good person, as good as I could possibly be. I'd always feel terribly bad if I did something wrong and got into trouble, at home or at school, and I would pray and ask God to glorify me, not really knowing what I meant by that.'

At sixteen, Judith borrowed from a schoolfriend a copy of Lopsang Rampa's mystical book, *The Third Eye*, and was immediately influenced. 'I believed in all of that,' Judith recalls. 'I thought about reincarnation a lot and when I was about eighteen I went to a spiritualist meeting and also had a bit to do with the Theosophical Society. By the time I started [work] at J Walter Thompson, I had also become interested in astrology and the occult.'

On tour in New Zealand, Judith and Ron had spent time reading books and listening to audio tapes. Judith absorbed the philosophy of living a moral life, abstaining from alcohol and mind-altering drugs, meditation and a strict diet. She resolved to aspire to these principles for the rest of her life. Judith now realised she'd found many of the answers she'd been looking for and, three months later, without telling her parents, she was initiated as a disciple of Ron's Master.

For Judith, it was a metamorphosis. For the first time in her life, she had the direction she'd craved for so long. Her vegetarian diet brought her food cravings under control; she had started to express herself musically and the path was fulfilling her spiritual needs. On top of all these positive aspects in her life, Judith Durham was head over heels in love.

'It just amazed me how different my life had become in the few months since I'd left The Seekers,' Judith says. 'The path seemed to vindicate my decision to leave the group. It had been such a monumental decision for me, and yet I realised that, for those four years, I had been disguising myself, playing a role. Because of that, I was not really acknowledging my own needs. The Seekers was never a terrible experience for me, it's just that it wasn't enough. I loved what I was doing and I knew I did it well, but I was basically doing it to please other people and denying myself.'

The things that had caused Judith so much misery during her years with The Seekers – her health and her weight – were no longer such dominant issues after Ron had come into her life. The natural vegetarian diet and fasting had replaced her need for medicines and antibiotics, and nerve tablets were a thing of the past. When Ron introduced Judith to the path, her spiritual needs were met. She was finally a very happy person.

With their successful New Zealand tour behind them, Ron invited Judith to join him on a two-week nature-cure regime at Hopewood, a health farm in Wallacia, New South Wales. 'When I was on that last tour with The Seekers, after talking to Ron that first night, he unexpectedly visited me in my dressing room,' Judith says. 'That in itself was a novelty, because no one ever came to see me as a rule. Wouldn't you know it, I was eating fish and chips! It was something I'd never normally eat and it was certainly something you never did in the theatre. It was a real taboo. I had sat there feeling embarrassed about it after Ron had walked in, when he dropped a book in front of me called *The Miracle of Fasting*. The author was Dr Paul Bragg, who, at eighty, was a picture of glowing health. Fasting was something relatively new and revolutionary in the seventies and Ron told me he fasted one day a week. He wanted to try an even longer fast. When he came to Australia and found out about the health farm at Wallacia, he was very keen to go.'

The two travelled to New South Wales and the first thing they did at Hopewood was have an iris diagnosis, to reveal their body's trouble spots. The results were analysed and Judith and Ron were told they should have a seven-day fast. They had expected to be able to take things a day at a time, so their jaws dropped! Seven days without food! There was a time, not so long ago, when Judith didn't want to face seven *minutes* without food! Like so many other times in her life, here she was going to another extreme. Their regime was basically just water every day, starting with hot water first thing in the morning and then cool water for the rest of the day.

'It was absolute torture!' Judith says. 'I had a terrible time. I just couldn't wait for the seven days to end. They'd told us our hunger would go away after the second or third day, but mine didn't and I was ravenously hungry. There was segregated nude sunbathing, so I thought I'd spend some time lying in the sun. My legs went numb, I had ants crawling all over me. You have no idea! It really was a terrible experience for me. I had to have foments for the awful back and shoulder pain I started to experience. They alternate hot and cold towels on you, to increase your circulation. I had this terrible lethargy, couldn't muster the energy to go for walks like some of the other people did.'

Judith and Ron watched a bit of television and did a lot of talking, having been warned not to go too far from the centre. They attended all of the in-house talks, which were very informative, and raw food was stressed. When their seven days were finally over, they were brought off the fast very gradually, under supervision. On the first day, they were allowed equal amounts of water and juice. The next day, it was 75 per cent juice, then fruit and finally salads. Food never tasted so good!

Although it was an ordeal, Judith was pleased she'd been able to complete the fast. She saw how it had worked for some of the other guests. One woman was seeing wrinkles in her knees for the first time, after years of arthritic swelling. Another was on the tenth day of her fast and had discovered boundless energy. Other people had managed to give up smoking. While the fast hadn't done anything to lessen Judith's cough, she was staggered by the weight she'd lost. Her eyes sparkled, she was more energetic and she was slim. It was a crash course in the alternative way of life and Judith had learned much.

After their fortnight's rejuvenation Judith and Ron returned to Melbourne and immediately resumed rehearsals for the forthcoming Australian tour. Their success in New Zealand had exceeded Judith's highest expectations and she was hopeful that Australia would accept her transition to solo singer with as much grace. The tour, at best, was a disaster. It was presented by Arthur Tait, who had originally envisaged that Judith would go on the road without musicians, just singing and playing piano for her audience in an intimate setting. What eventually went out under his banner was a vastly different show from the one he had hoped to promote.

'It was John Ashby's idea to turn the show into what was essentially a variety bill, with me as the headliner,' Judith says. 'It was his idea to bring Tommy Reilly, Dick Emery and Glen Weston to Australia as my support acts. Suddenly it became a very expensive tour. John struck a deal where I would be on seventy per cent of the profits, but there was no guaranteed fee. By the time we were ready to tour, the Channel Nine special had been screened and that's the image people had of me as a soloist, which was a far cry from the confident and versatile performer I'd become on stage.'

It was very evident once they hit the road that people just weren't going to come. There were half-full houses everywhere, so different from the New Zealand tour, where the TV special had not been screened and extra concerts had to be added to meet the demand. Audiences did not respond well to Dick Emery, who'd been brought out from England by Ashby. He was unfamiliar to Australian audiences then and, despite his excellent stage act, his material was very blue, totally unsuitable for a Judith Durham crowd. But the reviews weren't all bad. The Melbourne *Sun* acknowledged that Judith 'wowed her fans', but noted 'there seemed a lack of colour and depth'. The *Age* remarked that she had 'what it takes to make an audience shout and whistle for more'.

'I wasn't really happy with the deal John had done for the tour,' Judith says. 'I understood that I was on a high percentage of the profits, but I also had to stand the majority of the losses myself. I told John that if I lost money I really would have to let him go as a manager, because he'd put me in that position. Because of the half-full houses, I lost nine thousand dollars on that tour and that was the end of my business association with John. He was aware by now of my romantic involvement with Ron and he just removed himself from the picture and returned to London. It broke both our hearts at the time. We were finally saying goodbye for good. John was going home through America and Ron and I were going to England via India.'

After wrapping up in Australia, Judith and Ron headed for the Punjab, in India's north. There, initiates would go to see their Master. On special occasions, as many as 250,000 people would travel from all over the world to hear the Master give his discourses. 'It was a truly wonderful experience for me,' Judith recalls. 'I was an initiate and this was a consolidation of what I had embraced, in one hit. It was an eye-opener, travelling to India and seeing beyond the transit lounges. To actually be in the cities and see these teeming millions of people and the way they lived, the dust and the barrenness of it all. For the people there, so many of them handicapped in some way, life is such a slog.

'We arrived at the colony and found it was just incredibly imbued with love, people wanting to serve without question of money. Like everyone else, we wanted to spend some time in service to the Master, so, during the six-day stay, we joined in some menial tasks, like carting sand around. We were just two of thousands and thousands of people, no better than anybody else, no worse. It really was a fantastic experience in every way.'

In contrast with many alternative religions, their Master's path placed initiates under no financial obligation and their accommodation and food were provided free of charge. Here, everything was made out of love, as service to the Master, whose teachings advocated a vegetarian diet, with no eggs or alcohol. Staying on their raw-food diet was quite a challenge for Judith and Ron, considering the lavish vegetarian meals that were served at the guest house, but they stuck to salad and fruit during this first visit.

Leaving for England, Judith had concerns about how to explain her trip to India to the London media. Only a year or so earlier, The Beatles had found themselves at the centre of a media furore over their involvement with Maharishi Mahesh Yogi, whose transcendental-meditation lectures they'd attended in London and whose ashram in Rishikesh, India, they had visited. Judith was advised to state simply that she'd visited her Master in India, but the question was never asked by the journalists who met her at Heathrow. At the airport, she also met Ron's mother Vicky and brother Patrick for the first time. In preparation for their three-week Savoy booking, Ron moved back home with Vicky and Judith checked into a hotel. On 29 April, Judith made her solo cabaret debut.

'The shows went very, very well,' Judith remembers. 'I was initially daunted because the Savoy stage is so huge and it was the first time I'd had to work a stage that big. I'd done concerts on my own, but never cabaret and I didn't feel as confident at first as I'd have liked to have been. I was beginning to think perhaps I should have done some of the other clubs first and then hit London, but that's not how it turned out. I really would have liked to have done longer shows in London too, perhaps a couple of hours, but Eddie was adamant that it would be too much. Just like with The Seekers, he believed that 50 minutes was as much as I should do, and the Savoy only required 30 minutes.'

In the Savoy audience one night was the American vice-president, Hubert Humphrey, who was unaware of Judith Durham's musical history, but extremely impressed by her performance. He was reported to have stood up at the end of the evening, thrown his glass on the floor and announced, 'That girl's damn good'. The next day, Humphrey's press agent approached Eddie Jarrett and booked Judith to sing aboard a barge on which his press entourage was to be given a Thames-eye view of London. However, Jarrett told Judith that mounting a suitable sound system on board the barge proved impossible and, to Judith's disappointment, the show was cancelled. Judith followed her Savoy season with week-long cabaret stints at the Fiesta Club in Stockton and Mr Smith's in Manchester, and both bookings required further band rehearsals to accommodate the four or five encores demanded each night.

Still unresolved was Judith's recording future. Eddie Jarrett had received offers and expressions of interest from all of the major record companies in Britain and told Judith she could virtually take her pick. Also, while touring New Zealand, John Ashby had been told there was strong interest being shown by A&M Records. This relatively small American label run by Herb Alpert and Jerry Moss had in its stable The Carpenters, Burt Bacharach, Herb Alpert and the Tijuana Brass, Carole King, Liza Minnelli and Claudine Longet. Judith had her heart set on signing with an American record company because they wouldn't automatically associate her with The Seekers in projecting her own image. In her mind, America would be the springboard for her solo recording career.

Those days were long before the advent of fax and Judith entered into negotiations with A&M by mail. 'Letters went backwards and forwards between A&M and Eddie for months,' Judith says, 'but nothing seemed to be coming together, so I decided to fly to California and meet with Jerry Moss. We reached an agreement whereby A&M would pay my airfare if I signed with them, which seemed fair to me, so off I went to America, on my own!'

Judith flew from London to Los Angeles for the meeting, enjoying the company of Cliff Richard, who coincidentally sat next to her on the flight. She met with Jerry Moss at A&M's studio complex on North La Brea Avenue, where the offices had been built in Charlie Chaplin's old movie set. With no management ties in America, Judith elected to do her own negotiations with A&M. She was aware of the deals some of the English labels had offered Jarrett for her services and resolved that, if

A&M could broadly match them, she'd sign. Judith met with Moss and his lawyer and the meeting went very well. Judith needed to push hard to get them to match the English offers, and at one point Moss's lawyer remarked that she would make a good attorney herself. With her new confidence had come a growing ability to assert herself and she had learned from experience not to cave in when she strongly believed something was not fair.

Moss showed some concern when Judith played him a tape of her Stockton Fiesta show, which was brimming with cabaret numbers and ended with 'Tzena Tzena'. He appeared worried about the image Judith would have on record, although nothing was said. Discussions over, Moss took Judith to lunch and, fanatical about her mainly raw diet, she ordered a large raw salad. Moss was sneaking glances at his watch by three in the afternoon, while Judith chomped her way through the remaining half of her lunch! The chomping didn't lose her the deal and, by the time she left America, it was clinched. A few weeks after arriving back in London, Judith received the contract. Any other singer, after signing a major recording contract in Hollywood, would go out and paint the town red. Judith bought a set of matching luggage!

A&M had signed Chad Stuart to produce Judith's first album. As one half of Chad and Jeremy, Stuart had enjoyed great chart success in 1964 and 1965 with hits such as 'A Summer Song', 'Willow Weep for Me', 'Yesterday's Gone' and 'If I Loved You'. With Judith's album, he would be making his debut as a producer.

Judith set about trying to find songs for the project, and, with no manager to advise her that it wasn't the done thing, she traipsed around all the major music publishers in London, looking for material. Through a process of elimination, she found six songs she was happy with and hoped that, by the time she arrived in America to record, Chad Stuart would have found a few more.

'Before going to Hollywood for the sessions, Ron and I decided we'd have a short holiday on the Continent,' Judith says. 'We had planned to go through France, Belgium and up to Scandinavia, because I'd never been there. Our *International Vegetarian Handbook* from the Vegetarian Society in London listed all the vegetarian restaurants, guest houses and health-food shops worldwide. It had become our hobby, trying out as many of them as we could. We went off by train and when we got to Denmark we decided to go and have lunch at a little raw-food guesthouse we'd read about that was just outside Copenhagen, called Hummelgarten. We were overpowered by the smell of garlic coming from this place, but it took a long time before we could find anyone who spoke English.

'We eventually found out that the woman who'd established the place had cured herself of cancer with a raw diet and garlic, and people came from all over the world looking for a cure. Instead of just having lunch there, we ended up staying for the whole ten days, just eating the raw food and masses and masses of garlic. We reeked of it! We had a great time there. The lounge had a piano and every evening Ron and I would play and I'd sing to these people who couldn't understand a word of what we were saying or singing but just loved the music. We ended up doing two hours each night while we were there and I had this flash that, if people who couldn't understand a word of English were content to sit for a couple of hours, why wouldn't English audiences? We returned to London and put it to Eddie, but he still insisted a two-hour concert was over the top and he didn't think promoters would be interested.'

When Judith and Ron arrived in Hollywood for their six-week A&M recording project, they found that Richard Clements had been hired as the arranger and the session musicians read like an industry *Who's Who*. On drums they had Hal Blaine, on keyboards Larry Knechtel and Joe Sample, and one of their five trumpeters was Buddy Childers, former lead trumpeter with Stan Kenton. 'When I went into the studio, I realised A&M were going to record the album at thirty i.p.s. [inches per second] instead of the usual fifteen,' Judith says. 'That showed a major commitment. They spared no expense, giving me a thirty-six-thousand-dollar budget. I was on raw food and had been fasting, so my voice was very clear and the sessions were a real joy. There was only one occasion when I clashed with Chad, over one of the bars of "Take Care of My Brother". It got a bit tense but, to my amazement, one of the musicians in the orchestra eventually piped up and told Chad I was right, and it was all resolved.'

During their six-week stay, Judith and Ron shared a house with a pool that A&M had found for them in the Hollywood Hills, only a stone's throw from LA's famous vegetarian restaurants. An A&M publisher, in a discussion with Judith about material, suggested that she put her piano skills to good use and write a song for herself – and a seed was planted in her mind. The next day she and Ron attended a meeting with people who were on the same 'path' in a house on the outskirts of Los Angeles, and they listened to a discourse about feeling love in your heart for everybody.

'The following morning, I woke up with the words and the melody of a song in my head,' Judith says. 'I called out to Ron and, when he came in from his room, I sang the chorus. I actually asked him whether he'd heard it before, because I'd never thought up a song on my own before and I worried that I was remembering someone else's tune. I stayed in bed and ended up composing the whole song there, and called it "Let Me Find Love". When I got up, I wrote it down and then Ron and I sat at the piano and worked on it. I'd written some very simple chords, and Ron expanded them to make them richer. When we'd finished it I asked Chad to consider it for the album, but, because our return flights to Australia were booked, we had to leave. Chad mixed the album and then sent the tapes of a backing for "Let Me Find Love" to Melbourne, so I could add the vocals there. We actually did do that, but it never sounded quite right and, because of the distance between us, it couldn't really be corrected. So it never made it on to that album.'

The main reason Judith and Ron were travelling to Australia was that they had been secretly planning their wedding. That momentous decision was made in London. On the evening of 21 July, as Neil Armstrong stepped down the ladder of the Apollo 11 lunar module on to the dusty surface of the Sea of Tranquillity, Judith accepted Ron's proposal of marriage.

'Ron had actually proposed once before,' Judith says. 'It was a few days earlier, when I was staying with my aunt and uncle in Southwold, on the coast of Norwich, and he rang me one day. Now by this stage, I was hoping he *would* ask me, but I had hoped he might propose in person! It was typical, unconventional Ron, deciding he missed me and asking me to marry him by phone. I told him to ask me again later on, which probably knocked his confidence a bit. I knew he was hesitant because he was scared of my knocking him back, so in the end I pushed him into it. I said, "Go on, ask me." I had accepted, but we didn't say anything while we were in Hollywood. The people at A&M, when they heard we were married, sent telegrams expressing great surprise. They saw us working very formally together in the studio and had no idea there was any romantic involvement.'

As soon as they arrived in Australia, Judith and Ron began planning the wedding, which was to take place just five weeks later. Hazel was delighted with the news and took great pleasure as the proud mother in ringing the newspapers to announce the couple's engagement. Judith wanted to marry in Melbourne's Scots Church, where Hazel and Bill had married thirty years before, but the only available time for a wedding was

Friday, 21 November, at five in the evening. That was peak hour in the city, so Judith's plans for a low-key, private affair flew out of the window.

'We really didn't plan very well,' Judith admits. 'I returned to Australia and had only a matter of weeks to organise my wedding dress, Beverley's matron-of-honour dress and a reception. If I'd had my wits about me, I would have flown from London to Paris and picked up a dress there before going to Hollywood, but I was so caught up in planning the album that it didn't occur to me. Ron's mother Vicky and his brother Patrick flew out from England. We met them in Sydney and took them sightseeing to Bondi. Patrick, who was Ron's best man, was a textile salesman in England, who also worked semiprofessionally as a stand-up comic and sometimes wrote one-liners for other performers. Unbeknownst to us, he was thinking of staying on in Australia. There were more of Ron's relatives in England who would have liked to have been at the wedding, but we just couldn't afford to bring everyone out. We would have had to hire the *Fairsky* to get them all there!'

Five hundred fans turned out to see Judith and Ron marry and traffic came to a standstill at the top end of Collins Street. The bride unintentionally kept with tradition and was half an hour late. She had been held up by the hairdresser and ended up doing her own hair and Beverley's, too. Upon her arrival with Bill, who was beaming from ear to ear the entire time, Judith was swamped by well-wishers, reporters and photographers.

'It was a lovely experience,' Judith recalls. 'Travelling in the car with Dad and arriving at the church. As I rounded the top of the aisle and looked up, Ron turned around and flashed me this most fantastic smile, a real bond between the two of us. He's told me since that it did start to cross his mind that I mightn't turn up. He and his brother were waiting in the anteroom at the church and after thirty minutes, he started wondering whether I'd had second thoughts. I didn't find that out until we'd been married for 24 years.'

Leaving the church, Mr and Mrs Ron Edgeworth waited patiently, smiling for the throng of newspaper and magazine photographers to get their shots, which turned up on front pages across the nation the next morning and in the following weeks. All she wanted was a happy home, filled with music, Judith told reporters. Yes, she said, she would like to have children, but only if they could fit in with her career. A reception followed at Melbourne's Southern Cross Hotel, with fifty relatives and close friends taking part in a singsong around a grand piano.

Judith had asked her father if she and Ron could have a vegetarian wedding breakfast, but Bill was not keen. He and all his friends were meat-eaters and he wasn't comfortable with the notion of an entirely herbivorous celebration. As a compromise, though, he agreed that the wedding cake could be vegetarian. Before the wedding, Judith met with the chef at the Southern Cross. He had never made a vegetarian cake before and was a bit baffled. Flicking through his recipe book, he came up with a fruit-bun recipe that didn't require eggs, which he cooked and iced – but, no matter how good it looked, it was still a bun! With the weight of the decorations on it, it started to sag as the night wore on and Bill made constant jokes about it.

During this visit home, Judith and Ron heard from Max Bygraves, who was performing in Australia. He invited Judith to perform on his television show back in London. Eddie Jarrett considered *The Max Bygraves Show* a perfect vehicle for Judith and the deal was clinched. It meant, however, that the newlyweds would have only a few days for a honeymoon. Judith and Ron spent their wedding night in Melbourne, and the next morning Judith had the first inkling of the offbeat life she would lead as Mrs Ron Edgeworth.

'I had no idea Ron wasn't a breakfast person,' Judith says. 'I always woke up ravenous, could hardly wait to eat breakfast, and here I was, married to someone who couldn't care less. That morning, I ended up having wedding cake and bits of carob confectionery with the remains of the apple cider. That was really the start of the Aquarian and the Cancer getting together. I like to plan everything and stick to tradition and ended up spending my life married to someone who is very spontaneous and untraditional.'

The following day, their families came to the airport for a tearful farewell. The pair left Melbourne for Fiji, where they were to spend just three days in the idyllic splendour of remote Castaway Island, before flying on to London to begin rehearsals for the Bygraves show. Their plans were thwarted again, this time by weather. On the speedboat ride from Nadi, Judith's bare skin was exposed to the harsh tropical sun. Not long after the honeymooners had arrived at the island, Judith found she was severely sunburned.

'I spent my honeymoon slapping on creams to help the sunburn heal,' Judith recalls with amusement. 'I could hardly be touched. We had a little thatched burro [hut] right on the beach which was just beautiful, with its white sands, rippling sea and blue skies, but I wasn't able to get out in the sun much at all. The other shock for me was the burro, which was built with the toilet right in the middle, without any soundproofing. I almost died of embarrassment every time I went to the loo, within earshot of my new husband. It wasn't anything like I expected my honeymoon to be!'

Judith and Ron flew from sunny Fiji to snowbound London late in November and moved into a small basement cottage behind 28 Enford Street. Judith immediately began rehearsals for *The Max Bygraves Show*, which was being made by Thames Television and had a budget of £25,000. The network was making a concerted effort to break Bygraves into the lucrative US television market. Other guests on the show included the American comedian George Burns, whose television show with Gracie Allen had been essential viewing in the Cock household in the fifties. Another was the actor Jim Backus, who was not only the voice of Mr Magoo, but also the dithering Thurston Howell III on *Gilligan's Island*. For the special, Judith performed 'My Happiness' as a duet with Bygraves. Public reaction was favourable and Bygraves asked Judith to record the duet, but despite lengthy negotiations, those plans were later shelved.

As 1969 drew to a close, Judith was only a matter of days away from the release of her first post-Seekers solo single and the A&M album. In the end-of-year UK chart ratings, The Seekers were Number 1 on the list of top British LPs with *Best of The Seekers*, above The Beatles' *Abbey Road*, but Judith had no idea: her head was miles away from the pop charts.

With the dawn of a new decade, Judith had the entire world of music at her feet. She hoped that she wouldn't find herself in competition with her past, but, throughout the seventies, the spectre of The Seekers would loom like a sword above Judith Durham's head, frequently cutting down her plans and wounding her pride.

9. MUSIC EVERYWHERE

Music, sweet lovely music,
I hear your music everywhere,
I feel it surging, softly urging
My mind to wait till all is still.
Then you will come to me,
And we will share,
That lovely music everywhere.

– 'MUSIC EVERYWHERE'
RON EDGEWORTH AND JUDITH DURHAM

The Edgeworths' pretty hideaway cottage was a hub of creative activity at the start of 1970. Ron had moved from his mother's house his old upright piano, which he had inherited from his uncle, and the newlyweds spent many hours playing and singing together. It was in this cottage that the couple would write 'What Could Be a Better Way', their second songwriting collaboration. Judith undertook a hectic schedule of television and club appearances in readiness for the release of *A Gift of Song*, which was preceded on 9 January by a single from it called 'The Light Is Dark Enough'.

It was not Judith's ambition to become a Top 40 star once again, nor was it her choice to release a single from the album. The discussions she had held with A&M Records in America left her with the understanding that the company intended to market her as an album artist, in the vein of Judy Collins. Meanwhile, A&M had opened a London office and had decided to use Judith's album as a major launching vehicle for the company there. Naturally, huge emphasis was now being placed on the ex-Seeker connection, instead of promotion of Judith as a 'new artist'. But comparison with The Seekers was inevitable. It was also unfair, given the difference in style.

As a result, little attention was paid to the single and, while *Top of the Pops* filmed Judith performing the song, it was never screened. The album was released a few weeks later and it didn't take long for Judith to realise it was going to sink. Critically, *A Gift of Song* was a success. *New Musical Express* ran a review that praised Judith's 'beautifully sung set of eleven songs'; while Melbourne's *Listener-In TV* hailed it as a 'splendid showcase for her talent . . . a voice with an appealing purity of tone and a singing style which is refreshingly open and free from affectation'. It was just that the public found it hard to accept Judith Durham singing anything but Seekers-type songs.

'The press seemed to be concentrating on the amount of weight I'd lost rather than the musical path I was choosing to take,' Judith explains. 'I was seeing myself as a concert artist, but I was being channelled into variety again. The album was designed as a springboard to the concert stage, but people seemed to be looking for happy, bouncy numbers.'

A&M had also realised that *A Gift of Song* was not going to work quite the way they'd planned. They were prepared to finance another album, but first they needed another single to try to lift Judith's recording profile. They were aware that there really wasn't another single on the album, so they put Judith together with The Hollies' producer Ron Richards, and asked him to suggest material. Two possibilities were Mike D'Abo's 'Bonny Face' and Elton John's 'Skyline Pigeon'. Judith did ask whether 'Let Me Find Love', which had narrowly missed inclusion on the first album, could be the B-side. Richards was so impressed by the song that he suggested it should be a contender for the A-side. A&M agreed and 'Let Me Find Love' became the A-side.

Studio time was booked and on the morning of the session Judith and Ron turned up at Abbey Road's huge Studio One, where The Beatles had always recorded. They found a fifty-piece orchestra and an eight-voice choir, but no producer. A short time later, Judith was informed that Ron Richards had suffered a nervous breakdown that morning and wouldn't be able to work. Another producer was brought in and, despite the fact he knew nothing about the song, the session went well. 'Music Everywhere', the song Judith had helped Ron complete during their first rehearsal together, was recorded as the B-side. Both arrangements were done by *A Gift of Song*'s Richard Clements, who was visiting London.

The next day in Abbey Road's mixing suite, everyone was dismayed to discover a lag in the drum track. The studio was so large that the drums were playing slightly out of sync because the baffles had been set up incorrectly. Not only that, but A&M was concerned that the song was too long and asked for a verse to be removed. They asked production novices Judith and Ron to return to the studio to chop a chorus. The problem was that the song had four choruses, one after the other, and on each one Judith changed key to build the song to a climax. They removed one of the choruses, but felt the song had been ruined. A&M were equally unsure of its chances, but decided to release it nonetheless.

Again, the press loved it. *Record Mirror* wrote, 'Judith Durham has a very celestial voice entirely suited to this number ... her voice goes soaring away while the backing builds to solid fever pitch and everything trembles on the brink of an almost semi-religious feel.' Again, Judith found resistance from radio and television. To make matters worse, 'Let Me Find Love' was released on the day that The New Seekers made their debut with 'What Have They Done To My Song, Ma?' While Bruce had returned to writing jingles and Athol was hosting a TV show in Australia,

Keith Potger had formed the group the previous year to capitalise on The Seekers' name, joining forces with three male and two female singers, including Australian pop stars Marty Kristian and Peter Doyle.

Suddenly, Judith was in competition with The Seekers, albeit in a new guise. Instead of reporters asking her about her new single, they were asking her what she thought about The New Seekers. 'Let Me Find Love' sank without a trace, while the new group's version of 'What Have They Done To My Song, Ma?' hit the Top 10.

'We were told "Let Me Find Love" had been chosen for the Record of the Week segment on the next *Kenny Everett Show* on BBC1,' Judith says. 'Ron and I tuned in and the last part of this horror story was when they got to Record of the Week: Kenny Everett came hopping on in a kangaroo outfit. He put the record on and played a few bars, then threw it on the floor and jumped on it. He said, "That was the worst record of the week, folks" – and I was just mortified.'

One day, a few weeks later, quite out of the blue, Judith received a call from Dick Katz, a highly respected agent with the management company MAM. A&M Records had requested that Judith be handled by MAM instead of Eddie Jarrett. The agency looked after Dusty Springfield and other big names of the time and it was Katz who had been recommended. He was a well-known pianist in his own right, Judith knew his name from BBC broadcasts in Australia. Katz understood Judith's musical needs and expressed concern about her management set-up. Judith was becoming disenchanted with Eddie Jarrett's reluctance to expand her artistic boundaries, and by now there was no love lost between them. Keen to move on, Judith met with Katz and a new partnership was formed. Katz was instrumental in developing Judith's act. He raised her fees and began shopping around for a major television opportunity to compensate for her recording dilemma.

Katz negotiated Judith's own television special with London Weekend. While the budget – and therefore Judith's fee – was small, the special would give her the mass exposure her records weren't able to provide. London Weekend hired Brian Izzard to direct the special, which was called *Meet Judith Durham*. Izzard hired as Judith's guests her old friend Tommy Reilly, pop star Dave Dee, pop group Harmony Grass, Malcolm Clare and his dancers and a children's percussion group from the Bonneville School in London. Music for the special was a mixture of songs from Judith's albums and her own favourites.

'I was very lucky to get my own Special, but looking back, it was too contrived for my personality,' Judith says. 'The programming was wrong.

The second number in was the kids playing percussion, which was possibly a turn-off at that point in the show. I didn't question the way the show was put together at all. I just more or less did what they asked of me. I put myself in their hands, and as a result the special didn't really reflect what I might have chosen. But it was all good experience and Brian Izzard was very helpful. From that point on, thanks to his help, I developed more confidence in chatting on a microphone to a live audience.'

Riding on the publicity generated by the TV special and the efforts of the A&M-appointed publicist Tony Barrow, Judith and Ron undertook a cabaret tour through Britain, opening at Talk of the North in Manchester. The reviews were positive, especially one in *Record Mirror*, which read, 'They twice demanded her return and literally gave her a standing ovation. Why? Because Judith has a nice girl freshness, possesses a crystal-clear voice with diction to match, is infectiously friendly – and has talent.'

A week's booking at Sheffield's Bailey's Club was followed by a week at Blackburn Cavendish, which saw the *Blackburn Times* reviewer claim, 'For the first time ever, a capacity crowd at Blackburn Cavendish just couldn't get enough of her. Judith Durham had hit town and the audience just couldn't stay down.' The management of one of the clubs told Judith they'd never seen any other act go so well, except maybe Shirley Bassey or Gracie Fields.

The tour was completed with one-night stands at St Albans City Hall, Gravesend Woodville Hall and the Golden Garter in Manchester. Through it all, Judith and Ron referred to their vegetarian handbook for accommodation, staying in charming, homely guesthouses. They ate at rustic health-food restaurants up and down the country, sowing the first seeds of the nomadic lifestyle that was to come.

When Ron Richards was well enough to work again, A&M Records organised for Judith to record her second album at Air London studios. This time, in a bid to beef up Judith's image, the company brought in the arranger Christopher Gunning. Where *A Gift of Song* had been a laid-back effort, the new album was planned to be more orchestrally challenging. Judith selected her material from music publishers in London, her own repertoire and songs offered to her by A&M. For this album, Judith settled on 'What Could Be a Better Way', one of her first compositions with Ron, and some of the songs she'd featured in her concerts. Judith decided to call the album *Climb Ev'ry Mountain* after the song that had been so ecstatically received in her stage shows. Unlike *A Gift of Song*, which was recorded live with an orchestra, *Climb Ev'ry Mountain* had its musical tracks recorded first, including an expanded brass section, and vocals were laid down later. Unaware that Judith was married to a talented musician, Christopher Gunning had booked two session pianists. The first was Reg Dwight, just before he changed his name to Elton John, and Judith was told during the session that 'Skyline Pigeon' was his song. The second pianist was Dudley Moore.

On a train trip to Manchester, where Judith was to appear on a TV show, Ron by chance sat next to Peter Burman and discovered Burman was in partnership with Michael Rouse, who staged concerts by Juliet Greco and Cleo Laine. Taking the opportunity, Ron discussed Judith's dream of presenting a one-woman show. Burman and Rouse agreed to back them. Judith had envisaged doing one concert on the quiet in a 200-seater venue like the Tap Room in Bath, and was stunned to find that her promoters had booked four 2,000-seater venues, including Fairfield Halls in Croydon, Bournemouth Winter Gardens and Bristol's Colston Hall.

'I was very concerned when I realised how big these venues were,' Judith remembers. 'I was thinking it would be a sort of try-out but Peter and Michael believed it was going to do well, and booked four major venues. I worried that I might end up with egg on my face. When the tickets went on sale, they sold out very quickly. We were amazed, and so were the promoters.'

For the show, Judith and Ron had rehearsed all types of material, including the aria 'Io Son L'Umile' from *Adriana Lecouvreur*, a few standards from Judith's jazz days, and both classical and ragtime piano pieces that would show a side of Judith Durham that few audiences had seen. The crowd reaction and the reviews for those first four shows were fantastic, and Judith was over the moon.

Not long after that, Michael Rouse contacted Judith to let her know that Australia didn't have a representative for the Rio International Song Festival, to be staged in Brazil in October. Eager to represent her country for the first time as a solo performer, Judith was selected as a contender. Initially, she intended to sing Mike D'Abo's 'Bonny Face', but permission was denied and she settled on Peter Pye's 'There He Is'. Pye was a former member of The Honeycombs who had supported The Seekers in the early sixties. As a member of The Honeycombs, Pye had rivalled The Seekers for chart positions with hits like 'Have I the Right' and 'That's the Way'. His renewed association with Judith came about because he was following the same spiritual path.

'Rio was one of those places I'd always wanted to visit,' says Judith.

'Unfortunately, we weren't there during carnival time, but we were really struck by the city's contrasts. On the one hand, there were the dusty backstreets and the poverty and on the other the white sands of Copacabana and the magnificent Sugarloaf Mountain with its cable cars. On the surface, the scenery was beautiful, but the city also had its rough side. When we arrived there, we thought we'd be typical tourists and we went along to a show that advertised voodoo. A few minutes after we arrived, the show was cancelled because the performer had died, presumably due to some sort of black-magic ritual. That was our first inkling that perhaps we shouldn't have really gone to Rio.'

The Rio Song Festival was staged at a local football stadium and attracted a crowd of more than 50,000 people. In a hotel lift, Judith exchanged pleasantries with Paul Simon, who was one of the official judges. This was four years after he'd written 'Someday One Day' for The Seekers. Simon and Garfunkel were at their creative peak, having just topped the charts around the world with 'Bridge over Troubled Water'. She and Ron also struck up a friendship with Ray Conniff, who was another of the judges. Judith remembered all those teenage parties and dancing classes where Conniff's music was played. Come show time, Ron Edgeworth had the magical experience of conducting the sixty-piece orchestra that was backing his wife's performance of 'There He Is' for the contest. The winner of the day was Argentina. The host country, Brazil, was placed third, Britain was eighth and Australia – represented by Judith Durham – was placed ninth.

'I can remember noticing how many people in this huge audience were wearing red,' Judith says, 'and how aggressive the audience was. I was very happy with my performance, but a fight broke out while I was singing and somebody was hit over the head with a camera. The audience got restless because of the disruption and started to boo the people fighting.'

By the time the incident made the papers, headlines around the world screamed JUDY DURHAM SONG FLOPS and JUDY BOOED OFF STAGE. 'It was a misinterpretation of the facts,' Judith says. 'In hindsight, it's interesting that I put myself in that situation. Song contests should be to judge songs, not singers, but it was a wonderful experience in its own way.'

Leaving Rio behind them, Judith and Ron boarded a plane for Australia, via Los Angeles. On that flight, someone asked whether they were headed for Machu Pichu. They had never heard of the place, but were shown intriguing maps and photos by their fellow passenger, who described it as the lost city of the Incas, discovered high in the Andes at the turn of the century. Typical of the Edgeworths' nomadic lifestyle, it seemed like a good idea at the time. When their flight stopped in transit in Lima, Judith and Ron left the plane and headed for Machu Pichu.

'It was another wonderful experience,' Judith recalls. 'We were able to see one of the wonders of the world, and the incredible way this city had been built on the peaks of mountains [and] the way these huge blocks of stone had been laid together in perfectly straight lines, without cement. Ron was challenging me to go higher, to go the extra distance, and we climbed to the highest peak, which seemed as if it was about a kilometre straight up. Being one of the earth's power centres, there was a very spiritual feeling about the place. We ended up spending the night in a little hotel at the top of the mountain peak, with lightning and thunder all around us. Incredible.

'When we got back to Lima, we pulled out our vegetarian handbook again and found a vegetarian restaurant. The girl there didn't speak English, of course, so we made clucking noises like a chicken and drew a picture of a hen and an egg and shook our heads vigorously as we pointed at them. We ordered two lunches, not knowing what we'd end up with and, once again, we were delighted.'

From Peru, Judith and Ron flew to Los Angeles, where photos were taken for the front and back of the *Climb Ev'ry Mountain* sleeve. Again, the people from A&M expressed concern that Judith didn't have a manager and seemed uneasy over her choice of material. The photo session over, the couple flew on to Australia for Christmas and the New Year.

Early in 1971, Judith and Ron returned to England and spent a few nights at the Dorchester Hotel before taking a six-month lease on a house in Highgate Hill in north London. It was at the Dorchester that Judith wrote two more songs. One night, filled with the sadness of yet another tearful farewell to Hazel, Bill and Beverley at Melbourne Airport, she wrote, 'It's Hard to Leave'. Feeling creative, she also wrote 'When Starlight Fades', based on a phrase that, a couple of years previously, her mother had suggested might make a good song.

'Mum knew I was writing songs,' Judith says, 'and she'd heard my first song, "Let Me Find Love", because I sang it at my wedding reception. Back in London, I opened a letter from her one day and in it she had suggested I write a song with the phrase "When starlight fades, the day comes in from somewhere". It was a very hard phrase to find a tune for and I didn't do anything with it for a long time. That night at the Dorchester, after I'd written "It's Hard to Leave", I was thinking of

Mum's suggestion again and the melody just came to me. All of this took place in the bathroom, I have to tell you! I was just thrilled with the two songs and I wanted to sing them to Ron, but it was four in the morning and I didn't dare wake him.'

Within weeks of Judith's arrival in London, 'Climb Ev'ry Mountain' was released as a single and the new album was issued. *Climb Ev'ry Mountain* was a more powerful album than *A Gift of Song* and it was enthusiastically received in Australia. *Listener-In TV* called it the 'best thing she has done since leaving The Seekers'; while the *Melbourne Age* wrote, 'It's an album of which she ought to be proud ... she still sings with that eternal, infernal, virginal freshness and the dozen tracks recorded are genuinely melodic, potted philosophising.' But in Britain it was a different story. The critics gave it a unanimous thumbs-down. *Record Mirror*'s reviewer claimed, 'Miss Durham sings in tune, but I can detect not an ounce of feeling ... choice of material is unusual, but the execution dull and cold.' *Melody Maker* dismissed the album, especially the title track, with 'One is sorry to hear Miss Durham, a fine singer, battling with this crumbling ballad.'

The criticism of the record didn't bother Judith, who welcomed any feedback at all. She had felt a little out of her depth with Chris Gunning's very complex arrangements, particularly as the songs on *A Gift of Song* had been so simply arranged. Once again, she decided that, if recording success was going to elude her, she should return to the stage, where audiences responded so positively and where she felt most at home.

Judith and Ron had very successfully tested the waters with the four one-woman shows. Now, with a five-piece band and the giant MAM agency behind her, Judith mounted her first full tour of Britain, with twenty one-woman shows, kicking off with a February date at London's Royal Festival Hall. 'The bigger promoter came in with a better offer for a longer tour, which Peter Burman and Michael Rouse weren't able to match,' Judith says. 'I felt sad about switching promoters, because they'd been so supportive, but it was business and MAM made a very, very good offer.

'The second lot of shows was as well received as the first four had been. It was a big test for me, vocally, to sing for two hours, but it was enormously satisfying. The musicians we booked could all double on other instruments and it was only then that I discovered Ron could play the trombone. We had an organist who could play trumpet and a guitarist who could play banjo and suddenly we could change from an orchestral sound to a lovely little jazz band. Ron and I talked about traditional jazz

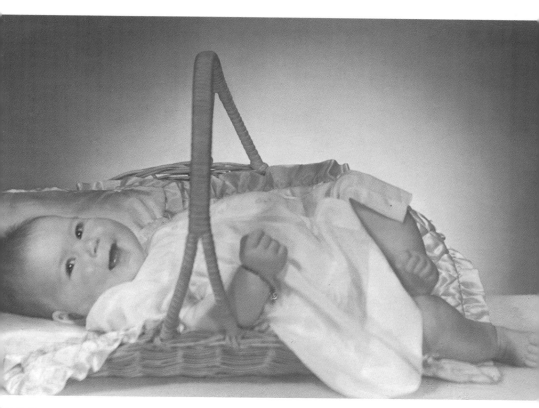

Above Judith Mavis Cock and that famous smile, aged six months. *Durham collection*

Left Judith at nine, mastering her tambourine technique. *Durham collection*

Below Judith's class at Fahan School, Hobart, Tasmania. Judith, aged eight, is the second girl from the left in the front row. *Durham collection*

Above The Cock family – Hazel, Beverley, Judith and Bill – reunited at Essendon Airport during The Seekers' first Australian tour, May 1965. *Herald & Weekly Times*

Left Sixteen-year-old Judith in a dress she made herself. *Durham collection*

Above The Seekers in their first appearance on *The Ed Sullivan Show* in America, 1965. *Simpson collection*

Right A publicity photo of The Seekers in 1967. *Robert Whitaker*

Below The Seekers then and now: in front of Melbourne's Myer Music Bowl, where they drew a crowd of 200,000 people in March 1967, with the line-up returning in the nineties. *Durham collection*

Left Ron and Judith flanked by their Mothers on their wedding day, 21 November 1969. *Durham collection*

Right A publicity shot of Judith in 1972. *A&M Records*

Left Judith and Ron in London, 1969. *Simpson collection*

Right Cliff Richard and Judith, 1970. *TV Week*

Left Judith outside the Hampton Rehabilitation Centre, 1990. *Brendan Beirne*

Right Judith on stage in 1993. *Bob King Photography*

Above Judith with her sister's family, (*Left to right*) Ben, Belinda, Bev and Tony Sheehan, after the filming of *This Is Your Life*. Channel 9

Right Judith with Marianne Faithfull, backstage at Melbourne's Forum Theatre, 1996. *Durham collection*

Below Judith presents the Duchess of York with a copy of the first edition of his book, 1994. *Derek Rowe*

Left Judith takes a final bow at the Royal Festival Hall, London, during her Mona Lisas tour of the UK 1996. *Durham collection*

Right A relaxed Judith Durham takes a break from rehearsals, 2003. *Bryan Siebel*

in our early rehearsals together and, although we agreed it was our musical roots, we didn't think it was challenging enough to pursue as a career. We included a medley of trad jazz to close the first half of our show and we realised how much we loved it. It surprised us to find jazz still so much in our blood.'

Reviews were ecstatic. A review for her Brighton Dome concert raved 'Anything anyone can do, Judith Durham can do better and she proved it in front of nearly 3,000 people'; while *Melody Maker* gushed that, on stage, Judith looked so fragile as to be incapable of producing the mellow, rich, full tones she did. 'I see her now emerging as a singer in her own right and receiving acclaim equal to, if not in excess of, her previous success with The Seekers,' the reviewer concluded. Tell that to the record-buying public! Judith had now hit her stride as a concert performer, fulfilling one lifetime ambition, but it was completely at odds with her recording career.

'On one hand, The New Seekers had been launched and I was being criticised and compared to them,' Judith says. 'On the other, the concerts were a resounding success, but, because the three singles and two albums had been released and nobody supported them, I was seen to have failed as a recording artist. Only the people who came to the one-woman show would have been aware of the success. One of the August shows, at the Octagon Theatre in Bolton, was filmed by the BBC and broadcast as a half-hour special.'

Judith's other problem was cabaret, which really was her bread and butter. Clubs were prepared to pay top money – usually £2,000 a week – for the privilege of presenting Judith Durham in cabaret, but, more often than not, it was with the proviso that she sing Seekers songs in her act.

'I had an overwhelming sense of prostituting myself,' Judith says. 'More and more, I was having to rely on The Seekers to get these bookings. I didn't want to be known for those songs alone, but they were the reason I was being booked. I was also competing more and more with The New Seekers. On occasions, we'd both be considered for the same booking and they'd win out because they had The Seekers' name. That happened on more than one occasion, but I remember specifically that I lost a season at the Talk of the Town and a London Palladium show for that reason. I was constantly asked for my opinion of The New Seekers, even though it really had nothing to do with me. I saw them on television once or twice and I thought they were very good – very professional and very good singers. It seemed a shame to me that they had The Seekers' name, which led to a lot of confusion. I was competing with them, but it was needless competition, because they had their own audience. They actually appealed to a much younger audience than The Seekers had and The Seekers' name really couldn't have been much help to them.'

With *Climb Ev'ry Mountain* faltering, Judith threw herself into a hectic round of television promotional spots, appearing on *The Joe Brown Show*, *Stewpot*, *The Golden Shot* and *The Spinners*, as well as a Cliff Richard television special.

A&M Records believed that, in order for Judith Durham to succeed as a recording artist, she needed a hit single, which, to date, her two A&M albums had failed to deliver. It was their suggestion that Judith go back into the studios and record a cover version of Carole King's 'You've Got a Friend' as her next single. King, who was also an A&M star, had included the song on her multi-platinum *Tapestry* album and it had already been a Number 1 hit for James Taylor in 1971. But Judith didn't want to cover other people's material simply in order to have a hit, so she turned it down.

Towards the end of 1971, Judith and Ron realised that by continuing to live in England, they were simply inviting comparisons with The Seekers – both old and new. Judith was beginning to crave respite from public scrutiny and, besides, their earning power was constantly being diminished by Britain's tax laws. Together they sought legal advice on the possibility of setting up a Swiss company. It was not their intention to use Switzerland as a bogus tax shelter. Indeed, they resolved that, if their business was to operate from Switzerland, they should also move there to live. In order for that to happen, they were told, they would have to apply for Swiss residency, but that would necessitate their having to live somewhere else for a few months.

Settling on Annecy in the South of France as their new base, Ron packed the couple's possessions into the specially ordered, sky-blue, right-hand-drive Citroën they'd bought duty-free in Paris at Easter in 1970. On arrival in Annecy, they moved into a little apartment on the edge of a lake, known as Villa Lac Mer. Judith caught a cold not long after moving into the apartment and, having consciously dispensed with antibiotics and medications since Hopewood, opted for a two-day fast to get over it. Two days later, she felt better but decided she may as well stay on the fast for a while longer. She ended up remaining on the fast for three weeks, with Ron joining her for the last sixteen days.

'I really didn't know a lot about fasting,' Judith says, 'other than it was good for me. By Day 21 of this fast, I was very weak, I ached all over and my lips were completely dried out. I later learned how dangerous fasting that way is. Suddenly, we had begun a long fast without the proper preparation, such as having enemas, eating only fruit and salad, and so on. We could have done ourselves a lot of harm. But it did wonders for me in so many ways. At the end of it, Ron remarked how dainty I looked. That's a term nobody had ever used to describe me before. I was down to seven stone two pounds and all of a sudden I was able to wear the beautiful clothes that were sold in the French boutiques.'

The fast was also creatively inspiring for Judith, who took to writing songs with renewed fervour. The basil plant on her windowsill inspired 'Oh Basil Blues', which would become a staple of her one-woman show. She wrote a song about her father's passion for golf, called 'What Is It About Golf' and completed a song for peace called 'How Long', which Ron had started writing in London. On Day 19 of the fast, with their Swiss residency approved, Judith and Ron drove across the border to register their new company, Troph World AG – later to become Troph Promotions in Australia – and to open a bank account at the International Credit Bank of Geneva. While staying overnight in a Geneva hotel, Judith was inspired with the tune of a song that she originally saw as a gospel but that would ultimately resurface many years later as her anthem, 'Australia Land of Today'. Judith and Ron drove all over Switzerland, looking for somewhere to live. They ruled out Zürich and Geneva and headed across the Alps to the Italian sector.

The rustic seclusion of Lake Lugano immediately appealed to them and it was here that they decided to set up home and base themselves, before flying to Los Angeles to meet an agent introduced to them by A&M.

Back in Annecy, just as they were packing up to relocate, Judith had a phone call from home. Her father Bill had suffered a stroke. Beverley, now a working mother with two young children, had her hands full and Hazel, herself battling deteriorating health, wasn't coping well. Could Judith come home? The news was devastating for Judith. She wanted to be there for her family, but for the first time since their marriage she and Ron faced being separated. In addition, their LA plans looked like being shelved for a while. Ron decided that, although he would miss his wife, he really should remain in Europe and find a home near Lake Lugano for Judith to return to. He drove Judith to Milan airport and the two bade each other a tearful, wrenching farewell.

'Dad was still in hospital when I got back to Australia,' Judith recalls. 'His stroke had been very serious and he had a blood clot somewhere in his neck. His speech was very bad, but he cried when he saw me. It was so touching really. I'd never seen him cry before. He really was happy to see me. I was living back in Balwyn with Mum and stayed on after Dad came home from hospital, trying my best to encourage him to modify his high-cholesterol diet.

'After I'd left Australia following the wedding, Mum had gone through some of the books I had in my bedroom, looking for vegetarian cookbooks. She'd seen what a difference the new diet had made to me and wanted to try it. Instead, she found some books relating to the path Ron and I were on and it made a lot of sense to her. She was always open to alternative ways, much more so than Dad. With each letter I received from her in England, she appeared to get closer to the path and to becoming a complete vegetarian. By the time I arrived home, she had been initiated. But Dad was a different matter. He stuck with his traditional diet and we really could have lost him after the stroke.'

Back in Switzerland, Ron had found an apartment in the hills above Lake Lugano and had moved in their belongings. He had desperately missed Judith in the weeks she'd been in Australia; so, with their new home ready and waiting, he boarded a plane and flew to Melbourne for a tearful reunion. As Bill recuperated, Judith began developing the idea of presenting her one-woman show in a Melbourne venue. She hoped there might be some way of staging the show just once so Hazel could hear 'When Starlight Fades' for the first time on stage. Ron had never acted as a promoter before, but he was confident he could present the show. He contacted the Michael Edgley organisation, which had just acquired the Comedy Theatre in Melbourne, to see whether there was a one-night vacancy. As luck would have it, the theatre was vacant for a week. Ron booked it and set about organising press advertisements and working out some new musical arrangements.

Judith's first Australian concerts for almost four years attracted a lot of media attention, much of it focusing on her happy marriage and spectacular slimming diet. Judith and Ron had taken their raw-food diet a step further and were now sprouting their own wheat and grain and making raw cakes. They bought sunflower and sesame seeds to sprout, ground birdseed and turned kilo after kilo of nuts into nut cream by blending them with honey and water.

Judith opened *An Evening with Judith* to a full house and the next morning got one of the best reviews of her career from the *Melbourne Sun*.

Their reviewer wrote, 'Judith Durham was wonderful. Hearing her as one of a quartet, however famous, was no introduction to the enchanting entertainer we got to know on Saturday night ... Do see her.' That evening, the Melbourne *Herald* claimed:

> Judith Durham parted the dark clouds on Saturday night ... She had all ages standing on their seats, roaring their approval. It was far more than just a welcome home. It was a signal that a world class entertainer had burst on the scene.

Among those roaring their approval were Hazel and Bill, who were astonished by the concert performer Judith had become and thrilled with the reaction she was getting on her own. Interestingly, the journalist who wrote the *Herald* piece had not attended the concert, but, during an interview with Judith, took her word for the positive audience reaction. It worked, and for the remainder of the week the house was fully booked. To accommodate the extra bookings, two matinées were added. Performing four two-hour shows in two days was a real test for Judith, but she breezed through them. Only one newspaper – Melbourne's *Truth* – was negative. Its social writer called the show 'suburbia let loose' and suggested that Judith give her gowns to Granny and start dressing her age!

'I was still very much the ex-Seeker returning home,' Judith says, 'but the audience reaction was just amazing. The shows went very, very well and being able to have Mum and Dad there was very special. Beverley had started singing jazz at Smacka Fitzgibbon's restaurant the year before and one night, when Mum and Dad were in the audience, I got her up on stage and we sang "Coney Island Washboard" as a duet. I just loved that week there and, because of the raw-food diet, I had the most amazing energy. I was able to do two two-hour shows on days when I was staging a matinée, and that was something I'd never have been able to sustain before.'

With a handful of rave reviews, Ron returned to Edgley and, at very short notice, set up a national tour of the one-woman show. From 26 February to 3 March, they played the Theatre Royal in Sydney and one reviewer wrote, 'Sydney has only until Saturday to enjoy a rare, brief appearance here by a local lass who can outmatch in entertainment value a great many of the "name" acts we import.' From there, they moved on to Festival Hall in Brisbane, where the *Courier-Mail* called the show 'two hours of fun'.

Next on the agenda was a stint at Hobart's Theatre Royal, where, many years earlier, Judith had played the mirror in *Snow White* and the principal rat in *The Pied Piper*. This time, she made sure she didn't miss any cues! A week's stint followed at Her Majesty's Theatre in Adelaide before the one-woman show's tour wound up with a week at Her Majesty's in Perth.

Once their tour was under way in earnest, and now that Bill was on the mend, the couple discussed picking up the threads and making that trip to Los Angeles, before going home to Switzerland. However, during their Sydney season, Judith and Ron were invited to a press luncheon, where Ron sat next to a representative of a major shipping line, who enquired about Judith's interest in singing on a cruise. Ron's initial reaction was to turn it down. He learned, however, that this was a millionaires' cruise on a one-class liner – the SS *Mariposa* – and all that would be required of them was three concerts between Melbourne and San Francisco. It wasn't Los Angeles, but it was close. After realising the fun they might have, Judith and Ron decided to accept. It was a decision that would change the next decade of their lives. They planned to spend two weeks holidaying in San Francisco and then travel on to Los Angeles to explore the possibility of mounting the one-woman show in California and finally to meet the important agent who had expressed great interest in Judith some months earlier.

When their Australian tour wound up in Perth, the couple decided that instead of flying back to Melbourne, they would fulfil one of Judith's childhood daydreams and catch the train across the Nullarbor Plain. Their first stop was the West Australian gold-mining town of Kalgoorlie and there they decided to spend a night before resuming their train trip the next day. From Kalgoorlie station, Judith and Ron caught a cab to the nearest motel and, as they pulled up, there was a knock at the car window. The first person they met in Kalgoorlie was the motel's owner Colin Crisp, who had been the tour manager in Australia and New Zealand for The Seekers in the mid-sixties. Judith had intentions of playing tourist for the day, but, once word got around that she was in town, requests for just one show began to filter in. For the sheer hell of it, she and Ron decided to play together in the local hall, their first time ever without backing musicians. Their night at Kalgoorlie Town Hall was such an overwhelming success that they agreed to a second show. To publicise it, Judith wrote a poem, which they read on local television:

When we arrived in historic Kalgoorlie,
We were looking a trifle unruly,

When someone who saw us, began to implore us,
We'd love just one concert – truly!
So on Saturday we did a show,
So that all of Kalgoorlie could go,
But the crux of the matter,
Was the hall should be fatter,
And many missed out – what a blow!
Now on Tuesday at eight, once again,
We'll be there till about half past ten,
And we hope you will show,
'Cause we want you to know,
That Kalgoorlie we love – see you then!

'We ended up staying in Kalgoorlie for a week,' Judith says. 'While we were there, the council announced they were giving me a mayoral reception and all the local dignitaries came together to make speeches. The nice thing was that The Seekers had meant so much to them, but they'd also been able to see me from a different perspective, as a solo performer. It was very touching.'

Bidding the west goodbye, Judith and Ron reboarded their train for Melbourne and, while rattling across the Nullarbor, Judith wrote another song. During their week in Kalgoorlie, someone had presented her with a Tex Morton poem called 'The King of Kalgoorlie', which hailed the landmark statue of the old gold digger Paddy Hannan, who had died of thirst out in the desert. It was Tex's poem that Judith set to music. The freedom she felt, so far away from London and The Seekers, was so liberating that Judith often pinched herself for reassurance that all this was real. In four short years, she had met and married the man she loved and had finally found a way of life that embraced her beliefs. For the remainder of the train trip, she and Ron enjoyed gazing out of the window at the Nullarbor's natural wilderness and dreaming of the property they'd bought during their recent Queensland trip, which would one day become home.

Since their marriage, Judith and Ron had continued reading books relating to spirituality and diet, but had expanded their educational agenda to include textbooks on self-help philosophies. In America, Ron had found two revolutionary books that eventually became a cornerstone in the foundation of their shared life. One was *How I Found Freedom in an Un-Free World*, which offered advice on the search for fulfilment. The other was *How to Prepare for the Coming Crash*, which predicted a forthcoming depression, a fairly off-the-wall concept in the early seventies. According to this book, cities would be unsafe places to live during the oncoming depression and only those who had stocked up would get through the tough time ahead. Looting in the streets would lead to a scarcity of food and only those who were prepared would survive.

During the one-woman show's tour of Australia, Judith and Ron's raw-food diet saw them eating a lot of Australian tropical fruit, much of which came from Queensland. After their recent Brisbane dates, they had taken ten days off and headed north, hopeful that they might find a five-acre lot where they could perhaps grow all their own fruit and become self-sufficient.

'We'd met somebody in an organic-fruit shop in Melbourne, who suggested we contact a man named Ron Bush on the Sunshine Coast,' Judith says. 'We looked Ron up when we were there and he was very, very helpful. We met for a cup of tea and really hit it off. We ended up spending ten days with Ron and his wife Flo and little daughter Cathy, roaming all over the place looking at blocks of land. At first, they had no idea who I was, so their helpfulness was very genuine. They were typical generous-hearted country people. We trudged through the undergrowth in the pouring rain with him, getting leeches all over us. We soon realised that five-acre blocks of land, like the one we had in Lara, just weren't sold on the Sunshine Coast at that time and what was available came in 50- or 100-acre lots. While we were there, we saw a newspaper advertisement headed GET AWAY FROM IT ALL. It was for a large acreage in the hills near Nambour and it included an old homestead, a running creek with natural pools and waterfall, and a few fruit trees. It was everything we were looking for and it sounded too good to be true.

'We fell in love with it the moment we saw it and bought it, all eighty-seven hilly acres of it. Years earlier, it had been a banana farm and there was still a quarter of an acre of bananas there. The homestead was very run down, but that didn't bother us. We weren't buying it with a view to living there, but rather as somewhere we could come for sanctuary if we needed it and, eventually, as the place we would retire to in our old age.'

As their train drew in to Spencer Street station, Judith and Ron knew that, no matter where their nomadic lifestyle took them next, they finally had roots. They had one last emotional farewell with Judith's family and off they set on another of those adventures that had become a trademark of their married life.

10. GOIN' OFF TO SEA

Goin' off to sea,
Soon we're goin' to sail on a tide ocean wide,
Soon we'll glide on the blue,
That's what we're goin' to do.

– 'GOIN' OFF TO SEA'
JUDITH DURHAM

The thought of exploring musical possibilities in America had occurred to Judith and Ron on several occasions before their trip to San Francisco. After Judith had recorded A Gift of Song in Hollywood, she had received a telegram from an American agent named Dan Cleary, who was anxious to represent her in the USA. A&M's desire for her to remain in London as the crowning glory in their London stable prevented her pursuing her prospects. The cruise to San Francisco was a means of eventually catching up with Dan Cleary in Los Angeles – or so they thought. But first the holiday in San Francisco. Judith and Ron boarded the SS Mariposa at Woolloomooloo on 11 July and set sail for America.

'We had a great time on the boat,' Judith says. 'The shows went very well and it was a very enjoyable cruise. The shipping line immediately offered a second cruise, to Alaska, but we were keen to make the most of San Francisco while we could. The medley of jazz numbers we'd featured in our one-woman show had rekindled our interest in the music and on arrival in San Francisco, we asked our hotel doorman if he could suggest a good place we could visit to hear some jazz. The doorman suggested we shouldn't look further than Earthquake McGoon's, a club just down the road co-owned by Turk Murphy, the legendary jazz trombonist, and pianist Peter Clute. McGoon's was a jazz lover's Mecca, but, despite its renown, its overheads were high and it was run on a shoestring budget. It wasn't uncommon to notice Pete missing from the piano – he'd be unblocking the toilets – and at the end of each night it was Turk who would drag out the rubbish bins.'

Murphy was Frank Traynor's idol and Judith knew well the respect he commanded in jazz circles. Earthquake McGoon's was their first stop and, as soon as Judith and Ron walked through the doors of this unique nightclub attraction, they fell in love with trad jazz all over again. 'The minute I heard Turk's band playing I said to Ron, "I just have to sing with this band,"' Judith says. 'It was the first time in years I'd been exposed to full-on, San Francisco, two-beat, sousaphone–banjo jazz and I found it incredibly infectious.'

In a moment that must surely have taken her back to the Memphis in

Melbourne in 1961, Judith nervously approached the bandstand and introduced herself to Murphy as a singer from Australia who used to sing and record jazz in Melbourne many years before. Could she sing with the band? It was *déjà vu* all over again when Murphy looked her up and down and suggested that she come back on a quiet night. Undeterred, Judith and Ron enjoyed the rest of their night at McGoon's, listening to the music and dancing on the crowded dance floor. In the ensuing days, they wandered along to the jazz sessions held on the San Francisco piers and hit the jazz spots at night.

A couple of days after their arrival in San Francisco, Judith met up again with Dave Guard, the former member of the Kingston Trio. Guard offered Judith and Ron rent of a cottage in the grounds of the house he and his wife now owned in Portola Valley, on the outskirts of San Francisco, and the Edgeworths moved in, with plans to stay just a week or two.

One Sunday afternoon, after Ron had seen an advertisement for an afternoon jam session at Pier 23 on the docks, he and Judith set off. The band featured pick-up musicians, but they were very good and, when they launched into Bessie Smith's 'Reckless Blues', Judith jumped up and sang it with them. Unexpectedly, she received a standing ovation after only one chorus. There was no dance floor at Pier 23 and, after Judith's performance, a member of the audience told her he loved her singing. But he said, "I wanna dance to your music." Judith was on her way to the toilet at the time and, while in there, was struck once again with inspiration. Her admirer had triggered a song title with his remark. The next morning, while lying out in the sun in the garden, she put the phrase to music and wrote a verse and chorus. 'It just came to me out there in the sun and it was finished in about half an hour,' Judith says. 'I sang it to Ron and he helped me write the chords for it.'

Another night, Judith and Ron moved on to a pub called the Rose and Thistle, where once again Judith sang a few songs. 'These venues were very low key, but the people they attracted really knew their jazz,' Judith says. 'I was getting incredible reaction from these people, who kept asking me why they hadn't heard of me before. The exhilarating bit for me was getting this level of appreciation from people who had no knowledge of my musical past and didn't associate me with The Seekers. They had no expectations of me and I had no past to live up to. That night at the Rose and Thistle, I had just finished singing "Just a Closer Walk with Thee" and there was a big round of applause that just didn't stop. Then suddenly this drunk stumbled through the doors. He stood there looking stunned as the audience clapped and clapped and he thought it must have been for him, so he took a bow!'

Encouraged by the response from the enthusiastic jazz audiences, Judith decided she'd try her luck again at Earthquake McGoon's. She knew Turk Murphy had given her the brush-off, but persistence had paid off for her in the past and it was worth a try now. She deliberately chose the next 'quiet' Thursday night to approach Murphy and he reluctantly agreed. Like Frank Traynor and so many other jazz greats, Murphy was inundated with requests from singers who wanted to sing with his band and he usually didn't encourage them.

Without rehearsal, Judith stuck with the safety of the blues and performed 'Reckless Blues', 'See See Rider' and 'I Wish I Could Shimmy Like My Sister Kate'. Her sit-in at Earthquake McGoon's was a resounding success and even Turk Murphy was impressed. This tiny girl with long hair could certainly belt it out with the best of them and he was aware his audience liked her. For Judith and Ron, the experience was extraordinarily uplifting. They left the club that night and drove around San Francisco for hours, reliving the experience, finishing up with guacamole at the 24-hour Mexican restaurant at the Fairmont Hotel.

'We were on the most incredible high,' Judith says. 'After I'd sung, I went back to my table to sit with Ron and listen to the band. In the break, Turk's pianist Pete Clute came and joined us and asked if we did an act. In reality, we didn't, although we'd had that experience of working together, just the two of us, in Kalgoorlie. Pete explained that there was a private function at the club the following Monday and he hadn't managed to book anyone for intermissions so far. Were we interested? The way it worked at McGoon's was Turk's band played for forty minutes and then there'd be a twenty-minute intermission that usually featured a banjo player. Then there'd be another forty minutes of the band, and so on, with the intermission act playing five sets.'

Just for fun, Judith and Ron accepted the booking. They hadn't performed much jazz for years and had little in the way of arrangements, but, for sentimental reasons, Judith always carried with her the chord book that John Tucker, one of the University Jazz Band members, had helped her put together all those years ago in Melbourne. All through the following weekend in Portola Valley, they plundered the book and rehearsed as many jazz and blues standards as they could, throwing in the odd torch song for variety. Especially for the show, they learned songs such as 'Body and Soul' and 'Can't Help Lovin' Dat Man of Mine'.

The following Monday night, they played five sets at Earthquake McGoon's and went down a storm. In Judith's set were songs such as Ma Rainey's 'Jelly Bean Blues', Bessie Smith's 'I've Got What It Takes' and 'Cake Walkin' Babies From Home', along with 'Gimme a Pigfoot and a Bottle of Beer', 'After You've Gone', 'Body and Soul' and 'He's Funny That Way'. In each song, Ron would be featured in a solo, although he didn't know some of the tunes. 'How does this one go, Jude?' he'd whisper. But the audience loved them. They thought the cute Australian girl could sing up a storm and the tall English guy was pretty darn good on the piano, too. Best of all, they really knew their stuff, even if they were baffled how such a young Australian girl could sing old-style American music with such authenticity. By the time she'd finished, both she and Ron knew that a change in their musical direction was imminent. In performing jazz again, they had unleashed dormant energies and emotions and musically blended them to each other and their audience.

A short time later, they received a call from Pete Clute, offering them a residency at McGoon's, because the resident banjo player was taking a holiday. Judith and Ron jumped at the chance and celebrated by buying themselves a new Mercedes. 'Buying a Mercedes in America was a very extravagant thing to do,' Judith says, 'but we saw it in a car showroom and decided we just had to have it. It was a beautiful, silver, two-door coupe 300SL and we justified the expense because we figured we'd be doing a lot of driving in America in the coming months. I woke up the next morning and looked out and saw it gleaming in the morning sun and said to Ron, "What have we done?" But stepping back into jazz after so many years was very liberating for both of us. Ron started getting into the music more and more and was getting a great deal of artistic satisfaction from it and I loved the freedom. I was truly being appreciated as an artist, by people who weren't looking at me and seeing the girl from The Seekers.'

The pair opened at McGoon's in September as the resident intermission act, organising their repertoire so that Ron had the opening spot playing piano solo, as he had studied pieces by Fats Waller, Jelly Roll Morton and James P Johnson. He'd seldom played stride piano before but was able to develop his left-hand technique there on Clay Street. For the remainder of the evening, Ron would take solos between Judith's vocal choruses. Judith also stayed on the stage when Turk's band returned, and sang the first two songs of the band's set. Word started getting around about these two Aussie musicians who played and sang jazz. Even Phil Elwood, the hard-nosed critic on the *San Francisco Examiner*, was impressed. Reviewing one of the shows, he wrote, 'Miss Durham seems to have perfected pitch and no rhythmic inconsistencies. Combined with good taste and a willingness, in fact enthusiasm, to interpret and improvise, it makes her a quite sensational performer.'

But Judith's anonymity was short-lived. It took only a few busloads of tourists passing through Earthquake McGoon's for word to reach Turk Murphy that his new 'discovery' had in fact been a famous pop singer. Three weeks after the start of their engagement, Turk eventually confronted Judith and asked if the rumours were true. Judith's heart sank as she confessed that, yes, she had been a member of a pop group called The Seekers. Far from being angry that he'd been duped, Turk was star-struck. He thought it was nifty that someone famous might want to sing intermissions in his club. His main concern seemed to be that perhaps he wasn't paying them enough. Not that Turk was any stranger to having famous people sitting in. In November that year, Woody Allen contacted Turk, as he often did, to enquire hesitantly whether he might sit in on clarinet with the band. Turk welcomed him, as always, and Judith was delighted to meet someone even more shy than she was.

'Performing on the same stage as Woody Allen was a big thrill,' Judith says. 'He was very humble, not really believing he had any special talent on the clarinet. He played very much in the New Orleans traditional jazz style, very authentic in the vein of George Lewis. Another night, Clint Eastwood came in and Turk introduced us. He was a big fan of Turk's and he would come up from his home in Big Sur and have a relaxed night every now and again. He was so incredibly good-looking, but much slighter and more delicate than I would have imagined. He was the first big movie star I'd ever met and he was very complimentary about my voice. He told us how much he had enjoyed our set.'

Judith and Ron settled into a long residency at McGoon's, still enjoying sit-ins around town with other local bands. One of the stranger American customs they had to get used to, particularly at McGoon's, was receiving tips. 'A lot of up-and-coming acts in America virtually rely on tips to make a living,' Judith explains. 'It took some getting used to, reaching out to shake someone's hand and having a fifty-dollar note put in it.

'I was in a dilemma for a while, trying to work out whether I should keep the money or give it back. But giving it back, I was told, would offend someone who had done it as a means of expressing appreciation. We ended up keeping the tips. Ron would be asked to play requests and people would give him money as a way of saying thank you.

'Before long, I tried singing "I Wanna Dance to Your Music" at McGoon's. I felt a bit wary of doing my own material there, because the place was renowned for traditional jazz, but it turned out Turk was a bit of a composer himself and he didn't mind at all. Ultimately, before we left San Francisco, Turk gave me two of his tunes and asked me to put words to them.'

As resident singer, Judith often mingled with the audience after her performance, and became accustomed to being stopped and heartily congratulated. Once, she was stopped by an American woman who gushed her praise. Sitting within earshot was an Australian woman who remarked, 'Oh, you should have heard her with the three boys in the group', whereupon the American woman disdainfully replied, 'I don't care about no group. She's great on her own!'

By the time Judith and Ron had worked McGoon's for six months, they were ready for a break. With so many patrons wanting to meet her, and having to yell to be heard above Turk's band, Judith's voice started to suffer and she needed to rest it. It was Ron's idea to utilise the time off by putting a band together and recording some tracks, in response to hundreds of requests from the McGoon's audience and in the hope that a bouncy, two-beat jazz record would show another side of Judith Durham that few of her fans back in Australia and the UK knew existed.

Realising they would be staying in San Francisco longer than they had originally intended, Ron and Judith moved from Portola Valley to a stilt home in the artistic colony environs of Mill Valley. After contacting musicians, writing arrangements and assembling a band, they hired a tiny recording studio in San Francisco's Chinatown and got down to work.

To save money, they decided to produce the tracks themselves, although they had very little knowledge of the processes involved. Outside their difficult encounter with 'Let Me Find Love' in 1970, they had next to no experience at the console and, before long, it showed. Initially, four tracks were put down and Ron went down to see record companies in Los Angeles, where the big deals were done. Most showed interest, but wanted them to complete the album and come calling again. The two decided to go ahead and complete an album, but decided they would first surprise Ron's mother and spend Christmas of 1973 in England, where the family was gathering for the festive season. They were looking forward to surprising Ron's brother Pat and his new wife Angela, who had flown there from Australia.

Judith and Ron flew from America to Switzerland, where Judith saw their Lake Lugano apartment for the first time. They fired up their trusty sky-blue Citroën DS21 and drove to London, rolling up outside Ron's mother's house singing Christmas carols at the front door. After so long on raw food, they broke their diet and ate a curry, their first cooked meal in two years. They enjoyed a magical family Christmas, and, filled with the spirit of such a happy occasion, drove back to Switzerland.

Ten days later, they flew back to San Francisco to complete the album. They had a fixed line-up now, comprising Jim Goodwin on trumpet, Jerry Butzen on trombone, Phil Howe on clarinet and soprano sax, Ed Turner on banjo and Bill Maginnis on drums, with John Moore replacing Tom Rutley on sousaphone and string bass, and Ron on piano as leader of the band. The tracks they laid down included many of the songs Judith had sung at McGoon's. The album kicked off with 'I Wanna Dance to Your Music' and also included another blues song Judith had written called 'Mama's Got the Blues'. Their primary problem was that the sound engineer, Stephen Eldridge, who had recorded the first four songs, had returned to Boston for Christmas and wasn't coming back. In his place for the rest of the album was an inexperienced engineer, and leaks on the vocal track made it impossible to record overdubs. Judith and Ron were still proud they'd completed the album when – to their shock and horror – they discovered they had mixed the entire album in mono!

Meanwhile, Judith and Ron had received a phone call from Robin Blanchflower, who'd worked for A&M Records in London when Judith was signed to the label. Blanchflower had since left A&M and joined Pye Records and wondered whether Judith was interested in recording for Pye. Ron explained that, by coincidence, they had a new album almost completed and that when it was ready they would send it on to him for consideration. That arrangement in place, they realised their botched album needed a lot of work and resolved to take the tapes to Boston en route to London, to have them remixed in stereo by Stephen Eldridge.

So, after packing up their house in Mill Valley, they loaded the Mercedes to the roof and set off for Boston. They had not gone very far when the weather started to get very hot and Judith became worried that the master tapes in the back of the car might melt in the heat. They decided to buy a car fridge to put the tapes in and pulled up at a supermarket. Judith took the tapes in with her to make sure they bought the right size car fridge. She saw one that looked ideal but it was very high up on a shelf. Without thinking, in a move that could have demagnetised the tapes and erased everything they'd recorded, she put the master tapes down on the supermarket fridge on top of some frozen chickens!

The car fridge was crammed into their already crowded car and off they went, hurtling along the freeway towards Boston. Judith navigated while Ron drove and, as she read the map, she noticed how many American cities she knew from song titles or movies or television shows – places such as San Francisco, Laramie, Cheyenne, Chicago. She realised that very few Australian towns had been commemorated in the same way. On that trip to Boston, Judith thought Bendigo sounded like a good word for a song and wrote 'Bendigo-O', as well as a song for Melbourne. These were the beginnings of an *Australian Cities Suite* that would take shape over the next two decades.

Having broken their raw-food diet in London, they were allowing themselves a lot of treats – in Judith's case chocolate. Driving along in the car munching on chocolate, Judith was pondering about how fat she'd become since Christmas. Nevertheless, she was enjoying the chocolate so much that she wrote 'It's Fun to Be Fat' on the back of a scrap of paper. Passing through Lake Tahoe, they noticed that Elvis Presley was performing a Mother's Day concert. There were still tickets available, but with a deadline to meet in Boston they didn't stop and see the show. It remains one of Judith's biggest regrets to this day.

There was method in their madness, travelling to Boston. They'd heard a couple of years earlier from a fan in Hobart who had suggested that, should they ever get to Boston, the Hippocrates Health Institute run by Dr Ann Wigmore was well worth a visit for raw-food enthusiasts. Known as the Wheatgrass Institute, it would become world-famous in years to come for its wheatgrass therapy, which enjoyed some success in curing cancer and other illnesses. For the three weeks they were in Boston, Judith and Ron lived at the institute, enjoying the homegrown raw foods and learning more and more about health and survival. It was here they learned of the importance of enemas in a fasting regime, so that toxins are not reabsorbed. For six days, they stuck to a juice fast, drinking mostly wheatgrass and watermelon-rind juices.

Stephen Eldridge was available to remix their album only between midnight and dawn. So, by day, they read and slept, before working in the studio through the night. One morning, as they emerged bleary-eyed from the darkened studio, Eldridge remarked to Ron, 'It's going to be a beautiful day. What a shame to have to sleep it away.' He turned to Judith and said, 'There's a song title for you', and before long 'It's Going to Be a Beautiful Day' was born.

'We had a great time mixing the album in Boston,' Judith says. 'The people who owned the studio were very interested in the album and in managing me. They took copies of the mixed tapes with them to New York to see if they could do anything there. They were very supportive. The problem they had was that, while all the record companies loved the album, it was really a jazz record and there wasn't much they could do with it at the time. We heard the same story in LA, too.'

With the album remixed in stereo, the Mercedes was garaged in Boston and Judith and Ron flew home to Switzerland. Ron forwarded the tapes to Pye, who had decided to Judith's delight that 'I Wanna Dance to Your Music', backed with 'Mama's Got the Blues', would be the first single. Meanwhile, in London, a cousin of Ron's had died and he and Judith decided to bring his mother Vicky and grieving Aunt Olive to Switzerland for a holiday. It was while Judith was outside their apartment, cutting her mother-in-law's hair, that Vicky Edgeworth solved Judith's biggest dilemma: what to name her jazz band. Vicky's suggestion of the Hottest Band in Town was music to Judith's ears.

Judith liked the idea of having a song for her band, à la Alexander's Ragtime Band. A short time later, while returning from a day trip to Ascona with Vicky and Olive, she wrote the future album track, 'The Hottest Band in Town' on the back of an envelope. She and Ron liked Ascona so much that, after their relatives had flown back to England, they returned and found a house they liked called Ca' del Sass' (house of rock), built into a rockface overlooking Lake Maggiore. Soon after, they left Lugano and moved in.

For a short time they were parted while Ron returned to London in the Citroën to finalise contracts with Pye. At home in Switzerland, Judith decided to buy her very first grand piano, a second-hand Bechstein. It was a dream come true. Meanwhile, Ron had visited Harrods in Knightsbridge and wandered around the musical-instruments department trying out the merchandise. He was wearing his old jeans and his scruffy appearance prompted a curt salesman to ask him to stop playing the pianos. Without batting an eyelid, Ron left the salesman speechless by casually announcing he'd take the brand-new Bechstein, thanks very much! Where other married couples were content with 'his and her' towels, the Edgeworths had 'his and her' grand pianos!

It had been two years by now since Judith had seen her Mum and Dad. With an album ready to come out early in 1974, she decided to fly home alone to Australia to see them. Wishing to remain as anonymous as possible on what was only to be a quick, three-week personal visit, Judith left Milan airport wearing a wig and dark glasses. She was anxious to avoid any airport fuss and had planned to slip through customs, into a cab and arrive at her parents' Balwyn home undetected. Her flight stopped in Singapore in transit and, after takeoff for Melbourne, an announcement was made that a passenger was in labour and the flight would have to land at Darwin, the first available airport. This meant Darwin would be Judith's first port of entry into Australia and, as was the rule in those days, routine health checks would be made there. Judith carried with her a letter exempting her from smallpox vaccinations on health grounds, but, as she had been in transit in Singapore, she now was required either to be vaccinated or to be quarantined for fourteen days.

Judith angrily had to opt for the latter and was held in East Arm Quarantine Station, a few kilometres out of Darwin, for fourteen days and not a minute less. With her luggage flown on to Melbourne, her only clothes were those she was wearing on the plane. All alone, she turned this waste of time to her advantage. She began a five-day water fast, swam daily in the compound's pool and, as well as writing 'Quarantine Station Blues', finally wrote the words to Turk Murphy's tune, 'Some Other Time'.

'I was so cross I had to be quarantined,' Judith says. 'I had planned to spend three special weeks with Mum and I'd lost two of them because of this ridiculous situation. What capped it off for me was that, on the fourteenth day, the first plane out of Darwin to Melbourne was six hours before my quarantine period was actually up and they wouldn't let me catch it. I had to wait until the following day. It was wicked, it really was.'

Judith arrived back in Melbourne on 21 November – the day of her fourth wedding anniversary – and was reunited with Hazel and Bill. Since they would be apart on their anniversary, Ron wrote, 'A Theme for Judith', as a tribute to the woman he loved. A cassette of the song awaited Judith on her arrival in Melbourne.

'I had the most marvellous time with Mum,' Judith says. 'It was a very precious time, catching up on the past couple of years. I was able to talk to her about all sorts of things: our family history, her feelings about being a mother, our health, the path. We had long chats and we both felt great by the time I had to leave. I'd rung Ron and told him I was stuck in quarantine and that I was going to have to stay a little longer in Australia to compensate. We agreed we'd meet each other in New York just before Christmas.'

Until her last two days in Darwin, Judith's disguise had worked, but as soon as she arrived in Melbourne she was inundated with reporters and photographers and stories of her incarceration appeared in newspapers all over the world. The national and international press also carried a story claiming The Seekers would re-form following a $750,000 offer for a TV show and world tour. Their English accountant told the press he was trying to get the group back together, but Judith Durham had shown no interest. In a later interview, Athol Guy told Melbourne's *Sun* that the group had received several offers to re-form in the past two years, but that he had not seen Judith in a long time. 'She seems to have some bug about past associations with the group,' Guy said, 'which is a little hard to understand since she has not really published anything in her own right since we broke up.'

Judith was hurt when she read stories like these, although she secretly hoped the boys had been misquoted. She still felt that no one understood her personal needs or had appreciated her devotion and loyalty to The Seekers when she had been a member. Sensing that a new burst of Seekers publicity might overshadow her forthcoming album, Judith tried to distance herself from the reunion reports, but was eventually pinned down by London's *Reveille* newspaper. 'I have my memories,' she told *Reveille*. 'I want to remember us as we were. It's like remembering a favourite holiday. It's never the same when you go back.'

Judith and Ron were reunited in New York, where they attended the International Jazz Festival at the New York Hilton and spent a white Christmas, before flying back to London for the release of 'I Wanna Dance to Your Music', the single taken from the album *Judith Durham and the Hottest Band in Town*. Having to perform live to promote the album, they put together a British line-up of the Hottest Band in Town in great haste.

They handpicked some of the cream of the London trad-jazz scene, all great players.

Aside from Ron on piano, Judith's new band featured Phil Franklin on drums, Dennis Field on cornet, Terry Pitts on trombone, Hugh Rainey on banjo and guitar and Bob Taylor on sousaphone and string bass. Judith was delighted to include on clarinet and soprano sax her old friend from her Ken Colyer days, Sammy Rimington, who had by now become an international jazz star himself. Judith also signed an agency deal with Colin Hogg, who was well known in jazz circles as the agent for bands such as Acker Bilk, Alex Welsh and Chris Barber. Coincidentally, Hogg had taken over Eddie Jarrett's original office at 235 Regent Street, after Jarrett had moved to Savile Row.

To promote 'I Wanna Dance to Your Music', the Hottest Band in Town

THE JUDITH DURHAM STORY: COLOURS OF MY LIFE

appeared on several television shows, including the BBC's *Nationwide*, Thames TV's *Today* and *Sunday Night at the London Palladium*. On *The Benny Hill Show*, they performed the single and 'Cake Walkin' Babies from Home'. The single didn't chart, but it did receive a great deal of airplay and was used as a dance track by the Young Generation on Rolf Harris' show.

Reviews were mixed: *Disc* wrote, 'The voice is unmistakable. It was a great shame when The Seekers broke up, we can but hope that this marks the return of their leading lady to the music business.' *Record Mirror* played it safe by calling the disc 'earthy', while the *Staffordshire Evening Sentinel* dismissed it as 'a totally unsuitable vehicle'. Nevertheless, the Young Generation danced to it throughout an entire London Palladium season headlined by Ethel Merman. Judith had made a major mark as a writer, and in years to come the fans and friends Judith had left behind in America would jealously guard their copies of the albums, which were given pride of place in their collections of Bessie Smith and Ethel Waters.

With their first round of appearances and artwork for the cover of the album complete, Judith and Ron packed the Citroën for their return to Ascona. On the night of their departure, they decided to have a look at London's 100 Club, a venue being considered for a Hottest Band in Town show. They spent an hour or so inside the club and found when they returned to their car that they'd been robbed. The Citroën had been rifled and missing were their passports, travellers' cheques and two of Judith's stage dresses. More distressing for Judith was the loss of the pearl pendant that had been a gift from Hazel and Bill, and had featured so often in early Seekers publicity photos.

They finally made it back to Switzerland and, elated with the success of the single, Judith rang Hazel in Melbourne to let her mother know that 'I Wanna Dance to Your Music' had helped her find her niche. Two days later on 18 March, Judith's brother-in-law, Barry, phoned with the devastating news that Hazel had died. Hazel's already bad health had deteriorated rapidly in the previous two years and, while her life had been under threat constantly, her death still came as a shock. Judith's dilemma was whether or not to return to Australia for her mother's funeral. Only three months earlier, they had spent three happy weeks together.

'It seemed that trip to Australia the previous year had been a settling of our relationship,' Judith says. 'It was a moment when I was being given the opportunity to say goodbye, without realising that's what I was doing. Aside from Ron, Mum was my best friend and her death left a huge gap in my life. But on the spiritual path I follow, which Mum also followed, death has a different meaning than it does for a lot of people. I view death in a positive way, to an extent. I grieved for Mum, but by remaining in Switzerland I was able to concentrate on the positive aspects of it all.

'I found it very hard to play the piano for a while after Mum's death, because it reminded me of her so much, and her encouragement with my music. For a time, it was also very difficult for me to sing "After You've Gone", because I was reminded of her calling out for it from the kitchen when I was a little girl.'

Four days after Hazel's death, *Judith Durham and the Hottest Band in Town* was released. Once again, Judith and Ron packed up their Citroën and headed for London, where a showcase performance and a small jazz tour awaited them. So too did mixed reviews for the album. The *Hendon Times* loved it, claiming 'She is superb ... a dynamite set to explode in a new minefield of talent. Fabulous Judith, keep it blues.' *Melody Maker*, on the other hand, was positively acerbic:

If this is the Hottest Band in Town, we're in for a mighty cold winter. Judith Durham was and is one of the classier singers to crack the hit parade. Yet this record amply proves the lady should stick to what she can do best, for this little foray into trad jazz is nothing short of disaster.

Referring to the album as 'a stilted, embarrassing affair', the critic claimed Judith came over 'like a society lady in a back street disco'.

On 28 March, Pye Records introduced Judith and Ron and the Hottest Band in Town to the media with a showcase reception at the famous jazz club, Ronnie Scott's. The performance was a resounding success, moving the jazz critic Bob Eborall to write:

The music scene audience at a party at London's Ronnie Scott's Club was very impressed with Judith and her Hottest Band in Town, consisting of British jazzmen. They yelled out for an encore, which doesn't happen every day with such a hard showbusiness audience.

Two nights later, Judith and the band played at London's 100 Club, which would later become the birthplace of punk rock in Britain. For Judith, it was a great thrill performing at the same club where all the greats of the trad jazz scene had played. Again, their performance was greeted with wild enthusiasm and it seemed that Judith Durham the jazz singer was back in business. Pye Records had been pleased with the success of the album and had asked for a second one to capitalise on its success. With recording sessions booked through May and June, Judith and Ron took the Hottest Band in Town on the road in April, for a six-date tour that played to full houses and received glowing reviews.

The tour behind her, Judith headed back into the studios to record *The Hottest Band in Town Volume II*. This time, she would record three of her own songs, 'The Hottest Band in Town', 'It's Going to Be a Beautiful Day' and 'Chase Those Blues Away', the latter having come to her while she was cleaning the bath one afternoon in Switzerland! Some standards were chosen and Judith also included a song she'd learnt at Earthquake McGoon's, called 'Louisville Lou (The Vampin' Lady)'. Ron's arrangement of 'Papa If You Can't Do Better' came into the repertoire after Turk Murphy's trumpet player, Leon Oakley, included an early version on a tape for her. Rounding out the set were two old Bessie Smith favourites, 'On Revival Day' and 'Nobody's Blues But Mine', as well as her own fine piano version of Scott Joplin's 'The Entertainer', which had been recently popularised in the film *The Sting*. The final track was Irving Berlin's 'What'll I Do', which had been used as the opening song in the movie *The Great Gatsby*. Pye was anxious to have the song as a single for Judith and many hours were spent remixing it in the studio and adding echo to get that old 1920s ballroom feel. The single was finally completed and Pye released it ahead of the new album, but in a masterstroke of bad planning, the company also released a version by Des O'Connor on the same day. Again, Judith's 'masterpiece' sank without a trace.

With the album completed and the decision made to release 'It's Going to Be a Beautiful Day' as its second single, Judith and Ron packed up and flew to Australia. There, Judith was to make her acting debut in the television drama series, *Cash & Company*. Ron's brother Patrick had stayed on in Australia after Ron's wedding in 1969 and, having worked as an actor for a couple of years, had made a name for himself as a scriptwriter. With his partner Russell Haig, he formed his own production company, Homestead Films, whose first major project was *Cash & Company*, a goldfields drama being made for the Seven Network and starring Gus Mercurio, Serge Lazareff, Penne Hackforth-Jones and Bruce Kerr. Patrick wrote an episode, entitled 'Golden Girl', with both his brother and sister-in-law in mind. He cast Judith as goldfields singer Sarah Simmons, with – surprise, surprise – Ron as Charlie Owens, her pianist. In the hour-long episode, Judith would be required to sing her own composition 'When Starlight Fades', as well as 'Maggie May', 'Home Sweet Home', 'Oh! Susannah', 'The Lord Is My Shepherd' and 'Rock of Ages'. The director for the shoot would be Simon Wincer, now a world-renowned Hollywood director, who would be very understanding of Judith's 'first-night nerves' as a TV actress. Before filming got under way, Judith got wind of Turk Murphy's first Australian tour and, through an arrangement with the promoter Kym Bonython, was made surprise guest artist at several of Murphy's concerts in Melbourne, Sydney and Adelaide. Judith's appearances with Turk attracted a lot of publicity and when she met him at Tullamarine Airport one of his greatest fans – Frank Traynor – turned up, seeing Judith for the first time in many years.

After Turk left the country, Judith and Ron began work on *Cash & Company*. Part of the filming was done at Emu Bottom Homestead in Sunbury, Victoria, and the remainder was shot on a set in a Melbourne city building that had been taken over by Homestead Films. Filming was completed in two weeks and most mornings they were required on the set by 5.30, often working through until late in the evening.

'The television role was a big challenge for me,' Judith says, 'having never really acted in front of a camera before. Gus Mercurio was just the most wonderful person to work with. Penne Hackforth-Jones and the others were terrific too and the story was very well put together. Ron was the surprise packet, though. Everybody was so impressed with his spontaneity and wit on camera, the way he performed what he was doing. It was only a small part, but he put so much into it.'

In the little spare time she had, Judith enjoyed being at home with Bill and greatly admired the way he had adapted to his new life without Hazel. Bill had found new strength in his growing fondness for Dulcie, an old friend of his and Hazel's from their Shell Company days. After so many years of devotion to Hazel and the sacrifices he made, Judith and Beverley were very supportive of this renewed friendship.

Filming ended just as Judith was being splashed across the pages of the daily newspapers again, with yet another story about The Seekers re-forming. Again, the press made much of the idea that Athol, Keith and Bruce were interested in singing as The Seekers again, but that Judith Durham was emphatically against the idea. The interviews she did before leaving Australia were to have promoted *Cash & Company* and her jazz album, but the press preferred to concentrate on her refusal to rejoin The Seekers.

On the way home to Switzerland, Judith and Ron stopped off in India once again to see their Master at the colony, where people live in the Master's spiritual environment and do service. 'Our path is a path of meditation, with the Master being our spiritual guide,' Judith explains. 'To be in his presence is the ultimate physical experience. As our path's an inner one with meditation as its focus, it is not necessary to ever see the Master, but it is wonderful to have that opportunity if you can. We valued our visits to India very much. They gave us the chance to remove ourselves from the full-on pell-mell of show business and spend time in a spiritual world. Many people would go and hear the Master's discourses and we were happy to be one of up to two hundred and fifty thousand people. To actually be in the Master's presence in a smaller group is very unusual and we were very lucky to have had that experience twice.

'The path has been such a very important part of my life with Ron. It's a practical scientific path, the journey to God realisation. There are many gurus but not many "Perfect Masters", and people must make their own search. I believe if you are ready you will be brought into contact with a teacher. In that way, it was my destiny to come into contact with Ron and, through him, to have found a path that is totally right for me. The karmic aspect is that things that happen to you in this life are the result of unpaid debts and credits from previous lives. Karma continues life after life and you are caught up in an endless cycle of births and deaths, debts and credits you've had with all the souls you come into contact with in each life. That's what helps me to come to terms with all the things that happen to me in this life. It gives me a tremendous sense of acceptance and peace and worthiness about my life, and a goal far beyond anything tangible or material.'

After six days with their Master, and filled with renewed spiritual awareness, Ron and Judith returned to Ascona to prepare for their British tour and the release of the new album. Within days, they found themselves back on the treadmill again and before the year was over, they would need all the inner strength they could draw on. First of all their drummer, Phil Franklin, phoned them from London to give them more bad news. There was a major audio fault on one of the tracks on the album and, just as Judith was to kick off the tour to launch the album, Pye had recalled 2,000 copies because of a 'pressing fault'. So, when Judith and Ron arrived in London early in October to start their Hottest Band in Town tour, Judith was promoting an album that wasn't available in record stores.

To her horror, Judith found that while she and Ron were away Pye had decided that 'It's Going to Be a Beautiful Day' was too long to be a single and had edited the instrumental passage out, and in doing so had accidentally stretched the master tape. It was this edit that had resulted in the 'pressing fault' on the album and may also have contributed to the single's bad reception. Typical of the canning the single got was a review from the *Herts & Cambs Reporter*, whose reviewer wrote:

> It's Going to Be a Beautiful Day – well, it was until I heard this new single from Judith Durham. Let's face it, where has Judith got herself by going solo – absolutely nowhere. And if she keeps on producing this sort of rubbish, she will do it to the end of her time.

The four-week tour, taking in England and Scotland, lost money. The dates had not been properly advertised and numbers were down. Still, the shows received rave reviews and audiences were ecstatic; but the tour was capped off when, typical of Judith's regular encounters, she was abused in a Scottish petrol station by a woman who was incensed that she'd 'broken up' The Seekers. On another date, she was mistaken for The New Seekers' Eve Graham and asked to sing 'I'd Like to Teach the World to Sing'!

Already that year, Judith had lost her mother; she and Ron had been robbed; her single had been ruined; her album had been recalled, badly affecting her tour; and she was fighting a losing battle with the press over her reluctance to rejoin The Seekers. The boys had even announced they would re-form the following year with a new female singer replacing Judith. But there was worse to come. First, the silver Mercedes they so loved, which had been taken out of storage and shipped to them in London, was wrecked upon arrival. On the docks, someone had started the engine, oblivious of the fact that the car had been drained. The engine seized, causing £2,000 worth of damage.

Eventually the car was repaired and returned to Switzerland, but, while they were still in London, a much bigger disaster struck. One morning, while Judith was ironing, Ron was reading a newspaper in his mother's kitchen. He was horrified to find that the International Credit Bank of Geneva had collapsed. Suddenly, overnight, Judith and Ron had lost all their money.

'We didn't have a bean,' Judith says. 'It was such a shock with no warning at all. All the money I had made from The Seekers had been put into that bank and, although we'd used a lot of it on our travels and making the albums, we lost all our savings. We had always been able to make professional decisions according to what we thought was right, financing our own albums and going wherever we wanted. Suddenly, that freedom no longer existed and Ron and I became totally reliant on work.'

As Christmas 1974 approached, a phone call came out of the blue from the Australian promoter Malcolm Cooke, who had been tour manager on The Seekers' 1965 Australian tour. He was interested in having Judith as an attraction at the 1975 Summer in the City festival in Melbourne. Judith and Ron jumped at the offer. With no money of their own for airfares, they suddenly had a way of getting back to Australia, where they had a property, family and, most important of all now, work. So that Australian audiences could see Judith Durham as the international jazz singer she had now become, Ron persuaded Cooke to include the English line-up of the Hottest Band in Town in the deal. Things, finally, were looking up.

Back home in Switzerland, the couple tried to take stock. They had no ready cash and, for the time being, no work. They decided to put Judith's five-acre block of land in Lara on the market, but its sale was many weeks coming. In the meantime, they could only tough it out in Ascona, as frugally as they could. One blessing was their earlier instinct to stock up on survival food. Having read *How to Prepare for the Coming Crash* and believing a worldwide depression was looming, Judith and Ron had begun stocking their Ascona home with seeds to sprout. They'd learned new methods of sprouting from the Wheatgrass Institute in Boston and were now able to put them into practice so that when the depression came, they could survive by being self-sufficient. Through the weeks ahead, they lived on sprouted lentils, alfalfa and mung sprouts, all painstakingly prepared by Judith, but it didn't stop them giving in to the temptation of Swiss Suchard chocolate for dessert!

The drama, however, wasn't quite over. Their Swiss residency permits were up for renewal and, this time, the Swiss government was questioning their right to residency status. Permits were granted annually and the authorities claimed that in the past twelve months Judith and Ron had been out of the country too much. The Swiss government altered their permits to visitor status, which effectively meant they would have to leave Switzerland immediately.

'Now we were not only broke, but homeless as well,' Judith says. 'We had to get out of our agreement with Pye Records, because they had totally breached their contract and as a result I had virtually thrown away two good albums. So there we sat, pondering our future.'

Ron phoned their friend Ron Bush in Queensland to ask his advice about making the house on their Nambour property habitable. It could be done, Bush told them, but it would mean a lot of hard work. This was the plan, but, as fate would have it, it would be quite some time before they would begin the renovation process and have their first taste of life as residents and landowners in Queensland.

After the money from the sale of the Lara land came through, the Edgeworths packed up their home. The pianos and other bulky items went into storage, to be sent on to Melbourne later, and the rest of their belongings were packed into their two cars. With Judith driving the Mercedes and Ron behind the wheel of the Citroën, the two travelled in convoy through France to London. They stayed for a time with Vicky in East Ham before flying to New York, en route to what they hoped would be a fruitful 1975 in Australia.

11. CHASING THOSE BLUES AWAY

The blues get everyone,
When everything goes wrong,
But do you make it fun,
Tryin' to make them move along?

– 'CHASE THOSE BLUES AWAY'
JUDITH DURHAM

After spending the first two weeks of 1975 in America, Judith and Ron flew in to Melbourne on 16 January, ready to open the first of three nights as the headlining act at the Summer in the City concerts at Melbourne's Myer Music Bowl.

Judith had less than a week to enjoy her private life before she was innocently embroiled in a new controversy. Her Hottest Band in Town tour was booked to travel round the country to Victoria, New South Wales and Tasmania from 30 January through to 15 February, but already there had been a hitch. A Bendigo concert had been scheduled for the 1,200-seater White Hills Technical School but Judith and the band were banned by the school's principal, Mr Dingle, who objected strongly to the group's name. Seizing a perfect publicity opportunity, much was made by the tour's publicist of the principal's objections. The story made the front pages of most of the Australian daily newspapers and many more throughout England.

Mr Dingle told the press that a number of functions held in the White Hills school hall had attracted 'types that have caused damage'. The school council had ruled that any function that resembled a pop concert would not be allowed in the hall. The booking fee, which the promoter Malcolm Cooke had paid to the school, would be returned, Mr Dingle promised.

Furore mounted over the issue, with Judith pointing out that she felt slighted by Mr Dingle's assumptions about the type of audience she would attract, and she pointed out that Ron's dear white-haired mother had thought up the band's name! Bendigo's mayor stepped in and offered Bendigo Town Hall for the concert, but, as a 600-seater, the venue was too small. A cable arrived from nearby Eaglehawk Council, offering not only the use of their town hall, but a civic reception honouring Judith as well. While this was being considered, Judith took part in a phone-in on the local radio station and talked to callers offering her their support. When the radio show ended, Mr Dingle phoned to let Judith know the ban had been lifted by the school council, with the proviso that her promoter guarantee to be responsible for any damages. The night of the concert, Judith's song 'Bendigo-O' brought the house down.

With the tour now firmly in place, Judith Durham and the Hottest Band in Town kicked off with three shows at the Myer Music Bowl. Their all-star supporting bill included the Australian singers Kerrie Biddell, John Farnham and Colleen Hewett. Outdoor concerts in Melbourne in January are always a risky proposition and inclement weather conditions kept crowds away, but the shows were enthusiastically received.

During the ensuing tour, Judith was faced with a barrage of press reports announcing that the original Seekers had finally re-formed, having replaced Judith with a Dutch-born Australian singer named Louisa Wisseling. Billing themselves as Seekers '75, they had made an album and, by mid-year, they had reached Number 1 on the Australian charts with their single, 'Sparrow Song'. Despite the fact they never approached Judith directly to discuss re-forming, the three men claimed in interviews that they were tired of Judith's constant knock-backs.

'Suddenly, I was back on the defensive,' Judith says. 'Everywhere I turned, people were asking me what I thought of this new lot of Seekers and did I regret leaving the group? Still no one understood why I had to get out. For the four years I'd been with The Seekers, I did it to the exclusion of everything else. I was immensely proud of what we had achieved as a group and part of me was worried that with someone else coming in, I would be written out of the history books. In England people had confused me with the girls from The New Seekers and people were unsure who sang what hit. Now I sensed it could happen all over again with the Australian line-up. I felt a bit better about it when I realised they were being billed as Seekers '75, because it drew a line for people. The credit for the records we made in the sixties would remain with the four of us and this new line-up was not really a continuation.

'I tried to explain in interviews that I needed more varied fulfilment from my work, which is part of the reason I left the group. In some ways, I felt sorry for Louisa. I was an established singer, battling the comparison, but she was a relative newcomer and her big step into the spotlight was accompanied by comparisons to Judith Durham. So often she'd be photographed with the guys and there'd be a shot of me in the article, as the original singer. It can't have been very satisfying for her either.'

The Hottest Band in Town tour was a successful but gruelling one and Judith and Ron were to learn quickly that taking a seven-piece band on the road in Australia was an expensive procedure. By the time they'd finished, they realised how fragile their band structure was and faced some difficult decisions.

'I realised at the end of that tour that it was probably the last time I would be able to work with The Hottest Band in Town,' Judith says. 'The band had come out from England, but not all of them were full-time musicians. One of them was a teacher and could only work with us during school holidays; another had a drinking problem, which affected his work. Even if I had been able to put together a band of fully professional musicians, I really wasn't able to offer them permanent work. I was effectively at another crossroad in my career.'

Judith had no further work lined up at the end of the Australian tour so Ron arranged another shipboard cruise to America – this time aboard the *Mariposa's* sister ship, the SS *Monterey* – and he and Judith agreed to keep the nucleus of the band: Phil Franklin on drums and Bob Taylor, the sousaphone and string-bass player, who was also a dab hand on the trumpet if necessary. 'We were able to work, just the four of us, a fantastically effective group,' Judith says. 'We played on the ship and it was our intention to audition and perform like that in the States if necessary. We thought up the name Hot Stuff, to avoid using my name, with all its Seekers connotations, and to reflect the fact that we were all "hot" jazz musicians. The idea of the group was great in principle, but as soon as we got to Los Angeles Bob Taylor told us he had girlfriend trouble back in England. So we gave him a week's wages and off he set to sort it out, and that was the last we ever saw of him! It was now just me, Ron and Phil, and we didn't really have an act.

'We had no idea what to do next. I thought perhaps we should record a new song as a single, as a means of promoting The Hottest Band in Town albums. I wrote a song called "I Love You" and contacted the players from the original Hottest Band. The three of us drove to San Francisco to meet up with the guys and we went into a small studio to cut the song, with our arrangement of "Gloryland" as the B-side.'

Judith and Ron loved being back in San Francisco and, after their short visit, found it hard to leave this city that held so many happy memories – but they had to move on. Once back in LA, Ron began the arduous task of pounding the pavement, trying to shop a deal for the single and albums with the major record companies. While Ron was in one of those meetings, Judith waited patiently in the car downstairs. Twilight was descending and she was reflecting on this fruitless, soul-destroying mission. Everyone seemed to like the records, but didn't quite know what they could do with them. There just wasn't a pigeonhole they could slot a jazzy Judith Durham into at this point. It broke Judith's heart that, although their music made so many people happy, they couldn't get their records out there for the mass market. There in the car, she put her thoughts into words:

> It used to be, when I was small,
> I'd give a smile, they'd give me all.
> The world was soft, the days were long,
> And someone cared where I'd belong.
> And when I'd thirst, they'd quench for free,
> And when I'd yawn, in bed I'd be,
> I'd outstretch arms, they'd reach for me,
> And I'd have ears for every song.
> You come of age, and on life's pages,
> You write with blood you can't afford.
> At every stage, you crawl to score,
> You bet your life, to get you more.
> 'Someone Cared'

Finally, Liberace's manager, Seymour Heller, showed keen interest in 'I Love You' and in Judith as a performer. Negotiations began immediately. Heller loved the record and believed that Judith would be a perfect supporting act for Liberace. Not only did Heller want the single and Judith as his star pianist's support act, but he wanted to secure Judith's recordings for the remainder of her career and at a very low royalty. Again, warning bells rang. She was concerned that, while Heller loved the record and the work she was doing, he effectively wanted to pin her down for the rest of her life. The negotiations dragged on and on, and eventually Judith had to walk away.

By now there wasn't enough work to keep Phil Franklin gainfully employed and no real prospects in the United States for Judith and Ron. They had no record deal and no management and, worst of all, no money. Packing up yet again, the two moved back to London and took up the lease they'd bought in 1970 on a flat in Bury Street, St James's.

They had not made a lot of money by letting the flat. When they learned it was vacant, the estate agent who handled it explained she had evicted the previous tenants. For some months, a newspaper advertisement headed LONELY AT CHRISTMAS? had given the flat's telephone number. For several weeks after Judith and Ron moved in, calls came in from 'lonely' businessmen and they realised that a prostitute had been operating a call-girl racket from the flat. In the coming months, Judith and Ron tried to clinch a deal for their 'I Love You' single, but to no avail.

Everywhere they turned, they met obstacles. The mainstream music industry didn't seem to care that audiences loved this music – jazz seemed to be a dirty word. Yet, ironically, Judith and Ron had great difficulty gaining acceptance in the genuine jazz circles outside the US.

In desperate need of work and a permanent base, at last they resolved to return to Australia, thinking they would start making their Nambour home habitable. They sold the flat, packed their belongings, shipped the pianos and some furniture to Queensland, and flew home to Melbourne. The Citroën wasn't far behind them, on a ship, while the Mercedes was stored in London.

Breaking the news to Judith's father that they were home, but would live in Queensland, was difficult, but Bill helped them pack their still unused wedding presents and waved them goodbye as they set off for what they hoped would be a brighter time ahead. Arriving in Queensland, they discovered that the Nambour homestead had deteriorated in the four years since they'd last seen it and needed more work than they realised to make it habitable. 'It really was a terrible mess,' Judith says. 'It was an ancient weatherboard house and it had rats and bats and spiders everywhere, even the odd snake. We realised we couldn't live there, so we rented a flat in Brisbane and drove up to work on the property on weekends.'

Judith and Ron arranged for two walls to be knocked out inside the house and began scouring wreckers in search of second-hand floorboards and French windows. For a time, they investigated the possibility of becoming totally self-sufficient, making enquiries about solar hot water, a gravity feed from their creek for irrigation, and composting. Later, they moved from Brisbane and took an apartment in Coolum, to be closer to the property.

It was in this apartment that Judith made another monumental decision in her life. After many months of deliberation, she picked up a pair of scissors and cut the long hair that had been her trademark since the mid-sixties. 'For a long time prior to that, I would walk up to Ron with scissors in my hand, saying will I or won't I,' Judith says. 'I felt like I needed a change and one day at Coolum I just did it. Then I went to a hairdresser and had it permed and just loved the freedom. For once, having showers or swimming wasn't a hassle any more.'

However, there was a surprise in store for Ron, who was invited to compose the music score for the new Australian film *Raw Deal*, being written and produced by his brother Patrick.

In the few weeks Ron was away, Judith threw herself into completing the renovations. 'The walls had been knocked out to make a larger living area,' Judith recalls. 'When Ron went away, I realised supervising a renovation was a bit beyond me, because I'd never done anything like it in my life. I decided the house wasn't really big enough and I had another room stuck on the back, but it still wasn't working out the way I'd pictured. I remember ringing Ron and telling him I'd done it and already wanted to renovate my renovation! Our intentions were very good, though. We had all the renovations done using recycled materials because we wanted to keep the homestead as authentic to its period as we could.'

Eventually the funds for renovating ran out. Judith and Ron had exhausted the money they'd made from the sale of their London flat on airfares and builders and suddenly they needed to find work again. Fate stepped in when a call came from Turk Murphy in San Francisco, offering them several months' work at Earthquake McGoon's. After packing up one more time, the two flew back to San Francisco and began singing jazz at Turk's club again. Within a fortnight of their arrival in America, Judith received a heartbreaking phone call. Her dad had died.

'It was just devastating,' Judith says. 'Mum was ready to go when she died, having suffered so much for so long, and, in an odd way, her death was a relief, but it was different with Dad. He had been so looking forward to his retirement, playing golf and enjoying himself. I've always felt an awful sadness that Dad didn't get to do what he really wanted to do. I didn't have the money to fly home for the funeral, so we just had to carry on with the McGoon's job and leave everything to Beverley and Barry again.'

Their initial booking at McGoon's stretched into eight months and was a musically liberating and fulfilling time. In those months they lived, first of all, in an apartment in Haight Street and then, realising their stay would be longer, they shipped the Mercedes to San Francisco and moved into a much larger modern home in Foster City, overlooking the canal. When their stint wound up in 1977, the two were told their left-hand-drive Mercedes was prohibited from import to Australia and they had to sell it. To get the best price they could, they had it detailed and polished and, handling the car with kid gloves, set off for a Mercedes dealer in the city on the day before they were due to fly home to Australia. They pulled up at traffic lights beside a big lorry, not noticing that the truck driver was indicating a turn in front of them. Crunch! In those few seconds, their expected profit diminished and the Mercedes was sold for much less than it had been worth an hour earlier.

Having calculated their losses, Judith and Ron flew to Melbourne to a tearful reunion with Beverley and Barry and the saddening prospect of putting their parents' Balwyn home up for sale. On returning to Queensland and settling into a new apartment in Brisbane, Judith learned that an agent, Wally Wrightman, was interested in handling her in Australia. He was bowled over by 'I Love You', which by now had been released in Australia by Festival Records, the company that had released her last four albums. Wrightman travelled to Brisbane for discussions with Judith and Ron, and began to arrange bookings. A big tour was organised, with flights to Melbourne and Sydney for television appearances. During the last year away from Australia, Judith had performed only jazz, blues and gospel, and had excluded her popular hits from her shows; however, at her new agent's insistence, she reluctantly returned them to the act. But, by the end of the tour, she realised how uncomfortable she was feeling singing the songs of The Seekers when they were so out of context. When she withdrew them from the act, her shows were cancelled.

'Musically, I just wasn't happy at that time,' Judith says. 'Two things were of major concern to me. One was the way Ron always slipped into the background when we were in Australia. He had received so many accolades for his playing overseas and I really wanted his name included in the advertising for my shows to give him credit for his wonderful playing. But there was always reluctance. The promoters were only interested in billing Judith Durham. And, secondly, they always placed unnecessary emphasis on The Seekers. I still felt uneasy about singing those harmony songs in an essentially jazz act. They seemed so out of place. But the minute I tried to suggest I would do an act without Seekers songs the work started drying up.'

It was difficult in Australia for Judith to move on. It had got to a point where, whenever she did interviews, she would know as soon as she walked into a studio whether the interviewer had seen the show. If they hadn't seen her perform on her own, interviewers would take the angle that, because Judith hadn't had hit records on her own, she must regret having left such a successful singing group.

'During that tour, I had a show in Tamworth,' Judith recalls. 'I turned up for a television interview to promote the show and the first question the interviewer asked me was, "Do you regret leaving The Seekers?" That was his first and only question. It just floored me, so I asked him if perhaps he could ask me another question. With that, he stood up and started packing his stuff up and then he and the film crew just walked out. That was the end of the interview. Dealing with this kind of negativity became a constant battle.'

Judith and Ron moved into the property at Nambour, although the renovations had not been completed. They connected the electricity and telephone, but spent many months without hot water. Their lounge room leaked through the ceiling, their water tank kept running out of water and snakes were always a risk. The renovating funds had long since dried up and, with shows being cancelled in Australia, Judith and Ron realised they would once again have to look further afield for work. They accepted a booking to perform jazz as a duo in New Zealand, in a two-week season at the Shoreline Cabaret Club in Auckland. It was there that they considered their options and resolved to follow their hearts back into jazz.

'Jazz had really become our musical life again by then,' Judith says, 'but it was absurd, trying to perform it in Australia. We were attracting a Seekers audience, most of whom enjoyed what we were doing, but still expected me to sing Seekers songs as well. To please them, I was having to sing The Seekers songs in the act, but as a result we had trouble attracting the jazz crowd. They couldn't take us seriously if we suddenly launched into "Georgy Girl" in the middle of the act. The irony was, the act really was geared towards the jazz crowd. The music we were presenting was mostly authentic and internationally we enjoyed great acceptance. But the minute we were back in Australia I was The Seekers girl and Ron was the piano-playing husband in the background. The miracle was that, once they got there, the audiences loved the show and we sold a lot of the [Judith Durham and the] Hottest Band in Town albums at the venues.'

In December 1977, Judith and Ron took their first major steps towards jazz autonomy when they appeared as a duo at the Australian Jazz Convention, being held that year in Hobart. For the first time, they could honestly say that singing jazz in Australia was a sensational experience.

'I felt at last we were being appreciated by Australian jazz audiences,' Judith explains. 'Jazzers come from all over the world to the conventions and we were playing to an audience of serious jazz lovers who responded so incredibly well to us. Best of all, these real-jazz fanatics were cheering Ron's playing. He'd been cheered overseas many times, but never before in Australia. In fact, even with the Hottest Band in Town shows, he was hiding his light under a bushel.

'Initially, he'd been feeling his way with that style of music. Ron had been more of a sophisticated, modern-jazz player before I met him – he'd even recorded with Alexis Korner's All Stars! When we played at McGoon's that first time, he really had to get his left hand going, refining a stride style of playing that he wasn't accustomed to. Overseas, he received so much praise for his playing, but he didn't rate himself as highly as other people did. The convention in Hobart really changed all that for him. Suddenly, he was being cheered in his own right for this incredible playing.'

As is usual at the Australian Jazz Convention, the final concert was taped and aired on radio by the Australian Broadcasting Commission. The producers were so impressed with Judith and Ron that they invited them to stay on for a full concert of their own, which would also be broadcast as a radio special. During their time in Hobart, Judith got the chance to perform with Beverley, who was by now a fully fledged jazz singer in her own right. It was the first time she'd sung with her sister since 1972, when she called Beverley up from the audience at Melbourne's Comedy Theatre for their duet.

While in Tasmania, Judith and Ron met jazzers from overseas who were planning to go to the annual Breda Jazz Festival in Holland. The pair decided that they too would head for Holland in May 1978 and present their music as a piano-and-voice duo.

Having arrived in the Netherlands, Judith and Ron made their way to Breda, and Judith brought the house down with several international jazz bands. While they were there, they also met up again with a fan they'd first encountered at Earthquake McGoon's.

'We first met Stan King in San Francisco,' Judith says. 'He was a lovely well-to-do, middle-aged, silver-haired New Yorker. He came bounding up to me after hearing us at McGoon's, saying "I don't care who you are, I want to marry you!" He wasn't serious, of course, but he knew his jazz very well and he just loved the music we were making. Stan runs his own textile-design business and his position allows him the freedom to travel around the world, going to all the jazz festivals. Nowadays, he's become a musician himself, playing washboard with his own group. Stan was leaving Breda and going on to Paris, so Ron and I decided we'd join him, just for a few days' sightseeing.

'We'd seen Paris before and loved it, but this time we all went to some jazz clubs, where Ron sat in playing with some really great Paris musicians, and I sang as well. Again, Ron got the most amazing reaction from audiences, who recognised that his playing was exceptional.'

From Paris, Stan went home to New York and Judith and Ron travelled on to London to see Ron's mother. While they were there, they received a phone call from Stan, inviting them to stay with him in Manhattan. It would give New Yorkers the chance to hear their music. Their new friend organised sit-ins for both of them at Manhattan jazz clubs and in no time at all people were starting to talk about these two unknowns from Australia who were pretty darn good.

Stan King also approached the organisers of the prestigious Newport Jazz Festival and persuaded them to create a showcase spot for his two new finds. The organisers agreed to let the two Australians appear in the traditional jazz section of the festival, playing in an outdoor marquee in New Jersey. Judith and Ron were delighted and viewed the Newport Jazz Festival as the highlight of their jazz career so far. Judith felt she was treading in Mahalia Jackson's shoes, after seeing her in the 1958 film, *Jazz on a Summer's Day*. They were to play two or three songs as the opening act, before the main stars of the event – and most of the audience – arrived. The two began their set in front of just fifty people, who were there waiting for the big names to begin, while hundreds more roamed around outside, many picnicking on the lawns. After just one song, something remarkable began to happen.

'It was really incredible,' Judith remembers. 'This small crowd just went crazy at the end of the first song and people started coming down the lawn into the marquee to watch us. The audience just kept getting bigger and bigger and these people were applauding and clapping and cheering every number. We were so thrilled that we stayed on and instead of doing two or three songs, as planned, we played for an hour. By the time we'd finished, we'd had three standing ovations from an audience of more than three thousand people.'

The public weren't the only ones who were impressed by what they'd heard. *Cashbox* magazine described them as 'very fine and well received'. The *New Jersey Jazz Journal* wrote, 'Judy Durham and Ron Edgeworth, fresh from Australia, took the early arrivals by surprise, and entertained with a solid hour of blues, ballads and swing ... they brought the tent down, figuratively speaking. A special treat.' But for Judith, the most satisfying review was the one that appeared in the *Mississippi Rag*, singling out Ron's playing. Its reviewer wrote, 'Pianist Ron Edgeworth is something special, playing a very capable Morton-cum-stride piano style that was at once engaging and refreshing. He reminded me very much of the young Dick Wellstood.'

Elated at their reception, Judith and Ron were also delighted to find that, unbeknown to them, the festival organisers had taped their performance for archival purposes. Mind you, Ron thought he would never have played so well if he had known the set was being recorded. This was no multitrack professional job, rather a quarter-inch tape recorder of dubious worth; but the Edgeworths managed to persuade the promoters to let them have the tape. Just possibly, they thought, they might be able to mix it and release it on record. If not, it would always be a wonderful memento of the most exhilarating performance of their shared musical life so far.

The two months Judith and Ron had planned to be away from Australia had now expired, but they were having a ball. With nothing but a leaking roof and a Seekers-hungry cabaret audience awaiting them at home, the couple took up Stan King's offer to spend summer with him in his Manhattan apartment, while his family holidayed on Fire Island. For the next few weeks, Stan helped organise sit-ins and gigs for them. They turned up one night at Brown's Bar, a trendy restaurant and bar in New York, where for many years Woody Allen has done an unpublicised and unpaid Monday night sit-in. Allen was pleased to know Judith was in the audience and would have liked her to sing with the band, but the bar's owner wouldn't allow it. Sit-ins and impromptu performances were entrenched in New York nightlife, but not at Brown's Bar, it seemed. Down the road at Jimmy Ryan's one night, Judith was in the audience when Ella Fitzgerald got up for a jam. Another night, Sarah Vaughan was in the audience while Judith performed.

After four months as Stan King's house guests, Judith and Ron realised they would need a place of their own if they were to stay on in America: Stan's family were returning home after the summer and, besides, they'd imposed enough. They were ecstatic with American audiences' reaction to their work and had found the musical satisfaction they'd been yearning for in working together as a duo. They both agreed that perhaps America, where Judith's Seekers past was not so conspicuously remembered, would be the place to stay. Judith had loved her New York experiences, but wondered whether it was really a city where she and Ron could put down roots.

'Musically, it was a very satisfying place to be,' she says, 'but there is something about New York people that I've never been able to put my finger on. New York is a very tough city and I noticed after we'd been there for a while that I didn't seem to be the same smiling person I had always been. There's a tough attitude you need to adopt in order to survive in New York and it really wasn't something we could acquire easily.'

Their search for accommodation led Judith and Ron to two charming young women who had a nice apartment to rent, one that could certainly house a grand piano. After an enjoyable chat with the women, Judith and Ron paid a $2,000 bond on the flat and were told to move in the following Saturday morning. They rolled up at the same time as eighteen other couples who had also paid the nice women $2,000 each for the same apartment! The nice women, of course, had disappeared with $38,000.

Judith and Ron soon got the message that, for the moment, New York wasn't their town. America was still very much the place they wanted to be, so, rather than find another apartment in New York, they invested their money in a luxury motorhome. With their musical life so reliant on travelling, it seemed like the logical answer. Besides, winter was about to fall on New York and the idea of being able to escape the snow was very appealing. They found a motorhome that was everything they were looking for and more. It had its own shower and flushing toilet, generator, television, carpeted walls, floors and ceiling and every mod con, including a blender in the kitchen bench. Best of all, it was big enough to house their electric keyboard. Finally the Edgeworths had a home.

Before leaving New York, Judith and Ron invited Ron's brother Patrick and mother Vicky to fly in from England and spend a travelling holiday with them, driving south. The motorhome comfortably slept four and the family set off from New York, driving along the east coast of America. They visited Washington, DC, Atlantic City, Norfolk, Charleston, Jacksonville and Savannah, staying in recreational-vehicle parks along the way. They stayed for a time in Miami and Fort Lauderdale, before moving down to the most southern tip of Florida, through the islands known as Keys.

'We just loved Key West,' Judith says. 'It was more touristy than what would normally appeal to us, but it seemed like a very artistic community, quite alternative. The lifestyle was very laid-back and the weather was just wonderful.' Standing watching buskers at sunset, Judith was struck by the immediacy of this level of entertainment and would have loved to give it a go. But for now she couldn't muster the courage; instead, she wrote 'Key West', a poem:

We stood and watched a sunset, watched with all the rest,
We stood and watched a sunset, we were in Key West.
The water looked so soothing, the orange sky was best,

The water looked so soothing, we were in Key West.
The juggler threw his fire-sticks, musicians strummed in vests,
The juggler threw his fire-sticks, we were in Key West.
We clapped our approval, coins were tossed to rest,
We clapped our approval, we were in Key West.
Everyone was mellow, yes, you might have guessed,
Everyone was mellow, we were in Key West.

When the holiday was over, Judith and Ron drove Patrick and Vicky back to Miami, where Vicky flew home to England and Patrick to Australia. The couple then drove back to Key West, where they planned to undertake a long fast. For inspiration Ron bought two interesting books – *Rational Fasting* and *The Mucousless Diet Healing System*, both by Professor Arnold Ehret. Judith started her fast while they were on the road back to Key West, and began reading the books.

'The books took quite a different approach to many of the other health and fasting books we'd read,' she says, 'and it stressed the importance of only fasting for short periods of time, until the body had cleansed itself of toxins, and then extending the fasting period. Instead of persevering with the 30-day fast I had set out to do, I decided to take the advice given and break the fast after only five days. I followed the recommended transition diet for eight weeks, which Ron did with me. Arnold Ehret had experimented on thousands of patients at his sanitarium in Switzerland in the early 1900s and had worked out that, in a clean body, the perfect diet would be ripe fruit and uncooked, green-leaf vegetables. However, the transition from a sick body would be through a predominantly cooked fruit and vegetable diet with dried fruit, until the body becomes more cleansed and better able to tolerate the raw diet. I would have to give up my nuts and grains, but luckily I didn't have to forfeit my beloved olive oil or decaffeinated tea and coffee.

'We both felt the best we'd ever felt and we had a new perspective on health foods and vegetarianism. I thought perhaps I might have finally found the answer I'd been looking for. I truly believed in eating the foods I'd been eating to date, but my problem was that my hunger was never fully satisfied. I had always craved food and had an aggravated stomach. It didn't seem to matter what I ate, I just never felt as though I'd had enough. So, instead of having a weight problem, I had traded it for a hunger problem. It was something I always had to deal with. The mucousless diet didn't clear my cough up, but it did help control my food cravings. Ultimately, that diet became a way of life for me and it has given me such great control over my health that I seldom need medication. These days you can buy ready-made soya milk, and I've added that to my diet.'

With a new health-food regime in place, Judith and Ron left Key West in search of work in nearby Boca Raton. Through a lawyer they'd met during their New York performances, they found a new agent, who booked them into Bubba's Jazz Club in Fort Lauderdale and on Florida's lucrative condominium circuit.

'Performers could make a whole career out of the condominium circuit if they wished,' Judith says. 'Florida is the state where a lot of older people go to retire. These condominiums are real luxury affairs with every amenity, including splendid auditoriums. The audiences we played to on this circuit were just amazing and we often got standing ovations. They loved the fact that we were Australian and young and yet we knew how to present very American material in such an authentic way.'

While still in Florida, Judith and Ron concentrated heavily on their songwriting. Often, at twilight, they'd drive their home to a remote beach somewhere, start the generator, set up the piano and play and sing to their hearts' content. From those dusky sessions came Judith's 'Baby, When You Look at Me' and Ron's 'In Your Love' and 'Got Them Blues'. Their lawyer put them in contact with a local author who was interested in helping them write the book for a musical they were slowly putting together. They ended up with a script that didn't feel quite right and had to set the project aside for a while, but the exercise brought their dream of writing a musical a little closer to fruition.

They also listened back to the Newport tape and decided to write to the New Jersey Jazz Society, who had been involved with the Newport Jazz Festival, seeking authorisation to use the tapes of their showcase performance as the nucleus of a new album. With permission granted, they headed to Miami's famed Criteria Studios, where the Eagles, The Bee Gees and many other big-name bands of the seventies had recorded. They spoke with a recording engineer, who acknowledged that the quality of their Newport tape was very poor, but not totally beyond salvation. In the coming weeks, the three worked on the Newport material and the tapes from the Hobart concert. Ultimately, they ended up with eight inspired vocal performances and Ron's dazzling piano solo, 'Mood Indigo'.

By the time Judith and Ron left Criteria, they had produced their third album – all paid for on credit card! Giving their album – and their act –

a name had been a major issue for some time. Concerned that audiences would be expecting her to sing Seekers material, Judith was at first reluctant to use her own name on the album, although the two did consider calling it simply Judy Durham and Ron Edgeworth. Finally, they settled on *The Hot Jazz Duo*, which they believed reflected the mood of what they were doing. From that point on, their duo shows were also billed with the new name.

With the master tape of their *Hot Jazz Duo* album in their hands, Judith and Ron decided the time had come to move on again. Spring had arrived and Los Angeles seemed like a good starting point for placing the album with a record company. En route to LA, they detoured to Colorado, having contacted the organisers of the Summit Jazz Festival, who'd agreed to add them to the bill of the festival in the Rockies, near Aspen. While in Colorado, they also played at Zeno's jazz club in nearby Denver and, before leaving, the local jazz fraternity honoured them with a special concert of their own before an invited audience.

'After one of our shows there, we met a woman in the audience who was a handwriting expert,' Judith says. 'She asked if I had any samples of my handwriting she could read. I showed her a letter I'd started writing and she was just amazing. She told me she could see conflict in my professional life and that my problem was that I felt I hadn't made my mark in life yet. She was right, too. I had been in a dilemma musically for such a long time and what she said encapsulated how I really felt. This woman knew nothing of my history and wouldn't have known of The Seekers, but she picked up on my professional uncertainty. I realised I hadn't really made my mark, musically speaking. I had done it with The Seekers, but I never felt it was really making my own mark.'

Judith and Ron moved on to Los Angeles, where a reunion awaited them with Ron's brother Patrick, who was now a sought-after film and television writer. He was in America to work with the film producer George Miller, of *Mad Max* fame. The two brothers had a wonderful time showing each other the sights of LA, while Judith embarked on another of Arnold Ehret's short fasts and concentrated on perfecting the new fruit-and-vegetable regime from the book.

Judith vowed that she would stick to the Arnold Ehret diet for the next three years, until she turned forty. If it hadn't cured her eating problems and helped her health, she would eat anything and everything she could get her hands on! She built in one concession: she would allow a break in the diet in the unlikely event she and Ron should ever end up back in Paris, knowing she wouldn't be able to resist a French breakfast. Little did she know!

Songwriting became another focus for the pair. Ron perfected some chords for 'I Remember', his favourite of Judith's compositions, while Judith wrote verses for 'Let Me Find Love', the song that started her off as a composer in her own right. Many other songs were written over those weeks, before they headed north to the beautiful Three Rivers community, where they took part in a jazz festival. During this performance, a fight broke out among a local Hell's Angels gang, causing a tremendous ruckus. Later, after Judith's performance, one of the gang members caught her eye and remarked in his gravely voice, 'Lady, you gotta whole lotta lung', which remains one of Judith's favourite compliments to this day.

While they were in Three Rivers, the well-known American jazz chronicler Steve Fleming wrote an article on them, which was later used as the liner notes for the *Hot Jazz Duo* album. Fleming described their sound as 'astonishing', adding:

> Ron's forceful, full-bodied bass stride piano works on equal footing with Judy's broad powerfully executed vocals. This is not a vocalist with piano accompaniment, it's two extraordinary talents that, forged together, form one hard-driving unit. Edgeworth is quite simply all Durham needs behind her.

They had been invited to Three Rivers by a German banjo player named Leuder Ohlwein, and they discussed with him their intention to move on to Europe, where the jazz scene was more concentrated. Leuder told them Germany was thriving with jazz and suggested they might consider Düsseldorf as their base. From Three Rivers, Judith and Ron took advantage of their new motorhome and the freedom it allowed, and drove on to San Francisco for one last look around before moving back down to Los Angeles.

While still in Three Rivers, Judith had told Leuder that she'd been tempted to busk in Key West and he urged her to try it sometime, to broaden her perspective as an artist. Knowing she'd soon be leaving America, where she enjoyed relative mainstream obscurity, Judith realised it was now or never. She and Ron picked an appropriate kerb in San Francisco, parked their motorhome and ran an electric cord into a nearby shop. Ron played piano on the pavement while Judith stood singing the blues and jazz.

'It was a great experience and very humbling,' Judith says. 'It really was another dimension in performance. I found I had to be immune to anyone who just walked past me without looking or stopping. It was hard at first to be detached from people putting money in the hat. They knew that was expected, but there's an art to not looking them in the eye and making them feel pressured to give you something. On stage in my normal shows, I'm deliberately working to people, but busking on the street requires a much more contained performance.

'I realised for the first time how many excellent performers are out there on the streets and in subways, with no hope of performing anywhere else. It made me grateful that I have concert halls and theatres and clubs to sing in. My voice carried around the corner of this street and I was approached later by a couple of Australian tourists who'd only arrived in San Francisco that morning. They told me that the day before, on Sydney radio, someone had asked what had happened to Judith Durham. The next thing they knew: they were hearing me in San Francisco, singing on the streets!

'I was very happy to find that I could pull a crowd in that situation. We were very close to the kerb and a couple of cars driving by parked for a while with their windows down, before driving on. It's a very genuine appreciation from passers-by. They give you money if they like you and that's it. They don't have to pay their money first and then see whether they like you. I wonder sometimes whether that's the fair way to do it, even with concerts. Let people book seats and then pay what they like on the way out!'

From San Francisco, it was down the coast to Los Angeles. But Judith and Ron had begun encountering problems with their luxury motorhome: the maintenance bills were horrendous, there were major troubles with the generator, and the roof leaked. They decided to sell up and take their friend's advice and check out the jazz scene in Germany. Dubs of their *Hot Jazz Duo* album had been sent to the major recording companies in California and, while feedback was sensational, they again faced the problem that the music industry in LA did not know how to market the product.

Once they had sold the motorhome, they made arrangements to visit Vicky Edgeworth in London before travelling on to Germany for a look around. There had been a longstanding invitation from the upmarket London jazz nightclub Pizza on the Park, and Ron contacted the owners to arrange a season on their return to London. The last thing Judith did before flying out was visit a Los Angeles hairdresser to have some style put back into her short hair. The hairdresser showed her a photograph of a multilayered, shaggy look and then proceeded to cut it several times shorter. To her dismay, Judith left for London with a punk hair-do!

'Pizza on the Park was a great club to perform in,' Judith says. 'The pizza restaurant was upstairs, and downstairs was a very plush nightclub room with two grand pianos. There was a resident pianist, who would play two-piano material with Ron. We were back in London again, but we wanted to keep up the style of show we'd been presenting in America. As usual, we did three one-hour sets, with Ron having solos in the middle of many of the songs. The venue didn't want to bill us as the Hot Jazz Duo, because the name didn't mean much in England, so I had to settle for being billed as Judith Durham. It concerned me for a while, but we were very well received and only occasionally did I find Seekers fans asking for the old hits.'

For a time, Judith and Ron stayed with Ron's mother in East Ham before moving into a flat in Soho. Later, in 1980, they accepted a Christmas and New Year booking for the Hot Jazz Duo in Bahrain, in the Persian Gulf. The promoter had booked a hot-jazz band with some great players as well and everything was looking good.

'Of course, we got there to find that everybody knew Judith Durham, the ex-Seeker was coming,' Judith says. 'There was a huge press and television turnout and we learned on arrival that the promoter had also booked me into an enormous local cabaret room as Judith Durham, and every seat in the place was sold. He'd also done a sponsorship deal with a cigarette company, which horrified us. They had me over a barrel. I had been billed without my permission, but, if I refused to do the show, I'd look bad. We got around it by teaching the musicians the chords for Seekers songs and incorporating them into our jazz show. But for me it was just the crystallisation of the ongoing problem I had. There was no way people would let me have a strictly jazz career.'

At the same time, however, the booking opened Judith's eyes to the fact that she had an international name, strong enough to draw big crowds in countries where she'd never previously considered performing. Judith and Ron then returned to London before travelling to Oslo for another jazz booking. When the season was over, they took a boat from Norway across to Germany and picked up a hire car to take them to Düsseldorf. There, they enjoyed the hot jazz but, surprisingly, found it wasn't a city they could ever call home.

'We just couldn't relate to Germany as a place to live,' Judith says. 'Ron had spent time there when he was in the Irish Fusiliers army band in the late fifties, but there was something not right for us about settling there. We had the hire car, so we just moved on.'

Heading back to London, the Edgeworths hadn't planned to go through Paris again, but they had unlimited mileage on the hire car and the idea was just too tempting. With plenty of spare time to look around, Judith and Ron found more jazz than they could have hoped for and a more creative ambience than they'd noticed on their previous visits to Paris. Within days, they had found a new home. They returned to London, packed their belongings and caught the ferry across the English Channel and the train to their rendezvous in the French capital. Here, they would begin another chapter in their life together. *C'est si bon!*

12. PARIS NIGHTS

Those Paris nights,
Strung with those Paris lights,
Where we strolled by the Seine,
In the warm gentle rain,
Under those Paris skies,
Where we found true love lies,
In our hearts it was there,
All along, free to share.

– 'PARIS NIGHTS'
RON EDGEWORTH AND JUDITH DURHAM

Judith and Ron were no strangers to the allure of Paris. Judith had been there in her days with The Seekers and she and Ron often passed through it for a day or so in transit between Switzerland and London. It was there, in 1971, that they bought their beloved Citroën. This time, however, they were struck by the sheer magic of this most romantic of French cities, and felt totally at home. They went flat hunting and found an agent who thought she might have the perfect apartment for them. There was just one thing she thought would put them off the place, but she didn't want to mention it until they'd seen it. The apartment was on the fifth floor of a very old building on the Left Bank and she had to entice them up all these stairs. There, in the middle of the lounge room, was the piece of furniture that had deterred so many prospective tenants in the past: a grand piano! Delighted with their good fortune, Judith and Ron signed the lease that day.

'It really was a beautiful place to live,' Judith says. 'It was very quaint, with exposed beams and a bedroom up a little ladder on a mezzanine. It also had a big sun terrace that overlooked the street below. We'd spend a lot of time out there, and we could watch the crowds around the street performers beneath us. One man used to turn up regularly with a box of glass bottles. He'd smash them on the pavement, roll around in the broken glass and then his mate would pass around the hat. There were another two guys, who would turn up with a llama and a ladder and they'd try coaxing the llama up the ladder. Being a llama, of course, he'd love to climb anything and when he got up there, with his four paws on the top rung, their act was over!'

Like Key West in America, Paris afforded Judith and Ron a multicultural, artistic and creative environment in which their music could flourish. Before long, they were booked to perform at Le Petit Opportun, where they'd sat in during their brief trip to Paris with Stan King. The club's owners had extended an invitation to Judith and Ron to return any time they liked, and so they did. They also spent several weeks as the resident act at Carol's Paradise, one of the many clubs that thrived in the underground wine cellars of Paris, known to the French as les boites. It was run by a tall, black model who was no stranger to the catwalks of the leading French fashion houses. It had been Carol's ambition to set up her own jazz club and, in no time at all, her establishment had become one of the venues where the chic jazz crowd gathered. Carol's started at midnight and continued until four, and afterwards Judith and Ron would walk home across the Seine with the lights of Paris surrounding them. Paris never slept; it was always busy, even at that time of morning.

One of the Paris jazz critics became a regular visitor to Carol's. He reviewed the Hot Jazz Duo's show for *Le Canard Enchaine* and called it *'fantastique'*. On each return visit, he would ask Judith to sing 'My Funny Valentine' for him. Another regular was the heir to the Pernod fortune, who befriended the couple and invited them to his home. Because Judith was Australian, he nicknamed her Kangaroo.

While in Paris, Judith and Ron received a booking from a Zürich supper club and they jumped at the chance to return to the country that had been their home for so long. They had also noticed, while reading Arnold Ehret's fasting book, that the foreword was dated and signed at Monte Verita, in Lugano. Ca' del Sass', which had been their Swiss base for many happy years, was in Ascona, near Lugano, right next to the Hotel Monte Verita. Their curiosity aroused, they took advantage of their Swiss booking to research further. They had been told that there had been a vegetarian colony on Monte Verita at the turn of the century and that the hotel had been built on the site of this curative establishment.

'We managed to track down a book that showed this nudist and vegetarian colony,' Judith says. 'It had literally been a few hundred yards from where our house was. Apparently, thousands of people from all over Europe had gone there seeking cures all those years before, people like Lenin and Trotsky. It was renowned. We also found that it was there that Arnold Ehret had done so much of his ground-breaking work. It was so coincidental that we ended up, so many years later, studying his books, having lived almost on the site where he wrote them.'

For Judith, Paris also lived up to its reputation as a gourmet's paradise, and, within hours of arriving in the city, she had had her first French breakfast. Much as she wanted to stick with Arnold Ehret's diet, a good morning meal in Paris was too much of a temptation. Many more French breakfasts followed in the coming weeks and before long she had started to put on weight again. After strictly adhering to Ehret's mucousless eating programme, Judith's change in diet resulted in an increase in her mucous levels, and, even more worrying, she had detected what she thought was a small lump in her breast. She was determined not to undergo medical examinations for the lump, uncertain of the treatment foreign doctors might prescribe. Coincidentally, she had been reading Joanna Brandt's world-renowned book, *The Grape Cure*, and, seeing a natural alternative, put the diet to the test.

'On the grape cure, you really eat nothing but grapes for the whole time,' Judith says. 'Just my luck, grapes were out of season when I decided to go on the cure, but the book did say you could get by with raisins and grape juice. I soaked raisins and drank grape juice for about a week. When Ron realised I was serious about it, he went off wandering around Paris and came back with a couple of boxes of Californian grapes and I threw myself into it in earnest. As time went by, I felt better and better and, after two weeks, the lump went away. By the time I'd been on grapes for thirty days, I found my food cravings had actually disappeared and grapes were all I wanted to eat. The book recommended a maximum of six or eight weeks on grapes and because I was feeling so good I thought I'd stay on it for the maximum time.

'My energy levels just got higher and higher. We were living on the fifth floor with no lift and I was able to leap up the one hundred and four stairs two at a time to the top, and my awareness increased tenfold. It had the most incredible effect on me. My looks improved, my singing voice became even clearer and I was so in tune creatively. It gave me a new insight about how what we eat can have such an influence on our health and made me realise what a perfect food fruit is. Towards the end of the cure, I found my consciousness had been raised to an amazing level. My concentration had never been so acute and I could focus in a way I never had in the past. Just as I was finishing, Ron also joined in on the grapes. He ended up doing even longer than me and feeling boundless energy. His eyes were so clear.

'Ultimately, I think I stayed on the cure a little too long. Once I passed a certain stage, I started to feel very weak. In my final week, I felt a real detachment from everything, like I wasn't worried whether I carried on or not. It wasn't a suicidal feeling in any way, just this sense that nothing was keeping me in this world. I felt I had no ties anywhere and no ambitions to do any more.'

Joanna Brandt gives specific instructions in her book for coming off the cure and Judith followed those to the letter. She gradually introduced other fruits – such as vine-ripened tomatoes – and then salads and leaves. She had survived for so long on just grapes that she became aware, each time she introduced a new food, just what effect it was having on her body and of the different vibrations the food gave off.

It came as a surprise to Judith one night to be singing jazz in a Paris nightclub and to have someone in the audience call out for her to sing 'Georgy Girl'. The Paris jazz circuit had given her a new identity, but there would always be English and Australian tourists, no matter where she went in the world.

'I realised that, almost fifteen years later, my association with The Seekers was still as strong as ever,' Judith says. 'It really got to a stage where I couldn't use the name Judith Durham to sell a show without inviting people to come along expecting to hear Seekers songs. I still loved those songs, but it seemed so incongruous in a jazz show and I always felt inadequate singing them without the boys, as if I couldn't do them justice.

'I saw myself as a fully fledged jazz singer by now and I really only wanted to sing the music of the twenties and thirties, and some of the songs I'd written with Ron that fitted into that idiom, but I couldn't. Whenever I performed in an English-speaking country, I was expected to sing Seekers songs. We'd be full on into a jazz set and then suddenly we'd be singing "A World of Our Own". As far as being a bona fide jazz artist, it destroyed my credibility to be including sixties songs in the act.'

It was Ron who first suggested that, if Judith truly wanted to get away from her identification with The Seekers and their songs, she would have to consider changing her name. Their Hot Jazz Duo identity worked to an extent, but, if the couple ever wanted separate billing, Judith Durham would be instantly associated with The Seekers.

'I realised finally that leaving The Seekers in 1968 didn't automatically mean I was leaving The Seekers' material,' Judith says. 'I mean, I understood that people loved those songs and it was a compliment in a way; but, all these years later, I really was trying to do something different. I discovered what it meant to be typecast. I was selling myself on one name and giving them something different altogether. Leaving The Seekers didn't mean I could leave the material behind, so it seemed the only option was to leave The Seekers *and* Judith Durham. We thought about Judith Edgeworth for a long time and came up with some other alternatives. In the process, we toyed around with some fun names, like Marilyn and Clyde Dancer and really silly ones like Lola DeLovely and Snakehips McGee. But seriously, we just couldn't seem to settle on the perfect name.'

It was one day, while walking around Paris with Ron, that Judith passed a hotel and caught sight of a sign that gave her the answer. If she ever needed to change her name, she'd found a new one – Lutetia Concorde. She filed it away for future reference.

By now, the Edgeworths had spent nine months in Paris and Judith was beginning to feel musically unsettled again. She was restless and knew in her heart that she once again needed to change her musical direction.

'It came as a bit of a shock to Ron,' Judith says. 'I told him one day that I felt I'd come to the end of the road as a jazz singer and I needed to do something different. What that was, I wasn't sure, so I told him I wanted to have a year off without working, to sort out my musical life. Since we'd been performing jazz, Ron's standard of playing had gone through the roof and it didn't take him long to realise he could easily carry on as a solo performer. As a trade-off, I told him I didn't mind where we lived in the world, so he opted for us to come home to Australia. In the back of my mind, I had an idea that perhaps I could become a singer-songwriter, but I didn't want to rush into it. I wanted to have a year out to do other things, like reading books and writing songs and just finding out what felt right.'

Leaving Paris was difficult for them both. They had become very settled there and were now thinking that perhaps it might be their permanent home. They had many happy memories of their magical Paris nights. But it was again time to move on. Before leaving, they wandered around the fruit and vegetable markets that had been their shopping centre for so many months, saying their goodbyes. The French stallholders, who'd so enjoyed Judith and Ron's attempts to make themselves understood, hugged them and wished them bon voyage. They returned to London and faced more farewells, saying goodbye to Ron's mother Vicky, family and friends.

Judith and Ron had left Nambour in 1978 with plans to spend just two months away from home. They were returning four years later. In that time, Queensland's airports had been upgraded and, for the first time in their married life, they were able to fly directly into Maroochydore. Their first shock was picking up their cherished Citroën and finding it had become a home to a family of rats. They found an obliging mechanic, who cleaned and tuned the car, and then set off for their Nambour property, looking forward to settling back into rustic domesticity. It wasn't long before they were confronted with their second shock.

Assuming they wouldn't be away from the house for long, Judith and Ron had not covered their furniture or taken any of the precautions people usually take when planning a long-term absence. They returned to their homestead to find leaking roofs and gutters, rusted appliances, faulty power points and still no hot water. Their fridge had become a rodent paradise, thriving with families of mice, and their wardrobe full of clothes had provided a four-year banquet for the local moths and silverfish.

'The renovations hadn't been finished when we'd gone away in 1978,' Judith says, 'so we still had a lot of makeshift devices all over the place and all these repairs on top of it. I was determined we weren't going to spend money until we had the means to do the house up properly, so we just had to make do the best we could. The hot water wasn't connected, so we worked out a way to have a shower under a hose hooked up outside. It was fine in summer, but not a lot of fun when the weather started to get cooler. Then we had an army shower inside, using hot water from the kettle and buckets!

'When the wiring was being installed, I had gone mad planning lots of dimmer switches, two-way switches, outdoor floodlights and double power points for our recording equipment. But when we came back we couldn't use the interior power points, so we brought a lead up from under the house, where our one working point was located. We attached a series of extension leads and double adapters to it and plugged in everything we needed. We ended up with quite a sophisticated external wiring system in the end!'

Doorknobs had been removed from all doors when Ron and Judith hired painters in the late 1970s and new ones had never been fitted. Judith worked out a way of using cotton reels for doorknobs, stringing two together through the holes in the doors and adding some of Bill's old golf tees to keep them in place.

'We used our tea chests and polystyrene fruit boxes on their sides as bookshelves, and for cooking we used Ron's old two-ring electric stove from his army days. The problem was, whenever I turned the stove or the iron on, the lights in the house went dim. If I wanted to iron, I had to do it when I wasn't cooking! We had a double sink and double faucet, but they hadn't been installed so we rigged up two plastic basins in the kitchen and just threw the water over the side of the front veranda when it was finished with. Our fridge was a very old one we'd plonked in there for when we were just spending weekends at the property. We cleaned out the mice and got it working again, but it didn't have a handle. I found an old concrete smoother that one of the workmen had been using and screwed that on to the fridge as a handle. It looked pretty good.

The thermostat wasn't working, though, and I had to remember to turn the fridge off and on every couple of hours. I also had to remember to put the bowls and towels out to catch the drips from the leaking ceiling when it rained.'

In an area already renowned for power failures, they sometimes spent nights with just candles to light their way, but it didn't bother them. Judith and Ron had their work cut out for them, but at least they were home and they were happy.

'It was pretty makeshift, but we had a lot of fun,' Judith says. 'One major mishap was an accident Ron had while sawing some wood for the old combustion stove we had installed. He was outside using a circular saw when I heard this scream, so I raced to the power point and pulled the extension cord out of the socket. The saw had gone deeply into Ron's leg, but luckily the denim in his jeans stopped it from doing too much damage. I managed to get him to hospital and they stitched him up.'

Their first Christmas Day at Nambour was unlike any other Judith and Ron had ever celebrated. The subtropical conditions were ideal for an outdoor feast and their Christmas dinner was fresh pineapple, watermelon and mango. Judith was by now perfectly content to stay at home for several months, venturing out with Ron only for meetings connected with the path. Mostly, she enjoyed the solitude and was happy to spend time on her own when Ron was out doing gigs. He'd begun accepting solo work in Brisbane, Noosa and Maroochydore, travelling to and from Nambour in the Citroën. Often, he spent a night or two away, playing piano with the Mileham Hayes Jazz Band, with whom he also made an album. He spent the rest of his time playing solo or in trios on the Sunshine Coast, building up his own following of fans who marvelled at his exuberant style.

Judith had decided not to make any public appearances for a year and, within weeks of being home in Nambour, was turning down another bid for The Seekers to re-form. This time, it was a $1 million offer for just a few shows. The producers of Hey Hey It's Saturday also asked Judith to take part in a Seekers tribute show without her former singing partners, but she turned this down too.

Judith revelled in her new-found freedom. She had never had this much spare time on her hands and relished the opportunity to be herself in such isolated surroundings. Dressed mostly in shorts and T-shirts, with no makeup, she spent her days doing housework, playing the piano, swimming in the natural rock pool, lying in the sun and reading books on health and organic gardening.

'It was a wonderful period in my life,' Judith remembers. 'Having the chance to live up there in the wilderness, absorbing things I wouldn't normally have had the opportunity to enjoy. I became quite domesticated, doing ironing, sewing and dusting, things I'd never had time to do properly in the past. We didn't have a television, so I would either listen to talkback radio or sit at the piano and sing. I planted little herbs and tried growing a few veggies. I thoroughly enjoyed reading the organic-gardening books. I even gave some thought to developing the property and establishing orchards, but we never got around to it. We had a botanist come up sometimes and he walked with me around the property pointing out all these rare species of plants that we had growing wild. I learned a lot in that time about the forest and the different plants and wild berries. It really fascinated me and is something I'd love to have done if I'd not been a musician.'

After months of involving herself in these nonmusical passions, Judith returned to her piano practice, singing and songwriting with a new vigour. She wrote a song called 'My Darling' one night while Ron was working in Brisbane. He had often said to her that she was in every song he played and sang while he was away. Touched by his sweetness, she set out to surprise him with a song built around those sentiments.

'I was very proud of how that song turned out,' Judith says. 'When I sang it to Ron, he loved it. He said he thought it was the best song I'd written. The big thrill for me was that there were no chords he needed to correct or add for me. In the past, I had often sung a melody to him and he would work out the chords for me, but with "My Darling" I did it on my own and there was nothing Ron thought needed changing. That was a huge compliment to me as a songwriter, considering Ron's knowledge of harmonies and chord structures. He'd taught me a lot by now and I felt as though I'd come of age as a writer. There was another song that Ron had written, called "Tonight's the Night", and I surprised him by writing a verse to it while he was away. He loved it – and again he didn't change any of the chords.'

Being anonymous on the Sunshine Coast meant Judith could go shopping without makeup, and be known to the Nambour locals as Mrs Edgeworth.

'It struck me that this was the first time in almost twenty years that I could be in Australia and be myself,' Judith says. 'Very few people up there had the slightest idea who I was, other than being Ron's wife. They were very lovely, straightforward country folk and their friendliness was so genuine. No favours or special gestures because I was a public figure, just genuine niceness. It opened my eyes to how friendly and kind Australian people are. I'd spent such a lot of time overseas, where people were forever talking about what a friendly bunch Australians were and this was really my first opportunity to find out for myself.'

Judith also began to take an interest in Australia's history and was dismayed to learn it wasn't quite the way she'd been taught at school. In the seclusion of the Queensland forest, with just talkback radio for company, she gleaned a lot.

'I was flabbergasted by what I was hearing about the way Aboriginal Australians had been treated,' Judith explains. 'I was listening to Kath Walker, the Aboriginal poet who reverted to her tribal name, Oodgeroo Noonuccal. She was talking about how the Aboriginal people wished that they could share what they had with white Australian children. This was after white man had walked into Australia and literally raped and pillaged, stealing everything away from them. After all that, they still wanted to share with us. We just took it away from them, with no appreciation of the gifts that the land had to give us. We made heroes of white men who walked across Australia and starved to death in the process, men who knew nothing about the land. The Aboriginal people had trade routes going from the north to the south and they knew how to survive.'

Judith was horrified to learn that Aboriginal culling had taken place, particularly in Queensland, with sporting parties making a weekend pastime of shooting Aborigines, and that Aboriginal people were not given the vote till 1967. This was only the early eighties and already there was talk about Australia's bicentenary celebrations of 1988. Judith realised that white Australians were celebrating an event that the original black inhabitants couldn't feel part of. Australia was celebrating the white man's coming in and conquering the land, taking it away from the people who lived there, whose heritage it was. Many were celebrating the conquering of a nation, when Australia was invaded. These birthday celebrations would more or less be a period of mourning for the Aboriginal people and there was little regard for their feelings.

'The actual event was four or five years off,' Judith says. 'I still had a lot to read and learn before then, but already I was starting to feel that I didn't want to be involved in any official celebrations in 1988. It was something I really felt very strongly about. Sometime later, I read an interview with Robyn Archer, who said she planned to be out of Australia for most of 1988, because she didn't support what was going on. I understood exactly how she felt.'

Judith furthered her newfound interest in indigenous peoples by reading a short speech written in 1854 and attributed to the Native American Chief Seattle. Touched by the chief's knowledge of and concern for the environment, Judith began rhyming his speech and setting it to music. Within a week, Judith had composed *The Chief Seattle Suite* of five songs, including 'We Must Teach Our Children', which she recorded in 1994 for her album *Let Me Find Love*. It was some years later, when a friend did some private research, that Judith was to learn that the speech was not written by Chief Seattle at all, but by Ted Perry, a white American scriptwriter from Vermont in the USA.

'Ted Perry was commissioned by the Southern Baptist Church to write six film scripts in America and one of them was about the environment,' Judith says. 'I found that Chief Seattle had indeed written a letter to the president in the 1850s and a small portion of that letter was used in Ted Perry's speech, but the rest of the work was Ted's. The Southern Baptists didn't credit Ted Perry with the work and, to this day, even many of the Indian people believe that Chief Seattle wrote those words.'

Judith was able to contact Ted Perry and they talked for a long time about his speech. When *The Chief Seattle Suite* was finally complete, Judith gave Perry his first official recognition by co-crediting him as the song's author, along with herself and Chief Seattle. The chief's tribe knows of Ted Perry's work and Ted and Judith arranged for proceeds from the song's royalties to go to them.

In 1983, Judith also completed her *Australian Cities Suite*, which had begun all those years ago in America with 'Seldom Melbourne Leaves My Mind'. Included in it were songs for all the capital cities in Australia, but it would be some years before she settled on the final words of her anthem, 'Australia Land of Today'.

'It had occurred to me many times that Australia didn't really have a lot of Australian music in the popular vein,' Judith says. 'Brisbane made a bid for the Olympics using the American song "Somewhere Over the Rainbow" as their theme song. You got on a Qantas plane and you heard Hawaiian music. We really needed something in the way of an anthem and, to me, "Advance Australia Fair" didn't embrace all Australians. There are certain sections of our Australian community that would feel left out of that song. Some years before, I had taken the music I'd written in Switzerland for a possible gospel song and reworked the lyric as a fun song called "Australia Land of the Free". It was all very patriotic, about waving flags, giving someone a fair go, and it ended with "Australia's a land of repute ... bloody beaut!" But now it was the eighties and I decided to take my song very seriously, reworking the lyrics and calling it "Australia Land of Today".'

After fifteen months of solitude, Judith decided the time was right for her to return to the stage. During her lengthy absence, she had visualised the ways in which her shows could change and, having left her jazz days long behind, she opted for a show of her own entirely original material in all styles, hoping to establish a new musical identity.

Judith and Ron put together a band of musicians from the Sunshine Coast and hired a local studio to rehearse their material. During those rehearsals, she also wrote her a song for the Sunshine Coast, to include in her *Australian Cities Suite*. The rehearsals went well, but at the very last moment Judith reneged and had the band rehearse some Seekers songs, for fear audiences would be disappointed. She made her comeback at Blazes, a Sunshine Coast piano bar where Ron had enjoyed success as a pianist during Judith's hiatus. They played six shows at Blazes and discovered that their own music was very much accepted.

With her return to public life, Judith forfeited her anonymity in Nambour. She had enjoyed not being public property and not having constantly to stop and chat to people who recognised her. The locals were stunned when they realised that Mrs Edgeworth, who always popped in with her hair up and no makeup on, was Judith Durham. Judith noticed the faces of many of her local shopkeepers at the ensuing shows. Audiences seemed delighted with both Judith and Ron's songs and the enjoyment the two obviously got from performing them. In particular, they loved 'Australia Land of Today' and many asked whether they could buy it on disc.

'We thought about recording it as a single,' Judith recalls. 'I hadn't been in a studio very often to record since the Hottest Band in Town albums in 1973 and 1974 and I'd never really recorded anything quite as contemporary as "Australia Land of Today". We went into a studio in Brisbane to try to put it down, but it just didn't work. The people we were working with were very much into contemporary music and they tried the entire time to influence us to change some of the chords, but we didn't want to change our conception of the music. The recording process in the eighties was also very difficult for us to grasp. We had to put the drums down first and then the bass, followed by the other instruments, which was very peculiar to us. We'd never done things that way in the past and we found it very hard to set a tempo and get a feel for the song that way. We ended up scrapping the whole idea.'

Encouraged by the reaction at Blazes, Judith and Ron accepted a four-week season at Brisbane's New York Hotel and a stint at The Resort on the Gold Coast. Again, the audiences were ecstatic and Judith's confidence was bolstered by their positive response to the new material. But there was still that nagging doubt about using her own name. So, early in 1984, Judith summoned up the courage to perform publicly under an alias. She settled on Lutetia Concorde, the name of the Paris hotel she'd seen three years before, while Ron performed as Ronson Palando, the name Ron had toyed with using as a joke when he was dealing with those groovy Los Angeles music-industry types in the seventies.

'It was a hard thing to do,' Judith says, 'but I had to go through the motions to see how it would feel. I checked with a lawyer, who explained that, as long as I wasn't using it for fraudulent purposes, I could sing under that name. We were booked to sing on a late-night television show in Brisbane and we decided we'd try out the names. The host, Mike Higgins, kept a straight face and introduced us as Lutetia Concorde and Ronson Palando. Ron played as I sang "Paris Nights" and it all seemed to go well. We went on and did a couple of Brisbane restaurant bookings under those names – we even had posters printed up advertising us. Then, at one venue, we found out from a waitress that a girl who had come along one night had asked who Lutetia Concorde was. The waitress whispered that it was really Judith Durham! The girl replied, "Who's Judith Durham?" To qualify it, the waitress said, "Oh you know, The Seekers," and the girl replied, "Who're The Seekers?"!

'That was all I really needed to hear to make me realise that by now, in 1984, there was a lot of water under the bridge. There was a whole new generation of music fans who didn't necessarily know about The Seekers – or Judith Durham, for that matter – so our new names were put away for good. Perhaps there was a market out there that didn't readily identify me with the group and who wouldn't automatically expect me to sing Seekers songs. A market for our material.'

Just as Judith was adapting to the notion that The Seekers were fading into her past, the bubble burst. Out of the blue, in August 1984, Judith received a letter from Bruce Woodley, which expressed the feelings he had bottled up for more than sixteen years. In it, he openly poured out the anger he felt towards Judith for leaving the group, telling her how he felt she had let her three close friends down.

'I was really thrilled when I got a letter from Bruce,' Judith says. 'It had been such a long time since the boys had had any contact with me. I started to read it and, about halfway through, I realised he was unburdening something to me. I got such a shock to read that I had hurt the boys so much by leaving The Seekers. I always felt I had done the right thing, standing by the group for those four years and then giving six months' notice of my intention to leave. I always thought they understood my reasons for leaving, but it came through very strongly in Bruce's letter that there was no understanding at all. There was absolutely no conception of why I had to leave and it dawned on me that the public felt the same way. If the boys had trouble understanding it, then the public would have been completely bewildered.

'It was very upsetting for me and I felt sad for the boys. I thought when we split up that we would all go on and develop as people and find our own ways in life. It had never occurred to me that the boys would always have this sense of unfinished business.'

For years, Judith had been confronted with questions from the media, asking if she had regrets about leaving The Seekers. She reached a point where she began to wish they would ask her if she had any regrets about *joining* them! Whenever she was approached with an offer for a reunion, she would turn it down. Her resolve not to rejoin the group was simply a statement of fact, but it was possibly taken as an indication that Judith didn't like her former singing partners and wanted nothing to do with them. When The Seekers split, Judith assumed they would all pursue their own careers and, having had four very successful years together, would remain friends. It had been a jolt for her to realise that once the business ended, so did the relationship.

'I got to the stage, sixteen years down the track, where I began to think they just didn't like me,' Judith says, 'that they resented me for leaving when I did. I felt they didn't understand me as a person and had no appreciation of the years I had exclusively devoted to them. Nor did they understand the theatricality in me, that need for performance perfection. I'd heard that I had a reputation for being difficult to work with, which was another shock. The only times I could ever have been perceived as being difficult was when I questioned artistic things, and I was doing that for the benefit of the group as a whole, not just for me. Bruce's letter made me realise that the guys must have considered that I was the only key to their success. You see, I saw the world as a great treasure chest of opportunity and, for me, The Seekers was one of those opportunities, but never the only one. It was becoming clear to me that the boys would have been happy to have stayed in that group situation for the rest of their working lives.

'My decision to leave The Seekers was a very difficult one, but I truly believed when I resigned that I had done the right thing for the four years. It was more time than I had ever expected to devote to the group, but I stayed in that situation because I didn't want to let anyone down. When I got to the point where I just had to find myself as an individual and experience different types of music, I gave notice. I saw it as resigning from one job and moving on to another one, but the public, and perhaps the boys, saw it as a divorce.'

The letter from Bruce consolidated all the thoughts Judith had had over the years. She still felt misunderstood, but she didn't have much time to dwell on the past. Out driving in Nambour one afternoon, she and Ron stopped at a pedestrian crossing and, while waiting for people to cross the road, a truck slammed into the back of their car, causing substantial damage to the Citroën and leaving Judith with a neck injury. For several months, she battled constant pain and on occasions her left shoulder blade locked. Three years after the accident, Judith suffered major complications and was forced to lie down for more than a month. She was unable to lift her chin and had crippling pain in her left arm, which prevented her from playing the piano. Eventually, her immobility required traction.

In November that year, just a matter of weeks after receiving Bruce Woodley's letter, Judith and Ron were planning to celebrate their fifteenth wedding anniversary with a day out. They had planned a little sightseeing, a game of tennis and a picnic. In preparation for the day, Ron dropped into the local supermarket to buy food. Having paid, he took two steps from the cash register and slipped on a spilled drink, breaking his hip.

'He was taken to hospital and discharged later that afternoon,' Judith says. 'So I had to look after him at home. That was the end of our performing for quite a while. Ron was quite disabled by this fall. His ankles and feet were very swollen and he suffered numbness whenever he tried to sit for any length of time.'

With three months of rehabilitation ahead, Judith and Ron spent their time writing songs and planning the next step of their already chequered careers. Though the spectre of The Seekers would loom even larger in their lives in the next few years, 1985 would see them back in the recording studios and mounting a show based on their lives together.

13. ON THE ROAD AGAIN

All through life,
You have to learn to live with the pain,
For you know the sun
Will soon come after the rain.
Look for freedom within you,
Do what's right for you,
All through life be you,
That's all you can do.

– 'ALL THROUGH LIFE'
JUDITH DURHAM

Midway through the decade, the eighties were shaping up to be an era of consolidation for Judith and Ron. For the first time since their marriage in 1969, they had a permanent home and were able to stay in one country long enough to see the seasons come and go. Judith had time to devote to health and philosophical issues and her quest for knowledge had helped her finally discover herself as an individual. She continued to battle her ongoing conflict over The Seekers songs and her relationship with the boys, but professionally she had entered the most creative period of her performing life. In contrast to the seventies, when she was developing as an artist on a performance level, the eighties saw Judith moving away from mainstream show business and trying to find her own unique place in the world.

The seventies had also posed another major question for Judith and Ron: now they were beginning to nudge forty, were they going to have a family?

'We talked about starting a family often during the mid-seventies,' Judith recalls. 'We could see the pluses and minuses. The minus we always came back to was that having children would restrict our freedom to move around. We were very, very happy with our lives then and I found great joy in the lifestyle we had. Certainly we had professional worries and our finances had taken a bit of a bashing, but we were extremely happy as we were and we didn't see any particular reason to start a family, especially as it would mean we'd have to put down permanent roots.

'Perhaps if my career had consolidated itself a lot earlier, we may have had a family, but it just seemed to us that we needed to be free souls at that stage in our lives. I don't believe in abortion and obviously, had we had children, we would have loved them, but we were very aware of how people's lives change when children come along. Ron could clearly see how motherhood would change my life and he pointed out that, if we had children, I would be giving up my creative freedom.

'We made the decision not to have children and have never had any regrets. People think if you don't have kids you're losing out on a lot in life and I guess in some cases that's true. But I don't feel I've missed out on anything. Our belief in reincarnation also helped us to make that decision. We have been other people in other lives, even other species, presumably always having offspring. We think of this life as one of our millions of lives, so it's not essential for us to pack everything into one life.

'These days, it's quite common for women to elect not to become mothers and it's not questioned at all. I've only been asked why I didn't have a family maybe a dozen or so times in my life. Occasionally I've had the feeling that people have been reluctant to ask, probably thinking it was because of a health problem, but it wasn't: it was just our complete contentment with our life together the way it was.'

It was March 1985 before Ron's hip was mended sufficiently to allow him to resume work. During his convalescence, Judith received an offer from New Zealand to play the starring role of Maria in a stage revival of *The Sound of Music*, but she turned it down. She was enjoying the musical challenge of breaking new ground with Ron. Besides, since Ron's accident, Judith had been writing her own small musical based on the adventures she and Ron had enjoyed together.

Although still experiencing discomfort from his hip break, Ron helped Judith scout around for a venue to stage her musical. They settled on the Majestic Theatre in Pomona, Queensland's oldest theatre and one of a few on the Sunshine Coast that had grand pianos. The owner was Ron West, a theatre and cinema buff, and he and his wife Mandy often used the theatre to show silent movies. He and Mandy made the theatre available to Judith and Ron, and their local drama group built sets and painted scenery.

'It was just brilliant,' Judith says. 'It was a terrific success and the audience seemed to love it. The show was supposed to run for two and a half hours, but on opening night we were on for three hours. We did so much of the material we'd written on our travels, like "When Starlight Fades", "Paris Nights", "Oh Basil", "It's Fun To Be Fat". We enjoyed giving the audience an insight into our lives and they were in fits of laughter watching Ron's antics, and, while I'm no great actress, I enjoyed the patter we shared on stage. It was just like talking to Ron at home in our own lounge room.

'The main reason for creating that musical was so that we could present our own music with a purpose, which would get around the expectations of my singing Seekers songs. The irony of it was that people loved the show and enjoyed our songs, but they still asked why I didn't sing "Georgy Girl". It still hadn't solved that problem for me, but I loved having the chance to do it.'

The musical was so successful that it ran for fifteen nights and was reviewed by a local playwright and theatre critic, Ian Austin. Renowned in the area for his tough critiques, Austin was impressed with the show. Judith plucked up the courage to contact him to thank him for his comments and told him that she had long wanted to write a full musical. She asked Austin if he was interested in writing the book. He was delighted and, over the coming months, they worked together on a musical with an environmental theme, called *Gotta Be Rainbows*.

Work on the project continued for three more years and, although it is now complete, it has yet to be staged. Before long, Judith's sister Beverley came to stay at Nambour for a short break. Towards the end of her visit, they dropped into the Nambour Folk Club, which Judith had read about in the local paper. Judith had not long walked in when the organisers recognised her and asked her to sing. Unaccompanied, Judith sang her newly composed 'Sunshine Coast, You I Love' and brought the house down. Afterwards, she met Bill Hauritz, president of the Queensland Folk Federation, who later booked her and Ron for a concert at the folk club.

'In those days, we were ending all our shows with "Australia Land of Today",' Judith says. 'I was quite accustomed to everyone going crazy after we'd done it, but it was different in this club. The response was OK, but nothing over the top, and I wondered what had gone wrong. After the show, a couple of people came up and started laying into me about some of the issues raised in the lyrics. For instance, they felt the words "brother man" were offensive to women. They also questioned the line "Australia's the best place to be", which was divisive on a world scale. Ron started getting all hot under the collar, and told these people they had no right to speak to me this way, but I was actually lapping it up. It was the first really constructive criticism I'd had of the song, and I needed to know how people really felt about it. I'd set out to write it in the first place so we would have a song that would unite everybody who lives in Australia and I didn't want anybody to feel alienated. As a result, I stopped singing it for about two years, while I desperately tried to refine the lyrics.'

Hauritz had also expressed interest in promoting a series of concerts for Judith and Ron, and they jumped at the chance to test their original material on a concert audience. They had played mostly clubs to date and while the show was always extremely successful, Judith felt it was better suited to a theatre atmosphere, especially after the warm response to the musical at Pomona. After so many years of seeking the right management, Judith had begun to establish a manager–artist relationship with Hauritz, but his involvement in the inauguration of the Maleny Folk Festival was mushrooming and their association had to end. However, through Hauritz, Judith and Ron appeared at the first Maleny Folk Festival, which is now the biggest folk festival in Australia.

By the time 1986 rolled around, Judith had developed a keen interest in all aspects of promoting and touring a show. She had stood by for years watching other people do it, but had no real concept of the mechanics involved. Like her stint at busking in San Francisco, this was something she felt she needed to experience in order to add another dimension to her understanding of the music business. Adopting a *nom de plume*, Judith set about organising a small tour for herself and Ron through northern New South Wales. The commitment it required from her was a surprise.

'I really had no idea of how much co-ordination went into mounting a tour,' Judith says. 'It gave me an understanding of how many things had to be in place at the same time. I did posters and flyers to advertise the concerts, booked the halls, handled all the paperwork and, using my *nom de plume*, arranged the radio and press interviews for "Judith Durham". In the past, Ron had always handled the phoning around and the negotiations, but, from the time he was out of action with his broken hip, I'd taken over those things myself. This was another level completely, trying to put together a whole series of dates. It ended up being an enormous workload, with phone calls from morning to night. By the time it was over, I was exhausted, but very glad I'd done it.'

Having arranged and performed five civic-centre concerts, Judith took her learning a step further by delving into the publishing side of music. She swotted up on performing rights, mechanicals, recording contracts and 'legalese' in general. 'Back in London in the seventies, I met a lawyer who advised me to hold on to my own copyright material,' Judith recalls. 'I didn't go into it in any great depth then because I hadn't written many songs. But when I started cataloguing all our compositions to this point, I realised we had around a hundred and fifty of them between us and that there was potential income from them. Most of them weren't published and I wanted to know everything that was involved before I went any further.'

Armed with her new understanding, Judith decided to give recording another try. With Ron, she went into a recording studio in Byron Bay, to put down two of their songs, 'That's When I'm Near You' and 'All You Have To Do'. Again, the two had trouble getting tempos right and, while

ON THE ROAD AGAIN

the session was not as abortive as the previous year's attempt, it did not deliver the end product Judith was hoping for.

Having worked in and around Queensland for so long, Judith and Ron arranged their next booking in Sydney at the Don Burrows Supper Club. The last time they had performed in Sydney was as a jazz act in the late 1970s, before they returned overseas. It was there, looking out of the club's windows, that Judith had one of her premonitions: an image of the streets of Paris flashed through her mind for no apparent reason, yet within three years she was living there. This time, the club was changing its musical direction and Judith and Ron's singer-songwriter material fitted the bill. The problem was, the public weren't told that the musical emphasis of the club was shifting and Judith drew fans expecting to hear her singing jazz!

'The shows went well enough,' Judith says, 'and I was thrilled to find one night that Keith Potger was in the audience with his wife, Pam. I wasn't singing Seekers songs at that point, but I did ask Keith how he felt about my singing them on my own. After Bruce's letter and my awareness that the boys had been hurt by my leaving the group, I really didn't want to alienate them any further. I needed to know that they didn't see me claiming those songs as my own. Keith was very supportive and very happy for me to sing them if I wanted to. The boys, of course, had been singing them in the line-up with Louisa Wisseling, but they were doing it as The Seekers. If I was to start singing them again, I would be singing them under my own name and I just wanted his blessing. I then needed to get approval from Athol and Bruce.'

Judith got that chance in November 1986, when she and Ron accepted a six-week booking at Noah's Hotel in Melbourne. For Judith, this was another long-overdue opportunity to catch up with Beverley and Barry, and she enjoyed seeing her niece and nephews, who had grown so much. By now, her niece Belinda was following in the footsteps of her mother and aunt and showing great interest in singing and a real flair for art; while Ben, the youngest of the three children, had been influenced by Ron's piano talents and had become a fine stride and boogie player himself.

Throughout their season at Noah's Orchid Restaurant, Judith and Ron stayed in the hotel and one afternoon Athol Guy and Bruce Woodley dropped in to see them. 'I was thrilled to see them both,' Judith says. 'They didn't stay for my show, but we had a nice chat. I explained my quandary over singing Seekers songs and asked them how they felt. They both assured me I should be doing them if I wanted to, and that I had as much right to them as they did. That was enormously reassuring for me. From that point on, I considered putting them back in my shows. It solved a big problem in another way, because I still had trouble getting promoters to take me on if I wasn't singing Seekers songs.'

Reviews of the Noah's season were favourable, with original songs like 'Someone Cared' and 'All Through Life' being singled out. For Judith, the run was a successful one but the venue, being upmarket and charging accordingly, prohibited many of Judith's fans from seeing the shows. It was the following year that Judith finally found herself booked in a venue that felt absolutely right: the Troubadour in Melbourne.

'The Troubadour was a real milestone for me,' Judith explains. 'It was a real singer-songwriter's venue and we could perform our songs in an environment that was created for that. It was rare that I was able to perform in Melbourne in a real musician's venue with that feeling of authenticity about it, as opposed to the show-business-type venues I'd been working in for so long. At a lot of my restaurant shows, the emphasis had been on the food, whereas the whole focus of an evening at the Troubadour was the music. I actually felt like an artist, rather than an act.'

The shows went so well that six months later Judith was booked for a second Troubadour season. At the end of one of their shows, a fan called out a request for 'Georgy Girl' and, in unison, the rest of the audience let out a groan before the whole crowd dissolved into laughter. That was another major moment for Judith, who had finally found an audience that didn't come along to hear Seekers songs at all.

Judith and Ron stayed on in Melbourne for Christmas, before returning to the Sunshine Coast at the start of 1988. Since their last abortive attempt at recording, they had heard of the introduction of a new music technology known as MIDI, or musical-instrument digital interface, working via computer with software that can 'remember' how a note is played and can recreate it. Eager to learn more, they used their spare time in Melbourne to go around the local recording studios and music shops, working out which MIDI equipment would be needed in order for them to set up their own recording studio at home.

As the months of 1988 rolled by, Judith kept a low profile, working mostly at home with Ron on new material and arrangements. Refusing bicentennial engagements meant lost income, but Judith was determined to stick to her principles.

Later in the year, she was contacted by the organisers of Brisbane's Expo '88, the largest official bicentennial event, who had decided to end the closing ceremony with 'The Carnival Is Over' and wanted the original Seekers to re-form for the occasion. Judith turned them down, explaining that she was a solo artist. Not wishing to stir up any controversy, she chose not to mention her opposition to the bicentennial celebrations. A fortnight later, the organisers contacted her again, stressing that 'The Carnival Is Over' was definitely the song they were using to close Expo '88 and would Judith sing it solo?

By now, Judith was including all the hits in her shows and it was a tempting honour to have been asked as a solo artist to take part in such a major celebration. Knowing she was being put to the test regarding her personal boycott, she gritted her teeth, took a deep breath and, for the first time in her career, took what would be seen as a political stand. She explained that her main reason for taking no part in any bicentennial events was out of embarrassment over the Aboriginal issue. Within two days, her explanation had found its way on to the front page of the Brisbane *Courier-Mail*. The organisers, knowing they were getting nowhere, explained to Judith that, if she didn't sing the song, they would have no choice but to offer it to someone else.

Ironically, before her approach by the Expo '88 organisers, Judith was advised by an agent to put together a group of three young men and start touring as Judith Durham and The Seekers. 'The agent tried to sell me on the idea that there was a million dollars in The Seekers' name and I should be capitalising on it,' Judith says. 'He assured me that I'd make a lot of money and my problems with being booked would be over. I explained to him that, if I ever considered being a Seeker again, I would do it with the other three original Seekers, or not at all. Having turned down the Expo people a second time, I had a feeling something would be in the wind.

'Not long after that, I heard that the three guys had got together with the Australian singer Julie Anthony and sung "The Carnival Is Over" as the finale at the closing ceremony. Out of the blue one night, I had a phone call from Athol. He was at Julie Anthony's house and they were ringing to tell me that they would be taking part in a musical that traced the life of The Seekers and Julie would be playing my part. I was put on the spot a bit when Athol handed the phone to Julie. I told her I was glad that she was doing the musical and pleased they'd chosen someone with such a good voice. Then they told me they were going to do an album of the music from the show, with some of Bruce's new songs on it.

'I couldn't really do anything more than wish them well, but a short while later I heard another rumour that Julie was going to join the boys full-time. I just kept saying to everybody "Oh, no, it's a musical that they're doing with Julie and they must be recording the hits for a cast album." Then, early in 1989, it was announced that The Seekers were getting back together and Julie Anthony was replacing Judith Durham. I saw only one article that ever mentioned the musical and it was never written about again.'

Of course, along with this exciting announcement that Julie Anthony was now a Seeker came an 'endorsement' from Judith, who was quoted as having said she was delighted that Julie was taking her place in the group. At no time after that initial phone call had Judith ever been informed by the boys that The Seekers were back in business. This was a major jolt to Judith, who was about to be thrust back into competition with The Seekers, some 21 years after she'd left them. Suddenly, Judith was being hounded by the press. They weren't ringing to ask about her new songs, the musical she'd been working on or even her thoughts on the bicentenary: they wanted to know what she thought of Julie Anthony. That, and the old question: did Judith regret leaving The Seekers in 1968?

It was while she and Ron were interstate for Judith's sell-out concert at the Perth Concert Hall in April that a twenty-track album credited simply to The Seekers was released, just two months after the group had announced their re-formation with Julie Anthony. It featured nine rerecorded versions of the original group's hits, several new Bruce Woodley songs and collaborations, and a song by Keith. Judith now had a more serious identity crisis than ever.

'It hurt my feelings enormously that, although the original group was not singing them, our hits had been rereleased and were credited to The Seekers,' Judith explains. 'It was as though I had been a session singer on those original recordings. It's one thing to re-form a group with a new singer, but it's another thing entirely to rerecord the old hits, rewriting history in a way. It was almost as though I'd never existed.'

The new line-up released a single with 'Georgy Girl' as its flip side and again it was billed as The Seekers. Anyone picking up a copy of the original single – the one that had sold 4 million copies – would have no idea who the female singer was. There was nothing on those original records to identify Judith Durham, other than her voice. On the other hand, someone who knew that Judith had been the original female singer in The Seekers might buy the new version and assume she was singing on those tracks. Much later, Judith learned from fans that the album was on sale in Europe with Judith's photo on the cover.

Judith was no stranger to this kind of confusion, which she'd already encountered in her solo career. People often asked her for 'I'd Like to Teach the World to Sing', which was by The New Seekers, or 'The Sparrow Song', which was the boys with Louisa Wisseling. The public was confused enough, but now everything was going to become even more confusing. Judith resolved that, if in the unlikely event she would ever sing with the group again, her name would be billed.

'Ron was very supportive through that time, as were a lot of members of the public,' Judith recalls. 'He told me time and again to just sit it out and let the public be the judge, but I still felt like I was battling the same old problem. I understood that in their hearts the boys wanted to be singing The Seekers material in a group and I had the greatest admiration for Julie as a singer, but I was saddened by the way it was done.'

There were two more slaps in the face to come for Judith. First, the *Live On* album notes, retracing the history of The Seekers, made no reference whatsoever to her involvement with the group. The liner notes seemed to be written in such a way as to suggest that the 1989 Seekers line-up was recreating its own past. Second, an interview with Bruce Woodley appeared in a mid-1989 edition of *New Idea*, quoting him as saying that Judith had dropped The Seekers overnight and that it had taken them a long time to get over the shock.

He claimed that Judith had negotiated a solo recording contract before quitting the group and that she had not been approached by the Expo organisers to sing 'The Carnival Is Over'.

'That one absolutely floored me,' Judith says. 'There seemed no other point to this article than for Bruce to get these things off his chest. I just couldn't understand why he was speaking this way in interviews, but I decided I couldn't let it go on any longer without something being said. I phoned Bruce and expressed my disappointment. I asked him why he'd said he had no warning that I was leaving the group and he told me he had no recollection that in resigning I had given six months' notice. Press articles for more than twenty years had mentioned the fact that I'd given six months' notice, but Bruce couldn't remember it.

'I also reminded him that I didn't have a recording contract when I left The Seekers and assured him that I had never sought one while I was a member of the group. It was a full year after The Seekers broke up that I signed with A&M Records. And, thirdly, I let him know that I had certainly been offered the closing spot at Expo, which he told me he was unaware of.'

After setting the record straight with Bruce, Judith contacted *New*

Idea through a lawyer and insisted that, if they didn't print a retraction, they must allow Judith to tell her side of the story. The final straw came later in 1989, when a Queensland tour that Judith had taken pains to piece slowly together suddenly fell apart. The promoter pulled out. His reason was that The Seekers – with Julie Anthony – had recently toured in the same areas and everybody had heard the songs. After she had agonised for so long about putting Seekers songs back into her shows to appease promoters and the public, they were once more working against her.

It seemed to Judith and Ron that their only option was to go overseas again. Aware it had been some time since they had an English profile, they contacted a promoter, who backed a small-scale, test-the-waters tour of England, using British musicians. Considering she had little promotion, the tour did extremely well and Judith was heartened to find that her loyal fans were still there and that the name Judith Durham could still pull audiences. It was also the first time in several years that Judith and Ron had seen Vicky. They spent some happy, but brief times together, knowing that all too soon, there would be fond farewells again.

During the month they spent in the UK, Judith and Ron made some enquiries into the country's major recording studios and record companies. They found that, as in Australia, studios were using MIDI equipment and that record companies were more interested in signing completed albums than artists direct.

Upon their arrival home, they contacted computer experts and learned all they could about the MIDI process, before selecting the equipment that best suited their needs. By the time 1990 rolled around, they had bought a computer, sound modules, keyboards and string samples. With their recording studio almost functional, their next step was finally establishing their own company in Australia.

'I had learned so much about contracts and copyright since we'd been back in Australia,' Judith says. 'We just needed something in place to operate properly. I'd been trying to think of a name for the company for a long time, but always seemed to pick something that was already registered. It took five years. One day, I was swimming in the rock pool and I thought of the name Musicoast, which seemed appropriate because we were living for music and we were living on the coast. We registered the company and I designed a logo that reflected the way I feel about music. I ended up with sketches of the world with a heart in it, and a treble clef inside the heart. I took it to a graphic designer, who did the finished artwork, and then we were in business. All that was missing now was that elusive manager I still dreamed would materialise one day.'

Before leaving for the UK, Judith decided to phone promoters herself, in the hope that she could be promoted in concert venues. Knowing how well her concerts were being received made Judith more determined not to become a club performer, despite the lucrative offers. She was delighted to receive a call from the promoter Arthur Laing, who offered to back a national tour on her return from England.

Although Judith had been singing professionally for 27 years, Laing elected to promote the tour as Judith's Silver Jubilee tour, the 25th anniversary of her voice's first topping the charts in 1965 with 'I'll Never Find Another You'. Laing's offer was not without conditions. He would present Judith only if she featured Seekers songs in her show, along with some of the other songs she was identified with, such as 'Danny Boy' and 'Amazing Grace'.

'It was something I just finally had to come to terms with,' Judith says. 'The Seekers were also touring, so I really was in a catch-22 situation. We decided that we'd do a two-hour show that gave Ron his own showcase at the start and featured Seekers songs in between the standards and our original material. It ended up a well-balanced and varied show and we were really looking forward to getting out on the road.'

In the coming weeks, the pair booked and rehearsed musicians, while Laing put together a hectic series of dates. The 36 dates surpassed any pre- or post-Seekers tour Judith had ever undertaken, but she was ready for the challenge and confident she had the stamina. As Judith and Ron packed their hired van and prepared to leave Nambour and start the tour, Judith had another premonition.

'It was raining,' she recalls. 'I was slopping around in the mud, thinking how funny it was to be setting off on a glamorous tour, under those circumstances. I went back into the house just to check that everything was in order and, as I looked around the lounge room, I had this strange sense that this was the end of another chapter for me. I had an eerie feeling that I wouldn't be coming back to the house and I wanted to soak up the sight of those familiar surroundings that had been the scene of so many happy and sad times during the last nine years. I went back out to Ron and asked him to reassure me that we would be coming home again. He just laughed and reminded me that the tour was only for six weeks and that after our final Brisbane date we'd be back home again. I had no reason to doubt him, but I still had this feeling that I should have been covering the furniture and taking the sort of precautions you would if you were going to be away for a long time.'

Judith's Silver Jubilee Tour kicked off in late April. Ron opened each show with the *Warsaw Concerto* and a smattering of Fats Waller. He remained on stage to lead the band, as Judith worked her way through new and old songs from all areas of her musical life. The concerts were ecstatically received by the public and the critics alike. Most nights ended with at least one standing ovation and, by talking to fans after each show, Judith happily realised that she had hit on a winning formula, a concert that pleased everyone. The one-woman shows in the early seventies had had similar success but for Judith this was something even more rewarding because so much more of her own material was included.

With this tour, Judith arranged to have printed forms left on seats, so members of the audience could write down the songs they'd enjoyed most during the evening. She planned to collate those forms and possibly record the most popular songs on her next album.

The Melbourne Silver Jubilee date was set for 19 May at the National Theatre in St Kilda, and Judith and Ron were delighted to hear that tickets had been snapped up quickly. This concert, they felt, would be something special.

Indeed it was. That night, Judith and Ron could do no wrong. After the pair had been two hours on stage, the audience clamoured for more, and, after ten encores, there were simply no more songs to sing. Judith asked the audience 'Will we do the whole thing again?' and they roared their reply: 'Yes!' The two exited the stage after bringing the crowd to its feet for the third time. This had certainly been the best night of the tour so far and Judith and Ron were elated. What they didn't know was that the events that would take place in the 24 hours following this concert would change their lives for ever.

14. THE CRASH

So young to falter,
Too young to die,
Don't give in, come on fight,
Take my hand, hold on tight.

– 'HOLD ON TIGHT'
LORRAINE JAGER

Fate had always played a big part in Judith Durham's life and the afternoon of 20 May 1990 was no exception. It was fate that caused a delay that day as she and Ron moved on to Tooleybuc, near the border of Victoria and New South Wales, for the next date of her Silver Jubilee Tour. As the tour wound its way to Melbourne, Ron had been driving Judith in a rented red Toyota Lexcen, while tour manager Peter Summers had been travelling with the production crew. In Melbourne, the hire car developed engine trouble on the evening of the National Theatre show and, it being Saturday, mechanics were unable to fix it by the next day.

On Sunday morning, Summers had trouble getting another Lexcen and instead, settled on a white Fairlane to transport the three of them through the country areas. He had to let the truck go on ahead because of the delay, so Judith and Ron set off for Tooleybuc with Summers at the wheel, an hour later than they'd planned, still filled with the elation of the previous night's triumph. As they drove along the Calder Highway near Kyneton, 140 kilometres north of Melbourne, Judith was sitting in the back of the car eating salad, and reminiscing about the concert with Ron, who was in the passenger seat.

'We were just chatting,' says Judith, 'when Peter said, "Look at that," and we looked ahead and saw a red car in a stream of traffic coming the other way. It was further to the left than the other cars in the same lane and it appeared to be swerving. A second or two later, it did a sharp right-hand turn in front of us. I don't clearly remember what happened after that. I know I reached forward to grip the back of the seat in front of me and tried to hold on, but our car was jolting a lot. The last thing I remember was the red car being directly in front of us, but I didn't actually see us hit it. I'd closed my eyes and was clinging on for dear life.'

The next thing Judith knew, she was wedged between the two front seats of the Fairlane, lying face down. In agony, she was unable to move, but through the haze she could hear Peter outside the car, yelling, 'Judith, Judith! Oh, my God, Judith!' She was anxious to let Peter know she was still alive and frantic to find out what had happened to Ron. She lapsed into and out of consciousness until a doctor, who had been travelling a few cars behind the Fairlane, arrived and immediately administered a painkilling injection.

'As the doctor turned me over, I can remember my arm was under me and my wrist was just flopping,' Judith recalls. 'I was aware there was something wrong with my leg, but I wasn't sure what it was. The doctor wouldn't let me look at it. I was told later that it was badly smashed up and the bone was actually sticking out of the flesh, so that's why he was diverting my attention. I looked to my side and I could see Ron gasping for breath, clutching his chest. I was trying to get the doctor to do something for Ron, but, because of the painkiller, the words just wouldn't come out properly.'

Ambulances arrived and rushed Ron and Peter Summers to Kyneton Hospital, but Judith's injuries were more serious and the decision was made to airlift her by helicopter to the Road Trauma Unit of Melbourne's Alfred Hospital. Judith asked the doctor at the scene about the people travelling in the other car and was told the red Holden Astra had been driven by a young woman. Her repeated questions about the woman's condition were not answered and she feared the worst.

Upon arrival at Alfred Hospital, Judith was immediately prepared for surgery. She was dazed and shocked, and recalls a foggy conversation with the surgeons about the condition of her lungs and expressing her concerns about antibiotics. Judith had sustained severe fractures to her right wrist and left leg and was operated on for six hours. Next morning, she woke to find nurses busy at their work and felt such deep gratitude that they were caring for her. They unwrapped the mystery bandages on her arm and revealed a strange metal rod fixed into the flesh of her hand and forearm. Her forearm was supported vertically by a sling attached to a pole by the bed, and she felt the weight of a full plaster on her left leg. She was told she had a long metal plate and screws inside her leg and faced several weeks in hospital.

Between bouts of nausea caused by a bad reaction to anaesthetic, Judith learned the details of the accident, which had made front-page news around Australia and in many parts of the world. Ron, she discovered, had suffered broken ribs and a broken left knee and would be discharged from Kyneton Hospital in ten days. For now, he was confined to a wheelchair. Peter Summers had already been discharged, having received treatment for a bruised sternum and concussion. Judith also received confirmation of her worst fears: the driver of the other vehicle, a 26-year-old East Keilor woman named Joanne Bryant, had died in the accident.

'That was the most difficult thing of all to deal with,' Judith says. 'I was so aware of the karmic aspect of the accident. Even though the accident was through no fault of our own, our car was instrumental in this young girl's death. Our lives had been interlinked and yet we were never to know her. I believe it was our destiny to be in that place, at that time. In a funny way, I felt I was being prepared for it. On the tour, I'd been singing the verse of "All Through Life" – which goes, "All through life, you have to take the good with the bad" – and, in hindsight, it felt as though I was somehow being made ready for this accident. This was the bad bit. Knowing our vehicle had been the instrument of Joanne Bryant's death was emotionally confronting for me. There was the realisation that in this life I was inadvertently going to be involved in another person's death and it was hard to deal with at first. That was the thing that made me cry, more than anything else.'

Judith was informed that Joanne Bryant had been driving with the left wheels of her vehicle on gravel and the right wheels on the road. There was a slight lip and Bryant experienced difficulty getting her left wheel over the lip and back on to the asphalt. In trying to get back into the stream of traffic, she had overcorrected and spun into the path of the oncoming traffic.

Since the accident, the Alfred Hospital public relations department had been working overtime, dealing with nationwide telephone calls from the media and distraught fans. Television news services provided updates on Judith's condition continually and some radio stations paid tribute to her by playing her songs every hour. Eventually, the concern of the public prompted Judith to arrange for a bedside press conference to assure her fans that she was going to pull through.

'I saw so many press articles and the TV news coverage was so intense, that I thought I should make some sort of gesture,' Judith says. 'The hospital switchboard people were being driven crazy – they had been wonderful handling the media but all they could really say was that I was serious but stable – so I agreed to do a media conference. A makeup man came in to make me look presentable, I took a deep breath and I was wheeled out to face the cameras. The people from the press were wonderful, I have to say. Very caring and very respectful.'

Judith arranged to have flowers delivered to Joanne Bryant's funeral and, concerned about the young woman's family, enquired whether she could meet with her parents. 'After many days, we finally met and it was tremendously beneficial for them and for me,' Judith says. 'I learned that Joanne Bryant had been in the area at the time of the accident, doing

279

good and helping others. I needed to express my sympathy to them and they needed to talk to me. They had feared that I might harbour resentment against their daughter for my injuries and for having my tour ended so abruptly, which couldn't have been further from the truth. We had the chance to share our feelings and they really were very beautiful, very special people. I saw them twice at the hospital and, later on, they came to my shows.'

Ron had undergone surgery on his left leg and had been transferred to St Vincent's Hospital in Melbourne. After ten days in hospital, he was discharged on crutches. With his brother's help, Ron moved into a furnished apartment in South Yarra, near Patrick and across the park from the Alfred Hospital. Ron was now able to visit his wife and their reunion was an emotional one.

Each day, dozens of bouquets, letters and get-well cards arrived for Judith from family, friends and fans. The nurses marvelled at the floral arrangements as they arrived, each one more impressive than the last. By the end of Judith's first week in hospital, not only was her room filled with flowers, but they spilled out down the corridor as well.

Athol Guy visited Judith at the hospital and she was amazed to find that, on the day of the accident, he had been driving a horse float in the opposite direction along the same stretch of the Calder Highway. She also learned that Bruce and Keith had wanted to see her, but when they contacted the hospital they were told that for those first few weeks only close relatives were permitted to visit.

'I was sorry to hear they'd been told they couldn't see me,' Judith says. 'It made me realise that I saw them almost like family, even though we hadn't seen each other much over the years. I would have enjoyed seeing them as much as relatives. Realising this made me more aware that there was quite a bond there.'

Judith's main concern after her first few weeks in hospital was whether her voice had been damaged in any way. The morning after the operation, she was alarmed to find she couldn't speak properly and discovered that the surgery procedure had involved tubes being inserted down her throat. After a few days, her speaking voice returned but, because she was still on a drip and suffering nausea, she was unable even to think of trying to sing. Some weeks later, however, when she was able to move around in a wheelchair, she visited the hospital chapel and, away from too many ears, sang some scales and 'Amazing Grace' and other songs to test her vocal capabilities.

Judith was equally concerned about her piano playing. She begged doctors for reassurance that she would be able to play again, but they could give no guarantees. At this point, they were concerned that Judith wasn't eating enough bone-building foods and also tried to encourage her to use an asthma spray to dilate her lungs. Although she had always suffered with bronchiectasis, her asthma had reappeared after the long anaesthetic.

'I really couldn't face eating,' Judith says. 'Everyone was scared I'd just waste away and the bones wouldn't heal, but, because of the nausea I was experiencing, I'd just bring whatever I ate back up again anyway. I couldn't face my normal diet, which was basically fruit and green vegetables with olive oil, so I ended up having things that would normally congest my lungs, like muesli or toast. Then, when I could eat, I was worried that, if I insisted on eating only fruit and vegetables so my lungs would be OK, then maybe the leg wouldn't heal. I was in a terrible dilemma, so I thought I'd better follow the doctors' advice and adopt a fairly conventional vegetarian diet. The problem was, the food was not helping my lungs and asthma at all and I had to have physio for my chest. The doctors kept trying to get me to use medication, but to their dismay I wouldn't. Instead, I had to tip myself upside down each day and have steam inhalations.'

Intense media interest in Judith's wellbeing continued. She talked to reporters, posed for photographs and conducted nationwide radio interviews, all from her hospital bed. Early in July, she was pictured in daily newspapers being presented with a cake. A fine way to spend her 47th birthday!

After six weeks, the time finally came for Judith to have the fixateur removed from her arm. While doctors had given her exercises for her plastered leg, she had had none for her hand or wrist. It hadn't occurred to the doctors – or to Judith – that, as a pianist, she needed to retain her flexibility. As a result of being immobile, her hand had stiffened irretrievably and she knew there would be a long struggle ahead to regain even the most basic mobility. Judith also faced another problem. Removing the fixateur required surgery and the Alfred doctors were reluctant to put her through another operation, because her blood count was low. Although she was reluctant, Judith had no choice but to undergo a blood transfusion.

After two months, the plaster was removed from Judith's leg and a few days later, while doctors were doing their rounds, she mentioned that she was experiencing numbness in the tip of her left thumb. A week after her cast was removed, Judith was transferred to the Hampton

Rehabilitation Hospital, in one of Melbourne's bayside suburbs. Judith's surgeon, knowing her concerns about her piano playing, had chosen that highly regarded hospital partly because it had pianos that could be used in therapy.

The fifteen-kilometre ambulance ride was Judith's first encounter with traffic since the accident, and she found her mind wandering back to Joanne Bryant. She was acutely aware that she wasn't a road statistic, like Joanne, and it seemed wrong to her that news coverage focused on road deaths but made little mention of the people maimed – those people whose lives, and the lives of those around them, are ruined by road trauma. 'There is hardly any coverage of the injuries people sustain in car accidents,' Judith says. 'All those people will never be the same again. I believe if there was more of a focus on the living victims of road trauma, it would be a far greater deterrent to people than just knowing how many people have died.'

In her first few days at Hampton, Judith was the new girl, getting to know the ropes and meeting fellow patients, whose injuries were often far more serious than hers. 'I met so many wonderful, courageous people at the rehab,' Judith says. 'Some of the people had the most horrific injuries: Mary Mielak, who'd had a hip replacement; Susan who'd lost an eye. I also met a man, Rod Lockett, who'd been there for two years. His hands were reconstructed after a traffic accident. I was touched when he told me that years ago he'd been thinking of emigrating from Manchester to Australia, and, when his mate pointed me out on television as an Aussie, he'd said "Well, if they're all like her, I'm going"!'

Within a week of her being at the rehab, the numbness that had been confined to Judith's left thumb had begun to spread to her other fingers and her feet. She mentioned it again and, a week later, the numbness had spread right up to her knees. Knowing that Ron had had a similar experience caused by antibiotics in 1983, Judith told her doctors she believed her numbness was caused by a Vitamin B12 deficiency, a result of all the penicillin she'd had at the Alfred. Fearing the numbness might become permanent, she asked her doctor not to waste any time in subjecting her to tests but instead to give her a series of Vitamin B12 shots. Judith insisted on having these injections and was given seven shots over a fourteen-day period. Within a month, she had thankfully regained all her feeling.

Judith also had to get used to driving a wheelchair. At the Alfred Hospital, her broken wrist meant she couldn't handle a wheelchair by herself, so she was given a gutter frame [chair on wheels] in her last week there. She had thoroughly enjoyed racing it up and down the ward, working up quite a speed. At the rehab, she found herself back in a wheelchair and rose to the challenge of making it go faster and faster. She could be seen each day, racing from one telephone to the next, trying to keep in touch with the outside world.

'I managed to get quite fast in it after a while,' she says. 'I worked out a way to get up speed by moving the wheels with my hands and scooting my foot at the same time. One guy I met there had become such an expert that he was going around corners on two wheels!'

Within a few days, Judith had settled into the routine at Hampton. Her daily exercise regimen started at nine in the morning with ninety minutes of physiotherapy. Starting off very slowly, the physiotherapist gave her exercises for her legs, arms and hands, taking her to her threshold of pain on the stiffened joints and ligaments, then very gradually building the wasted muscles. Judith was still in a wheelchair and could not put any weight on her mending leg for some time. Months later, she would make the transition to crutches and try getting around the obstacle course outside.

Sessions with an occupational therapist followed the physio, using simple games and tasks, such as pressing a clothes peg or stretching her hand in a bowl of warm water, to strengthen her hands. Soon, after much hard work, the day of reckoning came and Judith approached the piano to play her first notes since the accident. With weakened fingers, she made her first pathetic efforts to play the simple but beautiful piano arrangement that Ron had written for 'When Starlight Fades'. It was a shock to find that she could no longer stretch an octave and that her fingers pressed down unwanted black notes because she didn't have the strength to lift them up and off the keys. Her occupational therapist had to devise some special exercises to help with these problems and, whenever Judith thought of it, she would stretch out her hand into an imaginary octave. She was determined to bring her technique as close as she could to her pre-accident standard.

Knowing what hard work lay ahead, part of Judith's daily occupational therapy programme was playing the piano and also, most evenings, she would play unsupervised. Many of the patients would gather around in their wheelchairs for a singalong and, before long, Judith was taking requests, roughly improvising those songs she didn't know by heart. The other big setback was to find how weakened her diaphragm had become from months of lying and sitting, and she found it hard to sustain the long notes required in proper performance. It was a heartbreaking experience at first, but she was convinced all would be well again in time. And it was.

'Early on, I was sharing my mealtimes with a fellow patient, Clara Cinaglia, who told me her son Frank was a wonderful singer,' Judith says. 'He'd had a heartbreak in his life and hadn't been able to bring himself to sing for nine months, which upset his mother greatly. She arranged for us to meet and he tentatively joined me at the piano and sang in this marvellous, earth-shattering tenor voice. He joined in the singsongs regularly from then on, even though he wasn't a patient, and we graduated to singing duets from *Phantom of the Opera* and had a marvellous time. It was wonderful for me to be able to share my music and it turned out to be great therapy for him too. He came back a few times after his mother was discharged and we had some wonderful musical experiences together. Frank and I remain friends to this day; sadly, Clara died in early 1995. Another patient was Chen Wei, a Chinese man who was a classical-flute student and I played some piano accompaniments for him as well, which reminded me so much of my days at school in the string trio with my schoolfriends.'

After Clara was discharged, Judith's next mealtime companion was a Greek woman named Angela Delonas. Initially, communication between the two was difficult. Angela's accident had caused her to lose part of her memory and she was undergoing speech therapy to regain her command of English.

'Every mealtime, Angela would struggle to tell me the same thing,' Judith says. 'She continually said a word that sounded like "pimms" and I just couldn't understand her. Eventually, I learned she was talking about some poems she'd written, which had been published in *Neos Kosmos*, Melbourne's Greek newspaper. One day, she brought me a poem "O Metanastis", which was written in Greek, and I realised that all along, she had been asking me if I might be able to set it to music. I thanked her very much, but politely told her I doubted if I'd be able to do anything with it. I explained how busy my life was and that I didn't speak Greek, which made things very difficult. But I asked her if I could keep it anyway.

'Within a day, I met someone else at the rehab who spoke Greek and I discovered the poem was called "The Migrant". She gave me a literal translation of the song, which was quite lovely. She explained, as Angela had done, that the Greek words were very emotional and I realised this was something I should take very seriously and give a real shot. I spent some time rhyming the English words and added a couple of thoughts of my own, being careful not to detract from the original message of the poem.'

Now, with a set of lyrics to inspire her, Judith set about working out a melody at the piano. Within a few days, she invited Angela to make her way to the piano and, both women sitting in their wheelchairs, Judith sang the completed song for her friend, half in English and half in Greek. Angela was thrilled and, with her blessing, Judith later included the song in her concert performances and recorded it for her seventh solo album in Australia, *Let Me Find Love*.

Another song came unexpectedly from Lorraine Jager, the sister of a patient, Irene Elliott, who had suffered a stroke and was paralysed down one side. Lorraine introduced herself to Judith one day and asked for a big favour. She explained that she had written a song for her sister about the onset of her illness and wondered whether Judith would sing it for Irene and her husband and their six children when they all next came to visit. Judith was happy to help out, but, when she was presented with a simply written-out manuscript for 'Hold On Tight', she feared the song was going to be very amateurish. She was astonished to find when she tried it on the piano that it was a professional and moving composition. Later in the year, she performed the song publicly for the hospital's Christmas party and, with most of her fellow patients and staff in tears, she discovered how its moving sentiment could reach out and give hope to anyone whose life had been touched by disability.

The weeks went by, and eventually Judith was allowed to tackle the outdoor obstacle course on crutches, in addition to spending an hour in the gym on an exercise bike, treadmill, parallel bars and weights, and the treat of starting exercises in the warm waters of the hospital swimming pool. Before calling it a day, Judith sometimes spent time in relaxation therapy with the psychologist.

Gradually, Judith grew stronger. By October, she was able to start making the transition from wheelchair to crutches. She was allowed home at weekends, to spend time with Ron, and was soon able to become a day patient at the rehab, attending sessions for eight hours a day, five days a week. That same month, Judith was contacted by the Royal Australian Air Force, who were staging a variety concert early in November to commemorate the fiftieth anniversary of the Battle of Britain and wanted her to be their special guest. Judith was delighted at the prospect of returning to the concert stage. After checking with her doctors, Judith accepted their invitation.

On 2 November, she appeared at the RAAF's *Reach for the Sky* variety benefit at the John Batman Theatre in Melbourne's World Trade Centre. The RAAF Central Band played a bracket before Judith made her first public appearance since the accident. Leaving her crutches in the wings, she walked on stage to tumultuous applause with the aid of a specially decorated walking stick, and sang for 45 minutes. Ron, by now on the road to recovery, was featured on piano with the RAAF band. The concert represented a milestone after such a long absence from the stage and Judith told the Melbourne *Herald Sun* how much she enjoyed the experience after having been so 'musically starved'.

Just two weeks later, Judith's doctors gave her the good news: although she still required more therapy, she could finally trade her crutches for a walking stick. On 17 November, surrounded by a battalion of photographers, Judith threw away her crutches and took her first unaided steps. To celebrate, she announced a set of 'Thank You, Melbourne' concerts, to show her appreciation to the friends and fans who had swamped her with letters and cards of support. For old times' sake, they would be held at the National Theatre in St Kilda, where she had performed so successfully the night before the accident, and part of the proceeds from the concerts would be donated to the Alfred Hospital's Road Trauma Unit. Judith and Ron and their band played to standing ovations at these concerts, and Judith knew then that, given time, her singing career would be back in full swing.

Having been temporarily disabled herself, Judith found she could now associate closely with other people with disabilities. When the Yooralla Society invited her to take part in their annual Christmas fundraiser, she readily agreed to be the featured guest at their *Carols by Candlelight* concert. This was the beginning of a long association with Yooralla, and an ironic one, given the cruel twist of fate that was to be in store for her husband Ron Edgeworth.

Early in January, Judith joined the veritable *Who's Who* of Australian show business in a Melbourne Concert Hall tribute to the legendary Hector Crawford, who was terminally ill. Crawford's *Music for the People* concert during Moomba 1967 had given The Seekers one of their proudest moments. Judith was given a true hero's welcome by the audience. By now, Judith had regained most of her piano technique and was writing songs with renewed fervour. Often, the beginning of a new song would come while she was exercising at the rehab and she would leave her therapy in search of a piano before the idea was lost. The early weeks of 1991 saw Judith compose a series of love songs, including one called 'Say You Love Me So', which she considers one of her finest songwriting achievements to date.

Judith was eager to begin work on her album, which had been thwarted by the car accident, and had been scouting around for a producer and arranger who could pull the project together. Ron's brother Patrick had worked on a film with the composer Allan Zavod and suggested him to Judith. The two met and began work on the album, sorting through all the songs that audiences had responded to so emotionally during Judith's concerts. The days were very full and long, but she thoroughly enjoyed them. During the day, Judith would complete her therapy at Hampton and then, after five, would catch a cab to Zavod's home recording studio in Toorak, working with him late into the evening and feeling a part of the family life Zavod shared with his wife Chris and son Zak.

When Zavod had to halt work on the album to fulfil a previous obligation, Judith channelled her energies into resuming the ill-fated Silver Jubilee Tour with Ron, playing to grateful audiences who had missed out the first time around. Late in March, Judith commenced her 38-date tour in Ballina, New South Wales. The tour, once again presented by Arthur Laing, wound its way through the country to New South Wales, Sydney, Canberra and Victoria, including a date at Tooleybuc, where Judith was to have performed on the night of the accident.

Being a full year later, it was no longer appropriate to bill the concerts as Judith's Silver Jubilee Tour, and newspaper advertisements were headed JUDITH DURHAM – THE VOICE OF THE SEEKERS. For Judith this was a necessity, to counteract the confusion over The Seekers with their various female singers. It was an attempt to re-establish Judith's credentials. While Julie Anthony had by now left The Seekers to have a second baby and resume her solo career, Judith was still in competition with the group. In June, just five weeks after Judith's accident, the announcement had been made that Karen Knowles, a former team member of Australia's high-rating children's television programme *Young Talent Time*, was stepping in as the latest female Seeker. Although she wished them well, Judith was always stumped when the media asked the inevitable questions regarding her feelings about the new female member of The Seekers. It was difficult to comment, yet she admired both Anthony and Knowles very much as singers.

The tour ended on 18 May at Melbourne's Dallas Brooks Hall, where

Judith was special guest star at a concert by the Welsh Choir, and she was honoured that the choir took such delight in presenting a new song she'd written called 'Wales'.

Judith had been approached by the New Zealand promoter Stewart Macpherson, who in 1985 had offered Judith the lead role in the New Zealand production of *The Sound of Music*. Macpherson was interested in touring Judith and Ron throughout New Zealand. Judith jumped at the chance. Before leaving, she was interviewed by a Melbourne journalist, representing the New Zealand magazine, *Listener & TV Times*. The article was published on the eve of the tour, which opened on 26 July at the New Plymouth Opera House, and Judith was amazed by what she read. In it, the journalist described Judith's image as 'mumsy' and her Queensland home as a 'social backwater'. The Australian rock historian Glenn A Baker was quoted as saying that nothing she did outside The Seekers had any fire. But that wasn't what upset Judith. The journalist also wrote that she had contacted Athol Guy and Bruce Woodley, but they had refused to talk about Judith. Athol and Bruce, it was claimed, bristled at the mention of her name. Bruce was quoted as saying, 'We have had a gutsful of that lady in the last six months. She has not wanted any involvement with the group to the point of refusing to do special events. She didn't want to know about the songs. But in the last eighteen months, since we resurrected the group, she has been trading off it.'

Judith was shattered. When she arrived in New Zealand, almost every time she was interviewed on television or radio, the article was mentioned. 'I just couldn't believe what I'd read,' Judith says. 'I couldn't believe Bruce would say that I was trading off The Seekers' name, when I had agonised for years about singing Seekers songs. I had lost work because I wouldn't sing them and, finally, I had asked the three boys for their blessing to sing them again.

'With the interviews I did on the tour, I just took a deep breath and explained that perhaps Bruce had been misquoted. I told interviewers I was looking forward to getting back to Australia and asking Bruce about it. That article made me determined to clear the air with the boys. I resolved to get together with them when I got back from New Zealand, to air any grievances we might have had. In the twenty-three years since the group had broken up, the four of us had never been together at one time, in one place, and I thought it was about time that happened. The sniping in the press had to stop and I wanted them to see that I was not the big ogre that they perhaps saw me as.'

The New Zealand tour, which saw Judith and Ron performing in theatres, was a big success. While they were touring, a local jazz club approached the couple and offered them their own jazz concert in an Auckland theatre, once the concert dates were completed. It was a big decision for Judith and Ron, who hadn't performed jazz material in ten years, in spite of so many increasingly lucrative offers from the jazz fraternity. Ultimately, Judith decided to accept the booking.

Her only concern was putting together an entire evening of blues, gospel and jazz standards and using a local band of musicians they'd never met before. The band was booked and, with the help of Judith's trusty chord book, a complete programme was rehearsed.

'It was like going back to my teen years,' Judith says. 'We hadn't done a jazz show for such a long time and the theatre was sold out. The audience was great and the revelation for us was the response Ron was getting. It still bothered me that in the shows I'd been doing in recent months he was not being satisfied musically. He had billing and opened the show, but, because it was always a Judith Durham crowd, the audiences were waiting for me and not taking much notice of Ron's wonderful playing.

'At the jazz concert in Auckland, Ron would be halfway through a piece and the audience would start cheering him. This was the right audience for him – a jazz crowd that understood the complexity of what he was playing and could appreciate his extraordinary talent. That really brought the whole problem to a head and when we got back to Australia we had some long discussions about our musical direction. We decided that, from then on, I would do my shows on my own and Ron would work independently. We would work together only in the occasional jazz show that I was offered.'

Home in Australia, while Ron threw himself into dedicated piano practice and building an extensive repertoire of his own, Judith was contacted by Keith Potger's cousin Barbara, who had run The Seekers fan club in Australia during the mid-sixties. Now a school teacher, Barbara had visited Judith in hospital and recently had heard her singing 'Australia Land of Today'. She was keen on getting hold of the music to teach her students. During the conversation, Judith mentioned her desire to get together with Athol, Keith and Bruce. Barbara promised that, the next time she saw Keith, she would try to get all the boys together and invite Judith along.

Judith resumed work with Allan Zavod on the album and told him of another project she wanted him to be involved in. An entrepreneurial fan had heard Judith sing 'Australia Land of Today' in one of her concerts and was so taken with it that Judith was asked to record the song for release on Australia Day 1992, with a special concert in which she could present her entire *Australian Cities Suite*, with choral backing provided by the Melbourne Chorale.

Finally, twenty years after the melody was written, the song was recorded with the choir in a Melbourne studio, with Zavod as producer and Judith as associate producer. The song was also recorded as an instrumental. A distribution deal was worked out with PolyGram Records and while the single – Judith's first recording (and the first on the Musicoast label) on CD – was being pressed she continued working on the album and making public appearances. Ron had spent some time in Sydney performing his own shows, and on his return he and Judith performed together at the York Jazz Festival in Western Australia, their first Australian jazz performance in more than a decade. As if to make up for lost time, Judith amazed herself by singing seven different programmes with seven different jazz bands she'd never met before.

'One of the bands was Japanese,' Judith says. 'They couldn't speak a word of English, but they were wonderful players. That's one of the most amazing things about traditional jazz music. All you need to know is the tune and the key and away you can go, even if you don't speak the same language. The reaction we got from audiences was electrifying. There was so much appreciation, which I thought was ironic – Ron and I had struggled for so many years to gain acceptance in the jazz world and finally we gave up; now, years later, the jazz fans had caught up with us and our jazz albums had become collectors' items!'

'Australia Land of Today' was released on 19 January 1992 with a special launch at Emu Bottom Homestead in Sunbury, Victoria, where, years earlier, Judith and Ron had filmed some of the scenes for *Cash & Company*. To Judith's delight, some Aboriginal friends helped celebrate the launch with a corroboree and she invited them to appear with her at her forthcoming Concert Hall show. A week later, on Australia Day, Judith launched the song to the public with a showcase performance at the Melbourne Concert Hall. Billed as her *Australia Land of Today* concert, the occasion marked the first public performance of her entire *Australian Cities Suite*. She was supported by her friends the Mona Mona Aboriginal Dance Troupe from Northern Queensland. Monty Pryor played didgeridoo when Judith debuted another new song, 'Australia Day Dreamtime', which told of the dream that Australia Day might one day fall on a date that Australians of all racial backgrounds could feel good about.

It was a time in Judith's life when she truly felt she had come of age as an all-round performer, for on the same weekend she appeared with Ron at the annual Montsalvat Jazz Festival in Victoria. They were interviewed for the festival's 'Meeting of the Masters' segment and performed a number of jazz songs. That evening, Judith played several rags in the Pianorama, along with Ron and many other top jazz pianists. Two days later, the two performed at Montsalvat with the first Australian line-up of the Hottest Band in Town. Judith was also able to perform duets with her sister Beverley, for the first time since the Hobart Jazz Convention.

Now a recording artist again for the first time in more than a decade, Judith was aware more than ever that she needed management. Her profile had been elevated to such an extent that it was a huge workload for her to handle her own negotiations, and at times downright embarrassing. Year after year, she had hoped that her dream of a good manager would materialise but in the meantime she struggled on, professionally disadvantaged by going in to bat for herself.

Judith had many in-depth conversations with the Yooralla Society's public relations manager Colin Stephen, himself a well-known Melbourne musician. She discussed with him the fragment of an idea she had of returning to The Seekers for a reunion concert, to mend bridges with her three bandmates and to give the public what they had been pressuring her for since the break-up. Ever since the car accident, Judith's realisation of what The Seekers meant to their fans, even twenty years on, was growing. She had even received a letter from a fan in England, who pointed out that John Lennon's death had meant The Beatles could never perform together again and what a pity it would have been had one of The Seekers died.

Judith expressed to Stephen, however, her grave concerns that, should she become involved with a group reunion, she might be swallowed up and lose her individual identity again, along with all she had worked for over many years. Her discussions with Stephen made her realise that, with careful management, Judith could blend with The Seekers but emerge again with her own career still intact. Besides, 1993 would be the 25th anniversary of the last time The Seekers sang together and therefore a good reason to re-form for a one-off event. She still wanted to have a social get-together with Athol, Bruce and Keith, but they were moving from state to state and she had a record to promote in Melbourne.

In the coming weeks, Judith was able to perform 'Australia Land of

Today' on television several times, including a performance with the Melbourne Symphony Orchestra, and was approached by many choirs seeking permission to perform it themselves. She received marvellous feedback from the public, many of whom told her they got goosebumps on hearing the record. Those television appearances prompted a phone call to Allan Zavod from his associate Steven Prowse. Prowse ran Television House, the production company owned by the TV personality John Young. Prowse had been watching Bert Newton's *Good Morning Australia* and said he was totally knocked out by 'Australia Land of Today' and wanted his company to be involved should there ever be a film clip. Zavod passed the message on and Judith called Prowse to arrange a meeting the following day, mentioning in passing how she was finding it hard to cope without proper management. The next day a surprise awaited her. When Judith arrived for the meeting, there was someone else in the room. Prowse introduced her to John Kovac, and, although she didn't know it at the time, she'd found her manager at last. Kovac happened to be working out of Television House on a TV pilot.

'John showed great interest in my song, and even called it a hit pick,' Judith recalls. 'I realised how musically attuned he was and I thought he had a very professional approach. I asked Stephen to call me a cab, but instead he asked John if he would like to drive me home, which gave us the chance to chat some more. Out of the blue, John told me he thought he might like to manage me and before he dropped me home he surprisingly mentioned the word "karma" in the conversation. I'd seen him as a hard-nosed businessman and suddenly he was showing me a spiritual side. I always try to view everything in life in the light of karma and I realised then that this belief system had some significance for John as well.'

Some weeks later, Judith was approached by the Australian television producer Brian Finch, who was putting together a TV spectacular to mark the official opening of the Great Southern Stand at the Melbourne Cricket Ground (MCG). He had heard 'Australia Land of Today' and loved it, and wanted Judith and the Melbourne Chorale to perform it before 100,000 people during the opening ceremony, prior to the World Cup Cricket final. Judith was delighted to accept the invitation and the spectacular event was internationally televised.

'I watched the telecast on television,' Kovac says. 'It went incredibly well and I was happy to see how much the crowd loved her. I really didn't know what to do about managing Judith at that stage. She was a very talented performer who desperately needed guidance, but I wasn't sure that I wanted to spend all my time working on one person's career. There were still other things I wanted to do.'

With her MCG triumph behind her, Judith set about completing her solo album, but soon she needed to contact Kovac to ask for some advice. Judith had an instinctive feeling that Kovac was the right manager for her and was thrilled to learn he was still interested in working with her. With Allan Zavod as her musical director, Judith played a series of low-key regional shows that Kovac had organised, to give him a chance to see her in action as a concert performer.

Then, out of the blue, Judith received a phone call from Barbara Potger, who had managed to arrange a time when Athol, Keith and Bruce would be in Melbourne together. For the first time in almost a quarter of a century, the four members of The Seekers sat and talked together. Over dinner in a Toorak restaurant, the 24 years they had been apart melted away with stories and jokes. Though the boys didn't know it then, Judith had in the back of her mind the thought that perhaps the only way to settle the score once and for all would be to do one more concert with them, the farewell concert they never gave the first time round. One show might just clean the slate for everyone concerned, but it was not something Judith would even contemplate if her relationship with Athol, Keith and Bruce was not salvageable.

'I needed to know whether there was still something between us on a personal level,' Judith says. 'I couldn't walk on stage to sing with them if I felt they didn't respect me or didn't like me any more. Simply to lend my voice to something to make money would be like prostituting myself, and I couldn't do it. An informal dinner was the perfect way for us to get to know each other again. It was a really lovely evening. We had a nice meal and I was thrilled to be able to sit around a table with the guys and talk. It seemed funny that I didn't join them for a steak and a glass of wine, as I would have in the old days, but in many ways, it was just like old times. We were older and stronger characters, and we had all changed since 1968, but that bond between us was still there. I used to think it was corny the way we were passed off in the press as a happy family, but they were like my brothers. Families often grow apart, but, despite the differences, there's always that amazing bond.'

There was no mention made that night of performing together again. Four old friends chatted about old times and, at the end of the evening, bade each other goodnight and promised to stay in touch. By now, the newest line-up of The Seekers was off the road, while Karen Knowles went to America to record an album. Athol, Keith and Bruce had returned to their individual careers: Athol and Keith both worked in public relations and Bruce was writing songs and involved in a project revolving around his own song about Australia.

True to his word, Athol Guy did stay in touch with Judith. He phoned to tell her of yet another offer being made for the four original members to get back together, this time for a Christmas parade. Athol was ringing merely to go through the motions of putting the offer to Judith and was surprised when she told him that this time the answer wasn't 100 per cent 'no'.

'It was a major step for me,' Judith says, 'but I was feeling so much better with John Kovac in the picture. I was getting a stronger and stronger sense that a reunion concert was the best way to cement the new relationship with the boys and at the same time give the fans what they'd been wishing for since 1968. Hopefully, this would put an end to what I believed was some resentment towards me and would lift the heavy burden of guilt I'd carried for all those years. I didn't necessarily feel a Christmas parade was the right way to go about it, though. I was thinking more along the lines of a big one-off televised show from the Myer Music Bowl.'

Kovac was aware of the monumental decision Judith now faced, but he encouraged her to follow her instincts. If a Seekers reunion was in any way a possibility, he would move heaven and earth to make it happen.

Soon afterwards, Ron returned to London for a couple of months. He had not seen his mother since 1990 and she had become very frail. He wanted to see her again and also wanted to perform in London. In one of their many transcontinental phone calls, Judith told Ron that she had finally decided to reunite with The Seekers and that it would be for a full tour. Ron's first concern was that Judith might risk losing touch with her own musical identity, but he gave the concept his blessing. By mid-1992, the wheels were set in motion for a small-scale get-together by the original Seekers. But neither they, nor John Kovac, could have imagined how incredibly difficult it would be to get the show off the ground.

15. THE CARNIVAL CONTINUES

We're back together again,
Sooner not later together again,
We're back together again,
Gone are the times out of sight, out of mind,
Doing fine back together again.

– 'WE'RE BACK TOGETHER AGAIN'
JUDITH DURHAM AND KEITH POTGER

Instinct told John Kovac that news of Judith Durham's reuniting with The Seekers after 25 years would cause a stampede at the box office, but what he didn't anticipate was the resistance he would encounter in selling the idea to Australian promoters. Kovac's early discussions with the promoters were met with a resounding indifference. The Seekers are getting back together? So what?

Promoters weren't very interested: to them, it was just another line-up of the band. Off and on for more than twenty years, The Seekers had performed with a passing parade of female singers and varying degrees of success. Reassembling the original group was no big deal, they said.

But Kovac knew that, for Seekers fans, this would be the event of a lifetime. The public had been asking for this reunion for more than two decades, even though there always seemed to be a Seekers line-up playing somewhere. Without detracting from the talents of the female singers who'd stepped into Judith Durham's shoes, he knew the sound just wasn't the combination the fans knew and loved. Only the four people who'd created it in the first place could satisfy the public's need.

It was the Melbourne-based promoter Michael Coppel who took the chance. The Seekers were a long way from his usual agenda: Coppel had successfully toured rock acts including U2, Def Leppard, Metallica and George Thorogood. He figured The Seekers might be a bit of a gamble, but he insisted the tour be of theatres only, with an itinerary of just sixteen dates, so it wasn't a substantial risk. With a promoter now in place, Kovac tentatively suggested that Judith get together with the boys for a rehearsal. 25 years is a long time and, before any more arrangements were finalised, he needed to know that the golden sound the four had once made together could still be reproduced.

He needn't have worried. The four Seekers assembled in Music & Effects, a small Melbourne recording studio, and, in harmony for the first time since 1968, sang a few tentative bars of 'I'll Never Find Another You'. Judith was nervous, wondering if she would be able to recapture that special technique of blending her voice with the three others, worried that the timbre of her now mature voice might no longer give

The Seekers that unmistakable sparkle. But she too was worrying needlessly. It was all there. It was an emotional moment for the four, and for the few witnesses present. The boys were unanimous in their praise of Judith and she was impressed by them, too. She admired their guitar work and the very characteristic sound of each of their voices, which were all so important to The Seekers sound.

For the next few weeks, The Seekers got together regularly at Bruce's house, rehearsing their hits and honing their harmonies. Aside from a few forgotten lyrics, it all fell into place remarkably quickly. In the meantime, John Kovac was negotiating the release of a greatest-hits package. Since the group had disbanded, the 89 songs the original line-up had recorded in the sixties had already been repackaged and rereleased all over the world a hundred times over. Kovac's idea was a commemorative album for the 1993 reunion. It would be the *Silver Jubilee Album* and he suggested to the group and EMI that they record two new tracks especially for it.

After much discussion, two songs were settled on. One would be a new arrangement of Bruce Woodley's 'Keep a Dream in Your Pocket'. The other would be a new song that Judith had written with the television personality John Young. In a moment of true inspiration, Young said he believed the group should have a new song called 'One World Love'. Kovac gave the title to Judith and, a week later, she presented Young with a complete song. After a few lyric changes in collaboration with Young, 'One World Love' was ready for recording. Judith was tempted to keep the new composition for her own album, but she had written it with The Seekers' harmonies in mind and, if everyone liked it, she was happy to record it as a group song.

Having been so busy, Judith found it difficult to believe just how long Ron had been away in London, although he had told her in his letters and phone calls how thrilled he was at the standard of his playing and how well his shows in London had been received. He spoke of his pleasure in striding around the West End and jogging in the local park. However, his return was now imminent. It was three months since Ron had left and Judith was in no way prepared for the shock that awaited her when she saw him again at Melbourne Airport. He had become terribly ill in the past three weeks from what he believed was a reaction to a week on antibiotics for dental trouble. Judith was devastated by his appearance and, in particular, the peculiar way his speech sounded.

Judith was completely overcome by the awful feeling that her husband was going to die. Without voicing this premonition, she urged Ron to consult a doctor as quickly as possible. He did, and was immediately referred to a specialist, but it took many weeks before a tentative diagnosis of motor neurone disease (MND) was mentioned. Judith and Ron had never heard of it, and the specialist told them that MND was the collective name for a group of diseases in which the nerve cells controlling muscles of movement are destroyed. These nerve cells – or motor neurones – occur in the brain and spinal column. With no stimulus from the nerves, those muscles weaken and waste away. He said the condition affects each patient differently. Sometimes the feet and hands are the first to become weak; other times it begins with swallowing difficulties, slurred speech, muscle-twitching or cramps.

Worst of all, he told them that the cause of MND was still unknown and at present there was no medical treatment available, even though research continued throughout the world. He said that, apart from Ron's theory that antibiotics had triggered it off, there were all sorts of other theories, including viruses, dietary and insecticide toxins, and immune-system and nerve-growth factors, and that the disease strikes one in every 50,000 people and in Australia affects 30 per cent more men than women. There was no prospect of any remission. The best they could hope for was that Ron might sometimes experience long periods where no further deterioration occurred. Although Ron did not take the doctor seriously, Judith was obviously devastated to hear that her husband might have only two or three years to live.

Despite the horror of the disease's consequences, Judith resolved to keep it quiet to see if any more obvious symptoms manifested themselves and, with Ron's encouragement, continued with the reunion as if nothing had happened. Ron did the same and continued his piano engagements, heartily welcomed home by his local fans. It was on one of these shows that his right thumb showed some weakness, a telltale sign that the MND was progressing to his hands. Ron turned to whatever alternative therapy he could find in the hope that he would be spared the disabilities and untimely death that MND would surely bring.

Hiding her anguish, Judith quietly slipped into Metropolis Studio in Melbourne with Athol, Keith and Bruce, and laid down the two tracks that would bring their recording tally to 91 songs. Another 23 songs from their back catalogue were chosen to make up the 25 tracks for their *Silver Jubilee Album*.

With the new recordings now in place, and a commitment from EMI, there was a chance they might actually make money from their back catalogue should their *Silver Jubilee Album* be successful. Now, Kovac had in front of him the major task of pulling together a national tour. Aside from the work The Seekers needed to do in relearning their old material, there were musicians to find and rehearse, costumes to be made, publicity to be organised and television appearances to be finalised. Kovac's problem was money. After spending a year working full-time on the television pilot, Kovac needed a cash flow. He was almost at the point of having to sell his own property to fund his business concerns. At that time it was very tough selling locally produced programmes to the networks and, with all the extra Seekers business to contend with, he did not have the time to pursue a sale for the programme he was co-producing.

Coincidentally, Judith had recently taken a friend's advice and had turned the largest room in the apartment into an office, buying a huge desk and office chairs, with the intention of hiring a secretary of her own. Now, with Kovac in need of a base for his wheeling and dealing, and her wanting to work together with him on this monumental project, she suggested sharing the facilities.

'I really wanted to work with John,' Judith says, 'especially as I always planned when I gave up singing to work behind the scenes in the music business. I found John to be a very remarkable operator in terms of his ability to sell people literally anything and everything. I also admired his entrepreneurial skills, his broad vision, and far-reaching perception of personnel and events. So I offered funds to solve the reunion cash flow problem.'

Kovac set about moving John Kovac Management into Judith's office and joining forces with Musicoast, which would act as the production company. Now, as well as being the star of the show, Judith was to become Kovac's personal assistant and financier of the project until they were more established.

'Judith and I developed a very good working relationship,' Kovac says. 'She's not only a great singer and composer, but she is also a very good secretary and coffee maker! We couldn't afford a secretary at first, so I would dictate all our correspondence and Judith would type it. When I was on the phone hustling people, Judith was poring over itineraries. Often, we'd be working around the clock getting everything together. With phoning and faxing to London, we'd sometimes finish at one or two in the morning, have a few hours' sleep and then be back into it by nine.'

For Judith, the pace was frantic but finally she had the chance to practise all the things she'd learned when she'd staged her own shows. 'John and I really did work night and day getting things started in those early days,' Judith says,' and it was tremendous for me to find someone who could be my manager, friend and partner at the same time. He's a real do-it man and very demanding to work with, an absolute slave driver, never stopping, determined to make it happen. Very early on in the piece he stuck his mission statement on the office wall:

Enthusiasm, excitement, passion, totally arrest the situation. Think repercussion long term. Phone answering twenty-four hours a day, seven days a week. Every matter is urgent and most of all, don't trust anyone.

'We were so busy, I literally didn't have time for anything but organising the reunion tour,' says Judith. 'I remember always running late for photo shoots and rehearsals because of it. The three guys all had their own business to attend to at the time. I'd stipulated that I would only do the reunion if John was handling management, so I didn't want anything to be the reason for further conflict between the four of us.'

To break the band in, Kovac arranged with Ford Australia for The Seekers to play a series of private functions, thereby generating cash to pay back Judith's initial loan to the group. By the time the group stepped out of their rehearsal studio and on stage for Ford, Kovac had made sure that there would be no confusion over which Seekers line-up this was. For this reunion tour to happen at all, the billing had to leave no doubt that this was The Seekers the public wanted to hear. It was agreed that the re-formation would be billed 'Judith Durham: The Seekers' Silver Jubilee Reunion'.

'It all came back to credibility,' Kovac says. 'The group had lost a bit of credibility over the years because of all the other re-formations and the situation needed to be clarified. This wasn't just the three guys with a new female singer, singing covers of the group's material. This was the four original Seekers, singing hits that they made themselves. The guys realised that the difference needed to be highlighted. It had been made clear to them that no matter how good the other girls were, and they were all great singers, it didn't have that magic sound of The Seekers.'

In January 1993, the *Sunday Herald Sun* in Melbourne carried a brief, unconfirmed news story that Judith was re-forming with The Seekers; then, on 27 February, the reunion announcement was carried in the nation's daily papers. The following night, The Seekers sang together in public for the first time in 25 years when they performed at the first of their private Ford Australia functions. They were the surprise entertainment for the evening and, without any warning, they were announced and walked on stage. The audience of dignitaries in the ballroom of Sydney's Park Lane Hotel were stunned. Once the crowd got over their initial shock at the realisation that these were indeed the four original Seekers, they settled down and the show was a great success. But for Judith something was missing.

'Something didn't feel right,' she explains. 'We would do the whole show and the audiences were loving it, but after "The Carnival Is Over" we'd just walk off. We'd be back for encores, but there was no standing ovation. I mentioned it to the guys and said that, whenever I finished my own shows, I'd receive a standing ovation, especially if I'd been singing "The Carnival Is Over". Something hadn't quite gelled in the way the show was put together. We worked on it and refined it and got it to that next level, where people were really moved by what they were seeing and hearing and our bows created more of an opportunity for them to show their appreciation.'

With the advance payment from the Ford Australia shows to boost their reserves, Judith was reimbursed and Kovac was able to set up his own office and hire a secretary, Irene Ruffolo, who also became tour co-ordinator and Judith's personal assistant on the road. They bought some stage equipment for the forthcoming shows and a wardrobe of costumes for the group. Judith was happy to be able to commission Beverley's daughter Belinda, who was by now fully trained in fashion design, to create four costume changes. Belinda had designed Judith's gowns for the Australia Day Concert and the MCG Great Southern Stand performance and, when fans remarked on them, Judith was proud to be able to mention her niece.

EMI Australia released 'Keep a Dream in Your Pocket' as a single and it picked up instant radio airplay. The *Silver Jubilee Album* entered the Australian Top 40. Before long, it had climbed to Number 3. By early 1994, it had passed double platinum, with Australian sales of more than 140,000 copies. By the end of 1993, the album was certified by the Australian Record Industry Association as the third-highest-selling Australian album of the year, after Jimmy Barnes's *Heat* and John Farnham's *Then Again*.

When Michael Coppel first announced the tour, the original sixteen-date itinerary had to be expanded to accommodate the anticipated box-office rush. There were now 38 dates, including four warm-up shows in

Victoria. Many of the concerts sold out within hours of tickets going on sale. The group played their first capital-city public performance at the Perth Concert Hall on 30 April. The next day, the *West Australian* carried a review that noted:

> It was a pretty slickly packaged presentation, without throwing away the warm, cosy feel that comes with any reunion party ... younger music lovers may consider The Seekers as Old Dags, but their songs are still jolly catchy, delivered with complete professionalism and the warmth of natural communicators.

The same concert was also reviewed by the *Australian*, whose writer said, 'Their famous four-part harmonies can still produce goose-bumps and Ms Durham is in glorious voice. Her crystal-clear articulation is almost a lost art.' After a second Perth show, the tour moved on to Adelaide's Festival Theatre, where the *Adelaide Advertiser* gushed:

> Judith Durham's voice has the metallic clarity and fineness of edge of a blue steel blade. Her intonation was spot-on all night ... all night long Judith Durham's laser beam voice showed itself to be an instrument of great power and beauty, a vehicle for her conviction and personal strength.

Hometown Melbourne was next, and, in reviewing their concert-hall performances, the *Age* was more critical: 'The band has invested little new emotional input into its songs.' It did, however, acknowledge the two standing ovations. And so it carried on. The tour moved on to Canberra, through Sydney, Brisbane and the Queensland coastal areas, Darwin, Newcastle and Hobart. On the way back, extra concerts were added in all capital cities. The reviews were glowing and business was booming.

Rolling Stone magazine ran a feature on The Seekers, noting that their tour had outgrossed Guns 'N' Roses' Australian jaunt, while the American trade magazine *Billboard* observed in an article published at the end of June that $1.4 million worth of tickets had been sold in the first three days of box-office trading, and public demand had pushed the itinerary for Australia and New Zealand to 87 concerts. *Billboard* interviewed Michael Coppel, who admitted he never expected such a reaction to the reunion. 'We're seeing people at these concerts who haven't been to a concert since The Seekers broke up in the sixties,' Coppel said. 'The main reason it's working is that it is not a museum piece or just a nostalgia episode. It is a very positive, credible, contemporary "good feeling" show that has come along at just the right time. The response to them has been truly inspiring.'

Before the New Zealand leg of the tour commenced, Judith celebrated her fiftieth birthday in Perth, with a bouquet of flowers presented to her on stage during the show at the Burswood Casino. Behind the scenes, the hotel made an egg-free birthday cake for her, entirely of chocolate-cream mousse!

That same day, she and Keith Potger were flown to the Kohuna Koala Park and given the honour of naming two baby koalas, who are now known as Georgy Girl and Keith Koala. By proxy, Athol and Bruce named two other koalas Pierrot and Columbine, from that elusive line in 'The Carnival Is Over' that has mystified people for decades. With only a couple of days to catch up with the news at home and the sadness of finding Ron's health so much more affected by the progress of the MND symptoms, Judith had to wrench herself away from home again, to face a full month in New Zealand. The New Zealand tour was as successful as their Australian dates had been. The *Silver Jubilee Album* went double platinum there, in the country that had always been supportive of the group. The entire tour was sold out and, for the few weeks they were there, The Seekers dominated newspaper and magazine covers.

For Judith, the time in New Zealand was interminable. She was seesawing between jubilation at the reaction from the group's fans and the devastation of having to leave Ron at home for a month. He had fortunately been able to accompany Judith for the group's Brisbane dates, but it was clearly evident that he was very sick. Ron had to face the ordeal of being in public and not being able to express himself as the Ron Edgeworth everyone knew. Not only were his legendary hands becoming terribly weak, but Ron was now experiencing great difficulty speaking. To Judith's joy, however, Ron was able to make the trip to Christchurch for six days with his brother. It was a treasured time.

But life had to continue, despite their personal tragedy, and, with the *Silver Jubilee Album* still selling, Kovac initiated the recording of a live-in-concert album, which would give fans some of the new material the group had added for the reunion. Kovac decided the album would be independently produced by Musicoast, Judith's production company, for EMI records. Kovac also extended the project to include a home video and from that came the idea for a television special as well.

Such was the demand for concert tickets that further dates were added throughout Australia. At one of the group's Melbourne Concert

Hall shows in August, sound and film crews moved in and captured The Seekers at their best, performing to a hometown crowd who just couldn't contain their excitement. For Judith, there was the added thrill of being able to spot Ron, Beverley, Barry and Belinda in the audience.

When the tour temporarily wound down, Judith resumed work on her solo album. In the months when the album had been put on hold for The Seekers, Allan Zavod had accepted an offer from America and Judith started recording the remaining three songs and final mixing of the whole album with Michael Cristiano, The Seekers' musical director and guitarist. Nightly, Judith would slip into the sound engineer Doron Kipen's Music & Effects studio to help Cristiano with arrangements and to lay down vocals. The track line-up for this long-awaited, all original solo album was finally settled. In view of Ron's tragic illness, Judith was overjoyed that he was playing on three tracks on the album, and had written the music of 'In Your Love' and the beautiful lullaby 'Slowly, Gently'.

Acting as co-producer with John Kovac and Simon Barnett, Judith was involved in the editing of The Seekers' *Live In Concert* video, working through the night to meet the release deadline set by Roadshow Music, who were the distributors. 'To get it finished in time, we all worked in shifts,' Kovac says. 'We'd work around the clock in the edit suite, Judith taking the first shift with Simon. She'd go home, grab three or four hours' sleep and then come back and I'd nip back to the office for a nap. We were all exhausted but it was worth it in the end.'

As soon as it was possible to get away, Judith, Ron and his brother Patrick made a flying visit to England to see Ron's mother, in the hope that Ron's speech would be clear enough for Vicky to understand. It was a traumatic two weeks for all concerned, considering Vicky's failing health and hearing, and Ron's great difficulty in enunciating even the simplest of words. Judith and Patrick were required to act as interpreters. But it was an important trip. Vicky didn't know it, but this could well be the last time she saw her son.

While Judith was in England, Kovac had managed to finalise a deal with Australia's Seven Network, who had agreed to package an hour of the video as a television spectacular. On 7 November, with the first leg of their reunion complete, it was announced that The Seekers would stage a final farewell tour, under the auspices of the promoter Paul Dainty. To cater for the huge demand, Dainty committed to the Our Last Goodbye tour, with a swan song on Australia Day 1994 at Melbourne's

Myer Music Bowl, the scene of the group's greatest triumph 26 years earlier.

Dainty told the *Sunday Herald Sun* that he had been fourteen years old and living in England when The Seekers had played to 200,000 people at the Bowl in 1967. 'It was a huge news event overseas,' Dainty said. 'I clearly remember reading about it. I'm thrilled to be part of The Seekers' history in the nineties, but saddened that it is the end of a tremendous era in Australian music.'

The live album and the Roadshow video were both released on 29 November 1993. The album was an instant hit. The *Sunday Herald Sun's* review proclaimed The Seekers' tour a music highlight of 1993, along with Guns 'N' Roses, U2 and Madonna. 'Durham's pure, soaring soprano was *the* sound of The Seekers,' it read. 'No other woman who fronted the group during her prolonged absence had any hope of replicating her voice.' By January, the concert album had hit the Australian Top 10 and been certified platinum. The video jumped into the music-video charts and within three weeks had displaced Michael Jackson's *Dangerous* as the Number 1 bestselling video in Australia. By the time it had sold 80,000 copies, The Seekers *Live In Concert* video had become the highest-selling music video in Australian history.

The surprising legacy of a video of the original group at last being made available for family use was that a whole legion of very young fans would emerge – toddlers as young as two and three would pester their parents by asking for the video to be played and replayed for hours each day!

On 20 December 1993 the Seven Network screened edited highlights of the video and showed it as the one-hour special, *Judith Durham: The Seekers' Silver Jubilee Reunion Tour*. Kovac invited Olivia Newton-John to introduce the special to viewers and she reminisced about the group's phenomenal past. The special topped its time slot in all capital cities, outrating the hit shows of the day.

Only weeks earlier, readers of Melbourne's *Sunday Herald Sun* had been shocked to read a news story about Ron's diagnosis and prognosis. Judith had tried hard to keep Ron's illness as private as possible, but it was inevitable that sooner or later a journalist would see him backstage at a concert, notice something wasn't quite right, and start investigating. When she was approached directly by the newspaper, Judith and Ron decided to go public in order to give wider recognition to the illness and raise public awareness of the need for funds for research into a cure.

It was through the press articles that followed that Judith and Ron were grateful to hear from many members of the public, some of whom had lost loved ones to MND themselves. They heard from fans, people connected with the church and practitioners of all kinds of therapies, all offering their help and support. Over the ensuing months, Judith had many conversations with a doctor, Malcolm Barr, who ultimately pointed out that he believed Ron's case provided urgently needed hope, support and insight for potential investigation, because of a relatively simple and previously unreported chemical reaction to a widely used antibiotic.

With sadness in her heart at Ron's crippling disease, Judith bustled backstage at the Myer Music Bowl on 26 January. Irene Ruffolo rushed into the dressing room to tell her that Ron had arrived. Judith went to his side and watched as her husband was helped by two ushers to the front row. She worried that this might be the last time he would be well enough to see her perform on stage. But, for now, he would join the crowd to watch history being made in Melbourne. The Seekers performed before thousands of fans at the Myer Music Bowl, a fitting finale to the staggeringly successful Australian leg of their reunion tour.

Two days later, in a column called 'Icons', the Melbourne *Age* made much of Judith's introductory speech before Bruce's song 'I Am Australian', in which she spoke of Australia Day 1968, when The Seekers were named Australians of the Year for 1967. Back then, Judith said, the group had been blissfully unaware that Aboriginal Australians had nothing to celebrate. For Aborigines, Australia Day was a day of grieving and invasion. The *Age* writer noted, 'What a star Judy is. How sublime ... she seems eternal ... The Seekers remain what they always were: a bunch of honestly likeable dags. Love you guys. Love you Judy. Love you to death.'

The Australian end of The Seekers' reunion was over and Britain was beckoning. John Kovac had negotiated a deal with EMI Records in Britain to release the *Silver Jubilee Album*, albeit with a slightly different track listing and a new title – *A Carnival of Hits*. Backing it was a £200,000-plus television campaign throughout the United Kingdom.

John Kovac had also investigated the possibility of staging a one-off Seekers showcase for the British public and had arranged for Paul Dainty to present the group with the British promoter Barry Clayman. The 5,500-seat Royal Albert Hall was booked for 14 and 15 April. One single press advertisement ensured that both concerts were completely sold out within hours. The Seekers would leave for Britain mid-March for five weeks of promotion, including several television programmes. With her *Let Me Find Love* album mixed and ready for release, Judith was to fly to

London to begin a gruelling round of press, radio and television interviews. Meanwhile, their *A Carnival of Hits* album was released and stormed the British charts, peaking at Number 4.

Judith was once again packing her bags for London and this time she was packing Ron's, too. Staring adversity in the face, they had decided to include Ron in the trip so he could see Vicky just one more time. At one o'clock in the morning on which they were due to fly out, Judith was finishing last-minute packing when she heard a thud and a cry. Ron had fallen in the bathroom, one of the frequent falls he was now experiencing; but this time he was in real trouble. His head was bleeding and his shoulder was causing agonising pain. An ambulance was called and Ron was taken to hospital, where doctors diagnosed a broken collarbone. Complete immobilisation of his shoulder was crucial, they said. Shocked at how the fall seemed to have worsened Ron's MND symptoms, Judith had no alternative but to leave him in hospital and fly out to Britain without him. Faced with a stressful parting and the loneliness of the empty seat next to her on the plane, Judith arrived in London and had the unenviable task of placating Vicky, who had been so looking forward to seeing her son.

Judith made constant international phone calls home during the five weeks she was away, but Ron's speech was steadily worsening and those calls were fraught with frustration as she tried to make out what he was saying to her. Between calls, Judith had to smile for the cameras and carry on with her heavy promotional commitments.

Standing ovations greeted The Seekers at both their Royal Albert Hall shows and such was the disappointment at the unavailability of tickets that Kovac committed the group to a complete British tour early in 1995. By now, Judith had given The Seekers' reunion much more than the original twelve months she had agreed to. Eager to ensure that this time around no fans miss out, she had agreed to future dates, but the reunion was put on hold to enable her to meet her commitment to EMI in releasing her own album. Her fans had been waiting for more than four years and Kovac was determined to deliver what had been promised.

Judith finally arrived home in Melbourne and headed straight for the hospital. She held her breath as she walked up the corridor to her husband's room, wondering how he would be after their weeks apart. In her absence, the need to use a speaking communicator, even to express his most basic needs, had become a part of Ron's daily life. For so long, Judith had been the only person who could comprehend Ron's affected speech but she now realised his symptoms had progressed to a point where even she could no longer understand him. His body had stiffened badly and he was very frail. Their first night together at home was a traumatic one. Totally unprepared for the new level of disability Ron had reached, Judith struggled to keep him comfortable, while coping with her own migraine and asthma, brought on by the exhaustion of jet lag.

Two days after her return from London, Judith's long-awaited album *Let Me Find Love* was released in Australia and, as always, she found the strength to meet a hectic promotional schedule. The album's reviews were all favourable: the *Sunday Herald Sun* positively glowed, remarking on Judith's vocals. 'Durham's voice remains a glorious God-given instrument . . . on *Let Me Find Love* another side of her artistry is revealed – her ability to write songs that will have emotions pounding inside any soul.'

In an Australian Associated Press article after the album's release, Judith was asked how it felt to reclaim her solo identity, to be 'just Judith Durham' again. The article quoted:

I think I've got an enormous sense of responsibility, particularly since our car accident when I realised that the contribution I've made over the years has been so valuable to people. Realising how music can affect people so strongly, how it can uplift them, how it can heal them, how it can be with them in every situation in their lives, how my voice has some quality which seems to transport them or express something for them that they want to say. It's gone far, far beyond just entertainment for me. It's become a mission in my life to do things well and do them responsibly and try to give people something they will value and benefit from in some way.

A national television campaign for *Let Me Find Love*, coupled with a gruelling Australia-wide schedule of interviews and in-store appearances, pushed the album into the Australian Top 40, a first for Judith as a solo artist. By mid-May, *Let Me Find Love* was in the Top 10.

By June 1994, Judith Durham had accomplished many of the things she set out to do at the beginning of the nineties. She'd mended bridges with her three musical partners, given their faithful fans the event they'd been craving for 25 years and had finally recorded an all-original album that she had overseen from inception to creative fulfilment. Most of all she had rid herself of the guilt she'd carried since 1968, when she had exercised her right to a life of her own.

What we will never know is whether, back in 1968, Judith Durham left The Seekers six months too early. With no hits in the can for the group, dwindling crowds and an outdated image, chances are The Seekers split would have been inevitable. By leaving at a time when The Seekers were still a cherished part of people's lives, she perpetuated their myth without really knowing it. To the fans, the break-up of The Seekers was like a death in the family and, like stars who die at the height of their fame, The Seekers were crystallised in the hearts and minds of their public. Time served only to magnify their memories.

Was it time, then, for Judith to bask in the spotlight that shone so brightly on her in recent times, and to rest even momentarily on her laurels? Definitely not. One thing Judith Durham has never been known for is taking it easy. Most of all, she was cherishing the time she had left with Ron, whose absolute support of her career helped make all her recent triumphs possible. Musically, Judith's life was at its richest, but her success was bittersweet. Judith and Ron had faced many challenges during their 25-year marriage, but none so daunting as the one confronting them now. When they had first fallen in love, they had resolved to be happy, to take life as it comes and, together, to play whatever hand they were dealt. They just never dreamed they would one day be playing a no-win hand.

16. SAY GOODBYE, MY OWN TRUE LOVER

Now the harbour light is calling,
This will be our last goodbye,
Though the carnival is over,
I will love you till I die.

– 'THE CARNIVAL IS OVER'
TOM SPRINGFIELD

In the months following Judith's return from the group's last visit to the UK the previous April, Ron Edgeworth's condition deteriorated even further, and he was permanently hospitalised. The thought of leaving him again tore Judith apart. They had seldom been separated in the first two decades of their marriage. And now she was aware that each tearful goodbye could be their last – such is the uncertainty of prognosis with MND.

Judith would have given anything to take Ron with her, especially as they could no longer have conversations by phone: Ron could communicate only through an intermediary because his speech had deteriorated so much. Of course, Judith had been looking forward to the joy of being able to give to the British public something they'd wanted to see for so many, many years – Judith Durham back on stage with The Seekers – but in her heart she yearned to be near her husband.

'If Ron hadn't been so encouraging about my work,' says Judith, 'I would never have been able to be separated from him. He constantly said on his talking computer that he insisted I always put my career first, but it was still hard to know what to do for the best, a real struggle. Ron's incredible attitude made everything easier. It was still a seesaw existence, though: one minute the euphoria of public life, the next seeing Ron's great difficulties as he became increasingly disabled. And always, the tears of parting at every farewell, in case it was the last time.'

In public life Judith had experienced many highs, and the group's appearances at the Royal Albert Hall just seven months earlier were up there with the best of them. Their two-night stint was a complete sell-out that made press and television news around the world and moved even Q magazine, a well-respected British music journal, to devote half a page to a review. Even though it wrote that she had 'a grin that suggests she sells Hare Krishna tracts on the street; she dances like a baby elephant and dresses like a less tasteful Bet Lynch', it remains one of Judith's most treasured critiques. The magazine still ended that paragraph by conceding, '... she sings like an angel – clear, rich and pure'.

'Those shows at the Royal Albert Hall were truly fantastic,' Judith says. 'They were really over the top with emotion. There was no suggestion at that time that there would be any more concerts, so the people who desperately wanted to see the group live, and heard about the concerts in time, were the ones who turned up. They were so warm and so responsive. It was such a thrill for the four of us to play the Royal Albert Hall, something we'd never done in the sixties. It was a wonderfully warm and happy environment for us to do our first full reunion concerts in the UK.'

Amid the euphoria, though, Judith was once again brought back to earth with a thud. Standing at the stage door signing autographs, she was confronted with a fan who told her, 'I've never forgiven you for leaving The Seekers the first time and I'll never forgive you this time, either.'

Judith returned from the UK tour and recorded 'Somewhere a Child Is Sleeping', a duet with the Canadian singer John McDermott, which was to be included along with 'Amazing Grace' on the CD release of her 1968 Hollywood recording *For Christmas With Love*.

Only a few weeks later, she was honoured by Tattersalls with an award for Enterprise and Achievement, in recognition of her anthem, 'Australia Land of Today'. The award included a payment of $2,500 to a charity of her choice, which Judith donated to the Motor Neurone Disease Association (MNDA) of Australia.

In October, Judith and The Seekers were invited to provide the pre-match entertainment at the 1994 Australian Football League Grand Final. So too were the RAAF Roulettes and Judith was thrilled to be invited to join them for their flypast rehearsal, much to the mock envy of the boys! 'I just loved the adventure of it,' Judith says. 'I had to wear an anti-G pressure suit and go through a medical checkup with an RAAF doctor. There was a lot of red tape involved in actually getting me into one of the aircraft, including full instructions on how to use the pressure suit, the goggles, breathing apparatus, and of course, how to open my parachute if necessary. I tried to look unfazed when I was told that I should use it on hearing the pilot say "eject, eject, eject"!

'Once I was airborne, in a Pilatus PC9 turboprop, I got to do two loop-the-loops, which was quite mind-boggling. Dad had been in the RAAF in World War Two, of course, and it was a great thrill for me to have that experience, and to have some appreciation of what Dad had gone through.'

Two days later, Judith returned to the Melbourne Cricket Ground, for her second triumphant appearance since 1992. This time she and the boys performed at the grand final, before a crowd of 95,000, and an international television audience of eight million.

The Seekers played four songs and were ecstatically received by the crowd of swaying footy fans at the MCG and those watching at home. They opened with 'Georgy Girl' and followed it with the best-known version of 'Waltzing Matilda', this time featuring Judith singing the lead that Bruce had sung on the Queensland version of the tune recorded so many years before. The group then performed 'I Am Australian' and, in keeping with tradition, finished with the national anthem, 'Advance Australia Fair', as the players from the competing teams – Geelong and the West Coast Eagles – stood in respectful silence. Judith had finally decided to 'go with the flow' on 'Advance Australia Fair', despite still feeling that the lyric 'for we are young and free' was something indigenous Australians could not relate to in their ancient land; and she was bemused by the idea of calling her home 'Girt By Sea'. Nevertheless Judith felt honoured to be representing the country internationally by singing Australia's official anthem.

Within a week, the four Seekers were aboard another London-bound flight, heading for one of the most hectic promotional tours since their reunion had begun almost two years earlier. Over eleven days, the group fulfilled dozens of press and radio interviews, and performed on several TV shows. Then, back in Australia, Judith enjoyed some precious time with Ron before the release of the first edition of this book. A literary lunch at Melbourne's Regent Hotel was held to launch the book and, sadly, Ron was unable to be there to hear his wife's emotional speech about her life. To make Ron part of her special day, Judith wore one of his shirts.

'Ron was such a major part of the story,' Judith says. 'It was so fortunate that during the writing of the book, I was able to read the whole volume to him over many hours. On his computer, Ron was able to tap out a few missing memories of our life together.'

The launch was followed by a nineteen-day national tour, which saw Judith faced with at least fifty media interviews, more literary lunches and several in-store signings, where she met so many appreciative fans eager to read details of her life that had never been previously revealed.

The book tour was finally over on 20 November, and the following day Judith and Ron were able to celebrate their 25th wedding anniversary together. Sixteen of the couple's closest friends crammed into Ron's small private room in Melbourne's Bethlehem Hospital and celebrated with grape juice, hummus dip and chocolate biscuits.

'It meant so much to us both to reach such a milestone in our life together. And for Ron it was very special to have so many friends in the room with him. He was very weakened by now and in such discomfort, but the special smiles he gave were a delight to us all and the bond between the two of us was so intense in that room full of flowers. I will treasure the memories always.'

The very next day, Judith boarded another plane to fly to London for the second round of interviews preceding The Seekers' long-awaited UK tour, still not knowing whether Ron would live another two years – or two days – with MND. This parting was particularly painful for Judith, who knew that on this trip she would not even be able to hear Ron's voice on the phone.

Judith sent a silent plea to the universe for guidance. She received a phone call from a trained nurse whose own life had been turned around by the inspiration of Judith's song 'Hold on to Your Dream'. Sandi Isaacs rang out of the blue, extending an offer of help. For Judith, this was a gift from heaven. Sandi was able to take over where Judith left off, and she calmly and tenderly nursed Ron through the most physically and mentally testing weeks of his life. Sandi tended to Ron's every need and, in the many overseas calls to update Judith on his condition, acted as his interpreter and link to her.

In London, despite her frenetic workload, Judith managed finally to catch up with her close friends and associates Tom Springfield, David Reilly and Robert Whitaker. She was able to give them each a copy of her life story, in which they had all played such a pivotal role. The group were especially pleased that Whitaker, now an internationally exhibited photographer, could accompany them on their promotional tour, just like old times. Great media interest was generated by The Seekers' pre-tour visit, but for Judith the days dragged. Her heart and soul were with Ron back in Melbourne, and she counted the hours and minutes till she could be with him again.

It was during this trip that Judith was able to meet with her Motor Neurone Disease Association UK counterpart, the Duchess of York. For 25 minutes, Judith and the hard-working duchess chatted in a private suite at London's Ritz Hotel. The meeting became a media event and the two MND activists posed for photographs of Judith presenting the Duchess with a first-edition copy of this book. The Duchess then humbled and delighted Judith with an offer to visit Ron in hospital within a few days, during her forthcoming fundraising trip to Sydney and Melbourne, on behalf of the MNDA.

However, a further conflict between her professional and personal lives arose for Judith. She yearned to be home with Ron, especially during the duchess's visit, but last-minute pressure for The Seekers to visit Ireland meant delaying her departure by another couple of days, making her wish impossible.

A few days later in Melbourne, on 2 December, the Duchess interrupted her public media schedule to allow for a private meeting with Ron in his hospital room. Judith's sister Beverley and Ron's brother Patrick were also present. By now, although Ron was barely able to move any of his muscles, he insisted that the duchess see some home-video footage of him playing piano for Judith so that she could appreciate their music and see him as he used to be, so vibrant and so talented.

'I was so impressed by the Duchess,' says Judith. 'In spite of having ninety MND patients and their carers to meet and speak to, she still found that special time for Ron and didn't break her promise to me. She's quite a woman. She gave me her address and telephone number and urged me to keep in touch and, ever since then, we have continued our friendship.'

The Duchess later told Britain's *Hello!* magazine:

> It was wonderful to meet him. Especially since his clear blue eyes, which were the only muscles working in Ron's body, said so much about his depth of soul. [The home video] was so moving, that I found it very difficult to control my emotions. It was lovely of him to show me how he was before this debilitating disease took hold. Ron's imprisonment was one of the worst examples of how the disease affects people. Here was a brilliant pianist unable to play or sing the tunes he knows and loves so well. [Judith's] huge character and personality were completely infectious. I so admire her strength and determination to support motor neurone disease sufferers in the future.

Judith found herself counting the minutes on the plane on 3 December, the day after the Duchess had visited Ron, as the group returned from England. She knew from many tearful telephone calls back and forth to Sandi that Ron had been close to death during the group's last rushed days in Ireland. He had been placed on a drip by the hospital staff and that was all that was keeping him alive. Ron had now lost his sight and Judith was faced with the sad reality that the tearful farewell after their anniversary was the last time their eyes could ever meet.

After her return to Australia, Judith spent every day and night in

Ron's hospital room. On 10 December, less than a week later, Ron slipped into a coma in the early hours, and at 7 a.m., with his devoted wife at his side, he died.

'Ron was unconscious for a few hours and then left me very peacefully,' Judith says. 'If there is such a thing as a perfect death, then Ron experienced it. I'm so grateful that I was able to be with him at the end. He knew I was there to share his last moments, and that was very special.

'Because MND strikes with the warning that the patient may only have a short time to live, we'd both done a lot of grieving along the way. It's a terrible sadness that Ron could not be released from physical devastation without being lost to me. But we'd both based our lives on a spiritual awareness and that helped us through. We believed that what happened was Ron's destiny and with that came acceptance. We held on to the perspective that there is a Creator and he is in control, with his eye on every sparrow. People of all religions around the world would identify with that.'

Newspapers in many countries carried news of Ron's death and ran tributes, while television news services screened footage of Ron's playing. A news feature in Melbourne's *Sunday Herald Sun* quoted Judith:

I want Ron to be remembered for his sense of humour. He was always trying to make people laugh and throughout his illness, he was making jokes. Ron was a kind and gentle man who wished everybody well. He was my best friend and a wonderful teacher. He enriched my life on so many levels and helped me become the person I've aspired to be.

Ron had requested that he not be given a formal funeral, and a few days later, with only Judith and close family and friends in attendance, Ron was privately cremated. To mark this next step on Ron's spiritual journey home, Judith arranged for their recording of 'My Buddy' to be played – the opening track of their *Hot Jazz Duo – Live in Concert* album. It was a fitting tribute to Ron's remarkable musical gift and the one performance that had meant so much to them both through the years.

Following Ron's death, Judith spent time with her sister Beverley and family. She focused her thoughts on the spiritual teachings to which she had devoted the past two decades of her life, and concentrated only on happy thoughts of Ron. 'I resolved that I wouldn't dwell on the sadness,' says Judith, 'but rather, the joy of the happiness that I had shared with

Ron, the happiness that Ron had always given to the world and the sense of being left behind while Ron had moved further along on his spiritual journey. I tried to truly say goodbye and throw myself into my work as much as possible. I had immense support from all those close to me.'

Although it wasn't easy, Judith managed to honour her commitment to perform in Christmas carols presentations in Newcastle and Adelaide, and helped promote the release of the Salvation Army charity album *Spirit of Christmas*, which featured Australia's top recording artists. The CD included Judith's recording of 'Hark the Herald Angels Sing', which ended up being one of radio's most played tracks.

On 26 January 1995 – Australia Day – Judith Durham was named as a recipient of the OAM (Medal of the Order of Australia) in the Queen's New Year's Honours list. 'I was delighted by the top-secret phone call I had received the previous September,' Judith says. 'I was alerted to the probability of the award being made and asked that, if so, would I accept? I was so glad to be able to share my secret with Ron and that he could know that I probably would soon add "OAM" to the "A Mus. A" after my name.' Judith felt the honour was slightly marred, however, by the fact that the award was announced on a day that signified grief for many indigenous Australians, and she took advantage of the perfect opportunity to voice her feelings during the media interviews that followed the announcement.

Early the following month, the 1967 TV special *The Seekers Down Under* was chosen to open the Melbourne Music Festival. Two screenings were held at the Longford Cinema in Melbourne, and Judith and Bruce Woodley were invited to open the festival officially and speak about the making of the special.

A couple of weeks later, family and friends attended a celebration of Ron's life at Emu Bottom Homestead in Sunbury Victoria, where Ron had written the music for a film, *Raw Deal*, and where he and Judith had filmed many scenes for their guest roles in *Cash & Company* so many years before. There, after a few words from Judith and Ron's brother Patrick, Ron's ashes were placed in the lawns of Emu Bottom Homestead and a small chestnut tree was planted on top. 'The tree will grow and flourish and bear many conkers, which Ron and his brother used to play with as kids in Bristol,' says Judith. 'For Ron's memory, and ashes, to take form in a growing tree seems at least a small way to immortalise him in our sight, while his music can live on to nourish our hearts. It's such a small token compared with the immensity of his genius.

'We used to joke about putting each other under the mango tree on our Queensland property, so I saved some of the ashes and scattered them there when I next had an opportunity.'

From then on, emotional issues remained private as Judith was busy preparing for the forthcoming Seekers tour of England. She was also trying to find time to devote to selecting material for a new solo album she would be recording for EMI later in the year in London. Judith was delighted to find that the legendary Gus Dudgeon, noted for his work on many of Elton John's most successful albums, was to be her producer.

Judith was disappointed, however, that EMI had requested that no original material be included on this album. This was to be a whole album of cover versions, the first time Judith had not included any of her own compositions on a solo album since *A Gift of Song* in 1971. The search for suitable material was an arduous one. Judith listened to literally hundreds of songs she had found herself, or that other people had recommended to her. There were many beautiful songs among them, but the task was to whittle down the choice to the twelve tracks that suited Judith's voice and style the most.

A fortnight later, Judith flew out of Melbourne Airport en route to London for The Seekers' five-date UK tour, presented by Barry Clayman Concerts in conjunction with Paul Dainty. The tour opened at Sheffield Arena on 23 March and, over the coming six days, The Seekers would play Birmingham NEC, Wembley Arena, Cardiff CIA and Brighton Centre. The Irish singer John McDermott, who had recorded 'Somewhere a Child is Sleeping' with Judith almost a year before, would support.

'It was such an emotional experience again, for us and the fans,' says Judith. 'Many of them thought they would never see us again and they showed such overwhelming gratitude. Many of them turned up at the stage door with photos taken thirty years before and many just wanted to be photographed with the group.'

Of course, back in her hotel room each night it was difficult for Judith not to pick up the telephone instinctively, to tell Ron how well the concert had gone. But it was a big thrill for Judith and the boys finally to play Wembley Arena in their own right: the last time they'd stood together on that stage was on 11 April 1965, as part of the *New Musical Express* Poll Winners' Concert. Many fans complained that the tour wasn't long enough. Why hadn't The Seekers played Bournemouth or Liverpool or Blackpool or Ireland? Judith felt sad that she couldn't explain to each and every one of them that, when the tour was booked, it was restricted to five dates because she had thought that Ron would still be alive, and she would naturally want to be back home with him as soon as possible.

The whirlwind visit was over in less than three weeks, and Judith and the boys arrived back in Melbourne on 1 April. There were just twelve weeks left before Judith would once again return to London, this time to begin work in earnest on her first solo project in more than a year. So much to do, so little time. She'd even decided on an image change, and, for the first time in fifteen years, Judith took a pair of scissors in her hand and cut her hair to shoulder length.

Judith felt unprepared, though, for the recording sessions ahead. She was unsure of the material she would be performing. She had never met Gus Dudgeon before and the musicians were unknown to her, too. She had also experienced trouble with her voice and quickly squeezed in some singing lessons before recording began early in July at the original EMI Abbey Road Studios in London. Judith felt a sense of history and immense gratitude for the facilities and technical gadgetry at her disposal when she walked through the doors for her first session there since the recording of the ill-fated single 'Let Me Find Love' and 'Music Everywhere' in 1969.

In her preliminary discussions with Gus Dudgeon, who hit it off with Judith right from the start, the song list was reduced to the final dozen. Having enjoyed the experience of recording Elton John's 'Skyline Pigeon' some 23 years earlier, Judith agreed on Dudgeon's suggestion to use one of John's many compositions with Bernie Taupin, 'Mona Lisas and Mad Hatters' – which became the inspiration for the album's title – and the Lesley Duncan song 'Love Song', which John had recorded in 1970. Having loved the original when it was released in 1965, Judith happily added Dudgeon's recommendation of Dovovan's 'Catch the Wind' to the final list, along with a new, gutsy arrangement of 'Turn Turn Turn', which she had first recorded with The Seekers for their *Come the Day* album in 1966. In a moment of true inspiration, she threw herself into a gospel arrangement of Carole King's 'You've Got a Friend', which A&M had unsuccessfully urged her to record in the early 1970s. This time, however, she had the talented support of a black choir. Other personal favourites that made it were Julian Lennon's environmental 'Saltwater' (which Judith had wanted to sing ever since she had bought Julian's single), Cat Stevens' 'Morning Has Broken', Gallagher and Lyle's 'Heart On My Sleeve' and a stirring gospel treatment of Jackie De Shannon's 'Put a Little Love in Your Heart'. The songwriters Charlie Dore and Barbara Dickson provided Judith with the haunting 'Someone Out There', and she looked forward to tackling the range required for 'Northern Lights', which eventually became the closing song in her UK concerts. The most emotional experience of all was working once again with a live string orchestra on the heartrending 'End of the World', which had been a hit in 1963 for Skeeter Davis. Judith made a friend for life in Bruce Baxter, who arranged the strings, and the orchestra leader Gavin Wright paid her a tremendous compliment when he told her that the sound of her voice was the sound that violinists tried to achieve with their instruments, and how inspiring they all found it to play with her.

During earlier London visits, Judith had made contact with Tom Springfield and this time she had asked him about two songs. She recalled 'Adios Amor', which Springfield had written with Norman Newell in the sixties and had submitted for consideration by The Seekers in 1967. Judith had always thought it was a beautiful song and, as the solo artist she now was, she was thrilled to have the chance to record it for her album.

The recording sessions were inspiring for Judith. 'It was roasting hot in London,' she recalls. 'The heat was relentless day after day, like being in Australia in the middle of summer. As each week went by during the trip, I became increasingly grateful for the opportunity to be a true artist, surrounded by such fantastic people and equipment to work with, first at Abbey Road and later at Metropolis for the overdubs and mixing. I'll be for ever indebted to Gus and Matt Howe for enhancing my voice and making the entire album such an enjoyable experience.

'The surprise of being able to make those classic hits feel part of me, especially imbibing the spirituality of Ian Lynn's inspired arrangement of "Morning Has Broken", has brought a real hunger to work with Ian again.'

They were in Studio 2 at Abbey Road, used almost exclusively by The Beatles in the sixties, and, with the exception of updated technology, unchanged to this day. There, during the recording of one of the quieter numbers for the album, the drummer, Dave Mattacks, asked everyone to stop and listen: surely that couldn't be 'Lucy in the Sky with Diamonds' he was hearing, could it? Sure enough, eerie strains of The Beatles song were drifting in the air. 'We thought maybe The Beatles were haunting their old stamping ground,' says Judith. 'It turned out to be Paul McCartney and George Harrison working with George Martin on *The Beatles' Anthology* and the sound from the old echo plates was leaking through the rear wall of the studio.'

In mid-September, Judith arrived home in Australia and was unable to face food properly for several weeks, having become unexpectedly ill on the plane. She had an alarmingly high temperature and was waking with night sweats, her weight dropping steadily. To her horror, she woke one day to find she had turned yellow, and was admitted to hospital for ten days with jaundice. For a time in London, Judith had been taking medication for nasal polyps and the antibiotics had a devastating effect on her. The specialist told her that the very antibiotic she had been prescribed had in fact caused big problems for her liver. It reminded her that Ron had suffered terrible side effects from a dental antibiotic, which, in his case, had seemed to bring on the symptoms of MND. Luckily, Judith's symptoms abated over the ensuing weeks.

Far from enjoying being looked after in hospital during the lead-up to the Australian release of her new solo album, Judith became involved in compiling a box set of the complete works of The Seekers and the home-video release of the 1968 film *The World of The Seekers*. Much of the hard slog that went into preparing these gems for release was done from Judith's hospital bed, with Judith's phone running hot to EMI in Sydney. They never realised where she was calling from, or that she had been surviving on nothing but ripe watermelon for seven days, the first food she could face in six weeks.

On 2 October, a few weeks after Judith had been discharged from hospital with a clean bill of health, The Seekers were paid the ultimate tribute by the Australian Record Industry Association (ARIA) with their induction into the Hall of Fame by Peter Asher, during a national telecast of the 1995 ARIA Awards. 'Seeing Peter again took me back thirty years,' Judith says, 'to when he and Paul McCartney stood and watched from the end of Abbey Road Number 1 Studio, while I finished playing "Maple Leaf Rag" on the piano. It was one of the proudest moments of my life – and Peter didn't remember it! But it was such an honour to receive the award, especially from someone as eminent in the music industry as Peter Asher. We all were very grateful to finally have the recognition of our peers in contemporary Australian music. I was quite nervous as I played my part in the group's acceptance speech.

'The questions from the press at the event made me think about how the industry had changed in thirty years, and it struck me that a major difference in Australia was the emergence of Aboriginal contemporary music stars, something to really celebrate.'

Prior to Christmas, the Salvation Army's *Spirit of Christmas* CD for 1995 was released, featuring 'Bambino', a hit for The Springfields in 1963, which Judith had recorded some weeks earlier on her return to Australia. The same month, the 1968 film *The World of The Seekers* was released on home video. Presumed lost for ever, the film had fallen into Judith's hands some years before. The refurbishing of Bendigo's Capitol Theatre in 1991 was celebrated with a major production featuring Judith's song 'Bendigo-O' as the finale. The show's producer had happened to find in his garage, wrapped for twenty years in garbage bags, the only known original 35-mm reels of the coloured film. Would Judith, by any chance, be interested? Judith stored it in her bedroom cupboard for the next five years, until its release by EMI/Roadshow. Only weeks later, EMI Records also released the five-CD/cassette box set, *The Seekers Complete*, which featured, for the very first time as a collection, every song The Seekers had ever recorded. Along with some surprises (such as the two sets of lyrics for 'Georgy Girl' used in the opening and closing sequences of the film itself, three 1963 radio jingles, and some never-before-released sea shanties from the same year), was the long-lost recording by Judith of 'This Is My Song', which didn't make it on to *Seen in Green* back in 1967.

'It was the greatest "gift" to me to be able at last to grab any song from our catalogue at short notice,' says Judith. 'Previously, I spent so much time ferreting around in old boxes of vinyl or ringing friends in hope they might have a copy of something I had forgotten the words to. Listening to "This Is My Song" made me cry on first hearing. I feared I was going to be embarrassed by it, because I knew the recording had been rejected in the sixties. Instead, I was moved to tears as I heard the beautiful Bobby Richards string arrangement, which I assumed had been lost for ever.'

Before the year was out, Judith would take a deep breath and finally speak publicly of her almost lifelong struggle with bronchiectasis, and its effect on her life. Earlier in the year, she had been contacted by Liz Dew, the founder of the now defunct POOPS (People Out Of Puff), offering her condolences regarding Ron's death. Liz invited Judith to speak at their lung-disease seminar for health professionals at Melbourne's Monash Medical Centre during Breathe Easy Week.

'Sadly, Liz lost her battle with pulmonary fibrosis,' says Judith, 'but it was incredible to have the opportunity to speak so openly about my lifelong cough instead of continuing to apologise for "having a cold" and disguising it. I also met a seven-year-old girl with the complaint, the first other sufferer I had met and one of many others who made contact. I learned a lot more about my condition and I shared aspects of my lifestyle with others and told them how I combine a career with the illness, with emphasis on my gratitude for the knowledge of the Arnold Ehret diet – my saving grace.'

With Christmas behind her, and another gold award on her wall for sales of *The World of The Seekers* video, Judith spent the early part of 1996 preparing for her forthcoming solo tour of the UK and the release of her *Mona Lisas* album, which were to be preceded by a UK media tour in February. From a South Kensington flat in London, Judith tackled once again the gruelling round of television, radio and press interviews. Despite the frantic pace, Judith found great enjoyment in planning her first solo tour in five years, and discussing her new solo album, her first in the UK for 20 years. There was great interest in Judith, but she was frustrated that the press seemed so mystified at her having done a 'covers' album. How she had longed to tell them that she had desperately wanted to record an album of new material as a contemporary artist. It was heartbreaking for her to realise she would not receive the airplay she could well have with new material. Nevertheless, she found reward in the reaction from the public and the press to her singing and really appreciated the quality of the production in every aspect, irrespective of the material.

Confident that she had done all she could to promote the new album, Judith was about to return home to Melbourne when she learned of an invitation from a Scottish radio station to be interviewed for a one-hour special they were planning to make about her career and the *Mona Lisas* album. It was an offer too good to refuse, so Judith delayed her return to Australia and flew to Scotland instead. She was thrilled when the announcer opened the special with a wonderful welcome and, 'Now, Judith, let's go all the way back to the start ...' She took a delighted breath, ready to talk about her piano playing and her childhood, when he continued, '... now how did you all get together?'! Needless to say, it was The Seekers' music that made up most of the playlist for this one-hour Judith Durham special!

When *Mona Lisas* was released in Britain, Judith was delighted to receive word that BBC Radio 2 were to name it Album of the Week, but she was told soon after that another album had been chosen instead. It was *The Beatles' Anthology*, Volume 1 – at least it was nice to compete with them again! But there was no time for Judith to dwell on these disappointments with her forthcoming concerts looming. This would be Judith's first major solo tour of Britain in 20 years and ahead were 28 dates across England, Wales and Scotland in 37 days. As so often before, to avoid disappointing anyone, Judith included a medley of Seekers songs in her show. But the largest part of her repertoire was the new material from *Mona Lisas* – new arrangements to rehearse, a few completely new songs and new stage wardrobe to consider, not to mention the finalising of tour arrangements.

In April, with many of these requirements still not fully met, Judith flew to London to begin a concentrated period of rehearsal with the band that had been put together for her. While she was concerned that she hadn't yet learned all the new lyrics by heart, she was elated to learn that Cliff Richard's musical director, Alan Park, had agreed to take on the role for her tour – the band would be great. Indeed they were. The British musician Joe Fagin had signed on to play bass, Keith Hayman would play keyboards and guitar, Val McKenna was to play guitar, with Jeff Seopardi on drums and percussion. The band would provide great backing vocals as well.

Unfortunately, until just one day before her tour began, Judith had no opportunity to find out how great her new band really was: she had completely lost her voice, even for speaking. Alan Park and the band had no choice but to rehearse the material dutifully night and day, presumably wondering whether the singer was ever going to show or whether she could indeed still sing these days! It was only the day before the tour began that Judith had the chance to sing the concert through with them, and they discovered of course that, yes, this woman really could sing – and how! With fingers crossed, Judith opened the tour on 1 May at the Royal Centre in Nottingham, and fears that her lack of rehearsal might affect the standard of the show proved unfounded: the show was an overwhelming success; the audience was demonstrative and emotional; the band were great; and Judith was revelling in the thrill of appearing in concert on her own again.

'I was in seventh heaven with a band and backing vocals of that calibre,' she says, 'as with the *Mona Lisas* album. Everything with the tour was of top quality, and I was on an emotional high the whole time, never wanting it to end. And always in the back of my mind was the thought that this could well be my last solo tour ever.'

The next night, at the Anvil in Basingstoke, the scene was repeated, and then again and again as the tour moved by bus through the British cities and towns, where many of the venues were familiar to Judith. She had played them with Ron during her one-woman-show tour in the early seventies, or with their Hottest Band in Town shows a few years later. 'The sequence of songs in the show needed juggling,' says Judith. 'It took until the fourth show before it all settled into a final order.'

From then on, it was standing ovations night after night. Judith received rave reviews from the critics and delighted audiences everywhere, and found she could relax and just enjoy the complete feeling of freedom that a solo tour always afforded her. The stage was her own. Judith's fans flocked to the concerts, many travelling from show to show. Each night, Judith received letters from people who had so enjoyed their first concert that they'd decided to follow the tour. One man travelled from Scotland and back four times; others came to ten of the concerts; and one fan Judith heard of had seen them all. So many people who loved Judith as a solo performer got to meet her personally at the many stage-door signings.

But along with outpourings of praise for Judith's concerts came the inevitable questions: 'When is the group coming back?' 'How are Athol, Keith and Bruce?' 'Is there going to be another Seekers tour?' Mixed with Judith's many solo albums and programmes to sign, there were well-loved copies of Seekers albums, and amid the pleas for her not to leave it another twenty years before returning for more solo concerts in the UK were the heartfelt appeals for her to bring Athol, Keith and Bruce with her next time.

More and more, Judith realised that, whereas for herself and for many of her fans there had always been a very clear distinction between her work as a solo star and her involvement with the group, for the public at large the dividing lines were very blurred. For most, Judith's voice *was* The Seekers and there were no Seekers without Judith Durham! In the 25 years since Judith had left the group in 1968 to pursue her solo dreams, she had been shown, always to her great surprise, how deeply and how personally the public had taken her decision to leave the group. And now, far from being surprised by the overwhelming success of The Seekers reunion, she expected it.

A great deal of soul searching had preceded her decision to rejoin the group in 1993, and now in 1996, in spite of the resounding artistic success of her present solo tour, Judith was beginning to resign herself to the idea that whatever would be would be. Judith had never thought, back in the sixties, of the role The Seekers had played in people's lives and how extraordinary it was that the group brought such happiness and comfort whenever they sang. 'In the three decades since,' Judith says, 'no other group had come along to fill the void, and more and more since 1993 I could see the genuine need for Seekers music in the community, to create a much-needed balance and to help make the world a better place.'

Deep down, Judith came to realise the inevitability of renewed association with The Seekers and the joys of a different kind that this would bring to her and the fans. It seemed to her that life had destined her to reunite with Athol, Keith and Bruce so that they could continue their role in the world. If her voice, as she was so often told, had the power to heal, then it would become her mission in life, not just her ambition, to reach as wide an audience as possible. Although she knew she could achieve a certain amount of that balance with her solo work, never could she achieve it on the same grand scale as with the group and its international popularity.

Somehow, Judith resolved to make it all work, to enhance the unique place she had rekindled in *The World of The Seekers*, and still, somehow, to enjoy her own musical world outside the group environment. As she'd told *New Musical Express* in 1965, her ambition was 'for The Seekers to carry on successfully, [for me] to achieve professional recognition solely through musicianship, and to sing all types of music well'. The most significant thing her 25 years away from the group had added to that ambition was to be true in her heart to her personal world of music, and to hold on to her dream. Finally, the time was right for those dual ambitions to be realised, although it would mean difficulties in adjusting to the roles she would now play, and a heavy workload juggling virtually two careers at once.

Judith knew too well that life has a strange way of never standing still. Her personal world of music had given her many dazzling highlights, but as with so many of them – her one woman show, her Hottest Band in Town tours and her appearance with Ron at Newport Jazz Festival among them – she knew that the next day, even the next month, the euphoria of this present tour would be a fading memory both for her and for her fans.

So far, the reaction from fans on her *Mona Lisas* tour had thrilled and delighted her and she revelled in the joy of giving her audience such a gratifying concert experience as a solo artist. But she had no warning of the response she would receive on the next night of her tour. Coming up for Judith was her concert at the Royal Festival Hall in London, her first at that venue since she had performed her one-woman show in 1971. Judith was looking forward to playing the prestigious venue again, but, compared with the incredible warmth of The Seekers' Royal Albert Hall concert, she anticipated a cold atmosphere and a blasé London audience, and didn't expect to relish the experience as much as she had enjoyed the dates that led up to it.

The concert was scheduled for 23 May and, after a sell-out performance the previous night in Cambridge, Judith and her entourage drove into

London. A delay unloading the equipment meant Judith's rehearsal would be rushed, and as she alighted from her taxi at the stage door she wondered what was in store for her. At 7.45 p.m., after a sound check – and rested from her forty winks – she was ready. She knew she was in good voice, but nothing could have prepared her for the incredible cheers and applause that greeted her entrance on the Royal Festival Hall stage for the first time in 25 years. She felt an almost overpowering warmth and support from her fans, so keen to hear her voice after so long. She forgot all about being nervous and sang like a bird.

Time seemed to fly as Judith worked her way through her show, to rapturous response from her audience. As the show drew to a close, Judith tried again and again to move into her encores, but was completely overwhelmed by the cheers from the entire audience, who had risen to their feet refusing to stop their applause. For ten mind-boggling minutes, Judith Durham basked in the spotlight as a packed house showed their appreciation for her music, for her courage, and for her just being there to make them happy.

Filled with the euphoria of her Royal Festival Hall concert, Judith completed the ten remaining dates on her *Mona Lisas* tour, which wound up on 6 June 1996 at the Apollo Theatre in Manchester. While nothing could surpass the reaction Judith had experienced at the Royal Festival Hall, she was elated by the resounding success of the entire tour. As so often in her solo career, she had again left critics raving. Of her Royal Festival Hall concert, *The Times* wrote that 'it was impossible not to be won over'; the *Manchester Evening News* glowed with, 'It is impossible to over-emphasise the sheer perfection of Judith's voice and interpretation'; while the *Liverpool Echo*'s critic found that '. . . in the 90s that famous spine-tingling voice is as soothing and soaring as ever'.

Home in Australia, Judith rose to the challenge of an invitation for her to appear in Melbourne as a surprise guest on stage with one of Australia's leading rock bands, Chocolate Starfish. Their lead singer, Adam Thompson, challenged her with the idea, and, neither of them really knowing how the audience would respond to the cultural contrast between the two artists, Thompson introduced 'Georgy Girl' and the band played the first half, with Judith walking on from the side of the stage to finish it with them. The audience went wild and Judith remained on stage to sing along with the band's Top 40 hit, 'Mountain', and later joined them on an encore of 'Burnin' Love'.

In September, as her *Mona Lisas* album was released in Australia,

Judith got together with the leading Australian songwriters Heather Field and Robert Parde and penned an environmental song, 'Hey Hey Hey', which would later be recorded by The Seekers. With a choir, Judith recorded 'O Happy Day' for the album *Spirit of Christmas '96* and, not long after, found herself back in a studio to record a new single, 'I Am Australian'.

The popularity of this anthem, which Judith had already recorded with The Seekers on the *25 Year Reunion Celebration* album and video, prompted EMI to ask Judith to join Russell Hitchcock and Mandawuy Yunupingu – respectively lead singers of the international chart-toppers Air Supply and the Aboriginal band Yothu Yindi – to record 'I Am Australian' as a single with the producer Charles Fisher. Within days of its release it had reached Number 17 in the Australian Top 40. For the first time since 'The Olive Tree' in 1967, Judith's name was in the pop charts!

Not long after, with 'I Am Australian' still high in the charts, Judith was delighted to be able, finally, to meet Marianne Faithfull backstage at the Forum after one of the singer's Melbourne concerts. The two icons, who had been chart rivals during the sixties, posed for photographs and chatted for an hour about the different paths they had taken in life.

During that year, in the little spare time she had between writing and recording, Judith resumed work on her musical *Gotta Be Rainbows*, recording all the songs from the show in demo form, with the producer/arranger Ricky Edwards, using many of Melbourne's best contemporary singers to bring the songs to life. She created a CD as the first step in the process of finding an international theatrical entrepreneur to stage a full-scale production.

During this prolific period in her life, Judith also wrote with many other artists, collaborating with Paul Brady and Paul Kelly – whom she had first met during the recording of *Spirit of Christmas '96* – Mark Holden, Eris O'Brien and Ross Wilson of Daddy Cool and Mondo Rock, the female trio Tiddas, Richard Pleasance, Benny Gallagher (who was touring Australia with Manfred Mann), even touching base with Mark Seymour. Judith was involved with the compilation of *The Seekers Down Under* and *The Seekers at Home* for release on home video, as *The Seekers at Home & Down Under*, before returning to the recording studio as a solo artist. She recorded the ballad 'Always There', donating the track for use as the theme for a film clip to mark the 75th anniversary of the Smith Family, a charity supporting the underprivileged, for use in its 1997 advertising campaign. The sentiments of the lyrics so perfectly embodied the message to the community of the work of this charitable organisation. Later, Judith oversaw the repackaging in Australia of her *Mona Lisas* album, to be retitled *Always There* and to include the new title track and 'I am Australian', replacing 'Turn Turn Turn' and 'Heart on My Sleeve'.

With the boys, Judith also recorded two new songs, which would be released as tracks on a forthcoming Seekers compilation. One of them was 'Far Shore', which had been written especially for the group by the former Easybeats members Harry Vanda and George Young, and for which The Seekers filmed their first-ever video clip. In April 1997, 'Far Shore' was released as a single in the week that a press conference was held in Melbourne to announce that Judith and The Seekers were signing a new recording contract with EMI Australia. The deal, reportedly the most lucrative ever offered in Australia, called for two new studio albums from the group, their first in thirty years. In addition, 'Far Shore' and 'Hey Hey Hey', along with a bonus interview with the group, became the third CD in the box set *Treasure Chest — The Essential Collection*, which also featured their classic sixties albums *Seen in Green* and *Seekers Live at the Talk of the Town*. *Treasure Chest* peaked at Number 7 in the national Top 40 and was later certified gold.

After an exhaustive round of media interviews, Judith flew to Los Angeles for another intensive songwriting burst, first with the legendary Californian drummer and producer Russ Kunkel (married to the singer Nicolette Larson), Stephen Bishop, Tony Joe White, Pam Reswick and Steve Werfel, and John Durrill, who took her to meet one of her idols from her teenage years, Phil Everly of the Everly Brothers, joining him in a memorable singsong around his piano. While in LA, Judith met up with Doris Tyler, who had worked as a publicist on The Seekers' 1993 Australian tour. Tyler introduced Judith to a young songwriter and performer, Jeff Vincent. This chance meeting led Judith and Jeff to write 'Calling Me Home', especially for The Seekers. Both writers felt that the song just seemed to write itself, so easy was the collaboration.

Back home in June and through the following two months, Judith and the boys travelled to and from the Melbourne recording studio, where songs for the first of their two new albums were being recorded with the producer Charles Fisher. With the multitrack tapes literally in their luggage, Judith flew to Nashville with their manager John Kovac, to meet up with Charles Fisher and Keith Potger at Reba McEntire's studio, Starstruck, for the mixing of the album by David Leonard, best known for his work with Prince on *Purple Rain*.

Meanwhile, during the making of the album, not only were The

Seekers filmed for a video to be released later in the year for home viewing and to form part of a television special, but also by the *60 Minutes* team for a major television feature on Judith and the boys. The twelve songs that made the final selection, out of a choice of more than a hundred songs originally submitted from all over the world, all had the unique ingredients that go into making a Seekers song: strong melodies, optimistic sentiments and superb arrangements, instrumentation and vocals.

The Seekers' first studio album in three decades would include as its first track 'Calling Me Home', chosen as the song the group would initially use to promote the album. Also featured were a cover of Rick Springfield's 'Speak to the Sky' and 'The Bush Girl', with Bruce Woodley's music set to Henry Lawson's poem. Two songs Bruce wrote with Michael Cristian – 'Gotta Love Someone' and 'Amazing' – were the perfect embodiment of The Seekers sound, while 'Future Road', with its message of hope and unity, was composed by Keith Potger, Trevor Spencer and Boyd Wilson. Keith also contributed 'The Circle of Love', which he co-wrote with Rick Beresford, and his own 'Guardian Angel/Guiding Light'. Keith provided another perfect vehicle for Judith's voice in 'Forever Isn't Long Enough (For Me)', which he wrote with Byron Hill. Through the inspiration of John Kovac, The Seekers wrote the lyrics for 'The Shores of Avalon', based on an old Gaelic song, and they revived the singalong feel of many of their early folk/country records with Paul Anka's 'It Doesn't Matter Any More', originally a posthumous hit for Buddy Holly. The album's final track would be a group version of Judith's moving ballad 'It's Hard To Leave', which she had written in 1971 and recorded on her 1994 album, *Let Me Find Love*. Once it was mixed, all that was needed was to settle on a track order and album title before the album would be ready for release. They agreed that for a title the optimistic sentiment of 'Future Road' was a perfect reflection of The Seekers in the late nineties, just as it had been in the sixties.

Around this time, Judith was asked if she would accept the honour of having a music studio named after her at the prominent Fintona Girls' School in Melbourne. Meanwhile, the network links in other countries and in cyberspace were buzzing with activity as fans spontaneously set up websites and even printed a magazine in tribute to The Seekers as a group and to Judith individually.

All the time, behind the scenes, unbeknown to Judith, a team of people was working tirelessly and secretly on a national television programme in tribute to her. Clandestine arrangements were made for many of the people who had played a special part in Judith's life to fly in to Sydney as guests on the programme. They included Judith's sister Beverley and Judith's niece and nephews Belinda, Tony and Ben, her brother-in-law Patrick Edgeworth, Athol Guy, Keith Potger and Bruce Woodley, her piano mentor Ronald Farren-Price, the entertainer Bobby Limb and the rock star Adam Thompson, and all the way from England, her first songwriting partner, David Reilly. In addition, the show's producers had secured filmed messages from the Duchess of York, Olivia Newton-John, Lynn Redgrave and Rolf Harris, with a special tribute from Australia's international recording star Tina Arena.

With everything in place, the surprise was worked into Judith's hectic promotional schedule. *Future Road* was released on 20 October, and the overwhelming demand saw it debut in the national charts at Number 4 and earn gold certification within days, and later to go platinum. Judith and The Seekers flew to Sydney to make a series of in-store appearances to promote the album. Surrounded by a crowd of three thousand people, Judith was enthusiastically signing autographs for excited fans when the Australian television personality Mike Munro, who had joined the endless queue, stepped in front of her and presented her with a bound red book.

It took Judith a few moments to register what the gold-embossed words on the front of the book actually said, and, as she looked up in amazement, Mike Munro quoted those famous words directed to her: 'Judith Durham, *This Is Your Life*'.

The events that were to follow into the evening – before a surprised and delighted studio audience – were filmed and broadcast three weeks later, to become the most watched edition of the programme for the year. Nearly 3 million viewers tuned in to see this story unfold and as the programme drew to an end, with many viewers having been moved to laughter and tears, Judith unexpectedly joined with David Reilly to sing a chorus of the song they had written thirty years before: 'Colours of My Life'.

17. LIVING THE DREAM

Maybe someday you will find
It's gonna be your turn
If you Hold on to Your Dream within your heart . . .

– 'HOLD ON TO YOUR DREAM'
JUDITH DURHAM

For Judith, the early part of 1998 was spent putting together the upcoming Seekers' 30th Year Anniversary tour of Australia, the first to feature new material from *Future Road* and their first to feature elaborate staging.

Much time was spent rehearsing the new songs and translating them to a live setting; and Noel Crombie, of the now defunct Split Enz, was commissioned to create a colourful set for the show, which featured a hand-sewn backdrop giving an illusion of stretching to infinity. To celebrate three decades since The Seekers had last recorded in the sixties, a special commemorative 30th anniversary yearbook was published, featuring previously unseen photographs of the group, with a pull-out scrapbook of memorabilia through the years.

Along with the classic hits and selections from *Future Road*, The Seekers opened the second half of the show by recreating their early days at the Treble Clef in Melbourne. Sitting in a corner of the stage with lamps to create an atmosphere, The Seekers played an acoustic set from their earliest repertoire, including 'When the Stars Begin to Fall', 'Myra', 'The Light from the Lighthouse' and a gospel medley.

The tour kicked off in mid-February with concerts in the Victorian towns of Horsham and Bendigo, before moving to the major cities with a run of six sold-out shows at the Melbourne Concert Hall. Of the 'Treble Clef set', the *Melbourne Age* wrote, 'There was a point, just after the interval when The Seekers showed how they have become tangible symbols of an Australia ethos politicians talk about but very rarely understand.'

During the Melbourne dates, the Performing Arts Museum staged a Seekers exhibition, featuring vintage posters, albums and scrapbooks and a display featuring the gown Judith had worn for the final week of Seekers shows at London's Talk of the Town back in July 1968. EMI Records presented The Seekers with a gold disc for 'A World of Our Own', recognising worldwide sales of 42 million copies of the song in all its configurations. The sell-out crowds continued as The Seekers moved on to Hobart, Sydney, Newcastle, Brisbane, Toowoomba, Canberra, Perth and Adelaide, with many extra shows being added along the way.

Only days after the tour ended, Judith, in her continuing role as National Patron for the MND Association, was called upon to launch both the publication *Motor Neurone Disease – A Problem Solving Approach*, at the start of MND Awareness Week, and the MND website.

A few weeks later, the group resumed the 30th Anniversary tour in New Zealand, for a series of concerts in Auckland, Wellington, Nelson, Dunedin and Christchurch. 'At times the audience was spellbound, entranced by Durham,' wrote one reviewer. 'Her distinctive, crisp voice has no equal. It is her gift. She may be 50-something, but she still looks the same as in the dizzy '60s heyday.'

The new material was received ecstatically by audiences and reviewers alike, except in Auckland, where the reviewer for the *New Zealand Herald* not only took exception to the inclusion of new material, but balked at two songs that are favourites with Seekers' fans:

> Durham still has the voice of an angel, a thing of radiant clarity which was a joy to listen to. But we longed to hear it sing songs we knew ... Selections from the band's recent history cluttered the programme and we sat politely through them ... a nauseatingly pompous anthem about being Australian and an arty thing with words by Henry Lawson.

The Seekers returned to Australia and ended the tour with a week-long season at Twin Towns in Tweed Heads on Australia's Gold Coast, amazingly their first ever genuine Australian club dates.

Soon after that, Judith was moved in another unexpectedly emotional dimension. She was contacted by her friend Simon Barnett, who had previously been involved in the production of The Seekers' 1993 reunion video. Now involved with the Bonnie Babes Foundation, a nonprofit organisation established to counsel families grieving after the loss of a baby from miscarriage or stillbirth, Barnett encouraged Judith to write a song for the organisation. She met the challenge and created 'I Celebrate Your Life', sharing the lyric credit with the Foundation's Rachel Stanfield-Porter and Simon Barnett.

> *Where do I start? How do I feel?*
> *Sad and empty, cheated and lonely;*
> *You were my life, you were my babe;*
> *I was so excited, I longed for you only;*
> *Did I do wrong? Why did I lose you?*

You lived here inside me – tears I still cry;
Friends couldn't know how much I was grieving –
Just you and mummy were saying goodbye

'Simon truly inspired me to write a song which would celebrate a little soul whose life was lost, while expressing the depth of sometimes very lasting grief experienced by bereft parents,' says Judith. 'I avidly read all the literature from Bonnie Babes in order to gain a deeper understanding, never having had a family myself or even ever knowing that desperate yearning to be a parent which so many experience.'

Only a matter of weeks later, in mid-August, Australians woke to national newspaper banners that read SEEKER STALKED. After many years of harassment by a fan and former business associate, Judith had been left with no alternative but to 'go public', albeit reluctantly.

On 19 August, Judith appeared in Prahran Magistrates Court to seek an intervention order against Margaret Dahlstrom, and told how Dahlstrom had delivered 42 doormats to Judith's apartment over a three-week period. Judith explained that she had first met Dahlstrom as a sixteen-year-old fan, and Judith had met her again in the late 1980s, when Dahlstrom promoted several concerts and even ran Judith's fan club. After Judith's 1990 car crash, Dahlstrom had acted as her trusted assistant, showing great kindness and thoughtfulness in dealing with Judith's day-to-day business during her hospitalisation and afterwards when Judith's normal life resumed. But in late 1992, out of the blue, Judith was contacted by the Victoria Police, who informed her that Dahlstrom was in trouble with the law on several counts.

'I started to be very, very worried, but still wanted to give her the benefit of the doubt because of her kindness,' Judith told the court, but she realised she had no alternative but to end all association and, from that period, Dahlstrom had begun harassing Judith and her family and business associates. It was a confusing situation, because, while Dahlstrom had followed Judith to London and attended all of the concerts on the *Mona Lisas* tour, she had also been contacting Judith's associates in the UK and making allegations against her in an attempt to blacken her name.

The magistrate, Noel Purcell, was satisfied that Judith was being stalked and granted a twelve-month intervention order preventing Dahlstrom from going within 200 metres of Judith's home. Outside the court, Judith braced herself to face the national media and told them that the harassment had devastated her and left her with no option but to seek an intervention order. 'When there is a person stalking you all the time, you're constantly looking over your shoulder and wondering if they're going to be there.'

For Judith, it appeared the nightmare was over, but her relief was short-lived. Two days after the intervention order was granted, Dahlstrom was sentenced to two months' jail, suspended for twelve months, for breaching it.

Four hours after the intervention order was granted, Dahlstrom phoned a friend of Judith's and asked him to tell Judith that she was going to commit suicide. 'She asked him to tell Judith she was going to overdose on pills and would be dead within two or three hours,' Senior Constable Sue Hay told Prahran Magistrates Court. About an hour later, Dahlstrom faxed a twelve-page letter to Judith. Along with the suspended jail sentence, the court reinforced the intervention order and called for the seizure and sale of Dahlstrom's computer and fax machine.

Within days, Dahlstrom had been interviewed by a national women's magazine and a national television current-affairs programme, giving her side of the story and claiming that she had sent the doormats to Judith because she felt she had been 'treated like one'. Meanwhile, Judith had been advised by her lawyers not to make any comment on the case.

'I can honestly say that I have never experienced anything like the humiliation and stress of being in court, and then having to face the media afterwards,' Judith says. 'I wanted to explain so much to the world, and I knew it was important therefore to talk to the media, but at the same time I did not want to blacken the name and life potential of another human being. I knew Margaret's court cases were pending for other serious charges, so I had to be very careful what I said for fear of prejudicing the trial she still faced. It was a fine balance and very frustrating.

'I was also torn – and still am to this day – between wanting to show my love and gratitude to someone who had supported me and my husband and my career, and wanting to protect myself from a very disturbing and threatening situation. How I wish Margaret a good life and contentment. May her wounds heal. I know that my song "Australia Land of Today" would not have been completed in the same way without Margaret and her daughter Fernanda's influence. I hope Margaret has found peace in her heart now.'

On 9 September, Judith appeared in the County Court following an appeal by Dahlstrom to the intervention order. Judith told Judge John

Dee that she feared for her safety. 'I am not well and I am very, very stressed,' she told the court. 'My memory is bad. I've lost interest in eating. I'm highly stressed and emotional.'

As well as appealing the order, Dahlstrom instituted civil proceedings for libel and a criminal charge of perjury against Judith in Melbourne Magistrates Court.

Judith told the County Court she felt that Dahlstrom was continuing to stalk her through the media and the legal system. 'There are no longer doormats but my life is completely invaded,' Judith said. 'The difficulty is that I am unable to publicly defend myself. I feel awkward that I cannot respond in these instances and it is causing me great concern because my livelihood, character and everything I stand for is at risk.'

The court also heard that Dahlstrom had distributed pamphlets announcing the first annual 'Doormats for Durham Appeal'. These pamphlets had been posted in shop windows, revealing Judith's home address. In a taped police interview played to the court, Dahlstrom said she stalked Judith in order to have her day in court.

The case was adjourned until the following day, when Dahlstrom took the stand and told the court that Judith was 'a parasite' and 'thinks she's God's gift to Australian music'. She further referred to Judith's solo career as 'a dead loss'. In appealing the intervention order, Dahlstrom said the exclusion zone covered by the order would prevent her from collecting her teenage daughter from school, and from attending hospital for psychiatric assessment for stalking. In another taped police interview played to the court, Dahlstrom said that Judith 'would like to see herself as on the same sort of plane as John Lennon'. The officer conducting the interview, Senior Detective Craig Howard asked her, 'Are you talking about the fact that John Lennon was assassinated by a fan?' and Dahlstrom replied, 'Yes, but I'm not deranged. I'm not violent.'

In delivering his verdict the following day, Judge Dee dismissed Dahlstrom's appeal and told the court that it was clear that she wanted to bring Judith to court to embarrass her and tarnish her reputation, and that her actions were vindictive and born out of malice. 'You have sought to deliberately besmirch Ms Durham's reputation on every occasion. To achieve your aims, you have been prepared to lie,' Dee said. 'You are revelling in the public spotlight from the notoriety this case has brought you.' He added that Judith was a truthful witness who had acted properly towards Dahlstrom.

Unfortunately, the drama was not quite over. Less than a week later, on 17 September, Dahlstrom appeared in Melbourne Magistrates Court to launch a perjury charge, claiming Judith had made statements under oath 'which were untrue and injurious'. The case was adjourned until mid-November, to give Dahlstrom time to 'prepare her case', but was later abandoned before reaching court.

Exhausted from weeks of stress – and out of pocket to the tune of almost $100,000 in legal fees – Judith eased herself back into work by accepting an invitation to contribute a track to the album *One Man's Journey*, a fundraising project by the West Australian Jaycees Community Foundation. The funds were to aid one of the founding members of the top Australian club act the Four Kinsmen, George Fay, who had been diagnosed with MND.

'The choice was an obvious one,' says Judith. 'I immediately thought of "Slowly, Gently" which seemed just so appropriate, with Ron himself having contracted the same fatal illness as George, and Ron having composed and performed the music, which in its own way is an emotional song of farewell. To put the track on my current album, in spite of his progressing paralysis, Ron had still managed to record his music on keyboard at half-speed. Then, with computer technology, my producer Michael Cristian brought it up to normal speed and we added orchestral sounds. It was made even more special by George Fay's producer, the wonderful Barry Crocker, adding their choir to the existing track.'

Judith also guested at a reunion concert by the Australian rock band Goanna, as part of the Melbourne Festival. Performing at the invitation of the group's lead singer, Shane Howard, Judith duetted with him on his composition 'Murri Time', which had earlier been such a favourite on her *Mona Lisas* tour.

'I was delighted when I heard that Judith had been singing "Murri Time" on her UK tour,' Howard says. 'The song is a dedication to the Aboriginal people of Australia and particularly my many Murri friends in Queensland, who have suffered great hardship since the colonisation of Australia. In the late nineties, she attended one of my concerts in Melbourne. I asked her backstage if she felt like joining us for "Murri Time", which she did. It was the first time I'd heard her sing the song and the experience was overwhelming. Such purity, clarity, conviction, humanity and beauty.'

The *Melbourne Age* reviewed the concert and noted:

> Another set highlight was Durham's captivating vocals . . . on Murri Time . . . It appeared the folks backstage enjoyed it too . . . greeting

her with such a loud cheer when she joined them after the song that the audience in the otherwise silent venue broke into laughter . . .

Howard, like many Australian performers, had grown up with The Seekers. When he had first started playing guitar, he had borrowed a Seekers songbook from one of his brothers and among the first songs he ever played were 'Red Rubber Ball' and 'I'll Never Find Another You'. 'I remember vividly attending a forum in Cairns in the early nineties, where the guest speaker was that great environmental advocate, David Suzuki,' Howard says. 'After he spoke, Judith and her late husband Ron played and sang their *Chief Seattle Suite* and I was deeply moved by the humility and earthy commitment this diva displayed.

'Rudyard Kipling once wrote, "If you can walk with kings, nor lose the common touch . . ." Such could be said of Judith Durham, who has scaled dizzying heights, yet kept her feet firmly in the earth. If I had one word alone to describe Judith, it would be "grace".'

Early in January 1999, only a matter of weeks after the Goanna concert, Judith once again performed 'Murri Time' with Shane Howard, this time at Warrnambool Performing Arts Centre in a concert and cultural celebration by the Tarerer Gunditj Project Association, which had been established two years earlier to help bring awareness and understanding of local indigenous culture. Howard was the association's founding member and chairman.

'I am so humbled by the love and sense of community and sharing among Shane and his friends and colleagues and I feel so privileged that the music has brought us all together,' Judith says. 'The Aboriginal people of Warrnambool are so beautiful to me, and how lucky I am that at last I no longer think as a brainwashed "white Australian". Shane is such a fine example of how to make music your life in service to bond all with joy and hope.'

Enjoying the respite from touring with The Seekers, Judith headed for Western Australia in February to co-headline a special concert at Perth Entertainment Centre with John Farnham, James Reyne, Col Joye and the British star Gerry Marsden, in aid of the Special Air Services Regiment, a high-readiness commando battalion who would later be deployed in Afghanistan, where their skills in tracking were used to good effect in hunting down members of the al-Qaeda terrorist network.

The day before the concert the performers were each given a plaque by the Governor for taking part in a special award presentation at Perth's Government House.

'It was all I could do to restrain myself from leaping on the beautiful black antique Bechstein grand piano there in the drawing room,' Judith laughs. 'It was so like my own piano, only even older, and in that setting I could have stayed there all day playing and singing to my heart's content. I sometimes think that I would be very happy living in just that environment, in a large bedsitter in one of Australia's amazing stately Government houses with daily access to a piano like that!'

Flattered as she was by the acknowledgment from the West Australian Government, Judith was finding herself more and more at odds with the Federal Government's stance on Kosovo refugees. The Immigration Minister, Philip Ruddock, had announced that Australia would make no special plans to take in refugees, relying instead on the nation's existing refugee policy. Later, the Prime Minister announced that safe haven would be provided in Australia for four thousand Kosovo refugees on a strictly temporary basis.

The Foreign Minister, Alexander Downer, had told the media that the decision had been made on humanitarian grounds, given the genocide and atrocities against Kosovo Albanians. When Downer said that Australia would not support or tolerate ethnic cleansing, at the risk of courting controversy, Judith was moved to write a letter to the editor of the *Sunday Herald Sun*, which appeared in the letters column on 9 May:

We should abhor the term 'ethnic cleansing' as much as all white Australians should abhor our employment of it in our not-so-long-ago dark past. When the British conquered Australia, they set about 'clearing the land' of Aborigines by committing monstrous atrocities, such as weekend 'culling parties' (under the guise of recreation) and poisoning fresh water supplies . . .

'Before the media referred to the tragedy of the 'ethnic cleansing' of Kosovo, there was never a clear term for these events in Australia. When Foreign Minister Alexander Downer said, 'Australia will never approve of ethnic cleansing', he did not seem to recall that Australia has been a prime perpetrator of this horrific evil. And it will remain so until our Government acknowledges the true history of Australia's settlement . . . and apologises . . . and until we confess in history books the unexpurgated truth regarding the generations of Aboriginal refugees and murdered Aboriginal civilians. I'd like to see a different kind of 'cleansing' . . . that of Australia's conscience.

The letter was signed 'Judith Durham, OAM' and in the coming weeks the newspaper was inundated with replies, some chastising her, others supporting her. One letter, from a Melbourne Justice of the Peace, completely missed the point:

Did Judith Durham have a problem accepting the adulation – and the money that went with it – from British fans who took her to their hearts? If this is what she thought of the British people, I'm surprised she was able to perform in their country.

'If I have any regrets in life it is that I have been so blindly racist for much of my life,' says Judith. 'I remember a sense of things being right with the world when we were taught in school in Tasmania about the very last Aborigine in that state being killed off. I thought, at nine years old, What a good idea! Now I try to make amends for my ignorance and prejudice, sometimes even through my music. I have recently composed a song called "White Doves", dedicated to asylum seekers and refugees who seek sanctuary in our shores. Every human being deserves to develop their full potential in freedom. After all, The Seekers were just four boat people when we went to the UK in 1964. We could have been turned away after a few months, but we were so lucky that the British people took us to their hearts with no official paperwork.'

As the controversy died down, Judith was thrilled to learn that Warner Music Australia would be releasing her three jazz albums on CD in June, complete with their original artwork.

'It was Ron's pioneering spirit that led us to produce our own albums for the first time in the seventies, and John Kovac promised Ron before he died that all the albums would be out on CD soon,' says Judith. 'I'm so grateful in particular that the album *The Hot Jazz Duo* showcases to the world Ron's piano virtuosity with all its unique exuberance. All three albums were our pride and joy and gave the two of us immense pleasure in the making. It is directly due to Ron's fearless venture into the unknown as a first-time record producer that I can now produce my own recordings.'

The reissue was met with enthusiastic reviews from the media. The *Sunday Herald Sun*, in its review of *Hot Jazz Duo – Live In Concert*, wrote, 'Edgeworth's stride piano style, broad and busy, is often a perfect foil for Durham's pure and unembellished vocals ... They obviously had a beautiful musical understanding that complemented their lives together.'

The online music site, *All Music Guide*, was gushing in its praise of the first of the three albums, *Judith Durham and The Hottest Band in Town*. Calling it an 'extraordinary album', its reviewer wrote:

> Durham belts these numbers out like a latter-day Ethel Merman only bigger voiced and with an excellent feel for the genre and the sound in which she's working . . . Her originals, 'I Wanna Dance To Your Music' and 'Mama's Got the Blues' are a match for any of those standards, at least in Durham's hands as a singer, and lead one to believe that she could've had a career scoring musicals, had she been born 40 years earlier . . . The album is also a dazzling showcase for The Hottest Band in Town, especially pianist/arranger Ron Edgeworth, who displays a love and familiarity with this repertory the equal of Durham's. There's not a weak moment on the album, which is a must-own for fans of big-band jazz or blues vocals.

With the CDs now in stores and selling, Judith announced in August her first solo concerts in Australia for seven years. The first would be an out-of-town concert at Barooga Sports Club, situated along the Murray River on the Victoria–New South Wales border on 8 August, and the second on 14 August, in the showroom of Melbourne's Crown Casino. With the talented pianist David Cameron as her musical director leading a five-piece band behind her, Judith presented a two-hour concert featuring songs from her past, a smattering of Seekers hits and a selection of original material that left the full house clamouring for more.

Opening with Abba's 'Thank You For the Music', Judith worked her way through standards ('You Belong To Me', 'Getting To Know You', 'Can't Help Lovin' Dat Man'), covers ('As Dreams Go By', 'You've Got a Friend'), gospels and Seekers hits, as well as several of her own compositions ('When Starlight Fades', 'I Love You', 'Let Me Find Love', 'Australia Land of Today') and, on piano, 'Maple Leaf Rag' and her own ragtime original 'Banana Rag'.

'It was hard to comprehend that this was the first time I had performed a full solo concert in Australia for so many years,' she says. 'Yet the reality of that was borne out when I saw in the audience people who had travelled many thousands of miles especially to witness the occasion. How I craved the artistic freedom and scope of the live solo situation, yet already The Seekers tour was looming large with its own flavour of excitement, so I could not tour the solo show. It was hard to believe that all the effort and thrill would last for just two special nights and be gone for ever.'

In September, Judith was invited to be a special guest of legendary radio and television host John Laws on his national nightly talk show *Laws*, on the pay TV Foxtel network. Fearing that Laws would want to focus on controversial aspects of the recent stalking cases, Judith was surprised and delighted to find that the host devoted the thirty-minute interview to her career and philosophies, and even put her on the spot by having her sing a few lines of 'Just a Closer Walk With Thee' unaccompanied.

Less than a month later Judith was back in the national spotlight again when, unrelated to the intervention order, Margaret Dahlstrom was sentenced by the Hobart Supreme Court to three and a half years' jail on 65 theft and deception charges. Judith was horrified and saddened to read in the newspapers that the charges included five counts of burglary, nine of stealing and sixteen each of forgery, uttering and obtaining goods by false pretence in Hobart and Launceston between August 1996 and May 1997. During the hearing, the crown prosecutor Tony Jacobs revealed that Dahlstrom had more than a hundred previous convictions for crimes of dishonesty, including burglary, and stealing from charities, medical centres, schools and corporations. On the current charges, Dahlstrom was ordered to pay compensation of $3,000 to the Teachers, Police and Nurses Credit Union, $4,650 to the Commonwealth Bank, $49,700 to the Trust Bank and a victims-of-crime compensation levy of $2,500.

Judith was informed of the court ruling by the *Hobart Mercury* while she was in Sydney and in an interview with them said, 'It is a big sense of relief. It is my fervent wish she comes out and leads a better life.'

Later in the year, away from a public agenda, Judith and her sister Beverley heard that the sentimental Cock family home, so full of memories, at 5 Georgian Court, Balwyn, was up for sale, and together they attended the auction, where the property was sold for $500,000.

'Dad always wanted to do wonderful things to the house which he and Mum had laboriously built to architect's plans to fit on the abnormally shaped block,' Judith remembers. 'But there was no money to spare on tradesmen, so Dad had landscaped and terraced the lawns and flower beds with his own hands and had laid the gravel drive. He would be out there weeding and watering and pruning whenever he could spare the time in the weekends – after his game of golf of course! And there was the willow tree in all its glory still – and Mum's Liquid Amber – all grown from their cuttings. How amazing to see that the property had been developed so luxuriously by other owners since we lived there. [There were] extensions and the dreamed-of swimming pool now, and even brick veneer instead of the white weatherboards, which Dad always painted himself to save money. As we wandered through our much-smaller-than-we-remembered bedrooms, the memories of our teenage years and of both of our bridal preparations came flooding back to us: Dad driving us to school and later to work in the mornings; Mum shelling the peas; my first romance at sixteen; Ron courting me; practising on the upright piano for hours and hours; even the memory of Margaret my stalker, then a wide-eyed innocent of only sixteen, coming to knock on my mother's door. So much of my history was lived between those walls now up for sale, and it was good to have that chance to pay our respects to the past and momentarily live out that dream of luxury that might have been for Mum and Dad.'

In time for Christmas 1999, The Seekers' manager, John Kovac, had negotiated the rights for the 1968 BBC *Farewell The Seekers* special, which had been televised live to an audience of 10 million people 31 years before. It was to be released in Australia as a CD and video titled *The 1968 BBC Farewell Spectacular*. The year ended with the album peaking at Number 12 in the national charts.

As the new year dawned, along with the general populace, The Seekers were preparing to celebrate the millennium in their own style. They would soon be embarking on a new greatest-hits tour, *A Carnival of Hits*. But first there were Australia Day celebrations to take part in. On 25 January – the night before Australia Day – the group performed Bruce Woodley's 'I Am Australian' live before the Prime Minister and an invited audience on the nationally televised *2000 Australian of the Year* spectacular; and on Australia Day itself they performed it again in the Alexandra Gardens as part of the celebrations.

The *Carnival of Hits* tour kicked off on 18 February with a concert at Her Majesty's Theatre, Ballarat, before the group flew to New Zealand for concerts in Auckland, Wellington and Dunedin, where the *Otago Daily Times* wrote:

> ... in a night of unbridled nostalgia, sentiment and spontaneous, singalong music making, there was enough to keep my spine and those of a near-capacity crowd fair humming for close to two hours ... Durham, as always, was the standout. That is not to deride the vocal talents of Athol Guy, Keith Potger and Bruce Woodley, all fine

musicians and superb harmonisers. But this quartet is not billed as 'Judith Durham and The Seekers' for nothing . . .

They returned to Australia and toured through Melbourne, Geelong, Hobart, Burnie, Launceston, Canberra, Tamworth, Toowoomba, Brisbane, Rockhampton, Mackay, Townsville, Cairns, Newcastle, Sydney, Adelaide and Perth, before extra dates at the Melbourne Concert Hall. Once again, the concerts were greeted with excellent reviews. The *Melbourne Herald Sun* said, '. . . as always, the evening belonged to Judith Durham . . . Her spine-tingling rendition of "This Is My Song" was a highlight.'

'It is always such a thrill to be in New Zealand,' Judith says. 'Since the very early days we have found a very loyal fan base there. One couple were asked to be interviewed on television about The Seekers song which meant so much to them. They had become engaged to "I'll Never Find Another You" thirty-five years before, and here they were on their anniversary of that day, and still so happy with our music in their lives. And – on an important domestic note – you haven't tasted green veggies until you've tasted them in New Zealand!'

During the tour, while The Seekers were in Queensland, Judith learned the sad news that her friend, the Aboriginal elder Uncle Banjo Clarke, had died in Warrnambool. Uncle Banjo was dearly loved by his Framlingham community, and was related to the one-time world bantamweight boxing champion Lionel Rose. Judith had first met Uncle Banjo at the Aboriginal activist Gary Foley's week-long seminar 'Understanding Black Australia' at Melbourne University in 1991. It was at the seminar that she also met Monty 'Boori' Pryor, who played didgeridoo in Judith's 1992 performance of her *Australian Cities Suite* at the Melbourne Concert Hall.

'I was impressed by the great respect and love bestowed upon Banjo by those close to him,' Judith says. 'For the first time in my life I understood the value of an elder to a community and how our white community often misses out on this opportunity to revere someone older and wiser, and to learn enduring values.' Much later, Judith discovered that her fellow Seeker Athol Guy had close connections himself with Banjo, having been brought up on a farm in Warrnambool. Athol's uncle had been best mates with Banjo so many years before.

On 10 April, the day of the group's Melbourne Concert Hall concert, The Seekers attended a special ceremony in their honour at the Alfred Hospital in Melbourne, where the group's name is officially commemorated in naming The Seekers' Orthotics and Prosthetics Department on the fourth floor, in recognition of the band's fundraising efforts.

Judith had only a matter of weeks to prepare for the next leg of The Seekers' *Carnival of Hits* tour, this time touring Scotland, England and Wales in late May and June, with concerts in Edinburgh, Glasgow, Newcastle, London, Bournemouth, Cardiff, Birmingham and Manchester.

Judith recalls, 'Ah, London. How special to be back. No longer to be "always window shopping" – but definitely "stopping to buy" in those legendary establishments, and to catch up with all the latest trends. And to be revelling in taking the Tube – taking me back to memories of my very first arrival in London in 1964.

'How lovely this was to be singing for all the British fans again. So many of them were following us from concert to concert, and we heard their stories and saw how many of them had linked together in new friendships with our music as their common bond. At last we could meet on their home turf many who travelled to the Antipodes several times to see concerts, and in particular said hello to all the gang who had dedicated so much of their time to publishing a magazine all about the group. So much love and thought went into those special little booklets, and many of the fans were even setting up their own Seekers and Judith solo websites and undertaking individual fundraising efforts on behalf of MNDA, in addition to the amazing generosity of the fans who gave to the MND volunteers collecting at all the venues.

'To link with Ron's relatives again and see long-lost friends is always the meaning of London for me too. England is like a home away from home – from the very first moment I set foot on those white cliffs of Dover – especially to hug my dear mother-in-law Vicky, and to have those treasured chats with her very close mate, Lloyd Huish. I would always treasure those last lingering moments in case it might be the very last time, and very sadly this time was indeed to be the last that I would hug dear Vicky.

'For me London also had great meaning in being with David Reilly for the first time since he'd made the huge effort to come all the way to Australia to surprise me on *This Is Your Life*. We always pat each other on the back for writing "Colours of My Life"! And, seeing Tom Springfield in person, I was able to give him my heartfelt personal thanks once again for the wonderful hits he wrote and produced for the group. He told me that he was always writing those hit songs especially for my voice, and it meant so very much to me to hear him say that in person, knowing how those songs still affect fans of all ages in the UK and all around the world.

'A magic day was meeting up in Chelsea with Tom himself and the legendary photographer Robert Whitaker. Sitting there between Tom and Robert, I knew I was with two modern-day legends who created a huge chunk of all the historic Seekers sound and vision. Together they represent a big influence on my own life. Dear Rob (the man I would gladly have married if he had asked me back in 1966!) took me under his wing next afternoon to shoot one of his unique "Whitographs". It was a very special session where he would shoot all thirty-six frames very quickly – capturing a multitude of different segments of my entire face and upper body – and he would later arrange the whole collection in sequence, in a framed composite of huge dimensions. It was a very proud moment indeed when I saw one of those finished Whitographs displayed nearly three years later in Robert's *Yesterday and Today* exhibition in Melbourne.'

Judith also found time to travel across the West Country to visit her long-time friend and former fan club president, Tim Hubbard, now, as an author and TV presenter, himself a celebrity. They joked about *swapping* autographs this time, as he proudly showed Judith the wonders of the Cornish scenery. 'Little did I know that life's mysterious network would reveal, two years later, that [the noted English author and journalist] Shelley Bovey would join Tim for lunch at that very spot to talk about their mutual involvement in my life,' Judith says.

Fans would travel from far and wide for those Seekers concerts. One fan made the trip from the Isle of Man, another from Aberdeen, another from Denmark and yet others from the USA. Shelley Bovey, whose bestselling books include *The Forbidden Body, The Empty Nest* and *What Have You Got to Lose?*, had heard about The Seekers concerts on Brian Mathew's *Sounds of the Sixties* Radio 2 programme and bought tickets for the Cardiff concert. That night, and over the coming weeks, memories of the sixties would come flooding back for Shelley. On the night of their engagement in July 1968, Shelley and her fiancé Alistair had celebrated by taking Shelley's parents to the Talk of the Town in London, to see The Seekers in what would later be revealed as the group's final week together.

'Nothing could have brought us more joy,' Shelley says. 'Mum and Dad were fans, too. Our table was right next to the performing area and it was magical seeing them live. The evening was a mixture of happiness and grief because the fourth member of our family was missing: my young brother Tony, who had recently died. The grief couldn't be talked about, but Judith's voice made me cry because it was so achingly beautiful. I can personally attest to the power of music to unlock emotions, however painful the feelings might be. I was devastated later when I learned that The Seekers were breaking up.'

Although Shelley met Keith and got his autograph on her *Talk of the Town* vinyl album in 1968, it wasn't until the year 2000 that she met Judith for the first time, backstage at the M.E.N. Arena. She interviewed her for a colour feature article in *Woman's Own* magazine. 'She was so honest, so funny and natural and self-deprecating, in fact, exactly the person I imagined her to be all those years ago. Because I am a musician, I was fascinated by the quality of her voice, by how much purer and fuller and richer it had grown, and was astonished to learn that she has a severe, degenerative lung disease. When I left, I felt I had made a friend.'

Judith recalls that meeting with Shelley Bovey quite vividly. 'One of the significant memories of the tour surprisingly, was the final interview I gave on the night of the last concert in Manchester,' she says. 'Shelley Bovey had driven from Glastonbury to see our concert in Cardiff and couldn't wait to see another. She and her husband Alistair travelled all the way to Manchester for the final concert of the tour, and she became absolutely determined to submit a major article about me to one of the British magazines. Against all odds, she somehow convinced me that she should interview me before the concert, and she told me how very much she appreciated my voice. She explained in depth how she had been unprepared for the effect that my voice would have on her, and the cathartic experience she had during the concerts. Little did I realise then that this was an experience linked to the relatively new field of music therapy, and on that final night of The Seekers UK tour I had actually met the person who would change my life in the most massive way conceivable within only three years.'

The UK tour finally over, The Seekers returned home to Australia, and in a surprise move Judith accepted an invitation to join the board of the world's first gender-specific biotechnology organisation, Women's Health Biotechnologies (WHB), having been approached and asked to do so by her friend Diana Abruzzi. The organisation's aim was to undertake research and development programmes with Monash University's Centre for Women's Health Research, focusing on common female disorders such as endometriosis, fibroids, pregnancy disorders and hormonal problems.

It seemed merely a minor hitch when Judith slipped and fell in her kitchen, breaking her hip and wrist. This was particularly inopportune because The Seekers were preparing to headline a $1,700-a-head dinner for Prime Minister John Howard at Melbourne's Royal Exhibition Building within days in September. Anxious not to let anyone down, Judith had an inaugural informal meeting with Diana Abruzzi to sign the papers for her role as a nonexecutive director; and also asked the dinner organiser and master of ceremonies, Tony Charlton, a TV personality and long-time associate, if she might be able to sing with The Seekers at the official dinner in her wheelchair. Her doctors advised against it.

Transferred to a private rehabilitation hospital after initial surgery at the Alfred Hospital, she had exercised diligently and was well on her way to full recovery when, just four weeks later, ahead of WHB's listing on the Australian Stock Exchange, Judith quit the board in a blaze of publicity with Diana Abruzzi. The same day, the Australian Securities Investments Commission placed an interim stop order on the prospectus for the company's $30 million float, following the hearing of a criminal charge of receiving secret commissions against the WHB's founder and former director.

Judith recalls, 'Diana had been the inspiration of one of my songs. Diana is chair of the International Women's Federation of Commerce and Industry [IWFCI], which is an international network to link women in business and to inspire them further in their pursuits. She asked me to write a song to empower women which I called "The Hand That Rocks the Cradle (Rules the World)". We had become good friends, and I must admit I hardly felt the need to question the integrity of the company Diana was spearheading and was about to commit her energies and focus to.

'She was passionate about the cause and it was inspiring for me to know I could do some good in the corporate world for the best of motives. Knowing Diana's ethics and abilities as I did, and knowing Diana's controlling influence as executive chairwoman would be very instrumental in the company's potential, I accepted the position for altruistic reasons as much as for the new experience of becoming a board member. I was devastated, and so was Diana, that we both had to reluctantly resign from our positions. My short-lived days as a corporate board member are now just a memory – and I must say that I would think twice and three times about taking on the same responsibility and serious commitment ever again. There are so many twists and turns in the business world, and I am relatively inexperienced to see potential pitfalls. I read every day about corporate collapses, and think, That could have been me!'

It was unique for Judith to be watching the Olympic Games from her hospital bed, sometimes with the nurses. Ironically, The Seekers had been suggested by the media as the perfect performers to close the Olympic Games, and newspapers also suggested the inclusion of other legendary Australian icons, including The Bee Gees, AC/DC and Dame Edna Everage. But none of these internationally recognised and loved artists were included. In a stinging attack in the *Sydney Morning Herald*, the closing ceremony's artistic director said, 'The Seekers are hardly looking to the future.' He told the reporter he was aghast at 'the idea of a grey-haired Athol Guy and a prune-like Judith Durham having the final musical word.'

'We had fun watching the rerun of the local ABC comedy series *The Games* with John Clark and the other actors portraying The Seekers as if we had been performing at the closing ceremony of the Olympics themselves,' Judith says. 'Great stuff. I was deceived into thinking Gina Riley was really me for about the first ten seconds of their performance. So much so that when my own voice came over the airwaves, while I was watching the opening ceremony of the Paralympic Games, I certainly didn't think it was me at all for at least a minute. I was thinking, That's a nice voice; but I just couldn't place it. Then I suddenly twigged that it was *me* singing Bruce's song "I Am Australian". A proud moment indeed. But I have to say, I would have gladly gone up there and sung it for them live from my wheelchair. They only had to ask me!'

Two weeks later, a wheelchair-bound Judith did indeed join Athol, Keith and Bruce as The Seekers to bring the 2000 Paralympic Games to a close. The event marked the end of a spectacular six weeks of competition featuring 4,000 athletes from 120 countries, in what the international media agreed had been the best Paralympics in history. It was a double whammy for Australia, which earlier in the year had hosted the 2000 Olympic Games, praised by the International Olympics chairman Juan Antonio Samaranch as the best ever.

The 'grey-haired Athol Guy and prune-like Judith Durham' joined Keith and Bruce to perform 'The Carnival Is Over' at the Olympics Stadium in the finale of the closing ceremony. The *Sydney Telegraph* echoed the sentiments of the nation:

The greatest sporting carnival the world has seen ended last night. Judith Durham brought the curtain down with the trademark

1960s Seekers hit, 'The Carnival Is Over', probably still wondering if the Gods of Paralympia decreed that she should break her hip and sing from a wheelchair.

In a front-page article, the *Sydney Morning Herald* wrote:

There seemed no more obvious yet no more irresistible note on which to conclude Sydney's late-blooming love affair with the Olympics and the Paralympics, than with the '60s hit, 'The Carnival Is Over'. The Seekers, the original and the best, provided a showstopper in every sense of the word.

Judith said, 'I was very proud to be there in my wheelchair and I felt so privileged to share the same disadvantages with all the many Paralympians and others who are permanently resolved to the confines of such a means of achieving one's goals. It opened my eyes to so many things, not the least being that time-honoured question, "What is 'normal'?" I started to feel normal in that venerable company after even that short time. It was mind-boggling realising what difficulties the athletes were overcoming to achieve their goals. I was a long way off their high standards. My biggest hurdle was trying not to get my long dress tangled in my wheels!'

The year 2000 – a year of mixed fortunes for Judith – ended with the thrill of having her song for the nation, 'Australia Land of Today', released on an album for the very first time, to celebrate Australia's Centenary of Federation, which was fast approaching in 2001. Judith realised her dream of having her former *Let Me Find Love* album remastered and repackaged, when Warner Music proudly released her self-penned all-Australian album *Hold on to Your Dream*.

18. HEY THERE, GEORGY GIRL

Give yourself a chance, and you'll succeed,
Confidence is all you need,
And oh, what a change there'd be,
The world would see
A new Georgy Girl.

– 'GEORGY GIRL'
MUSIC BY TOM SPRINGFIELD
LYRIC BY JIM DALE
(MOTION PICTURE OPENING SEQUENCE)

With *Hold on to Your Dream* finally released, and featuring a remix of Ron's song 'In Your Love' and a much-improved order of tracks, it was time to promote 'Australia Land of Today', for the Centenary of Federation. Australia as a nation was to celebrate the hundredth anniversary of the coming together of the six colonies of Australia to form a federation.

As the centenary year drew close, Judith was contacted by Councillor Claude Ullin, who had been a work colleague of Athol and Judith at J Walter Thompson back in 1962. Now the Mayor of the elite suburban precinct, the City of Stonnington, Ullin was keen to have Judith join the Federal Treasurer Peter Costello and other Parliamentarians at the city's Australia Day Citizenship Ceremony. He insisted that this should be the occasion that would officially launch Judith's *Hold on to Your Dream* album, with a special performance of 'Australia Land of Today' for Stonnington's sixty newly invested Australian citizens. Following Judith's performance of the song, which was filmed by several television news crews, she joined the federal treasurer for the official presentation. To each new Australian, along with his or her citizenship certificate, Judith presented an Australian native plant, and the Treasurer presented a copy of *Hold on to Your Dream*.

'Judith is one of our city's icons and I was thrilled she agreed to launch her album at such an appropriate ceremony,' Ullin told the media. ' "Australia Land of Today" is a wonderful song, and featured beautifully in the ceremonies, expressing the deep pride we all share for our nation.'

Less than a week later, Judith was asked by her friend Maria Sheridan to headline a fundraising concert for Amnesty International Australia, at Melbourne's unique Ceres Park in Brunswick. This is the Centre for Education and Research in Environmental Strategies (CERES), a community environment project designed to foster awareness and action on environmental and social issues affecting urban areas. Maria had been Ron's very caring occupational therapist during his illness, and she was also an active member of this special cause, which was dear to Judith's heart.

Judith recalls, 'I loved taking part in this concert for such an impassioned and altruistic cause. It is very humbling when an artist has an opportunity to use their gifts for a greater good for all humanity. Ceres was a perfect setting for such a community-minded event. I had never been there before, but I was fascinated to see not only a very attractive and functional stage and seating area, but to see the shared organic veggie-growing areas and markets and eateries which have been established for the benefit of all concerned. It was a magic evening and one I will remember for a long time because of my magnificent efforts on the keyboard! Out of the goodness of their hearts, the organisers had borrowed an electric piano for me – and with no sound check I ploughed into some rather rich chords, and let's just say the keyboard suffered a sort of indigestion! Luckily, everyone still clapped nice and loudly!'

Later, in February, Judith joined The Seekers for a special one-off concert at Spray Farm on Victoria's Bellarine Peninsula, with its expansive water frontage and spectacular views of the You Yangs, Port Phillip Bay and the city of Melbourne. More than 2,500 people watched the show, part of the annual Spray Farm Summer Festival. Days later, the group flew to West Australia to headline the *Concert on the Bay* at the Royal Perth Yacht Club, a fundraising performance for local charities, including the West Australia Variety Club, Lifeline and Mission Australia.

Back home in Melbourne, Judith had a lovely surprise in store. She was contacted by the producers of Granada Television's top-rating British talent contest *Stars In Their Eyes*, inviting her to tape a special 'good luck' message to one of their season finalists. In the programme, contestants perform a musical tribute to their favourite stars. Five people appear in each episode with the winner from each show going forward to a live grand final judged by telephone poll from the television audience at home. Annie Sheppard of Saunderton won her heat impersonating Judith singing 'Georgy Girl', and made it through to the final. A film crew taped Judith's message from Melbourne in which she congratulated Annie and said 'When I'm thinking of retiring I'll certainly know who to call!'

'Annie was paying tribute to me and doing such a wonderful job that I honestly thought she looked more like me than I did!' Judith says. Not only that, but I really think Annie has given me a rare gift – she has let me see myself as others see me. To see how the British audience welcomed her to their hearts, it was as if it were me too they were applauding. *Stars In Their Eyes* proves just how important "image" is for an artist, and seeing Annie as myself singing "Georgy Girl", I could see that in the sixties I had unwittingly created an image for myself. I was transfixed as I watched her recreate my hand actions, and I studied my hairstyle and my haute couture (very similar to one of my own handmade creations, I must say!). It made me realise that Annie was the perfect mirror. I wish everyone could have such a special surprise gift as Annie Sheppard gave to me.'

The filming complete, Judith threw herself into preparations for her first solo tour of Australia in more than a decade, her own fortieth-anniversary tour. A hectic round of media interviews was completed before Judith started rehearsals with her two musicians, musical director Brett Rosenberg and featured pianist Michael Harding, both on keyboards. The concert was devised to cover Judith's forty years of music, from her debut at the Memphis Jazz Club in 1961, through her legendary success with The Seekers, her orchestral recordings and trad-jazz shows in the seventies and her songwriting through the years, culminating with *Hold on to Your Dream*.

Tickets went on sale before Judith had finalised her repertoire, and, some weeks before the tour was scheduled to start, Judith's newfound champion, the journalist Shelley Bovey, heard about the concerts and was immediately struck by two conflicting thoughts: she had to be there, but she couldn't fly. The dilemma consumed her for days. 'I kept thinking, I'll die if I get on a plane,' Shelley says. 'I had always wanted to go to Australia, from the time I was a child, but never entertained it as a possibility. To imagine I might fly seemed the equivalent of a blind person imagining that one day she might see. On the other hand, I just knew I had to be there! I kept thinking of the opening lines of the *Hold on to Your Dream* album ... "You have to have a little dream to start".

'I had a little time on my side, so I took it one step at a time. I learned about flying from pilots, from psychologists, from the chief medical officer at British Airways. I treated it like a journalistic assignment. I saw a psychologist who specialised in fear of flying. I did a course. I did "test" flights to Dublin then to Belfast and I didn't die! But Australia? A psychologist friend advised against it, saying it was too far. Still that thought persisted: it was Judith's celebration and I had to be there.'

An Australian friend sent Shelley the tour poster – 'Musicoast Presents – A Very Special 2 Hour Concert'. She stuck it on her study wall and looked at it every day. 'I would read it, and try to picture myself sitting in a theatre in Melbourne, watching Judith on stage, and just shake my head in disbelief.' Yet the bookings were made, and Shelley was upstairs full of nerves, packing her suitcases for her journey into the unknown, when her husband Alistair called to her. 'He just pressed PLAY on the CD player and "Hold on to Your Dream" started,' Shelley says. 'From that moment I knew I could do it and that I would be on that plane and sitting in the Athenaeum Theatre. I got there, because I held on to my dream and for that I have to thank Judith, who changed my life.'

'Shelley had started to really impress me as a person of immense perseverance and courage,' Judith says. 'She had written letters to me, inadvertently displaying incredible determination in trying to get her interview with me in Manchester 2000 into a quality magazine in the UK despite being knocked back by so many editors who claimed Judith Durham was "too old for their demographic". I started to really admire this likeable and sincere professional who would write to me about how the knock-backs made her even more determined, and she just kept on and on until one day a newly published full colour two-page *Woman's Own* article turned up in the post from the UK. So I started to reason that, if she could achieve publication after all that resistance, then it just might be possible I would see her on the ground in Melbourne one day soon. I knew what it would mean to her if she made it. I really took Shelley's statements with a grain of salt, that my music had changed her life, and yet I encouraged her and kept that spark alive in my own heart that perhaps we would share a mutual moment of triumph at the end of my first concert on the upcoming tour. And we did!'

The more Judith thought about her fortieth-anniversary shows, the more it seemed incomplete to feature the hits of The Seekers without the boys. She tentatively broached the subject with her manager of having Athol, Keith and Bruce as her special guests for The Seekers segment of the concert and was delighted when they leaped at the opportunity.

She says, 'The boys helped me very much by so willingly and encouragingly lending their support. Through the years, Ron would often state a very positive affirmation that one day I would truly embrace The Seekers, even though I so often insisted that I would have to make it in my own right and that the boys had distracted me from my true path and The Seekers was a different "me". It took me until 2001 to see the light.

'And how could I have misjudged the boys in assuming they would have better things to do with their time? They all were so happy for me that I could celebrate in this way and they just wanted to make the whole thing a big success for me. It was the icing on the cake, and we contrived a means whereby I could transform the style of musical backing during my time-honoured trad gospel "We Shall Not Be Moved" so that it would start with me in the jazz club with a pretend sousaphone and banjo, and then transform into The Seekers' gospel harmony sound. It would be smooth sailing to welcome the three boys on stage in the middle of the song to sing "We're brothers together". No worries!'

But, a matter of days before the tour was due to start, Athol Guy contracted viral pneumonia and was confined to bed. Doctors had hoped to give him the all-clear in time to join the tour, but further tests revealed he had suffered a relapse. 'We were all so very worried for Athol, knowing what a strong constitution he usually has,' says Judith. 'Athol is always so reliable, and never one to shirk, so we knew this must have really knocked him for six.'

With only a day or two to go, Judith finalised her repertoire, and Keith and Bruce came to terms with the idea that they would have to sound like three, with Brett Rosenberg frantically working out all Athol's acoustic-bass parts on his keyboard.

The concerts would open with a scratchy old recording of the Fahan School madrigal group – featuring Judith – performing 'Lift Thine Eyes', a peeling acetate recording that Judith had kept since childhood and had recently donated to the National Film and Sound Archives (ScreenSound) in Canberra. An orchestral overture played by Brett and Michael would follow featuring 'Colours of My Life', 'The Olive Tree' and 'Australia Land of Today'. It would end with a verse and chorus of 'Hold on to Your Dream' sung live off stage before Judith made her entrance with 'Join in the Journey', a happy gospel co-written by Athol Guy, Judith and Michael Cristian with lyrics that wove the thread for the theme of the whole evening.

The concert was designed to move through Judith's entire musical history and included songs she'd sung as a child and as a teenager ('Forever and Ever', 'You Belong To Me' and 'Wonderful Wonderful'), songs from musicals she loved so much ('Climb Ev'ry Mountain', 'Getting To Know You'), trad jazz and gospel ('Moan You Mourners', 'Just a Closer Walk With Thee') and even her special Maria Callas aria, not attempted by Judith since her one-woman shows in 1971 ('Io Son L'Umile' from Cilèa's opera Adriana Lecouvreur).

Special guests Bruce Woodley and Keith Potger would join Judith on stage before the interval for a set that included 'When the Stars Begin to Fall', 'I'll Never Find Another You', 'A World of Our Own' and 'Georgy Girl'. The remainder of the concert featured several piano solos from Judith (including 'Maple Leaf Rag', 'Banana Rag'), several songs from Hold on to Your Dream, including some accompanied by Judith on piano, and an emotional jazz medley – including Judith's original classic composition 'I Wanna Dance To Your Music', the torch-song classic

'Body and Soul', and the American war time classic 'My Buddy'. This last one focused attention on Ron's sensational *Hot Jazz Duo* recording at the 1978 Newport Jazz Festival, with Judith singing live on stage to his spontaneous piano track.

The tour kicked off on 28 August at Perth Concert Hall, followed by the three shows at Melbourne's Athenaeum Theatre, Brisbane Concert Hall, Norwood Hall in Adelaide and one final triumphant concert at the Sydney Opera House on Saturday, 8 September. The reviews of the tour were among the best of Judith's long career, typified by the *Australian*, whose reviewer wrote:

> Judith Durham's ebullient performance at the Perth Concert Hall on Tuesday night demonstrates that our world can be just as happy because of the songs she continues to sing ... The sun that comes in from somewhere is Durham, radiant and bursting to share her music ... Here's a dynamic performer who wants to give of her very heart – which she does.

'From the day years ago when I saw published in a newspaper several architects' entries in a competition for the best design for a new Opera House to be built in Sydney, I dreamed of performing there one day as a solo star,' Judith recalls. 'Now my dream was to come true. The tour was a thrill from start to finish, yet I was "winging" it, as they say in showbiz, right from the word "go" in Perth: dropping music, losing my glasses, forgetting lyrics, spilling water – you name it, it happened to me on stage! It was an absolute hoot and totally unprofessional, so I couldn't believe how much the audiences clapped. I knew how underrehearsed I really was. I felt like the show was a complete sham – especially my attempts to sing my beautiful aria. I think the actress Amanda Muggleton would have done better, having starred as Callas herself. But the total delight and exhilaration of once again performing a whole show on my own, with that vast array of musical memories from my forty years as a performer, including the cameo roles of Bruce and Keith, and sharing it all with the talents of Brett and Michael, was just the biggest thrill.'

As the tour drew to a close, there was much excitement when Judith received an invitation from Australia's Governor-General, Peter Hollingworth, to attend a reception the following month at Canberra's Government House in the presence of the Queen and Prince Philip. Sadly, this wasn't to be. Following the tragic events of 11 September, the Queen's visit was cancelled.

When venues had been discussed for Judith's national tour, she had immediately suggested Melbourne's antique and stately Athenaeum Theatre, which was opened in 1924 and by 1930 had become the first theatre to screen 'talkies'. Now it had been classified by the National Trust, and Judith was aware of its intimate atmosphere and excellent acoustics. She made time before the tour to slip into the theatre to catch the writer/director Gary Ginivan's children's production *Puff the Magic Dragon*, based on the hit song made famous by Peter, Paul and Mary and performed by The Seekers during the first round of reunion concerts in 1993. Judith bought the show's merchandise and was impressed by the quality of the artwork. She contacted Ginivan and asked who had designed the *Puff* brochures and badge, and was directed to the renowned children's author and illustrator Michael Salmon. His long list of credits include 133 children's picture storybooks, activity books and educational titles, and a ten-year ABC television run with his own show *Alexander Bunyip's Billabong*, based on the character from his very first children's book *The Monster That Ate Canberra*.

Judith contacted Salmon and tentatively enquired whether he might be interested in designing the artwork for the sheet music of her 'Banana Rag' piano solo, which she was planning to publish through Musicoast. Within weeks, Salmon had produced finished artwork and was eager to work with Judith on more of her sheet music. In her continuing association with Salmon, Judith had found another perfect working partner for many projects long dormant, including her first children's storybook.

'Having spent the 1960s studying for school exams while listening to The Beatles, The Stones and yes, The Seekers, it was the then-duty of every Aussie boy to fall in love with Judith Durham,' Salmon says. 'When Judith rang me thirty-two years later to enquire about artwork, I shouted, "Thank you, God, you've sure taken your time on this one!" Now Judith and I and the Banana from the Rag are blissfully happy!'

Through Salmon, Judith met, via email, his business associate Frank Howson, the Australian screenwriter, producer and composer, now living in Los Angeles. Through the 1980s, Howson wrote and produced twelve films in Australia, including the AFI-nominated *Hunting*, *Flynn*, *Boulevard of Broken Dreams* and *Heaven Tonight*. Howson's songs have been recorded by many international artists and he has been awarded four gold albums. Early on in their email relationship, Howson told Judith of a poem he had written that was inspired by a visit to the Jewish

Museum of Tolerance in Los Angeles and had been accepted for inclusion in the International Library of Poetry's *Under a Quicksilver Moon* publication. He invited Judith to set the work to music.

'What a moving experience it was for me to set "André" to music,' Judith says. 'It felt like an important responsibility to peek into the past all those years ago during World War Two and expose something so precious and hidden for more than fifty years. I felt so privileged to be the melodic and harmonic vehicle for Frank's very beautiful piece as the music revealed itself to me. I wanted to make it playful in parts because André was just a young child when he died, but I also wanted it to show all the emotion that Frank himself had felt when he dissolved into spontaneous tears on exiting from the exhibition on that sunny day, wishing in his heart that André could have "seen today" too.'

'André' told the story of Georges André Kohn, an eight-year-old French schoolboy sent to the Auschwitz death camp in World War Two. At the selection in Auschwitz, André was sent to a special barracks, where twenty Jewish children were to be used in horrific medical experiments. They were later transferred to the Neuengamme concentration camp near Hamburg, where they were injected with tuberculosis cultures. In April 1945, with British forces less than three miles from the camp, all twenty children were brought to a school in Hamburg, injected with morphine and murdered.

'Judith emailed me a copy of the music and it was frustrating because, being a lyricist, to me it was just a series of pretty dots and squiggles,' Howson says. 'Fortunately, my wife knew how to play some piano and set up a compact keyboard in the living room, and that's how I first heard it. Even in this rough form the music was beautiful enough to bring a tear to a glass eye. As a teenage music freak in Melbourne, buying all the latest records, I had followed The Seekers' career and international achievements with great pride. All these years later, to have Judith write music to my words, and then to have that perfect voice sing them, was one of the great thrills of my life.'

With 2001 shaping up to be one of her most creative years, Judith decided to go for broke and start the ball rolling on another long-held dream, to publish a book about her journey with ill health, paying particular attention to what she had learned and put into practice over the years from the early-twentieth-century teachings of the German born Professor Arnold Ehret. She discussed it with Shelley Bovey, who had returned to England and was, coincidentally, in the midst of writing her new book on weight loss, *What Have You Got To Lose?* Bovey invited Judith to contribute to the book some of her own thoughts on maintaining weight loss and, on hearing what Judith had to say, the author offered to ghostwrite Judith's own book, which is now a work in progress.

Later in the year, Sony Music released *Rove (Live) – Some Music*, tracks performed live on the national TV programme *Rove (Live)*, hosted by Judith's publicly proclaimed supporter, the comedian Rove McManus. The album included, as a bonus track, Judith's 'Coulda, Woulda, Shoulda', which Rove had constantly referred to on the show through the year after it was revealed in the press that it was one of the most played tracks in the show's production office. During the year Judith accepted Rove's invitation to take part in one of his comedy sketches. He repaid the favour by introducing Judith at the first of her fortieth-anniversary concerts at the Athenaeum Theatre in Melbourne.

Between her solo projects, Judith had also been working on a new Seekers CD to be released by Sony Music, the group's first album of Christmas songs. Judith was delighted that Michael Cristian, who had produced the *Hold on to Your Dream* album with her, was to be the group's co-producer. Over many weeks, Judith and the boys sifted through material and rehearsed, before recording their final selection. *Morningtown Ride To Christmas* included as its title track a reworking of 'Morningtown Ride' featuring Christmas references. This came from an idea of Judith's, many years before on the Sunshine Coast, to sing the words 'Dreaming of Santa Claus riding on his sleigh' instead of 'All bound for Morningtown many miles away'.

Judith was thrilled to make contact finally with Nancy Schimmel, the daughter of the late Malvina Reynolds, the much-loved composer of this all-time favourite hit song. To alter the original lyrics, Judith needed Schimmel, now a composer in her own right, to grant official permission on behalf of her mother's estate.

The other tracks included 'Mary Had a Baby' (from the gospel opera *Black Nativity*) and 'There Are No Lights on Our Christmas Tree', a song Judith had remembered for forty years since hearing it sung live in the sixties by its writer, the Welsh folk singer Cyril Tawney, as well as the traditional Christmas favourites 'Santa Claus Is Coming To Town', 'Silent Night', 'Have Yourself a Merry Little Christmas', 'When a Child Is Born', 'Jingle Bells', 'Once In Royal David's City', 'The Little Drummer Boy', 'The First Noël', 'Rudolph the Red-Nosed Reindeer', 'Away in a Manger', 'O Come, All Ye Faithful', and a new version of 'Children Go Where I Send

Thee', which The Seekers had first recorded in the sixties and which Judith often sang with Frank Traynor's Jazz Preachers, having been inspired by the version on the *Black Nativity* album.

'As the sessions progressed I think that we could all tell we were making something very special,' says Michael Cristian. 'One of my most enduring memories was of the group rehearsing. They were gathered around my kitchen table discussing tracks and arrangements and then they would launch into song. Just Judith and the boys, two guitars and a double bass – acoustic, unplugged, raw. The sound was amazing, magical. It sent shivers up my spine and I knew that if I could capture that to tape we would have a very special recording. In the end, we did just that and I still get comments from people saying that when they hear it it's like the group is right there in their living rooms. As a producer, there can be no finer compliment.'

The album was released on 12 November, and that night The Seekers headlined *Concert of the Year*, a star-studded benefit at the Melbourne Concert Hall in aid of the Alfred Hospital (an establishment dear to Judith's heart for so many life-saving reasons) for the upgrading and development of its cardiology centre. Within three weeks of its release, *Morningtown Ride To Christmas* had become one of the ten most ordered albums in Australian record stores. By the first week of December it had settled at Number 18 in the national charts and had been certified gold. 37 years after they first stormed the charts, The Seekers were ending another year with a hit record.

As a solo performer, Judith ended 2001 as guest star at *Dancesport 2001,* which was televised nationally on Christmas night. This 59th staging of the Australian championships would determine Australia's representatives at the International Dancesport Federation World Event, the title all dancers aspire to. Competitors travelled from every state of Australia, as well as from New Zealand, Asia, New Caledonia, the United Kingdom, South Africa and the Ukraine, for their chance at a title.

When Judith wrote and recorded 'I Wanna Dance To Your Music', her dream had been to see it choreographed for Liza Minnelli in her Vegas act. But the reality was far from that. In fact, for many years, the song languished in a bottom drawer with no place to go. So Judith was grateful to the publicist Julie Cavanagh when, with some clever networking to the producer Margaret Lonsdale, she presented the idea that Judith might sing her anthem 'Australia Land of Today' in the opening ceremony at the international Dancesport championships. It led to the suggestion that one of the champion ballroom dancing couples, in a special Ginger Rogers and Fred Astaire routine, could dance to Judith's song 'I Wanna Dance To Your Music' while Judith sang.

'It's quite an adventure writing a song,' Judith says. 'Each one comes along with its own agenda. You never know where it will lead. On Christmas night 2001, I saw myself at the top of a flight of stairs "dancing to my music" on television, with a male dancer on each arm. Well, I wasn't exactly dancing. Let's say "swaying", with two talented dancers below me. Still – it gave an impression. And for me it was a dream come true – especially as Liza Minnelli just wasn't available, I guess!'

In February 2002, The Seekers reconvened for a very special one-off concert event, performing before 20,000 people in New Zealand, where they shared the bill with Engelbert Humperdinck. The show was staged in a picturesque setting at Taradale's Mission Estate, which was established in 1851 by the French Marist religious order.

'I couldn't wait to meet Engelbert,' says Judith. 'I was longing to hear him sing live in that magic open-air atmosphere. His band was fantastic and he put on an amazing show. It was so many years since we all shared the pop charts and I had always wanted to thank him for his kind compliment about "Walk With Me" on *Juke Box Jury* in the UK when he said, "That girl could sing anything." So I felt a bit like a groupie, sneaking a peek out of my tent every now and then, just in case he should happen to wander by! But it was "own-up time" I'm afraid – the big difference between meeting Engelbert in the sixties and in the noughties is mainly that Engelbert's son Scott is now the same age as Engelbert was then, and I am now old enough to be his mother! Oh, well, at least Scott has Engelbert's same good looks. I guess I had to come down to earth with a bit of a thud. Indeed four decades have gone by since "Walk With Me" walked with me!'

Early in March, Judith was able to bring to fruition her dream of recording her own song 'Wales, You're a Dreamland' with the Melbourne Welsh Male Voice Choir when she was invited to be a special guest at a one-off Melbourne Concert Hall performance. The choir was formed in 1984 and has grown from a small group of enthusiastic singers into one of Australia's most acclaimed male choirs with an on-stage strength of fifty to sixty choristers. Earlier in the year, in a radio interview, Judith had talked about her songwriting and mentioned that she had written a song about Wales and that she had sung it in concert with a Welsh choir only once, in 1991. When asked whether she planned to record it with a

Welsh choir, Judith said she would love to do so but had not had the chance to pursue the thought. The secretary of the Melbourne Welsh Male Choir heard about the interview, contacted Judith and subsequent discussions led to their invitation to Judith to sing with the choir in concert with the Camerata Symphony Orchestra under the baton of the choir's music director, Douglas Heywood. Heywood spent many dedicated hours orchestrating several songs from *Hold on to Your Dream* and rehearsing Judith's vocals with the choir and orchestra. For this concert, Judith also enjoyed the rare experience of rehearsing her own piano parts with the orchestra, as she was to alternate in the piano spotlight on the night with the choir's pianist Linda O'Brien. When the concert was announced, it became the choir's most successful evening ever, attracting two thousand people.

'I loved it,' Judith remembers. 'Such a privilege to be surrounded by the power of those sixty male voices, and the beauty of the eighty-strong symphony orchestra. Doug Heywood was so wonderful to work with. He inspired us all with his joyful mastery of our "cast of thousands", all joining forces to create that soaring wonder and majesty of the music. I was in awe from the start – right from the first evening when I entered the rehearsal hall and nervously took my first breath, hoping my voice would be heard in a room filled with a very Welsh male presence of sixty flesh-and-blood sets of very Welsh-sounding, full-throttle vocal cords! But on performance night in the Melbourne Concert Hall it was different. We delicately traced the beautiful cello part of Gerald Keunerman in "My Father's Last Words", and we roared in celebration at the end as we let rip with our very self-indulgent encore of "Australia Land of Today". I thank the choir from the bottom of my heart for letting me share in such a wonderful experience.'

So well received was the concert that the mastering expert Martin Pullen was asked to turn the live recordings made on the night into a fully mastered and mixed CD. Later in the year, *Melbourne Welsh Male Choir with Judith Durham – Live in Concert with the Camerata Orchestra* was released, featuring Judith performing 'This Is My Song', 'When Starlight Fades', 'Let Me Find Love', 'It's Hard To Leave', 'Wales, You're a Dreamland', 'My Father's Last Words' and 'Australia Land of Today'.

As soon as production on the CD was complete, Judith threw herself into rehearsals for her upcoming two nights at Taronga Park Zoo, Australia's leading zoological garden, as part of the 'Tower Twilight at Taronga' annual concert series. For these concerts, Judith once again teamed with Brett Rosenberg and Michael Harding in a two-keyboard combination with a grand piano to accompany herself on several numbers. The repertoire was very satisfying for Judith – a two-hour performance combining about a third of the programme of songs she was known for, with many of her own compositions from *Hold on to Your Dream*, plus some piano features, and a lot of fun on stage. For the first time, Judith performed Frank Howson's poem 'André', for which she had composed the music, and it was an instant hit with the audiences.

'I couldn't get over how much everyone seemed to be enjoying themselves,' Judith enthuses. 'The big thrill for me was to be autographing my albums for more than an hour after the show. It was such a lovely thought to know people had really appreciated hearing all the new songs. I even had one request for my "Banana Rag". Wow! It was a very hot night and my hands were very sticky on the piano notes, and every now and then there would be a big gust of wind, so I was often frantically clutching at pages of music and manipulating bulldog clips to stop the music blowing away. I found myself even rescuing a large moth from the grand piano keys at one point and handing it to one of my kind fans in the front row. He was a most willing "ambulance man" for the little creature. A very special memory.'

Frank Howson was equally thrilled. 'Judith sent me a copy of "André", as performed at one of the Taronga Zoo concerts,' he says. 'It was truly magical. It never ceases to amaze me how brilliant that voice is. So many singers I've worked with in the recording studio have had to do twenty, maybe more, takes in order to achieve a good vocal performance, and here was Judith singing a live vocal that was more perfect than it you'd have spent days in the studio trying to achieve it. I think she's one of the wonders of the world. I really do.'

The concerts over, Judith flew back to Melbourne and, the same afternoon, launched Motor Neurone Disease Awareness Week with a speech to the media. The Motor Neurone Disease Association had put Judith in contact with the golfing entrepreneur David Inglis, founder of the Australian Masters golf tournament. David had recently been diagnosed with a form of MND and was more or less single-handedly masterminding an online memorabilia auction and charity gala, to raise money for research into the disease. Judith met with David, who outlined plans for 'A Blue Night', a spectacular fundraising event in the Palladium Ballroom of Melbourne's Crown Casino in late May. The Seekers were included on the bill with the former Little River Band members Beeb Birtles, Glenn Shorrock and Graeham Goble, and Judith was looking forward to performing 'Australia Land of Today' as well as

Ron's composition 'Big Band Boogie' with a real big band led by Peter Sullivan.

'I saw in David Inglis a true hero,' Judith says. 'Anyone else might have been tempted to just sit down and give up, knowing he virtually had a death sentence hanging over his head. But, for David, the adversity had spurred him on to meet greater and greater challenges. He realised that the more money that could be raised in the quickest possible time, the more research could be achieved and the quicker the cure might be found. It was that plain and simple to David once he had made his very diligent investigations. He was always such a respected professional in his normal business life and he simply applied similar principles to the mission he was pursuing in finding a cure for MND.'

Less than a month after the MND gala, Judith was lending support to a charity fundraiser for the Gawler Foundation, a nonprofit organisation established in 1983 by Dr Ian Gawler, one of Australia's best-known cancer survivors, to further his work. Judith performed for the invitation-only patrons, with piano accompaniment from Allan Zavod.

'Zavod and I had a great time that night,' Judith says. 'He is so amazing, such a virtuoso of the piano. He was so much part of the recording of my *Hold on to Your Dream* album, as those songs developed into finished recordings; and there in that special room of dedicated Ian Gawler fans, full of loving hearts who believe that there is a better way for cancer sufferers through the Gawler Foundation, Allan Zavod just transforms himself into the epitome of the classical musician – controlled and artistic and so respectful of the music. I feel privileged to share the stage with him, just as I did when we shared the stage in the middle of the MCG [Melbourne Cricket Ground] back in 1992 when we launched our co-production of "Australia Land of Today" to the world for the very first time.'

In July, Judith was proudly on hand for the official release and launch of her sister Beverley Sheehan's first full CD, *Spreadin' Rhythm Around*, a compilation of tracks from the many albums on which Beverley has appeared over the years, as guest vocalist with an assortment of leading jazz bands. Judith says, 'I was the one to be given the enjoyable task of selecting the compilation of twenty of Bev's best tracks from all the different albums on which she had featured as special guest through the years. I took great delight in surprising her with the fully mastered compilation.'

Beverley was delighted. 'I'd been wishing I had an album of my own to present to people,' she says. 'So often after my shows people have wanted to take the music home with them, and I had no idea that the album really already existed in a way, and could be compiled from all my previous recordings with such wonderful Australian jazz bands. The CD seems to be giving people a lot of pleasure, and it makes it very special that Judy was the one to select all the tracks.'

Late in July 2002, Judith was devastated to hear that the producer of her *Mona Lisas* album Gus Dudgeon and his wife Sheila had been killed in a car accident near Reading in southern England as they were returning home from a fiftieth-birthday party. Unable to make it to Britain, Judith arranged for flowers to be delivered to Gus and Sheila's funeral. 'I have not been able to stop thinking about Gus and Sheila since the tragic news of their deaths,' she says. 'Gus was such a significant figure in my life at a very important time. So many connections were made through him and such a beautiful album resulted from his spirit of adventure, musical inspiration, creative thinking and people power. Full of humour and love of humanity and good times, he is and was a real force in the British music industry, in particular with the huge contribution he made in producing so many of Elton John's magnificent recordings. My life has definitely changed for the better because of Gus. I can trace the path of his influence continuing in my life strongly even today in so many subtle but definite ways, and I am very proud to be able to name him always as one of my friends.'

Funerals and bereavement had figured quite strongly in Judith's recent past. Judith had been told often over the years that her voice had been of great comfort and help to people in times of trouble, palliative care and bereavement and she was aware that her songs were featured quite often in funeral services. But it was particularly since the release of *Hold on to Your Dream* that she was realising the strong therapeutic qualities of her music.

Many songs from the album were often quoted, including 'My Father's Last Words', 'Let Me Find Love', 'Slowly, Gently' and the title track; but, in particular, 'It's Hard To Leave' was being singled out for bereavement. Judith knew that, over the years, 'The Carnival Is Over' had been played often at funerals, just as 'I'll Never Find Another You' had been played during wedding ceremonies, and she heard of other songs being used to bring comfort. But she was sensing more and more reaction to 'It's Hard To Leave' as 2002 began to unfold.

Judith had long been awed by stories she had been told about the effect of her voice and her songs on so many people, in so many ways.

In 1970, she received letters and gifts from an English fan, Allan Pennington, whose mother told Judith after his death that to hear her voice in concert once had been the only reason he had left the house in the two years prior to his passing. Another woman, Rita Murray, who had tried to bring a Higashi School to the UK for children with autism and had asked Judith to be a patron for their cause, told Judith how overjoyed she was that her autistic son, Little Tel, had responded to the sound of her voice. 'Hold on to Your Dream' helped another woman to overcome a major weight problem. Another heart-wrenching story was revealed to Judith by a woman who had been forbidden to grieve or even speak about the death of her brother, and who at last found those tears still deep inside waiting to surface at the sound of Judith's voice singing 'The Olive Tree'. These stories only served to make Judith more committed to the cause of the common good through music.

She says, 'I await inner guidance now as to what to sing and how to sing it. A friend of mine who is a numerologist told me once that I had healing power. I thought immediately of the laying on of hands and thought, No, that's not me. But, from all these stories I hear, I have now come to realise that my voice and the songs I'm inspired to compose may be the means of healing and emotional resolution for some people. So it's up to me to try to use my voice in the best way to help others. This musical path I'm travelling is more and more awesome as the years unfold.'

Out of the blue, Judith was contacted by an Australian music therapist, who was working with patients who have neurological impairments, children with developmental disabilities, and migrants in palliative and aged care. She was seeking permission to use lyrics from 'It's Hard To Leave' in a paper she was presenting in Britain in July 2002, at the World Congress of Music Therapy in Oxford.

'This very special letter, so professionally written and beautifully presented, literally changed my life,' says Judith. 'I found it hard to comprehend that a practitioner in allied medicine was asking my permission to quote my lyrics at a world conference of music therapists. In a flash, this was the impetus I needed to focus my attention on the possibility of a special purpose and role for my music and singing in the future. I already knew something of what The Seekers music meant to fans worldwide, through generation after generation, but I was still very mystified and confused about the drawers full of music and lyrics of the hundreds of songs I had been writing through the years. So many of them were inspirational, perhaps written to lift my own spirits or to encapsulate a special insight at a moment of awakening, which I might have experienced at different times in my life. What was I supposed to be doing with them all – with my own very personal musical life? That big question: would there really ever be a musical life for Judith Durham after The Seekers' journey was fulfilled to everyone's satisfaction?'

In discussion with Judith over a media release in the UK about quoting 'It's Hard To Leave' at the conference, and knowing Judith's strong link with Shelley Bovey, John Kovac was struck by the idea that Shelley could send copies of the *Hold on to Your Dream* album to the British media. Having had first-hand experience of the healing power of Judith's music, Shelley certainly seized the opportunity to spread the word to an eager UK audience, where Judith's albums were largely available only through import stores or online. Shelley had become the representative for Musicoast and, with Kovac's blessing, took over Judith's management, first in the United Kingdom and then internationally. She launched a publicity campaign for *Hold on to Your Dream* and before long Judith was being interviewed on radio stations across Britain, with many presenters playing tracks from the album and adding them to their playlists. The public and media alike expressed their longing for the opportunity to see Judith in concert in the UK as soon as possible. Having left contact details with the broadcasters, Shelley Bovey was inundated with requests from listeners for copies of the album and over the coming months many albums would be sold independently on import through Musicoast. The signs were already there that it would not be long before Musicoast would be signing an international record deal for *Hold on to Your Dream* in the UK so people could buy the CD in stores.

The popular UK magazine *Woman's Weekly* ran a piece on the healing power of music, reporting on the World Congress of Music Therapy, and quoting 'It's Hard To Leave' as a song 'singled out as one which has provided particular strength and solace for those in need'. And Simon Evans, music editor of the monthly glossy magazine *Choice*, wrote a glowing article about Judith.

> If there was one single most important ingredient in The Seekers' success it was the soaring, angelic voice of the group's lead singer Judith Durham. Given sufficient airplay ['It's Hard To Leave'] could do for Judith's solo career what 'Over The Rainbow' did for the late singer Eva Cassidy.

In light of so many changes in her musical life, Judith comments, 'I open my eyes every morning with a sense of expectation and it is challenging to meet the demands of each day. I could not do it alone. I used not to understand the lyrics of Barbra Streisand's song "People" – but now I truly do. I have become one of those people who *do* need people. I am indeed one of the luckiest people in the world. I am blessed to be sharing the load with such a special team of professionals. Yet, in my own professional life, the absolute majority of the people I really need are my beautiful fans. I have come to realise that, no matter how much music I make, without them I could not share any of it with anyone. I just feel blessed to be able to sing for people and touch their lives. It's all I've ever wanted to do.'

Judith Durham's elevated profile in Britain has sparked renewed interest in her as a concert artist and, with John Kovac's decision to take a consultancy role in Judith's career, Shelley Bovey, now Judith's manager, is presently sifting through offers from promoters in the UK and the USA to present Judith in concert in 2003 and 2004.

And so life continues to offer fresh and exciting challenges for Judith Durham. New chapters in her remarkable story are constantly unfolding and, as always, the colours of her life are forever changing – 'shedding black and grey to take on red and blue', of course, and every colour in between.

AFTERWORD

I have come to the conclusion that it is good to live a long life, so I am truly celebrating my 60th year. I know now that life is just like a jigsaw puzzle and it is only by living a long time that we are given the insight to figure the puzzle out and see how all the pieces fit together and to understand the roles we all play in each other's life.

When I think back to myself as that self-deprecating young woman who left Australia's shores in 1964 – so full of worries and insecurities and so much obsessed with food and physical self-analysis and so ungrateful at heart – I can see I needed a good wake-up call. The only way that was going to happen was for me to meet all the wonderful people along the way who would show me the answers in their own ways. But I had to keep my eyes open and be in a spirit of wanting to learn and improve and to be the best I could be. I knew I could sing and could play the piano well. No problem there. But there were so many lessons to learn – and so many time-honoured clichés were to prove their own truths. Yes it's true that life is indeed what happens to you when you're making other plans. It's true that we should look for the silver lining and laugh away our troubles. It's true that the very longest journey starts with a single step and that beauty is in the eye of the beholder (or, in my own experience, that ugliness is in the eye of the beholder!).

In fact, the affirmations contained in those wonderful 'Georgy Girl' lyrics have become more and more true of me as the years rolled by, as at last I learned to 'fly a little bit'. When I saw wonderful Lynn Redgrave in that movie, I so much identified with her Georgy Girl character. That was 'me' on the screen – she was the same kind of girl I believed I was. Funny how every other person who knew me didn't see me that way at all. I only found that out years and years later. Now I look at my past footage and I marvel at the image I see on the screen. How could my perspective have been so warped? How come I couldn't see that there was absolutely nothing to worry about? But there you are, you see. We do not trust in God that he alone should be the judge of who we are and how we should be made. He gives – and he takes away. And, as my dear late husband Ron said, he used to think that his piano playing was a gift – but after MND he realised that it was only on loan. So, while I have this body 'on loan from the Lord', I have so much to be grateful for. Thank God that I have woken up before it was too late.

Every single person I have met in my whole life has made me what I am today. I cannot take away even one of those precious souls without changing the whole of my life's path. I now see everyone as important. Doesn't matter who it is. There are the obvious ones, of course: my mum and dad and sister Bev, no doubt – it goes without saying they were my first teachers; and my beautiful, loving husband Ron, whose endless patience and wisdom meant he was my mentor and saviour in everything. But equally I am grateful to everyone who has joined me in my journey, no matter what role they played. Athol, Keith and Bruce, who for so many years I wanted to separate myself from – yet whom now I cherish and honour for what we all created together. How I love the special character of each one of them so deeply. It was legendary what we did, and still can do through our records and footage. It feels very special to think that people's lives have been really affected by The Seekers' music. What a privilege it is that the boys brought me into their midst.

There are so many other team members, too, who created our jewels with us: dear Tom Springfield, who wrote the songs especially with my voice in mind and was the producer of our special sound; Eddie Jarrett, who was the one to realise the broad international appeal of the group even though we were swimming against the trends way back then; John Ashby, who shouldered so much with me when I was still so paranoid; my dear friend John Kovac, who masterminded the reunion years and whose mission it was to bring The Seekers back to the starving public and thereby introduce our special music to new generations; beautiful Shelley Bovey, who told me her story of the deep grief she finally resolved through my singing voice and the fears she overcame through the songs I write, and who now as my manager has made it her mission to champion my cause and help to bring my music to the world so late in my life. And there is the amazing and dear Graham Simpson, who has brought my life to the written page. He has encapsulated in his own words for all eternity my entire Destiny, which I have lived to this day in this frail body.

How special it was to meet a six-year-old boy only the day before I wrote these words, who loves The Seekers music in just the same way as a six-year-old boy would have in 1965. Here I am, old enough to be his great-grandmother, with these golden tonsils in my throat – breathing, coughing, eating and sleeping every day. Yet I am here to fulfil my role to write my songs and to sing for you, no matter how old you are, or I am.

What a wonderful job I have. What a wonderful goal in life to share what I have been given in such a creative way. How blessed I feel that at last the veil has been lifted from my eyes and I can see that life is infinite and that we have an endless capacity to love and to give. There are no limits. God has granted this blessing. The more selflessly we give to others, the more joyful we feel inside. The more time we give to others, the more time we are given to share that joy. It is all a question of motive.

I thank you all: from the dear lady who stalked me yet brought my music to the attention of others, to my competitors and critics who made me strive more deeply and try harder; from those who turned away from me and helped me to search my soul more deeply, to those who challenged me to take on something purely for the good of others only to prove to me the truth that something good always comes back to you most unexpectedly.

Here I am – smiling with you all as I start to comprehend that life is not meant to be easy. We must be brave and face adversity with a smile. I will help you if you will help me to live out our lives with love in our hearts.

– Judith Durham
January 2003

'How we love you,' you're all saying,
'We remember yesteryears.'
How you hurt me and I'm praying,
You could know me shedding tears.
When I die, you'll all send flowers,
When I die you'll play my songs,
Talk of me for hours and hours,
Talk so right, yet do me wrong.
When I die you'll see things clearer,
Only then you'll know the truth,
How you held the memories dearer,
As I was when in my youth.
Yes, I sang my little heart out,
Trying to give the world a tune,
Never thought that when I'd start out,
I'd be crystallised so soon.
I've so many more to sing you,
Poems and dreams I've put to rhyme,
All my music gifts to bring you,
Yet I'm running out of time.
Give me just a chance to show you,
All the music given me,
Give me just a glance to know you,
Hear my life's long melody.
Please don't let the years pass by me,
Don't let life just slip away,
When I die you'll glorify me,
Why not hear my song today?

– 'Why Not Hear My Song Today?'
Judith Durham

You can help

You can make a much needed tax deductible donation to the Motor Neurone Disease Association in your area by forwarding a cheque to:

MNDA
PO Box 246
Northampton NN1 2PR
United Kingdom
Tel. 01604 250505
(www.mndassociation.org)

INDEX